J. N. J.

nach S. Herrn D. MARTINI LUTHERI
Deutscher Dolmetschung/ und Erklärung/
vermöge des Heil. Geistes/
im Grund-Text/
Richtiger Anleitung der Cohærentz,
Und der gantzen Handlung eines jeglichen Texts/
Auch Vergleichung der gleichlautenden Sprüche/ enthaltenen
eigenen Sinn und Meinung/
Nechst ordentlicher Eintheilung eines jeden Buches und Capitels/
und Erwegung der nachdrücklichen Wort/ und Redens-Art
in der Heil. Sprache/
sonderlich aber
Der Evangelischen allein seligmachenden Warheit/
gründ- und deutlich erörtert/
und mit Anführung
Herrn LUTHERI deutschen/ und verdeutschten Schrifften/
also abgefasset/
daß der eigentliche Buchstäbliche Verstand/
und gutes Theils auch
der heilsame Gebrauch der Heil. Schrifft
fürgestellet ist/
Mit grossem Fleiß/ und Kosten ausgearbeitet/
und verfasset/
von

D. ABRAHAM CALOVIO,

Im Jahr Christi cIↄ Iↄc XXCI.
welches ist das
5681ste Jahr/ von Erschaffung der Welt.
Zu Wittenberg/
Nicht uns HERR/ nicht uns/ sondern deinem Namen gib Ehre/
umb deiner Gnade und Warheit!

Gedruckt in Wittenberg/ bey Christian Schrödtern/ der Univ. Buchdr.

J. S. Bach and Scripture

Glosses from the Calov Bible Commentary

Main title page that appears in each volume of the Calov Bible Commentary.

J. S. Bach and Scripture

Glosses from the Calov Bible Commentary

Introduction, Annotations, and Editing
by Robin A. Leaver

Publishing House
St. Louis

Manufactured in the United States of America

Library of Congress Cataloging in Publication Data

J. S. Bach and Scripture.

Contains facsimilies of all marginal comments in Bach's hand with English translation and commentary.
Bibliography: p.
1. Bach, Johann Sebastian, 1685-1750—Religion and ethics. 2. Calov, Abraham, 1612-1686. I. Leaver, Robin A.
ML410.B1J18 1985 220.7 85-6706
ISBN 0-570-01329-1

1 2 3 4 5 6 7 8 9 10 PP 94 93 92 91 90 89 88 87 86 85

In memoriam
Christoph Trautmann
1933 — 1984

Contents

Abbreviations

BACH *Bach: The Quarterly Journal of the Riemenschneider Bach Institute.* 1970–.

BD Neumann, W., and H.-J. Schulze, eds. *Bach-Dokumente, herausgegeben vom Bach-Archiv Leipzig.* Supplement to *NBA,* 4 vols. Kassel, 1963–79.

BJ *Bach-Jahrbuch.* 1904–.

BR David, H.T., and A. Mendel, eds. *The Bach Reader: A Life of Johann Sebastian Bach in Letters and Documents.* London, 1966.

BWV Schmieder, W. *Thematisch-systematisches Verzeichnis der musikalischen Werke von J. S. Bach* [Bach-Werke-Verzeichnis]. Leipzig, 1950.

CTM *Concordia Theological Monthly.* 1930–73.

KB *Kritischer Bericht* of *NBA.*

Leaver A Leaver, R. A. "Bach und die Lutherschriften seiner Bibliothek," *BJ* 1975, pp. 124–32.

Leaver B —."Luther and Bach," *BACH* 9, no. 3 (July 1978): 9–12, 25–32.

Leaver C —.*Bachs theologische Bibliothek: Eine kritische Bibliographie (Bach's Theological Library: A Critical Bibliography).* Beiträge zur theologischen Bachforschung 1. Stuttgart, 1983.

LW *Luther's Works.* American Edition. Philadelphia and St. Louis, 1955–.

NBA *Johann Sebastian Bach: Neue Ausbage sämtlicher Werke* [Neue Bach Ausgabe]. Jointly issued by the Johann-Sebastian-Bach-Institut, Göttingen, and the Bach-Archiv, Leipzig. Leipzig and Kassel, 1954–.

SML *Sermons of Martin Luther.* 8 vols. Grand Rapids, 1983. Reprint of vols. 7–14 of the Lenker edition, Minneapolis, 1904–09.

Trautmann A Trautmann, C. "'Calvoii Schrifften. 3. Bände' aus Johann Sebastian Bachs Nachlass und ihre Bedeutung für das Bild des lutherischen Kantors Bach," *Musik und Kirche* 39 (1969): 145–60.

Trautmann B —. "J. S. Bach: New Light on His Faith," *CTM* 42 (1971): 88–99.

Preface

The Bible commentary once owned by the composer Johann Sebastian Bach is now in the Ludwig Fuerbringer Library of Concordia Seminary, St. Louis. It is *Die deutsche Bibel,* edited largely from Luther's writings by the theologian Abraham Calov, in three large folio volumes, published in Wittenberg in 1681–82. It is of immense importance to Bach studies since it contains the composer's marginal comments alongside particular Biblical passages, as well as underlinings and other markings. They reveal something of the innermost thinking of the great composer and illuminate his theological and devotional approach to his art. It also provides evidence for Bach's own commitment to the Christian faith.

Presented here are facsimiles of nearly all the marginal comments and corrections in Bach's hand, together with a selection of the most significant underlinings and other markings. This book is in two parts. The first is the introduction, which discusses the character of the volumes, how they were rediscovered, Bach's estimation and use of them, etc. The second part comprises the facsimiles, which include enlargements of the entries in Bach's hand and other interesting material, and detailed notes and commentary on each of the facsimiles. The material is cross-referenced throughout by the facsimile numbers in part two.

The main purpose of this book is to make the evidence concerning Bach's faith, life, and work that is contained in these volumes more widely available and to draw attention to some of the significance of the composer's handwritten additions and amendments. In preparing this edition I am particularly indebted to the late Christoph Trautmann, friend and colleague, whose pioneer work on the volumes is the starting point for any study of them. I am also grateful to Professor Howard H. Cox for communicating to me something of his work on the underlinings in the volumes and the chemical analysis of the inks of the handwritten additions and to Hilton C. Oswald, who has again helped me with the problems of translation. In particular the translations of appendixes 1 and 2 and those within the notes on facsimiles 1, 2, 3, 18, 33, 41, 43, 47, 53, 55, 63, and 64 are all his work. The remainder of the translations, where a source is not identified, are my own.

25 January 1985
Conversion of St. Paul

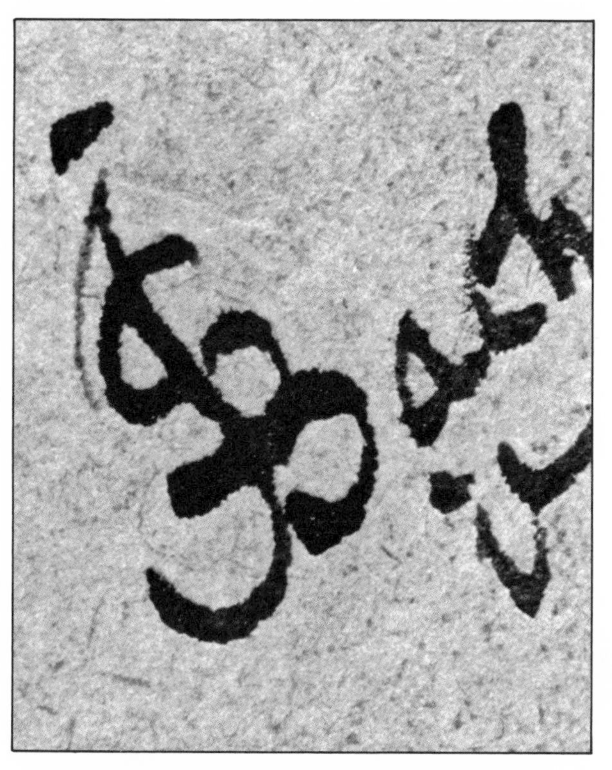

Introduction

In 1865, that is, 13 years before Spitta published his classic study of Bach,[1] Bitter wrote of the composer (in the paraphrase of his English translator):

> *He was in truth a sincere Christian; and his deep religious feeling is shown throughout his life. He was a zealous Lutheran; his healthy mind was not troubled with doubts, but he had not, like so many, passively remained in the church in which he was brought up; he had made its creed his own by faithful study and mature reflection; had embraced it with his understanding, and impressed it on his heart, and his life was shaped in conformity to it.*[2]

In practically every subsequent biography and study of the great composer a similar statement has been made or taken even further.[3] So Bach has been called "the classic Lutheran layman," "a sign of God," "the Preacher," "the Teacher," "the Theologian," "the first great German voice since Luther," and, more extravagantly still, "Bach, the Fifth Evangelist." Walter Blankenburg, in the Bach year of 1950, cautioned against "a faulty cult of a personality and a hero worship that turns backwards. To call Bach the 'Fifth Evangelist' testifies of a dangerous misunderstanding of his music: it serves the Gospel, but it is not the Gospel." But even he had to conclude that "for all of his creating and working, Bach was first of all a member of the Evangelical [Lutheran] Church."[4] And a few years later the same author wrote: "For all serious Bach research there is no question, that Bach's real spiritual home was orthodox Lutheranism."[5] In this Walter Blankenburg was simply expressing the commonly held view of Bach's faith and its expression in his life and work.

However, a serious question mark was placed over this generally accepted view by Friedrich Blume. In June 1962 he caused quite a stir when, in a lecture given at the Bachfest in Mainz, he asked rhetorically: "Did Bach have a special liking for church work? Was it a spiritual necessity for him? Hardly. There is at any rate no evidence that it was. Bach the supreme Cantor, the creative servant of the Word of God, the staunch Lutheran, is a legend."[6] Certainly, there was more than an element of truth in Blume's thesis, for much of the material written on Bach's faith and theology up to that time was in part legendary, part of the folklore of Bach studies. Bach's personal religion had always been assumed to be self-evident, requiring neither justification nor investigation. For example, no one seems to have questioned Bitter's categorical statement that Bach's "healthy mind was not troubled by doubts." There is just no evidence for such a sweeping statement. It is simply not known whether he did or did not have doubts about the Christian faith. But considering that even Luther was not immune to doubt from time to time, it seems fairly certain that Bach would have had his times of questioning the basics of the Christian faith.

The problem has been that instead of examining the facts of Bach's life and work objectively, many authors have simply written from within their own subjective religious—or non-religious—presuppositions.[7] Thus in 1938 the *Friends Quarterly Examiner* included an article by R. E. Witt entitled "Bach, the Quaker's Musician."[8] In 1966 loyal, devout Roman Catholics in Venice lobbied the Vatican's weekly, *Osservatore Della Domenica,* for his canonization—that he should be no longer "Johann Sebastian" but "Saint" Bach![9] Now clearly, Bach was neither a Quaker nor a Catholic, but Blume suggests that even though Bach worked for most of his life within the Lutheran Church, it is a misinterpretation of the man to regard him as personally committed to the Lutheran expression of Christianity.

What was it that caused Blume to question the traditional view of Bach, the committed Christian composer? His main piece of evidence was the new chronology of the vocal works of Bach, as established by Georg von Dadelsen and Alfred Dürr.[10] Blume concluded that as the result of the work of these men, "Spitta's picture of the supreme Cantor toiling away for years on end at the task of supplying his Leipzig congregations with cantatas has been destroyed."[11] This new chronology, which is scientifically based on an examination of the watermarks and handwriting characteristics of Bach's manuscripts, suggests that after his appointment as cantor in Leipzig in 1723, Bach spent the next five years or so in feverish activity, almost exclusively devoted to church music. The period from 1728 to about 1733 shows a distinct decrease in output, and after 1733 Bach apparently composed only a few occasional pieces. Such a revelation demands an explanation. For Blume, and others who have followed him, this is evidence that Bach lost his faith—or at least lost his vocation as a church musician—around 1730, if indeed he had any personal commitment before that time. Some have concluded that Bach was never particularly religious and have argued that the only place a man of his gifts and abilities could exercise them was in such church appointments as the Leipzig cantorate, and the fact that he held such a position does not necessarily imply any religious commitment on his part.[12]

However, the decline in the composition of church music revealed by the new chronology is not to be explained by positing Bach's personal rejection of the Christian faith. It is more likely to have been caused by the lack of understanding and sympathy on the part of the officialdom in Leipzig. Throughout his 27 years in Leipzig, there was hardly a time when he was not in dispute with one or another of the three governing bodies: the town council, the church consistory, and the university.

I have presented the relevant material in detail elsewhere,[13] but it would be as well to review the basic information here. Bach was elected cantor in Leipzig on 22 April 1723, but he was not the town council's first choice. Georg Philipp Telemann was preferred, and if the council could not secure his services, then it would turn to Christoph Graupner.[14] From the beginning Bach and the Leipzig officials interpreted the terms of his contract regarding the cantor's teaching duties in the Thomasschule in opposing ways. When Bach was officially installed on 1 June, there was an accidental departure from the traditional ceremonies. This was still being referred to 10 months later, giving the impression that there were some who thought it constituted a legal loophole by which their incorrigible cantor could be dismissed. About the same time, Easter 1724, Bach annoyed the officialdom of Leipzig by advertising that the Passion music on Good Friday would be performed in the Thomaskirche—for the second year in succession. But the local tradition was for the two principal churches of St. Thomas and St. Nicholas to share the Passion music in alternate years. Thus Bach had to bow to the dictates of tradition enforced by the council.

In 1725 Bach complained of unfairness regarding university duties, which he held were rightfully his since his predecessor had so operated. He wrote three letters of complaint to the elector of Saxony in an attempt to resolve the matter. Two years later, in 1727, the same matter was still causing problems, and Bach was again out of favor over the memorial service for the elector's departed wife.[15] In 1728 the consistory overruled Bach's right to choose hymns, and in 1730 the town council criticized Bach for laziness, and a member commented that "he shows little inclination for work." Bach replied with "A Short but Most Necessary Draft of a Well-Appointed Church Music with Certain Modest Reflections on the Decline of the Same." In this document Bach charged Leipzig officialdom with providing him with inadequate instrumental and vocal resources to work with. The same year, 1730, also produced his now famous letter to Georg Erdmann, in which he stated, "The authorities [in Leipzig] are odd and little interested in music. So I must live amid continual vexation, envy, and persecution; accordingly I shall be forced, with God's help, to seek my fortune elsewhere." After 1732 Bach composed nothing further in honor of the town council, and in the following year there was no entry on the St. Thomas cantor in the appropriate volume of the great Leipzig encyclopedia, Zedler's *Grosses vollständiges Universal Lexicon alle Wissenschafften und Künste.* The vast reference work reproduces musical information from J. G. Walther's *Musicalisches Lexicon oder Musicalische Bibliothek* (Leipzig, 1732), but the entry on J. S. Bach was not taken over by the great encyclopedia. Zedler's *Lexicon* was a prestigious Leipzig production, and therefore the omission represents something of an official snub for the Leipzig cantor. In 1733 he sent the Kyrie and Gloria of what later became known as the *Mass in B Minor* to the elector of Saxony, explaining:

> *For some years and up to the present moment, I have had the* Directorium *of music in the two principal churches in Leipzig, but have innocently had to suffer one injury after another... but these injuries would disappear altogether if your Royal Highness would grant me a title of your Royal Highness's Court Capelle, and would let your High Command for the issuing of such a document go forth to the proper place.*[16]

Bach's reasoning appears to have been that if he received such a title, the petty town officials in Leipzig would have to treat him with more consideration and respect. Then during 1736 and 1737 there was the long and bitter controversy in the Thomasschule between himself and Rector Johann August Ernesti, a man who disliked music and who was developing an un-Lutheran approach to Scripture.[17]

Such was a Bach's experience in Leipzig, and it forms the immediate background for a number of manuscript additions found in Calov's *Die deutsche Bibel* (see, for example, nos. 57, 70, 71, 72). With all this antagonism and misunderstanding from and by the town officials, it is hardly surprising that Bach's creativity waned. Therefore it is too simplistic to suggest that the new chronology "proves" that Bach lost his faith in God (although he was clearly aware of the possibility; see nos. 33, 67, 69). What is probably much nearer the truth is that it demonstrates that Bach lost faith in Leipzig officials who neither understood nor appreciated him.

Friedrich Blume came to his conclusion that Bach must have lost his faith in the early 1730s because of his presupposition that a truly Christian composer would steadily produce work for the church evenly throughout his life and that if he did not, then his faith and Christian commitment must necessarily be called into question. Alfred Dürr, one of the architects of the new chronology, took Blume to task:

> *This premise seems to be unsound. I do not see why a man should not be regarded as a church musician—and as fully conscious of*

> *his bent—just because when he first took office, he devoted superhuman energy to providing himself with a stock of practicable compositions of his own, to be repeated as necessary. Indeed, I doubt whether it would have been physically possible for Bach to continue such exertions throughout his life; and in any case, I cannot see how the known facts can be used to prove that Bach lost his vocation—any more than I can see that the converse would be true; that is to say, that writing church cantatas at regular intervals throughout the Leipzig period would have proved that he was a devout Christian.*[18]

The Christian character of a composer is not to be demonstrated by the frequency of his compositions for the church but rather by the quality, content, and nature of those compositions. Thus, after Blume had delivered his dissenting view, Walter Blankenburg could still state emphatically: "It is precisely the liturgical works of Bach's old age that come forward in the light of a conscious Christian affirmation of faith. . . . Studies of his works, above all the *Christmas Oratorio*, the *Clavierübung*, Part III, and the *Mass in B Minor*, in the research of recent times have made it absolutely clear that these creations in particular are motivated by a Christian faith and a Christian view of life."[19] Blume's thesis has therefore not been universally accepted,[20] although it has been widely influential. However, it did raise an important and fundamental question that needs to be answered: Where is the objective evidence, outside of the internal evidence to be discovered within his choral works, that will demonstrate clearly the composer's Christian faith and commitment? The evidence came to light just seven years after Blume raised the question when these Calov volumes were rediscovered.

The Rediscovery of the Bach Bible Commentary

How these volumes come to light is an interesting story in its own right.[21] On 25–29 June 1934 the Michigan District of the Lutheran Church—Missouri Synod met in Frankenmuth, Michigan. Frankenmuth was founded in 1845 by 15 settlers from the province of Middle Franconia, Bavaria, as a center for missionary work among the Chippewa Indians. They were among the many German missionaries sent to America by Wilhelm Loehe of Neuendettelsau. Over the years the town was expanded by other German immigrants, and the local St. Lorenz Lutheran Church thrived. There was a break with Loehe early on, and the church in Frankenmuth became one of the more important and influential parishes of the Missouri Synod.[22] A characteristic of early generations of immigrants was the close relationship various families developed with each other. Thus in 1934 Pastor Christian G. Riedel[23] of Detroit stayed with his cousin,[24] an elderly farmer then in his 74th year, Leonard Reichle. The Reichles were a well-established Frankenmuth family.[25] Leonard's father, Ludwig Michael, was born in Oberstenfeld, about 20 miles north of Stuttgart, on 24 August 1806. He worked with his father as a carriage builder until 1827 when at the age of 21 he left Oberstenfeld and eventually emigrated to America. He arrived in 1836 and settled in Philadelphia. He stayed there 11 years, was married in 1838, and became the father of three children: Louis, Christian, and Heinrich. In 1847 he migrated to Michigan, staying nine months in Ann Arbor. The following year the family moved to Frankenmuth, where Leonard Reichle was born on 5 November 1859.[26] He presumably worked in his father's carriage building business. On his father's death, 27 March 1879, Leonard went into business for himself.[27] In 1895 he was described as a "painter of carriages,"[28] so he presumably took up farming at a later date.

During Riedel's stay in Frankenmuth in June 1934, his cousin, Leonard Reichle, showed him an old folio German New Testament that his father had bought in Philadelphia. Trautmann[29] gives 1847 as the year of purchase, but I have been unable to verify it. Trautmann appears to have assumed the date on the basis of a statement made by Ludwig Fuerbringer, which was later pasted into the volumes (see below). However, the statement is not that specific, and all one can say for sure is that Ludwig Michael Reichle purchased the volumes in Philadelphia sometime between

1836 and 1847. Philadelphia booksellers did quite well by persuading penniless immigrants arriving at the port to sell their books for very little money.[30] That the volumes were sold and bought in America is confirmed by a now-erased pencil entry in each of the three books that includes a dollar sign, presumably a coded price mark:[31]

What Reichle had put before Riedel was a single volume, the third of the set, that is, the New Testament section of Calov's commentary. He explained that it had come into his possession when his father died in 1879. What the farmer and his family had not noticed over the years Pastor Riedel discovered almost immediately. On the bottom right-hand corner of the title page was Bach's monogram with the year 1733:

On 4 July 1934, a few days after returning to Detroit, Riedel wrote to his friend Paul Sauer in Chicago.[32] Sauer was the pastor of First St. John's Evangelical Lutheran Church in the city, a church with which he was associated for all of his ministerial life.[33] He was very musical and had a special interest in church music in general and the music of Bach in particular. In 1946 it was reported that his "library on Bach and his works is probably one of the outstanding collections in this country."[34] An address he gave to the Lutheran Young People's League on 26 April 1925 led to the founding of the Chicago Bach Chorus, of which he became president. On 23 November 1928 he gave another address that he hoped would lead to the founding of another Bach chorus, this time in St. Louis. It was given at Concordia Seminary just a few days before the cantata *Wie schön leuchtet der Morgenstern* (BWV 1) was to be performed in "Old Trinity" Lutheran Church, St. Louis, as part of the liturgy for the last Sunday of the church year. He spoke of "the sensational effect of the [Bach] cantatas on Missouri Synod Lutherans in Chicago" and gave his opinion of why this was so:

> *Bach, through his characteristic* motifs, *vivifies the text, as Luther says it should be. . . . Bach is the greatest musical poet that ever lived. To Bach a Bible-text suggests a clear picture; it becomes alive with action. And this Bach paints with the most astonishing wealth of musical color. Bach's recitatives, arias, and choruses are descriptive music of the most marvelous kind. He is the past master of bringing text and music into unison. . . . All this, then, is conclusive evidence of our high privilege and sacred duty regarding the Bach cantatas. We in Chicago are deeply cognizant of our great opportunity and obligation of reviving within the Lutheran Church our unexampled heritage of church music. The Detroit Bach Chorus and the Greater Cleveland Lutheran Chorus are equally enthusiastic. The opportunity of each of these three Lutheran choruses is, no doubt, greater than that of the splendid pioneer Bach choir in America, that in Bethlehem, Pa., founded by Dr. J. Fred Wolle. But the city of the greatest opportunity and therefore of greatest obligation in spreading this marvelous Lutheran music throughout our land and Church is St. Louis. I say this in all sincerity; for I believe that through the graduates of Concordia Seminary the Bach propaganda would most rapidly radiate throughout our country. As St. Louis, and not Wittenberg, is now the center of sound Lutheranism, so also St. Louis, and not Leipzig, ought to be the world's center for fostering Bach's genuinely Lutheran church music. . . . Turn your attention to these marvelous, genuinely Lutheran, orthodox cantatas of Bach, after Luther, God's greatest gift to our Church.*[35]

Therefore Sauer, a man of conviction and experience where Bach was concerned, was the natural person for Riedel to consult about the find in Frankenmuth. Furthermore, the two men apparently stood on friendly terms with each other and shared a common interest in Bach, since Riedel was involved with the Detroit Bach Chorus. Riedel informed Sauer of his encounter with the single (i.e., the third) volume of Calov's commentary in the letter dated 4 July 1934. This was an interesting coincidence, for Sauer had bought a copy of the offprint of Hans Preuss's *Bachs Bibliothek* from a secondhand bookstore just a few weeks earlier.[36] Although he was unable to identify them, Preuss revealed that the inventory of Bach's estate clearly records "Calovii Schrifften. 3 Bände."[37] Much correspondence that is no longer extant must have passed between various people. On 31 August 1934 Paul Sauer wrote to both Hans Preuss in Erlangen and Karl Straube in Leipzig announcing that one of the Calov volumes had been found and describing the interesting form of Bach's monogram on the title page.[38] Just over a week later, on 9 September 1934, Leonard Reichle wrote to Pastor Sauer and reported: "In my opinion the other two missing Calov [volumes] cannot be found in Michigan,"[39] that is, volumes 1 and 2 covering the Old Testament and the Apocrypha. About a month later, in a letter dated 2 October 1934, Hans Preuss acknowledged Paul Sauer's letter and its report of the find.[40] In the meantime the search for the other two volumes continued in Frankenmuth. On 13 November 1934 Riedel reported to Sauer that he had recently visited his cousin Reichle in Frankenmuth, who had now recovered all the Calov volumes, and each one had Bach's monogram on its title page. The two missing volumes had been discovered in a chest hidden in the attic of Reichle's home.[41] Presumably these two volumes were shown to the pastor of St. Lorenz Church, Frankenmuth, for verification. This was Emanuel August Mayer,[42] pastor since 1893, who for reasons best known to himself entered his name on the title page of the second volume, together with the year "1934" (see no. 78e). The news must have been communicated to Hans Preuss in Erlangen, for in 1935 he wrote:

> *A few years ago the three folio volumes of Calov's "Schrifften" from Bach's library, unidentified until now, were found in America—each with his personal signature—and these writings are Bible commentaries.*[43]

On 6 February 1935 Paul Sauer wrote to Ludwig Fuerbringer, who was then president of Concordia Seminary, St. Louis. Fuerbringer was born and brought up in Frankenmuth. His father, Ottomar Fuerbringer, had been the pastor of St. Lorenz Church from 1858, and Ludwig was born in 1864. After theological study at Fort Wayne and St. Louis, Ludwig was called and ordained to be his father's assistant in Frankenmuth in 1885. He succeeded to the pastorate on his father's death in 1892, but was called to Concordia Seminary the following year. E. A. Mayer then succeeded him in Frankenmuth.[44] Fuerbringer and Sauer shared a common interest in Bach. In the first part of his autobiography Fuerbringer wrote that in the 1880s "unfortunately, the great musicians of our Church, like Johann Sebastian Bach, were almost forgotten in those days, and I do not remember that [C. F. W.] Walther played Bach [on the organ] or spoke or wrote about him."[45] In the second part of his autobiography he records:

> *I like and value above all other music the Lutheran heritage bequeathed to us by Johann Sebastian Bach and other great composers of our Church. . . .*
>
> *And now we have a regular Bach Society, sponsored by the Lutherans of [St. Louis] and arranging an annual Bach Festival, when under the direction of William B. Heyne the immortal works of the greatest Lutheran musician and one of the world's greatest composers, the* Passion According to St. Matthew, *the* Mass in B Minor, *and other works, are offered.*[46]

Sauer had corresponded with Fuerbringer earlier about Bach matters. For instance, on 29 April 1929 he wrote to Fuerbringer about some typographical errors that had occurred in the printed form of the Bach lecture he had given at Concordia Seminary the previous November.[47] Within a few weeks of Ludwig Fuerbringer's receiving the letter of 6 February 1935, in which Paul Sauer had summarized the details of the discovery of the other two volumes, Fuerbringer wrote a short piece on the find for the journal *Der Lutheraner.* This appeared on 5 March 1935, and it reveals that Fuerbringer had been involved in the authentication of the find almost from the beginning:

Two days after [Riedel had contacted Sauer] I met P. Sauer . . . and P. Sauer, knowing my interest in Bach, shared the information with me. I said to him that if it is the same work that I possess and value highly, there should be three volumes. . . . Later, the two missing volumes were found.[48]

Thus it was fortuitous, as Fuerbringer points out, that the announcement of the find could be made just before the celebration of the 250th anniversary of Bach's birth on 21 March of that year. But the short article reveals that it was Fuerbringer's personal knowledge of the work in question that enabled the Reichle family to know what they should be looking for. Fuerbringer's set of Calov's *Die deutsche Bibel* is now in my possession. Each of the three volumes bears the signature "L. Fuerbringer." The first also carries the date "Dez. 1919," the year he received them, presumably as a gift, from his cousin, Ferdinand S. Buenger, whose signature is in the third volume, with the addition "St. Louis, Mo. 1878."[49]

Later that year an article appeared in the *Detroit News* by Henry George Hoch based on information supplied by Pastor Riedel. It also made somewhat misleading use of Fuerbringer's article and reproduced in large facsimile the title page of the third volume, which was the first to be found.[50] Fifteen years later Pastor Sauer wrote to W. E. Buszin and summarized the events of 1934–35 in order to

prove that the article of Henry George Hoch, in the Detroit News, *Nov. 2, 1935, is very inexact and erroneous. Riedel did* not *meet* me *at the Century of Progress Exposition, but* wrote to me Aug. 4. —*At the Century of Progress* I *met Fuerbringer, etc. Hans Preuss did* not *sent us word in spring 1935. He did* not *recognize Bach's signature; nor did he eventually find the* trail *of the Calov book "and by the time the Frankenmuth volume was identified,* he had *succeeded in locating the other two. The third volume, which contains the New Testament was 'lost.' . . . The third volume was known to be in Philadelphia about a century ago. There the trail ended and all trace of the book was lost, until Pastor Riedel happened to look at the signature in Reichle's book." Solch ein Unsinn, such a garbled story in the* Detroit News *by Hoch!*[51]

If one compares Hoch's account with Fuerbringer's, then it becomes clear that the Detroit newsman misunderstood the St. Louis professor's German. Sauer's statement that Preuss did not authenticate the volumes runs counter not only to Hoch's inadequate article but also to Fuerbringer's account in *Der Lutheraner* and to the statement that he wrote to be pasted into the volumes (see below). This must mean that either Fuerbringer misunderstood Sauer's communication to him about the content of the letter of acknowledgment he received from Preuss, dated 2 October 1934, or that Preuss sent a letter authenticating Bach's monogram to Fuerbringer rather than to Sauer in the spring of 1935. Whether or not Preuss sent such a letter to Fuerbringer, he nevertheless accepted the authenticity of the find in his booklet *Johann Sebastian Bach der Lutheraner,* first published in 1935.[52]

At the end of his article in *Der Lutheraner,* Ludwig Fuerbringer raised the question of where such valuable treasures should be kept. Perhaps he was influenced by Sauer's lecture a few years earlier[53] when he suggested that either Concordia Seminary Library or Concordia Historical Institute in St. Louis were the most suitable places.[54] It seems that negotiations between Fuerbringer and Reichle must have taken place about this time. However, pastors Sauer and Riedel apparently attempted to persuade Reichle to give the volumes to the Bach-Haus in Eisenach. But, Reichle was dismayed by the Nazi domination of Germany and its anti-Christian activities. He thought it inappropriate to send the Bible commentary to Eisenach "because the Germans are too godless."[55]

Eventually, in October 1938, Reichle presented the three precious volumes, which once belonged to Bach, to the library of Concordia Seminary in St. Louis. Reichle wrote to the president of the seminary that the volumes had been— or were about to be— sent to St. Louis:

Frankenmuth Mich. Oct. 18/38
Dear Dr. L. Fuerbringer D. D.,
Dear Sir,
Enclosed please bill of loading of the 3

Books Die Heilige Bibel. Dr. Martin Luthers Deutschen dolmetschung und Erklärung. D. Abraham Calovii, mit J. S. Bachs underschrift, diese Buchen kaufte mein seligen Father in Philadelphia. Er hat auch sehr fiel in diese Bucher gelesen. [Then follows biographical details about his father, himself, and other members of the family, mostly in German.]. . . *My Father died March 27, 1879, and the Books with many other things were left to me. . . . I wish you would write part of the history of these Books to paste in so that later any one who sees them can know who the donators are and please mail me a copy thereof.*

With best regards to you and your family,

Very truly yours,
Leonard Reichle.[56]

Fuerbringer wrote back to Reichle on 21 October 1938, stating that the volumes had arrived safely the day before and thanking him for the gift.[57] Because of illness it took Fuerbringer a little time to comply with Reichle's request. However, he wrote to Reichle on 13 February 1939 enclosing a copy of the piece he had written about the volumes and assuring him that it had been pasted into each of them.[58] It was written in German on Concordia Seminary letterhead notepaper:

This valuable work has been given to our library by Mr. Leonard Reichle in Frankenmuth, Michigan. It is particularly interesting because it was once in the possession of J. S. Bach, as is also indicated on the title page of each volume. Prof. Hans Preuss, in his article on Bach's library in the Festschrift *for Theodore Zahn, pages 103–129, mentions this work but could not indicate which work of Calov is meant and what happened to it. Through correspondence with him it has been established that this copy was really in Bach's possession and that the handwriting is genuine. How this work came to America can no longer be determined. The father of Mr. Leonard Reichle, Ludwig Reichle, came to America in 1836 and first lived in Philadelphia, Pennsylvania, where he probably bought the work. He then moved to Frankenmuth, Michigan, in 1848, became a faithful member of the congregation there, and as his son testifies, read diligently in this work on the Bible. After his death in 1878* [sic], *it passed into the possession of the above-named son, who gave it to our Seminary library in October 1938, on account of its rareness and historical interest.*[59]

Then followed the war years, and the volumes were put into a safe place—so safe, in fact, that in November 1950 the musicologist, Walter E. Buszin, who was then professor of liturgics at Concordia Seminary, had no knowledge of its whereabouts. He wrote to Pastor Sauer, who was then living in retirement in Oak Park, Illinois, to find out whether they had been presented to the seminary library or Concordia Historical Institute or whether they had been given at all.[60] Just exactly when and where they were rediscovered again is uncertain, but the fact that they were not shown publicly until November 1961[61] suggests that the volumes came to light again when the resources of the old library, Pritzlaff Hall, were being investigated in preparation for removal to the new library building, named after Ludwig Fuerbringer, which was opened in September 1962. I was informed of the existence of these Bach volumes, in the course of my research into Bach's library, in a letter of May 1967 from the late Arthur Carl Piepkorn, professor of systematic theology at Concordia Seminary. The following year Christoph Trautmann of Berlin was largely responsible for assembling an international exhibition, based on Bach's library, which was to accompany the 1969 Bachfest in Heidelberg. Knowing Preuss's comment that the three volumes were in America, but not knowing where they were located, Trautmann initiated an inquiry through the United States Cultural Mission in Berlin. The Information Agency for Libraries in Washington was approached in the spring of 1968, and the location of Concordia Seminary, St. Louis, was established.[62] Through his personal connections with the Lutheran Church—Missouri Synod, Trautmann requested permission to display the volumes in Heidelberg. He wrote:

An agreement for the loan of the books was quickly and graciously made. On the night of Oct. 2–3, 1968, the three folios were brought across the Atlantic on a turbulent flight in the personal custody of Dr. Alfred O. Fuerbringer [son of Ludwig Fuerbringer], *who was then president of Concordia Seminary. After more than 120 years the only books so far recovered from the official estate of Bach arrived in their homeland again—on loan.*[63]

While the volumes were in Germany, Trautmann conducted a detailed and painstaking search through all of them and discovered that they not only contained Bach's monogram but also various other marginalia and markings in the composer's hand. Thus the volumes assumed an even greater significance and importance. They were duly put on exhibition in Heidelberg in June 1969,[64] and Trautmann published the fruits of his research in the journal *Musik und Kirche.*[65]

I was awarded a Winston Churchill Fellowship to go to St. Louis in 1971 to work with the volumes for several months, and I have had the opportunity of examining them on subsequent occasions. A number of others have also worked on these volumes from time to time, but after the initial interest around 1969, they have not received the attention they deserve. Part of the problem is that unless one can actually examine the marginalia and underlining recorded in Trautmann's tables,[66] one cannot always assess their true significance. Similarly, the third volume of the *Bach-Dokumente* confines itself to giving just the four main marginal entries,[67] which suggests a limited importance to the source. For example, in a recent book Professor D. Arnold has argued: "A copy of a Bible with the annotations of the seventeenth century theologian Abraham Calov is dated 1733 with his monogram JSB on the title pages of the three volumes. Bach's own underlinings and comments are to be found. They have been used to show Bach's continuing faith in and deep knowledge of the Bible; but coming from the hand of such a seasoned campaigner, they look all too clearly like the texts to be used in a coming battle against the unmusical members of the Town Council."[68] If the four marginal entries were all that could be found in these volumes, then *perhaps* one could draw such a conclusion. One of the purposes of this book is to reveal the extent and nature of the additions, corrections, and comments that Bach made in his own hand and to draw out some of the implications they have for the understanding of the composer's life, work, and Christian commitment.

Description and Identification of the Volumes

As indicated above, the volumes are now in the possession of Concordia Seminary, St. Louis, and form part of the Rare Book Collection of the seminary's library, Ludwig Ernst Fuerbringer Hall, acquisition numbers 27911, 27912, and 27913. All three volumes are bound in well-preserved, blind-tooled pigskin, with "Vol. I," "Vol. II," and "Vol. III" blind-stamped on the spine of the respective volume. They once had clasps to keep the binding tight when not in use, but only the second volume now has them. At some time in the distant past, the second volume suffered an accident with oil, kerosine, or melted wax. But apart from making the lower third of the pages somewhat darker in color, the legibility of the print and handwritten marking is unaffected. Each volume is now housed in a specially made sturdy case for protection. The folio format of the pages is 195 by 330 mm. Inside the front cover at the upper left is "No. 2700" in red crayon, which may represent the sales or catalog number of the Philadelphia bookseller. The entry of "L.220.7" in each volume is the Dewey Decimal Classification number, and "C.165," later expanded to "C.1651," is the library author number. These were added when the volumes entered Pritzlaff Memorial Library and are now obsolete.

In the second volume the signature of "Ludwig Michael Reichle" appears, with the addition, "Halt im Gedächtnis Jesum Christ." In all three Leonard Reichle's ownership stamp occurs, and the signature "E. A. Mayer. 1934" is on the title page of the second volume. Ownership by Concordia Seminary Library is marked by its former name, "Pritzlaff Memorial Library," on boxed, round, and rectangular stamps on various pages throughout the volumes. These are, of course, in addition to Bach's monogram, "J. S. Bach 1733," which is found on all three main title pages (see nos. 2, 47, 55).[69] Disregarding dedications, prefaces, and other preliminary material, all of which is unpaged, the volumes have a total of 8,709 columns on 4,355 pages. The half-title page of the first volume is now missing (see no. 1), and the title page of the third is loose.

Until the rediscovery of these actual volumes, the identity of the Calov "writings" referred to at the head of the list of theological books in the inventory of Bach's estate,[70] which was drawn up after his death, proved to be a major problem. The rather vague entry, "Calovii Schrifften. 3. Bände," appears to suggest that Bach owned a collected edition of Calov's works in three folio volumes. Thus, when a folio volume of Calov's disputations from 1651 to 1658 came into the possession of the Bach-Haus, Eisenach, the director, Conrad Freyse, thought that it might have been one of the three owned by Bach.[71] Hans Preuss, in his pioneer study of Bach's library noted above, had to confess that he had been unable to find a folio edition of Calov's works.[72] No doubt Preuss was looking for a folio edition of Calov's collected writings and rightly discovered that no such edition was ever published. After Calov's death, a suitable funeral oration was delivered. It was later printed, together with a listing of his published works.[73] In this list only four of the titles were noted as being printed in folio:

[1.] Philosophia universa in tabulas redacta. *Lübeck, 1652.*
[2.] Biblia illustrata *(a Latin commentary on the whole of the Bible). 4 vols. Frankfurt, 1672–76. 2d ed. Dresden and Leipzig, 1719.*
[3.] Die deutsche Bibel D. Martini Lutheri . . . *Wittenberg, 1682.*
[4.] Scripta anti-Sociniana in unum corpus redacta. *Ulm, 1684.*

The third title above is now known to be the correct identification, but until the actual volumes were recovered, the possibility was disregarded for two basic reasons: (1) bibliographical and other sources do not indicate the number of volumes and thus suggest that it was a one-volume work, whereas, according to the inventory, Bach owned a three-volume set; (2) the title by which it is designated (which is, in fact, the half-title page [see no. 1]) gives the impression that the work is an edition of Luther's German Bible rather than the writings of Calov.[74] The first and fourth titles listed above were also dismissed as possibilities since they were clearly single volumes. Thus the conclusion that Terry reasonably drew was that Bach owned an incomplete set of Calov's *Biblia illustrata.*[75]

The notion that these volumes were Calov's *Biblia illustrata* persisted even after the rediscovery of the actual volumes. When the new library building at Concordia Seminary was opened in 1962, the program for the occasion included the following note: ". . . some extremely significant books were added, such as the three volumes of A. Calov's *Biblia illustrata,* which came from J. S. Bach's library."[76] When Trautmann received news that the volumes he was looking for were in the seminary library, he was told that they were of Calov's *Biblia illustrata,*[77] and when Alfred O. Fuerbringer took the set of books to Germany in October 1968, he experienced some difficulty going through customs control because the volumes did not tally with the description of them on the shipment documentation, which had *"Biblia illustrata"*![78] However, now that the actual volumes are known and clearly identified, all such previous speculation is rendered obsolete. Nevertheless, a number of misunderstandings persist.

To begin with, the set of books is frequently referred to as a "Bible," usually "Bach's Bible," but strictly speaking it is a Bible commentary. Certainly the half-title page, by which it is usually designated, begins by describing it as "The German Bible of Dr. Martin Luther," but it continues, "with the addition of the exposition to be found in Luther's writings, so that . . . everywhere the real literal understanding, and to a considerable extent also salutary application, of Holy Scripture, especially together with the inspiring words of that man of God [that is, Luther], is presented by Dr. Abraham Calov" (see no. 1). The main title pages are equally clear (nos. 2, 47, 55), as are the subsidiary title pages (see nos. 3, 43, 53, 64), and any superficial examination of the volumes will quickly reveal that it is a Bible commentary for study purposes rather than the straight Biblical text for devotional or other reading. Although it is customary to speak of the work as being in three volumes, to be strictly and bibliographically correct it should be described as six volumes bound as three: I–II, III–IV, V–VI.[79]

The editor of the volumes was Abraham Calov (1612–86).[80] Robert Preus describes him as "the most brilliant and influential theologian of the silver age of Lutheran orthodoxy, a veritable pillar of orthodox Lutheranism."[81] He studied at Königsberg and Rostock, after which he returned to Königsberg where he was professor, pastor, and eventually superintendent from 1641 to 1643. After six years as pastor of Holy Trinity Church and rector of the Gymnasium in Danzig, he was called in 1649 to be professor of theology in Wittenberg, where he later became superintendent of the churches in Saxony and "professor primarius," as the main title pages of *Die deutsche Bibel* state (see nos. 47, 53, 55, 64).

His writing activity was enormous, and he produced a whole library of commentaries, dogmatic works, polemical books and tracts, and a variety of other theological volumes. He was a doughty champion of Lutheran orthodoxy, and a good many of his works were polemical in content. For example, he wrote no less than 28 titles on the Syncretistic Controversy alone. His most important work, the *Biblia illustrata* (4 vols., Frankfurt, 1672–76), a vast Bible commentary in Latin, had its controversial aspect in that it was written to counteract and refute the *Annotationes ad Vetus et Novum Testamentum* of Hugo Grotius (Paris, 1641–50). Calov's principal dogmatic work, *Systema locorum theologicorum* (12 vols., Wittenberg, 1655–77), also has its particular polemical thrust against the theology of Georg Calixtus. This has led later scholars to dismiss him as a bitter dogmatician, ruled by his head and not by his heart. Thus, for example, F. W. Farrer, in his Bampton Lectures on Interpretation, characterized him as "a born heresy-hunter, one of those other people's bishops who think it their special mission to take in charge the orthodoxy of their fellow men. . . . This fury for polemics is the invariable result of a dead and formal theology."[82]

There is no doubt that Calov was a controversialist. There is also no doubt that he was not a cold and formal theologian but rather a man of deep piety and warm devotional life.[83] Certainly his writings are uneven, as Preus has stated: "Calov enjoys the distinction of having produced some of the most provocative and moving and some of the dullest and most repetitious writings of his day."[84] But again, as Preus reminds us, many of Calov's concerns were exactly those of Philipp Jacob Spener,[85] the father of Lutheran Pietism. Even among the dull passages of his writings there are warm flashes of piety and devotion. His catechetical writings for children, issued in Danzig and Wittenberg, are anything but exercises in dry, academic theology, and *Die deutsche Bibel* is pervaded by a warm devotional spirit. His *Biblia illustrata* is one thing, but in the words of Ludwig Fuerbringer, *Die deutsche Bibel* is "entirely different."[86] Of course, polemics are not entirely excluded. The Dedicatory Epistle, which is largely concerned with the doctrine of Scripture, spills over into anti-Roman Catholic polemic (see Appendix 1), and various controversial matters are raised elsewhere from time to time. But the overall tone and tenor of the writing is both practical and devotional as well as theological in content.

Calov's method is important to grasp. He is not the author so much as the editor of this complete commentary on Scripture. As the various title pages and the heading of the first index make clear, the substantial part of the commentary is taken from the writings of Martin Luther (see nos. 1, 2, 3, 43, 47, 53, 55, 64, 76, and Appendix 1, pp. 161–81). The commentary is essentially made up of quotations from Luther, either written originally in German or later translated from Latin into German (see no. 2), and where Calov, as editor, could not find a passage from Luther expounding the verse(s) in question, he has supplied his own commentary. In other words, the commentary can be seen as an edition of Luther's works arranged in Biblical order, with additional material from Calov. But even when Calov includes his own material, it is often largely dependent on the words of the Reformer, which are taken over virtually *verbatim* without either acknowledgment or quotation marks (see, for example, no. 58).

If the volumes are perused with the aim of discovering which edition of Luther's works Calov mainly employed for this commentary, then it quickly becomes clear that it was the Altenburg edition: *Aller deutschen Bücher und Schrifften des theuren, seeligen Mannes Gottes, Doctori Martin Lutheri* (10 vols., Altenburg, 1661–64). The tenth volume of this edition is an extensive index volume: *Haupt-Register über Herrn D. Mart. Lutheri Seel. Gesampte Teutsche Schrifften* (Altenburg, 1664).[87] The third chapter is a comprehensive index to the passages of Scripture on which

Luther either preached, commented, or lectured, arranged in Biblical order. This extensive index, which covers some 290 pages,[88] was clearly Calov's starting point in compiling this commentary. If one compares the passages referred to in this index with those that Calov has actually quoted, then one can see that in most cases he has followed the passage or passages recorded in the index. From time to time he quotes from the earlier Jena or Wittenberg editions instead of the Altenburg edition of Luther's works. But he could also have located those references through this massive index volume, since it includes cross-references to all the important previous editions of the Reformer's writings. For the commentary on the New Testament Calov also uses Luther's sermons on the Epistles and Gospels of the church year in his *Hauspostille* and *Kirchenpostille,* which were not included in any collected edition of Luther's works up to this time. It would not have been very difficult for a pastor like Calov, who year by year preached on these Epistles and Gospels, to locate the appropriate sermons of Luther in those two collections when commenting on a particular Biblical text.

The Place of the Calov Volumes in Bach's Library

There is evidence that Bach treated these volumes with special care. Even today they are in an excellent state of preservation, finely and robustly bound in pigskin. The fact that they are in such good condition suggests that Bach, and every owner since, treated them with care. But that is not to suggest that they were unused volumes. The underlining, corrections, and marginalia point to their continued use over a period of time. Another indication of Bach's care for the volumes is the number of corrections he made to the text in accordance with the errata at the end of the final volume (see, for example, nos. 6, 9, 30, 31, 34). These were not volumes to ornament his bookshelves but books to be used.

Yet another indication of the high regard Bach had for these volumes is that they head the list of theological books that was drawn up after his death in 1750.[89] Whoever drew up this inventory either had little knowledge of the books or was in great haste, for there are numerous errors in it. For example, at least four of the authors' names are misspelled; books by Heinrich Müller and Johannes Müller are considered together simply under "Müller"; and the library is grossly undervalued.[90] It is possible that the person who drew up the list sorted the books into some kind of order before listing them, but it is more likely that the inventory represents Bach's own classification of his books. The books are listed according to their format and size—folio, quarto, and octavo—and this classification undoubtedly represents their position in Bach's bookcase. The large folio volumes would have been on the bottom shelves to give stability, with the squat quarto volumes on the middle shelves and the smaller octavo volumes at the top. It appears that the compiler of the list simply worked along the shelves, noting the titles on the spines of the books and perhaps occasionally pulling out a volume to check its title page. The list began with the folio books thus:

[1.] *Calovii Schrifften. 3. Bände*
[2.] *Lutheri Opera 7. Bände*
[3.] *Idem. Liber 8. Bände*
[4.] *Ej. Tischreden*
[5.] *Ej. Examen Conc. Trid.*
[6.] *Ej. Comment. über den Psalm 3ter Theil*
[7.] *Ej. Hauss Postille*
[8.] *Mülleri Schluss Kette*

There is a further error to note here: The fifth entry was not a book written by Luther. It was the work of Martin Chemnitz, *Examen Concilii Tridentini* (4 vols. bound as one, Frankfurt, 1574), the classic Lutheran reply to the formulations of the Council of Trent.[91] Presumably, whoever used it last put it back in the wrong place among the Luther volumes. So if one disregards this work, some 18 volumes of the writings of Martin Luther are listed. But, as explained above, the Calov volumes in a sense represent another edition of Luther's works with the content arranged in Biblical order. It is true that where he has been unable to find a suitable quotation from Luther, Calov has supplied his own commentary, but even so, in Bach's day it was regarded as Luther's rather than Calov's commentary. Johann Gottlob Carpzov, archdeacon of the Thomaskirche until 1730, and Solomon Deyling, superintendent in Leipzig during the whole of Bach's cantorate, considered the commentary to be essentially an edition of Luther's works.[92] Bach evidently agreed with them, for in his library this three-volume commentary was carefully placed alongside his other Luther volumes. Thus, if these three volumes are added to the other folios of Luther, there were 21 fat folio volumes devoted to the writings of the German Reformer on Bach's bookshelves. But if one considers that the three Calov volumes amounted to six printed volumes and that the Altenburg edition of Luther's works (the second entry in the inventory), though normally bound in seven volumes, was printed in 10, then the total rises to 27. If one also adds the quarto volume of Luther's *Hauspostille* and the octavo volume of Johannes Müller, *Lutherus Defensus,* which were also in his library,[93] then something of the high regard Bach had for Luther and his writings can be appreciated. But these Calov volumes can provide further information regarding Bach's respect for Martin Luther.

In 1742 the library of the theologian Andreas Winkler, who died earlier that year, was sold by auction in Leipzig. Apparently Bach attended the auction and bought some books, for there is in existence a receipt in his hand that gives the details of his purchase:

> *These German and magnificent writings of the late D*[octor]. *M*[artin]. *Luther (that came from the library of the great Wittenberg theologian D*[octor]. *Abrah*[am]. *Calovius, which he probably used to compile his great* Teütsche Bibel, *and also, after his death, passed into the hands of the equally great theologian D*[octor]. *J*[ohann]. *F*[riedrich]. *Mayer)* [I] *have acquired for 10 th*[a]*l*[er]. *anno 1742. mense Septembris.*
> *John. Sebast. Bach*[94]

Here is the evidence that Bach purchased the Altenburg edition of Luther's works in September 1742. That it was the Altenburg edition and not another is confirmed by the following:

1. In the receipt Bach refers to the volumes as "Diese *Teütsche* . . . Schrifften des seel[igen] D. M. Lutheri." Of the Jena, Wittenberg, and Altenburg editions, only the Altenburg edition specifically mentions "German" on the title pages: *Aller Deutschen Bücher und Schrifften . . . Doctor Martini Lutheri.* The other two editions make no reference to language on their title pages.

2. Bach explains in the receipt that the edition of Luther's works he has just purchased was once owned by Abraham Calov, who may well have used these particular volumes of Luther to compile *Die deutsche Bibel.*[95] As noted above, even a superficial examination of the Calov volumes reveals very clearly that the main Luther edition he used in preparing this commentary was the Altenburg edition. Bach is well aware of this fact, for it is the main reason for his purchase, as he explains on the receipt.

3. Although the Altenburg edition was printed and published in 10 volumes, it was usually bound in 7.[96] Therefore, as the second item in the inventory of Bach's books mentions a seven-volume edition of Luther's works, one can state with reasonable certainty that it was the Altenburg edition that he bought in September 1742.

The three Calov volumes from Bach's library bear the year "1733." (Whether this represents the year of purchase is discussed below.) They were obviously highly treasured and frequently used volumes, for they contain Bach's carefully made marginal notes and underlinings. In 1742 the work was still important to him, so much so that when he had the opportunity to buy the actual set of Luther's works that had been owned by Calov and therefore most probably used to compile the commentary, he took that opportunity. Thereafter these two sets—the Calov Bible commentary and the Altenburg edition once owned by Calov—were kept together and given the place of priority in his bookshelves. The first two entries of the inventory drawn up after his death in 1750 read:

[1.] *Calovii Schrifften. 3. Bände*
[2.] *Lutheri Opera 7. Bände*

When the library was divided among the family, it is significant that these two sets of books were kept together. Even more important, they were both assigned to his widow, Anna Magdalena[97]—a distribution that almost suggests that because she knew how highly her husband regarded these books, she requested that they pass into her keeping.

Bach's Monogram and the Year 1733

There are five known examples of the intertwined JSB monogram, reminiscent of Bach's seal, which, however, is formed by the three letters being woven together with their mirror image:

The five examples can be divided into three groups:

Example 1 is found at the lower right-hand corner of the title page of one of Bach's copies of Elias Nicolaus Ammerbach's *Orgel oder Instrument Tabulatur* (Leipzig, 1571).[98] The form does not have the fluidity of the other two and therefore may well date from an earlier time when Bach was experimenting with the possibilities of the three letters. In particular, the first letter is clearly an *I* rather than a *J*. These were interchangeable letters, and *I* would be the obvious letter to experiment with first, since it provides a perpendicular for the formation of the letter *B*. This copy of Ammerbach is now in the library of Cambridge University and is further authenticated by an inscription on the flyleaf by Dr. Charles Burney: "This book which formerly belonged to Sebastian Bach was a present from my honored friend Mr. C. P. E. Bach, Musick director at Hambro 1772. C. Burney."

Example 2 occurs on a fragment in the possession of Professor Gerhard Herz of Louisville. It appears to be the bottom right-hand corner of a title page or flyleaf of a book or manuscript. Professor Herz has made a convincing case for its being from the flyleaf of the Leipzig copy of Ammerbach's *Orgel oder Instrument Tabulatur*. This work was known to have had Bach's signature at one time, but it had been removed by an unknown and unauthorized person during the later 19th century.[99] Here the first letter is an obvious *J*. The *g*-like *h*, the small crescent to the right of the upper part of the *S*, and the threes written with a concave upper bar, while slightly unusual, can nevertheless be paralleled in other Bach manuscripts, as Herz has demonstrated.[100]

Example 3 is the form of the monogram on the three main title pages in the Calov commentary (see nos. 2, 47, 55). It is very similar to 2, except there is no crescent on the *S*, the *h* is different, and the threes have a rounded top.

The fact that both 2 and 3 bear the same year, 1733, is both interesting and intriguing. One can take the date at its face value and assume that it records the year that the volumes came into Bach's possession. As was outlined above, 1733 was a "low" year for Bach and marks the beginning of a fallow period in which he virtually abandoned composing church music for some years. According to Blume's thesis, this decline in the composition of religious music is to be explained by the composer's abandonment of the Christian faith. But it is at this significant juncture that he purchased this Bible commentary. This suggests that in the face of unpopularity and misunderstanding, Bach was drawing on the resources of his faith and digging deeper into its foundation.

That the Ammerbach book also once bore a nearly identical monogram and the same date raises the possibility that the year does not represent the date that Bach took possession of all four volumes, that is, the three Calov volumes and the Ammerbach *Tabulatur*. As has been noticed earlier, the Calov volumes are in an excellent state of preservation, and there is little indication that they were owned by anyone else before Bach. But even allowing for the fact that such books stayed longer on booksellers' shelves than they do today, the time between 1681–82, when they were printed and published, and 1733 seems somewhat excessive (51 years). Therefore the question is raised: Could it be that these volumes came into Bach's library much earlier than 1733?

Since the Herz fragment bears a similar form of the monogram and exactly the same date, there are good grounds for thinking that Bach may have had another purpose for recording the year. Gerhard Herz has put the case well: "The fact that two out of the six extant titles from Bach's library show not only graphologically identical signatures but also the same year might give pause for reflection."[101] He also points out that during 1731–32 Bach and his family had to move out of their apartment while the Thomasschule was being reconstructed. Only a matter of months after the Bachs had moved back into the school building, the Saxon elector, Friedrich Augustus I, died (1 Feb. 1733). A four-and-a-half-month period of mourning ensued in which musical performances—inside and outside the churches—were drastically curtailed. Thus Herz concludes: "It seems at least to lie in the realm of possibility that . . . Bach used the sudden cessation of his hectic activities in early 1733 to reassemble and put in order his library and at that time penned his 'ex libris' into his best-loved books."[102] Therefore, if Bach purchased the Calov commentary before 1733, the fact that in this critical year these volumes appear to have been important to him again suggests that he was renewing rather than renouncing his faith. He apparently continued to do so, since nine years later, in September 1742, he specifically mentions this Bible commentary on the receipt he wrote after purchasing the very volumes from which its substance was quarried. Further, if the Calov commentary was in Bach's possession before 1733, it may have exerted some influence on his compositions, such as the cantatas in general or specific works like the motet *Singet dem Herrn ein neues Lied* (BWV 225) and the *St. John Passion* (see nos. 18, 63).

Bach and the Bible

Calov's Dedicatory Epistle (Appendix 1) is in effect an exposition of the doctrine of Scripture and a careful, if sometimes pedantic and repetitive, setting out of the principles on which the commentary was compiled and written.[103] The Scriptures are God's revealed Word to mankind, to be read, compared, believed, and acted on. "Thus the Scriptures function as the sole authority for the church, not merely by means of using Scriptural *words and phrases* in doctrinal statements but by believing, using, and living its *message,* which is divine truth itself."[104] This is a summary of the teaching on the Scriptures that Bach received during his schooling, which was based on Leonard Hutter's *Compendium locorum theologicorum* (Wittenberg, 1610 [see note on no. 65]). Bach's basic reverence and respect for the Bible is reflected in the librettos he chose for his cantatas, since "the decisive task of the cantatas consists not in narration or dramatic presentation of the events, but in an always new relation of this event to the men of the present."[105] It is also demonstrated in the two great passions. In the *St. John Passion,* although he does use some of the poetry of B. H. Brockes's *Der für die Sünden der Welt gemarterte und sterbende Jesus, aus den vier Evangelisten* (Hamburg, 1712), Bach rejects the poet's versification of the Biblical narrative and uses instead the direct words of Scripture. In his own carefully written manuscript of the *St. Matthew Passion* the Biblical text is written out in red ink.

However, there are those who remain unconvinced by such things and instead point to the inventory of Bach's books and suggest that as there is no Bible listed, it cannot have been very important to him personally. But it needs to be recognized that the inventory of Bach's books, drawn up after his death, is obviously incomplete and does not include all the books that Bach owned. His personal copy of J. J. Fux, *Gradus ad Parnassum* (Vienna, 1725), now in the Staats und Universitäts Bibliothek, Hamburg; his three copies of Ammerbach's *Orgel oder Instrument Tabulatur* (Leipzig, 1571), now in the University Library, Cambridge, the British Library, London, and the Stadt Bibliothek, Leipzig; and his Bohemian Brethren hymn book, *Ein hubsche new Gesang buch darinnen begrieffen die Kirchen ordnung unnd geseng* (Ulm, 1538), now in the Euing Collection of Glasgow University Library—none are listed in the inventory. It also does not include the many books Bach needed for his work in Leipzig, such as *Das Privilegirte*

Ordentliche und Vermehrte Dressdnische Gesang-Buch (Dresden and Leipzig, 1725) and *Neu Leipziger Gesangbuch . . . von Gottfried Vopelio* (Leipzig, 1682), or the copies of Luther's *Small Catechism* he would have used in the teaching of his children at home and in his teaching in the Thomasschule. It would appear that such books, in constant daily use in teaching his pupils or preparing for the services of worship, were not included in the inventory, presumably because they were not kept in the main bookcase with the others. The Bible would have been needed each day for family prayers and therefore most likely was kept on a table rather than on Bach's bookshelves. If so, it would not have been included when the contents of Bach's bookcase were listed.

It is probable that there were several Bibles in the Bach home. One, at least, has survived. Anna Magdalena Bach's Bible, printed in Eisleben in 1736 and stamped with gold letters "A. M. B." and "1738," is now in the Deutsche Staatsbibliothek, Berlin. Eleven years later she gave it to her son, Johann Christian Friedrich, on 20 Dec. 1749 with the following inscription:

> *As a perpetual memorial*
> *and for Christian edification*
> *A. M. Bach, neé Wulkin, presents*
> *this glorious Book to her dear son,*
> *Your loyal and affectionate Mamma.*[106]

The Bible was obviously greatly respected in the Bach home. What happened to Bach's own copy (or copies) will only be known if the actual volumes can be discovered. But to the skeptics who demand more evidence, one can point to the many volumes in Bach's library written by such authors as August Hermann Francke, Martin Geier, Heinrich Müller, and Martin Luther, which are collections of sermons on the Epistles and Gospels of the church year. In these volumes the portions of the New Testament on which the sermons are based are printed in full in Luther's German translation.[107] Thus Bach had access to the Biblical text in these books. He also owned another large, multi-volumed Bible commentary: Johann Olearius, *Biblische Erklärung* (Leipzig, 1678–81).[108] To these one must add the three Calov volumes within which much of the Biblical text itself appears. But the matter can be taken further since an examination of this Calov commentary reveals the evidence for Bach's having owned at least one complete Bible, that is, other than the edited texts that appear in the Calov and Olearius commentaries.

Calov's method is to quote the Bible text—a phrase, sentence, or longer passage—and then add Luther's comment (or his own) on the subject matter of the text. In many places Calov does not quote the Bible text in full but only that part on which he offers commentary. What is very significant is that in a number of instances in these volumes Bach has carefully added, from another Bible, the words Calov omitted. Genesis 13:4 is not given by Calov, so Bach adds the complete verse in the margin (no. 8). The central phrase of Exodus 5:23 is missing, so Bach supplies it (no. 17, see also nos. 20, 24, 32, 38, 48, 49, 69 [?]). Perhaps the most interesting example of Bach's completion of a Biblical text is found alongside Mark 10:29–30. Calov gives an abbreviated version of the two verses; Bach completes them in the margin:

> *Jesus said, "Truly, I say to you, there is no one who has left house or brothers or sisters or* father and *mother or* wife *and children and lands,* for my sake and the Gospel, who will not receive a hundredfold now in this time, houses and brothers and sisters and mothers and children and lands *with persecutions, and in the age to come eternal life."* (no. 61—the words added by Bach are given here in Roman type).

There are three important points raised here. There is the assurance that anyone who suffers loss because of commitment to Christ and His Gospel (1) will be compensated in this life and receive back immeasurably more than he has given up, (2) will at the same time have to suffer persecution, but (3) in the age to come will inherit eternal life. It is not known when Bach entered these Bible words,[109] but in practically every year in Leipzig he had to suffer personal attacks, misunderstandings, disrespect, and various other frustrations. What is notable is that he should choose to study these words that give the assurance that when a Christian suffers for his convictions and faith there will be compensations in this life as well as the certainty of eternal life to uphold him.

Here is evidence that Bach must have had a complete Bible that he used along with this Bible commentary and from which he copied missing verses or parts of verses into the margins of the Calov volumes. It further confirms that he looked to the Bible for support in living out his life from day to day (see nos. 37, 57, 58, 66, 70, 71, 72).

Marginalia and Underlinings

Scattered throughout these volumes are a number of marginal comments in Bach's hand that are of the greatest importance, for they point to Bach's interest in and concern for the integrity and significance of the Biblical text. Alongside Genesis 26:3 he remarks that he knows of a village called by the German equivalent of the Hebrew Beersheba (no. 10). The basic information comes from Luther's commentary on the verse, but Bach adds that he knows that the village is "about one hour from Erfurt." Leviticus 18:16 contains the prohibition of marriage between a man and his deceased brother's wife. Bach has written in the margin: "NB. The law (since it orders that a brother shall raise up his deceased brother's offspring) appears to be against this" (no. 29). There is an exception to the rule that Bach (and apparently not Calov) remembers. It is the exception that was the basis for the trick question that the Sadducees put to Jesus about the resurrection (Matthew 22:23-26). It is found in Deuteronomy 25:5–6:

> *If brothers dwell together, and one of them dies and has no son, the wife of the dead shall not be married outside the family to a stranger; her husband's brother shall go in to her, and take her as his wife. . . . And the first son whom she bears shall succeed to the name of the brother who is dead.*

This is another indication that Bach knew his Bible well and was a careful student of Scripture.

Four marginal comments have a direct connection with Bach's understanding of his art and profession. Alongside the great antiphonal psalm of redemption sung by Moses and Miriam in Exodus 15:20, Bach has written: "NB. First prelude, for 2 choirs to be performed for the glory of God" (no. 18). Gerhard Herz and Christoph Trautmann link this comment with the double-chorus motet *Singet dem Herrn ein neues Lied* (see note on no. 18). That may or may not be so, but it does indicate that the composer's custom of writing "S D G" (*Soli Deo Gloria*)—or variants of the three letters—at the conclusion of many of his works was no idle or empty formula. For him, like Luther before him, music was to glorify God (see note on no. 45).

The second of the four marginal entries occurs at the beginning of 1 Chronicles 25. This chapter presents the detail of King David's provision of 288 musicians for the worship of the old covenant. Bach comments: "NB. This chapter is the true foundation of all God-pleasing church music" (no. 40). In 1730 he had complained to the town council that the instrumental and vocal resources he had to work with in Leipzig were totally inadequate for "a well-appointed church music." King David had almost 300 musicians; Bach had barely 30 competent ones. How could the Thomascantor therefore produce church music that was pleasing to God?

A few pages further a third marginal comment with regard to music is found. It stands alongside 1 Chronicles 28:21, where David tells his son Solomon that he is "to use every willing man who has skill for any kind of service." Bach comments: "NB. Splendid proof that, beside other arrangements of the service of worship [*Gottesdienstes*], music too was instituted by the Spirit of God through David" (no. 41).

Fourth, 2 Chronicles 5:13–14 reads: "It was the duty of the trumpeters and singers to make themselves heard in unison in praise and thanksgiving to the Lord, and when the song was raised, with trumpets and cymbals and other musical instruments, in praise to the Lord, 'For he is good, for his steadfast love endures forever,' the house, the house of the Lord was filled with a cloud . . . for the glory of the Lord filled the house of God." The heading Calov gave to these verses is "How the Glory of the Lord Appeared After Beautiful Music." Bach has underlined the words "Beautiful

Music" and written in the margin: "NB. Where there is devotional music, God with His grace is always present" (no. 42). In other words, music is a bearer of the Word of God through which the grace of God is known and received.

There are other markings and underlinings that are connected with the role of music in worship. Calov heads the section 1 Chronicles 16:4–36, "The Appointment of the Singers and the Singing of a Psalm of Thanksgiving," and Bach has underlined various parts of the Biblical text (no. 39). He also underlined two important sections in Calov's preface to the Psalter in red ink: "Therefore the whole book is *called Psalterium, after the name of a musical instrument on which psalms, hymns, and thanksgiving are accompanied... to voice all kinds of beautiful melodies and arrange angelic songs.... Asaph, King David's Capelmeister*. . . . For even though Heman and Jeduthun were prophets . . . *yet they served in instrumental music-making as they had been ordered by David for the work of their office to perform this 'with harps, with psalteries, and with cymbals'* " (no. 44 and Appendix 2—Bach's underlining is in italics here). That Bach should pick up this connection between music and prophecy is very significant, and it links with his marginal comment on nos. 41 and 42. Prophecy, which is the proclamation of the Word of God, is seen as having a musical dimension. Taken together with the marginal comments referred to above, this gives us some insight into Bach's personal approach to the provision of music for the worship of the church. His relationship to his art in both performance and composition was not simply professional; it was also confessional. These markings in his own Bible commentary are intimate and personal reflections, to be shared only with his God and members of his family, and they show that his incomparable music was as much the product of his faith as of his unique and prodigious genius.

There are also a number of passages dealing with musical matters that Bach has not annotated or underlined but that were accessible to him through the topical index at the end of the third volume. Such passages are 1 Samuel 16:14–23, in which Saul was soothed by David's music, and which contains, in the comment, an encouragement to sing psalms and hymns in times of distress (no. 36); Psalm 150, in which the eschatological aspect of church music is expounded (no. 45); Luther's comment on Amos 6:5, which refers to the role of music in kindling the heart towards God and stirring the spirit through the Word of God (no. 54); and Colossians 3:16, where Luther again speaks of the function of music in the proclamation of the Word of God, asserting that music is to be identified with the Gospel rather than with the Law, and that music-making among the people of God is a sharing in the spiritual benefits of grace (no. 68).

The Question of Authenticity

All the entries in Bach's hand, and those that may well be his, are listed in the two tables on pp. 43–50. The first table deals with marginalia and corrections, the second with underlinings and other markings. There is evidence of hands other than Bach's in the volumes. For example, on Genesis 3:6–7 there are some words crossed out, probably by someone working in Schrödter's printing shop at the time the sheets were being printed (see note on no. 5). The corrections of Isaiah 25:2–3 may have been made by two different hands (no. 50). The change from *göttlich* to *geistlich* in Matthew 19:12 corresponds to Anna Magdalena Bach's handwriting, and a number of *nota benes*, written with the letters coalesced according to Bach's style, may have been added by another member of the family (see, for example, no. 66). There are also some pencil marks, which Trautmann suggests were perhaps made by Ludwig Michael Reichle,[110] and crude crossings-out in heavy red crayon by some immature person. These additional markings raise the question of authenticity and especially the question of the criteria for establishing whether or not an entry is in Bach's hand. Handwritten entries can be verified by comparison with other Bach manuscripts. The shape of the letters, the thickness of the lines, the strokes of the pen, and the density of the ink can all be compared with Bach's authentic manuscripts. The result of such comparative examination is that most of the entries listed in

Table 1 can be regarded as being Bach's.

However, the underlinings are much more difficult to evaluate. A simply drawn line by its very nature has no distinctive characteristics. But there is some help. Since Bach was the only writer who used red ink for marginalia in the volumes, one can be virtually certain that all the underlining in red is his. Bach tended to use a fine point on his quills, but since they were cut by hand, the thickness would vary with entries made with different quills. Therefore one cannot simply eliminate the thicker underlining in black ink as not scribed by Bach. Similarly, Bach appears to have used a dense black ink, but again, one cannot eliminate marking simply because the ink is of a lighter density, for entries made at different times with inks of different constituencies would produce this effect. However, where underlining or other marking appears in close proximity to marginalia or corrections with the same ink density, then one can with reasonable certainty attribute them to Bach.

Professor Howard H. Cox of Bethlehem, Pennsylvania, has been working on the problem of the authenticity of the underlining in these volumes. If the ink of the authenticated entries could be analyzed and compared with an analysis of the inks of the underlining and other marking, then some reliable answers might be found. But there was first the problem of finding a suitable laboratory that could undertake the necessary nondestructive ink analysis. Eventually Professor Cox was directed to the University of California, where such a process had been developed and used in connection with a Gutenberg Bible. The volumes were taken to the University of California in August 1982. Cox reports: "We tested 150 samples which I had selected. These included marginal writing, underlining, marginal marks, scribal symbols, signatures, etc. The results were much more complex than I had anticipated and, at that time, not very helpful. Many more authenticated entries were needed."[111] Cox has continued his research, expanding it to include other manuscripts that reliably demonstrate Bach's style and usage. "All these additional data are now making the ink analysis very useful and important. The inks of the underlining and marginal marks can now be coordinated with the inks of the marginal writing. A physicist at the University of California is collaborating with me in interpreting the ink analysis. This work is not completed but there are hopeful signs that a case can be made."[112] In due course Professor Cox will be publishing his findings. In the light of the present uncertain knowledge, we have reproduced in this volume as many of the authenticated entries as possible but only a few of the instances of underlining, concentrating on those occurrences that seem to be authentic. Nevertheless, some element of doubt must remain in these cases, as is made clear in the notes on the facsimiles in question.

Connections with Other Volumes in Bach's Library

There are many connections that can be made between these Calov volumes and other books that the inventory drawn up in 1750 indicates were in Bach's personal library. Amos 6:6 reads: "who drink wine in bowls, and anoint themselves with the finest oils, but are not grieved over the ruin of Joseph!" Bach has placed "NB" alongside the words "ruin of Joseph" (no. 54). According to the inventory Bach owned a copy of Heinrich Müller, *Evangelisches Praeservativ wider den Schaden Josephs* (Evangelical preservative against the ruin of Joseph) (Frankfurt, 1681). It seems likely that he placed the "NB" alongside the verse because he knew that Müller's volume of sermons took its theme from it and because the book itself was on his bookshelves.

His marginal note alongside Genesis 26:33, "NB. About one hour from Erfurt there is a village which has this name," demonstrates that Bach had an interest in understanding Biblical topography and geography in contemporary terms. This is confirmed by the volume in his library by Heinrich Bünting, *Itinerarium Sacrae Scripturae* (Helmsted, 1581), which is a description of the travels of prominent Biblical figures expressed in German miles (see no. 10; cf. no. 62). In Exodus 38:24–31 there is a summary of the amount of silver, gold, and bronze used in the construction of the tabernacle. The weight recorded in the text, eight tons of gold, is repeated by Bach in the margin. This also links with the Bünting volume, which includes an appendix comprising a treatise on the weights, measures, and monies of the Bible (no. 26, see also no. 27).

Although from time to time Calov may refer to a theological writer, or less often cite a passage from a particular book, it is extremely rare to find him recommending a complete book of any author other than Luther within the commentary. Revelation 14:6–8 was the portion of Scripture appointed as the Gospel for the Festival of the Reformation, celebrated each year on 31 October. Undoubtedly, Bach would have looked this passage up as he prepared for the annual celebration and may well have consulted Calov's commentary. In his comment on Revelation 14:8 Calov commends two books as excellent presentations of the truth of Lutheran doctrine over against the doctrine of the Roman Church. The first is Martin Chemnitz, *Examen Concilii Tridentini* (Frankfurt, 1574), and the second is Nikolaus Hunnius, *Apostasia Ecclesiae Romanae* (Lübeck, 1665) (no. 74).[113] Significantly, both volumes were to be found in Bach's personal library.[114] The Book of Revelation apparently had a fascination for Bach, for he owned an interesting work on this final book of the Bible: Caspar Heunisch, *Haupt-Schlüssel über die hohe Offenbarung S. Johannis* [mit]... *Erklärung aller und jeder Zahlen*... (The main key to the great Revelation of St. John with an explanation of each and every number . . .) (Schleusingen, 1684). The Book of Revelation is full of symbolic numbers, and each one is explained against the background of other Biblical numbers. Without going into the controverted area of number symbolism in Bach's works here, there is evidence in the Calov *Die deutsche Bibel* that Bach had more than a passing interest in such symbolic numbers (see nos. 14, 19, 22, 26, 27, 51, 52).

Bach and Luther

The large number of Luther volumes in Bach's library has already been mentioned.[115] The first two items in the inventory of Bach's books are the Calov *Die deutsche Bibel* and the Altenburg edition of Luther's works, which he bought at the book auction toward the end of 1742. Presumably, when he purchased this Altenburg edition, he already owned a set of Luther's writings in eight volumes.[116] The Jena German edition is the only collected edition of Luther's writings to be printed and issued in eight volumes at this time, and therefore it must have been this edition that was also in Bach's library. The Altenburg edition is virtually a reprint of the Jena edition with significant improvements and additions. It is extremely unlikely that anyone already owning the Altenburg edition would wish to purchase the Jena edition—unless he was an avid book collector—because the Altenburg edition contains all the material to be found in the Jena edition and extra material besides. Therefore one presumes that Bach already owned the Jena edition before he bought the more complete Altenburg edition in 1742. This means that after this year, Bach had many of Luther's writings in duplicate. Indeed, some of the Reformer's writings could be found in triplicate or even quadruplicate in Bach's library! The sixth entry in the inventory of Bach's books shows that the composer owned the third volume of the Wittenberg German edition.[117] This volume is almost exclusively devoted to commentaries on the psalms. Thus, if Bach wanted to read a particular psalm commentary of Luther, he could find it in the generous quotations in the Calov *Die deutsche Bibel*, vol. 1/II, and compare it with either of the respective volumes of the Altenburg and Jena editions and even with the third volume of the Wittenberg edition as well. That he had such extensive and easy access to Luther's writings suggests that Bach took the theology of the Reformer extremely seriously in his life and work.

In reviewing Hans Besch's contribution to the Friedrich Smend *Festschrift*, Walter Emery commented: "Even if Bach did buy this lot [the Altenburg edition] for his own library, it does not follow that he ever read it. Twenty years ago I myself bought an association copy that I did not want to read and am never likely to. I cannot see that this document [the auction receipt of Sept. 1742] does anything to dispel the doubts about Bach's religiosity."[118] But on the contrary, the receipt, together with the Calov volumes, does give the evidence that Bach bought this set for himself and that he read it alongside the three-volume commentary. At the same time these sources reveal Bach's concern for fundamental theological matters.

As has been stated above, the Altenburg edition of Luther's works is virtually an expanded reprint of the Jena edition. The 10 printed volumes of the Altenburg edition are arranged as follows: The first eight, which correspond to the eight volumes of the Jena edition but with additional material, are arranged in a basic chronological order. Volume 10 is the extensive index volume to the complete set. Volume nine of the Altenburg edition is the most important volume when the two editions are compared, for it contains the major omission from the Jena edition, Luther's *magnum opus,* his commentary on Genesis (1535–45), translated from Latin into German by Basilus Faber in 1557.

The Calov commentary contains an interesting marginal entry in Bach's hand that may well indicate that he compared the ninth volume of the Altenburg edition with the Calov quotation of Luther on Genesis 3. This chapter deals with mankind's fall into sin, and Calov gives a generous quotation from Luther on Genesis 3:7, which is a key verse with regard to the doctrine of original sin. However, in quoting Luther, Calov omits an important phrase, and Bach has written the missing words (given here in italics) into the margin alongside the passage:

> *The scholastics argue that [original] righteousness, when Adam was created, was not part of Adam's nature, but rather like an adornment or gift added to man, as when one places a wreath on a pretty girl, which wreath is not part of the nature of the girl but is something apart from her nature,* which comes from outside and without injuring her nature, *and can be removed again. . . . But this idea must be shunned like poison, for it minimizes original sin. . . . (no. 5)*

In the past I have argued that this is direct evidence of Bach's careful use and study of the writings of Martin Luther and that he must have compared the Altenburg edition, vol. 9, p. 79, with Calov's commentary, vol. 1/I, col. 32.[119] This argument now needs to be tempered by a subsequent discovery in these volumes. At the end of the third volume there are 10 fairly dense pages detailing errors to be corrected and omissions to be added to the printed text of all six parts. Both Trautmann[120] and the present writer, on his first encounter with the volumes, overlooked the first of these pages, which has underlining in red ink, including the words Bach added alongside Genesis 3:7—also in red ink! This red ink connection seems to suggest that the underlining on the errata page and Bach's marginal addition of the missing words were made at the same time, although the marginal entry seems to have been done with a different quill (cf. nos. 5, 77). Since the omission occurs near the beginning of the first volume and therefore is also among the first given in the list of errors and omissions, it could be argued that Bach looked up this list at the back of the third volume and began to make the necessary corrections to the text and additions to the margins at the appropriate places throughout the volumes, but soon gave up when the extent of this time-consuming activity became apparent to him. If that is so, and if the Calov commentaries came into his possession in 1733, the marginal addition alongside Genesis 3 was made soon after and therefore entirely without reference to the ninth volume of the Altenburg edition.

But there are too many uncertainties to be able to state that this was the case. To begin with, the year 1733 may not represent the date of purchase but rather the time when Bach reorganized his library.[121] Although there are corrections within the text of the volumes that follow those noted in the errata list at the end of the third volume, and although those near the beginning of volume 1 were made in red ink (see Table 1), Bach clearly did not try to transfer all the corrections into the body of the commentary. Indeed, one correction based on the errata list is made in black ink, and there are a good many others also in black that are not in the errata list. These mistakes were discovered by Bach as he actually used the volumes, and to do so he would have had to compare the printed text with a Bible and an edition of Luther's works. These corrected mistakes, which are not recorded in the errata list at the end of the third volume, indicate that it was Bach's practice to have more than one book open before him when he was engaged in Bible study. Further, the inventory reveals that the Calov commentary and the Altenburg edition of Luther's works were kept side by side in Bach's bookshelves, which implies that they were used together. The auction receipt of September 1742 confirms this conclusion. In it Bach takes the trouble to explain that he knows that the set of the Altenburg edition he has just bought was once owned by Abraham Calov and was the very edition that the Wittenberg theologian used to compile *Die deutsche Bibel.*[122] It is fairly clear that the first thing Bach would have done on taking the Altenburg volumes home would have been to compare them with his copy of Calov's commentary. If he took out the first volume of the Bible commentary, he would begin with Genesis. As was stated above, the distinctive feature of the Altenburg edition is that unlike any other previous edition it includes Luther's commentary on the first book of the Bible, and so the comparison would have begun with the ninth volume of the Altenburg edition. It is therefore possible that Bach made the marginal entry in 1742 shortly after purchasing the volumes. But the problem is that it is just not possible to know with certainty when Bach made the entry. What can be said with greater certainty is that it was made at a time when Bach was studying the book of Genesis,[123] and that study included checking the errata list at the back of the final volume.[124] What is of particular importance is the passage to which Bach has given his attention.

In his commentary on Genesis 3, Luther exposes the underestimation of original sin by scholastic theologians, and the words that Bach adds in the margin are part of an important illustration of this inadequate view. After Luther's death, Lutheranism was disturbed by a number of internal controversies. One of them was the so-called "Flacian Controversy," which was a fierce debate about the nature of original sin.[125] The controversy was resolved, along with others, in the Formula of Concord. After 1580 every Lutheran pastor, teacher, and church musician had to signify that he believed the confessional writings of his church, which were to be found in *The Book of Concord.* This included the Augsburg Confession, its Apology, the catechisms of Luther, etc.[126] But when subscription to these documents was demanded, special emphasis was placed on the Formula of Concord, for this document above all defended pure Lutheranism from the undermining influence of crypto-Calvinism and other false doctrines. For example, the religious oath required of all pastors and schoolteachers in Saxony included, among other things:

> *You shall promise and swear that you will abide and persist steadfastly, without any guile, in the pure and Christian knowledge of these lands as is contained in the original, unaltered Augsburg Confession, and repeated, explained, and preserved against falsification in its Christian* Book of Concord, *that you will do nothing against it either in secret or in public, even if you notice that others intend to do so, and will not conceal such opposition but reveal it at once and unsparingly. Though God may decree (may He graciously avert it!) that through madness and delusion you are diverted from such pure doctrine and knowledge of God either to the papists, to the Calvinists, or to other sects which are in conflict with the aforementioned pure confession and are singled out and condemned in the religious peace [of Augsburg 1555], you shall swear that in keeping with your oath you will at once and without fear report the same [i.e., your change of conviction] to the proper authority, await further orders and decision, and do all this with loyalty and without deception.*[127]

The first article of the Formula of Concord deals with the nature of original sin.[128] The end of the article emphasizes a particular section of Luther's commentary on Genesis 3 as a strong statement against any minimizing of the doctrine of original sin.[129] What is significant indeed is that it was this particular passage in Luther's Genesis commentary that Bach was studying in Calov's *Die deutsche Bibel* and at which he made the marginal addition.

Another connection with the Formula of Concord is found in some underlining at Romans 1:17 (no. 65), the verse that was of key importance in Luther's discovery of the doctrine of justification[130] (the underlining is given here in italics):

> *In short: namely, the* principal cause of God's salvation *in* word and power is the Gospel, *which is the* means of salvation. *But the* mer-

> itorious cause *is* Christ *and the* means from our side is faith *by which the revealed righteousness of Christ is received, but it is by faith alone: thus the* sinner *who* believes in Christ *is made righteous. The* form *is the* righteousness of Christ *which becomes our own by faith. The* final cause *is life and eternal salvation.*

The passage is derived from a statement in the Formula of Concord:

> *The only essential and necessary elements of justification are the grace of God, the merit of Christ, and faith which accepts these in the promise of the Gospel, whereby the righteousness of Christ is reckoned to us and by which we obtain the forgiveness of sins, reconciliation with God, adoption, and the inheritance of eternal life.*[131]

On 13 May 1723 the superintendent minister in Leipzig, Solomon Deyling, reported to the church consistory that Bach's theological views had been examined and that the cantor-elect had specifically subscribed to the Formula of Concord.[132] Just what form the subscription took is uncertain, but it must have been similar to what was required of Leipzig licentiates of theology:

> *I, N. N., swear to you . . . that I intend to follow without guile the sacred doctrine of Christ as this was handed down in the writings of the apostles and prophets and as it is explained in the prescribed Creeds, in the Augsburg Confession which was presented to Charles V in the year 1530, in its Apology, in the Schmalcald Articles, in the two Catechisms of Luther, and in the Formula of Christian Concord; to combat to the limit of my strength all godless, confused, heretical, and enthusiastic opinions . . . as truly as God will help me through his holy Gospel.*[133]

The marginal addition and underlining at Genesis 3:7 and Romans 1:17, and indeed all the other marginalia and markings, indicate that Bach's subscription was no empty formality. The Leipzig cantor made a point of studying carefully the fundamental doctrines of his faith and did so by reading the writings of Martin Luther with the aid of the Calov commentary.

Looking at the evidence of the marginalia as a whole, one is impressed by the insight they give of the man, his faith, and his attitude toward his profession:

> *In their terseness, Bach's annotations seem to span the nature of church music—its expressive means, its divine mission and liturgical foundation, its blessing. Addressed to no one but himself, they are the most personal reflections upon his art which have come down to us from Bach. What renders their discovery so remarkable is that they are not the expressions of youthful enthusiasm but the thoughts of the aging master . . . amidst the professional battles . . . they show the composer at the height of his achievements as a devout artist unshaken in his Christian belief.*[134]

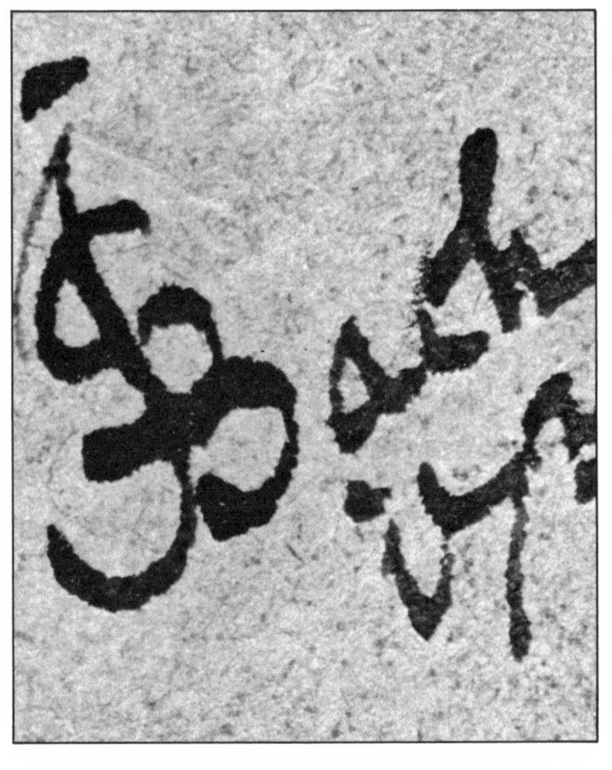

Notes

1. P. Spitta, *Johann Sebastian Bach, 2* vols. (Leipzig, 1873–80); translated by C. Bell and J. A. Fuller-Maitland, under the title *Johann Sebastian Bach: His Work and Influence on the Music of Germany, 1685–1750,* 3 vols. (London, 1883–85).
2. C. H. Bitter, *The Life of J. Sebastian Bach: An Abridged Translation,* trans. J. E. Kay-Shuttleworth (London, 1873), p. 46. The original German edition appeared in Berlin, 1865.
3. For examples, see the review article by W. E. Buszin, "Lutheran Theology as Reflected in the Life and Works of J. S. Bach," *CTM* 21 (1950): 896–923.
4. W. Blankenburg, "In the Sign of Bach," *CTM* 21 (1950): 366.
5. W. Blankenburg, "Theologische und geistesgeschichtliche Probleme der gegenwärtigen Bachforschung," *Theologische Literaturzeitung* 78 (1958): 396.
6. F. Blume, "Outlines of a New Picture of Bach," *Music and Letters* 44 (1963): 218.
7. See further R. A. Leaver, "Editor's Introduction," in G. Stiller, *Johann Sebastian Bach and Liturgical Life in Leipzig* (St. Louis, 1984), pp. 11–16.
8. R. E. Witt, "Bach, the Quaker's Musician," *Friends Quarterly Examiner* 1 (1938): 57–58.
9. Reported in *Weekend Telegraph* [London], no. 116, 16 Dec. 1966, p. 31.
10. G. von Dadelsen, *Beiträge zur Chronologie der Werke Johann Sebastian Bachs,* Tübinger Bach-Studien 4/5 (Trossingen, 1958); A. Dürr, *Zur Chronologie der Leipziger Vokalwerke J. S. Bachs,* 2d ed. (Kassel, 1976).
11. Blume, p. 219.
12. This is a point of view one frequently encounters in Bach literature emanating from East Germany; see, for example, W. Siegmund-

Schultze, *Johann Sebastian Bach* (Leipzig, 1976).

13. R. A. Leaver, "Leipzig's Rejection of J. S. Bach," *BACH* 3, no. 3 (July 1972): 27–39; ibid., no. 4 (Oct. 1972): 3–7; and the sources cited there.
14. On the political divisions surrounding Bach's appointment, see U. Siegele, "Bachs Stellung in der Leipziger Kulturpolitik seiner Zeit," *BJ*, 1983, pp. 7–50; *BJ*, 1984, pp. 7–43.
15. BWV 198 was written for this occasion.
16. *BD* 1:74; BR, p. 128.
17. See R. M. Stevenson, "Bach's Quarrel with the Rector of St. Thomas School," *Patterns of Protestant Church Music*, (Durham, N.C., 1953), pp. 66–77; P. S. Minear, "J. S. Bach and J. A. Ernesti: A Case Study in Exegetical and Theological Conflict," *Our Common History as Christians: Essays in Honor of Albert C. Outler*, ed. J. Descher, L. T. Howe, and K. Penzel (New York, 1975), pp. 131–55.
18. A. Dürr, "New Light on Bach," *The Musical Times* 107 (1966): 484–85.
19. W. Blankenburg, "Zwölf Jahre Bachforschung," *Acta Musicologica*, 37 (1965): 131–32; cf. W. Blankenburg, "Die Bachforschung seit etwa 1965, Teil III," *Acta Musicologica*, 55 (1983): 52–57.
20. Among the enormous number of publications written in response to Blume's thesis are, in addition to Dürr's article in note 18 above, F. Smend, "Was bleibt? Zu Friedrich Blumes Bach-Bild," *Der Kirchenmusiker* 13 (1962): 178–88; J. G. Mehl, "Johann Sebastian Bach—liberaler Humanist oder lutherischer Christ? Zum 'neuen Bachbild' Friedrich Blumes," *Gottesdienst und Kirchenmusik*, 1962, pp. 203–18; and G. Stiller, *Johann Sebastian Bach and Liturgical Life in Leipzig* (St. Louis, 1984).
21. Various accounts of the finding of these volumes have appeared in print, including H. H. Cox, "Bach's Bible," *Bach in Bethlehem Today: A Conference Report*, ed. A. Mann (Bethlehem, 1979), pp. 31–35; L. D. Miller, "J. S. Bach's Bible," *The Hymn*, 25 (1974): 14ff.; and C. Trautmann, "Bach's Bible," *American Choral Review*, 14, no. 4 (Oct. 1972): 3–11. But all of these accounts are heavily dependent on Trautmann's original article, Trautmann A and Trautmann B. What follows here is in part indebted to Trautmann but makes full use of material in the archives of Concordia Seminary Library, St. Louis, which, at several points, leads to modified conclusions. It is also an expansion of the earlier article, R. A. Leaver, "The Calov Bible from Bach's Library," *BACH* 7, no. 4 (Oct. 1976): 16–22, esp. pp. 20–22. Since this was written, Gerhard Herz has published his *Bach Sources in America* (Kassel and New York, 1984). His description of the volumes and their provenance, pp. 187–95, confirms the conclusions given here as against those of Trautmann.
22. See H. F. Zehnder, *"Teach My People the Truth!" The Story of Frankenmuth, Michigan* (Frankenmuth, 1970).
23. On Riedel, see *Der Lutheraner* 118 (2 Jan. 1962): 13; ibid. (13 Mar. 1962): 94; *The Lutheran Witness* 81 (March 1962): 118.
24. Evidence of the relationship is found in a letter of Paul Sauer to Walter E. Buszin, 23 Nov. 1950, Concordia Seminary Library.
25. See Zehnder, pp. 124, 125, 136, 137, 182.
26. Information from a letter of Leonard Reichle to Ludwig Fuerbringer, 18 Oct. 1938, Concordia Seminary Library.
27. Ibid.
28. Zehnder, p. 125.
29. Trautmann B, p. 91.
30. See H. Lehmann-Haupt, *The Book in America* (New York, 1951).
31. Trautmann reported the discovery. He also enlisted the help of the University of Pennsylvania Library to attempt to identify the Philadelphia bookseller, but without success; Trautmann B, pp. 91–92.
32. Reported in Sauer to Buszin, 23 Nov. 1950, Concordia Seminary Library. The letter is particularly important in that it contains Sauer's resumé of correspondence in 1935 and 1936 that is no longer available.
33. See *Der Lutheraner* 108, no. 24 (18 Nov. 1952): 13.
34. Worship bulletin, "The Service of Praise and Thanksgiving Celebrating the Fiftieth Anniversary of the Rev. Paul Sauer . . . July 28, 1946, at 7:30 o'clock," Concordia Historical Institute, St. Louis.
35. P. Sauer, *The Life Work of Johann Sebastian Bach: Lecture Delivered under the Auspices*

of the Lyceum Committee of Concordia Seminary, St. Louis, Mo. November 23, 1928 (St. Louis, 1929), pp. 9, 14.

36. See note 32 above.
37. See H. Preuss, *Bachs Bibliothek* (Leipzig, 1928), pp. 106, 108; BD 2:494; Leaver C, pp. 31, 37, 46.
38. See note 32 above.
39. Ibid.
40. Ibid. There is no indication in Sauer's resumé of 23 Nov. 1950 that Karl Straube responded to his letter of 31 Aug. 1934.
41. "In einer versteckten kiste in der garret." Ibid.
42. See *Der Lutheraner* 96, (24 Sept. 1940): 331–33; *The Lutheran Witness* 59 (15 Oct. 1940): 364–65.
43. H. Preuss, *Johann Sebastian Bach der Lutheraner* (Erlangen, 1935), p. 15.
44. On Fuerbringer, see *Der Lutheraner* 103 (27 May 1947): 176–78; *The Lutheran Witness* 66 (20 May 1947): 180–82.
45. L. E. Fuerbringer, *Eighty Eventful Years* (St. Louis, 1944), p. 89.
46. L. E. Fuerbringer, *Persons and Events* (St. Louis, 1947), pp. 257, 235.
47. Sauer to Fuerbringer, 29 April 1929, Concordia Historical Institute, St. Louis; cf. the quotations given at note 35 above.
48. L. E. Fuerbringer, "Das Schicksal eines Buches," *Der Lutheraner* 91 (5 March 1935): 76.
49. On Fuerbringer's library, see *Persons and Events*, pp. 253–54.
50. H. G. Hoch, "Lost Volume of Bach Found in Thumb Home," *Detroit News*, 2 Nov. 1935.
51. See note 32 above.
52. See note 43 above.
53. See the quotations given at note 35 above.
54. See note 48 above.
55. Reported in Sauer to Buszin, 12 Nov. 1950, Concordia Seminary Library. In the same letter Sauer commented: "I was so disappointed by Reichle's narrow-minded view, that I was not interested in meeting him in 1939."
56. MS in Concordia Seminary Library.
57. Carbon copy typed on the back of the first leaf of Reichle's letter of 18 Oct. 1938.
58. Carbon copy typed on the back of the second leaf of Reichle's letter of 18 Oct. 1938.
59. The original German is given in Trautmann A, p. 147; another English translation is in Trautmann B, p. 91. The notice was still in the volumes in 1971, when I first examined them. Since it was typed on acid paper and likely to damage the volumes, it was subsequently removed.
60. Buszin's letters are no longer extant, but Sauer's crowded replies to his questions, dated 12 and 23 Nov. 1950 (see notes 32 and 55 above), together with a letter by Alfred O. Fuerbringer, Ludwig's son and eventual successor at the seminary, dated 15 Nov. 1950, are in the archives of Concordia Seminary Library.
61. See M. Frick, "Three Volumes of Bach's Library Featured," *The Quad* 10, no. 9 (16 Nov. 1961). *The Quad* was the seminary's student newspaper. The article was based on the notice pasted into the volumes and on the article by H. G. Hoch in the *Detroit News*. It announces that the volumes, the clipping from the *Detroit News*, and correspondence between Reichle and Fuerbringer were to be exhibited in the reference room of the library.
62. Trautmann B, p. 89.
63. Trautmann B, p. 90.
64. See C. Trautmann, *Ex libris Bachianis: Eine Kantate Johann Sebastian Bachs im Spiegel seiner Bibliothek* (Zurich, 1969). The volumes were returned after the exhibition in October. Professor Gerhard Herz examined them in Concordia Seminary Library on 29 December 1969; see G. Herz, "J. S. Bach 1722: A 'New' Bach Signature," *Studies in Renaissance and Baroque Music in Honor of Arthur Mendel*, ed. R. L. Marshall (Kassel, 1974), p. 256.
65. Trautmann A; Trautmann B.
66. Given here in revised form on pp. 43–50.
67. *BD* 3:636–38.
68. D. Arnold, *Bach* (Oxford, 1984), pp. 58–59.
69. Not simply "JSB" as Arnold suggests in the quotation given at note 68 above.
70. See note 37 above.
71. C. Freyse, "Fünfzig Jahre Bachhaus," *BJ*, 1957, p. 185.
72. Preuss, *Bachs Bibliothek*, p. 108.
73. See H. Pipping, *Sacer decadum septenarius Memoriam Theologicorum nostri aetate clarissimorum renovatam exhibens*

(Leipzig, 1705), pp. 129–37; see also the graphic presentation of Calov's output of books in the frontispiece to the first volume of the second edition of his *Biblia illustrata* (Dresden and Leipzig, 1719).

74. Various sources, in referring to the work, quote the half-title page rather than the main title page and also do not record the number of volumes; for example, J. G. Walch, *Bibliotheca theologica selecta litterariis adnotationibus instructa* 4 (Jena, 1764): 184; H. Leube, *Kalvinismus und Luthertum im Zeitalter der Orthodoxie* (Leipzig, 1928), p. 329 n. 1.

75. C. S. Terry, *Bach: A Biography,* 2d ed. (London, 1933), p. 273.

76. See "Ludwig Fuerbringer Hall—Concordia Seminary Library," St. Louis, Mo., Sept. 30, 1962 (a pamphlet for the dedication of the library building), p. 7, and Errata, p. 7, lines 25ff.

77. Trautmann B, p. 89.

78. Trautmann B, p. 90.

79. See Leaver C, pp. 46–48. Some bibliographical sources omit reference to the number of volumes. A few mention the fact that it was issued in three volumes (e.g., M. Lipenius, *Bibliotheca realis theologica* 1 [Frankfurt, 1685]: 149; *Bibliotheca Mayeriana seu appartus librarius Io. Frid. Mayeri* . . . [Berlin, 1715], p. 3; [T. Georgi], *Allgemeines Europäisches Bücher-Lexicon* 1 [Leipzig, 1742]: 149), but only J. A. Fabricius, *Centifolium Lutheri* (Hamburg, 1728), p. 181, is bibliographically correct in listing it as having six volumes; see also note 74 above.

80. On Calov, see, for example, [J. H. Zedler], *Grosses vollständiges Universal Lexicon aller Wissenschafften und Künste* 5 (Leipzig, 1733): 304–08; Pipping, pp. 108–37; *Die Religion in Geschichte und Gegenwart,* 3d ed. (Tübingen, 1957–62) 1:1587; R. D. Preus, *The Theology of Post-Reformation Lutheranism* (St. Louis, 1970) 1:59–61.

81. Preus, 1:59.

82. F. W. Farrer, *The History of Interpretation,* Bampton Lectures for 1885 (London, 1886), pp. 364–65.

83. See Leube, pp. 322–34.

84. Preus, 1:61.

85. Ibid.

86. Fuerbringer, *Persons and Events,* p. 253.

87. E. W. Hammer, "Index, 1286 Pages: The Altenburg Luther," *The Lutheran Quarterly,* 1 (1949): 213–24.

88. Vol. 10, pp. 187–476. Hammer, p. 221, comments: "It would require far less space to list the passages which Luther has omitted!"

89. See note 37 above.

90. See Leaver C, pp. 10–15, and *passim.*

91. Leaver C, no. 5.

92. J. G. Carpzov, *Introductio ad libros canonicos Bibliorum veteris testamenti* (Leipzig, 1714), 1:18; S. Deyling, *Observationes miscellanae* . . . (Leipzig, 1736), p. 739.

93. Leaver C, nos. 28, 44.

94. *BD* 1:199; Leaver C, p. 42; see also H.-J. Schulze, "Marginalien zu einigen Bach-Dokumenten," *BJ,* 1961, pp. 95–99; H. Besch, "Eine Auktionsquittung J. S. Bachs," *Festschrift für Friedrich Smend zum 70. Geburtstag* (Berlin, 1963), pp. 74–79.

95. In the receipt, Bach refers to the Calov commentary as the "Teutsche Bibel," which are the main words at the head of the half-title page, now missing from the copy he once owned (see no. 1), and the short title by which it has been listed in bibliographical and other literature (see note 74 above).

96. See *Bibliothek J. F. Knaake. Abtheiluing I: Luther* (Nieuwkoop, 1960), p. 12; Hammer, pp. 213–14; Leaver A, pp. 127–28; Leaver B, pp. 25–26; *Bibliotheca Mayeriana* . . ., p. 78.

97. *BD* 2:505; Leaver C, p. 38.

98. See S. Godman, "Bachs Bibliothek," *Musica* 10 (1956): 756–61; S. Godman, "Bachs Copies of Ammerbach's 'Orgel oder Instrument Tabulatur,' " *Music and Letters* 38 (1957): 21–27.

99. Herz, "A 'New' Bach Signature," pp. 254–63.

100. Ibid., pp. 255–56.

101. G. Herz, "Towards a New Image of Bach," *BACH* 1, no. 4 (Oct. 1970): 22; cf. Herz, "A 'New' Bach Signature," p. 261.

102. Herz, "New Image," p. 23.

103. Calov's argument given here in Appendix 1 should be compared with Preus, pp. 255–403, which deals with the doctrine of Scripture in orthodox Lutheranism.

104. R. A. Bohlmann, *Principles of Biblical Inter-*

pretation in the Lutheran Confessions, rev. ed. (St. Louis, 1983), p. 46.

105. H. Werthemann, *Die Bedeutung der alttestamentlichen Historien in Johann Sebastian Bachs Kantaten* (Tübingen, 1959), p. 31.

106. Besch, "Auktionsquittung," p. 78.

107. See R. A. Leaver, "Bach's Understanding and Use of the Epistles and Gospels of the Church Year," *BACH* 5, no. 4 (Oct. 1975): 4–13.

108. Leaver C, no. 12.

109. In *BD* 3:636, Hans-Joachim Schulze suggests a date sometime after 1742 for this entry. However, more recently he has modified his position and now concludes that it is to be dated "no later than 1740"; see Cox, p. 33.

110. Trautmann B, p. 96.

111. Letter to the author, 29 May 1984.

112. Ibid. Since this introduction was written, Dr. Cox presented a paper to the Leipzig Bach "Wissenschaftliche Konferenz," on 26 March 1985, entitled "Tintenanalyse als neues Mittel der Bachforschung: Schrieb Bach alles, was an Eintragungen in der Calov-Bibel enthalten ist?" which will eventually be published along with the other conference papers. A more extensive account of Dr. Cox's researches is due to be published by UMI Press, Ann Arbor, in early 1986.

113. Calov also refers to Hunnius's work in his comment on 2 Thessalonians 2:3, which formed part of the appointed epistle for the Festival of the Reformation (no. 69).

114. Leaver C, nos. 5, 49.

115. See above, p. 25.

116. Leaver C, no. 3.

117. Leaver C, no. 6.

118. *Music and Letters* 45 (1964): 167.

119. Leaver B, p. 28; Leaver A, pp. 130–31.

120. Trautmann A, p. 160.

121. See above, pp. 26–27.

122. See above, p. 25.

123. See Tables 1 and 2. The use of both red and black ink suggests that Bach worked through Genesis on more than one occasion.

124. The underlining at no. 77 is, in the main, general rather than particular, in that it extends underneath the greater length of the line of type rather than being made underneath each particular error or omission, as one might have expected.

125. See F. Bente, *Historical Introductions to the Book of Concord* (St. Louis, 1965), pp. 144–52.

126. *Die Bekenntnisschriften der evangelisch-lutherischen Kirche,* 6th ed. (Göttingen, 1963); English: *The Book of Concord,* trans. and ed. T. G. Tappert (Philadelphia, 1959).

127. Quoted by C. F. W. Walther in T. G. Tappert, ed., *Lutheran Confessional Theology 1840—80* (New York, 1972), p. 73.

128. *Bekenntnisschriften,* pp. 770–76 (Epitome), and pp. 843–66 (Solid Declaration); *Book of Concord,* pp. 466–69, 508–19.

129. *Bekenntnisschriften,* p. 865; *Book of Concord,* p. 519.

130. See, for example, *Preface to the Complete Edition of Luther's Latin Writings* (1545), *LW* 34:336–37. The preface was accessible to Bach in German in the first volumes of both the Jena and Altenburg editions of Luther's works.

131. *Bekenntnisschriften,* p. 922 (SD iii 25); *Book of Concord,* p. 543.

132. *BD* 2:101.

133. See note 127 above. Bach's positive and negative subscription, dated the same day, 13 May 1723, to the Saxon Visitation Articles of 1593, which were particularly aimed against Calvinism, is extant; see *BD* 3:630–31 (cf. nos. 37 and 44). In Bach's library there were two volumes with expositions of the Augsburg Confession (Leaver C, nos. 17, 24), as well as various treatments of Luther's Small Catechism in other volumes (Leaver C, nos. 38, 45c-e, 46, 47).

134. C. Trautmann, "Bach's Bible," *American Choral Review* 14, no. 4 (Oct. 1972): 10–11.

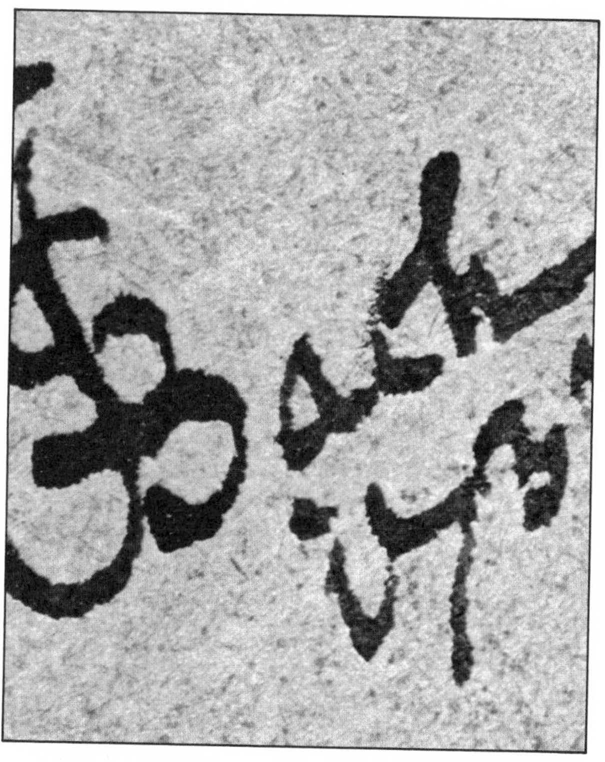

Table 1

Autograph Entries by Johann Sebastian Bach

Based on Trautmann A, pp. 155–58. The first column gives the number of the entry; the second, the number of the facsimile in this volume; the third, the reference in *Die deutsche Bibel;* and the fourth, the Biblical reference. The fifth column includes descriptions of the type of entry, according to the following code:

1 — personal notes
2 — missing text from either Bible verse(s) or commentary
3 — amplification or clarification of the text
4 — correction of typographical and other errors
* — typographical error listed in vol. 3/VI, signature Ddddij recto and following.

The sixth column gives the detail of each entry; and the seventh, the color of the ink. A question mark enclosed in parentheses after an entry denotes some uncertainty concerning its authenticity. Figures enclosed in parentheses are those printed in error in the text.

No.	Facs. No.	Col.	Bibl. Ref.	Type	Entry	Ink Color
		Vol. 1/I				
1	2	Title page		1	*J S Bach 1733*	black
2	5	32	Gen. 3:7	2*	*das von aussen hinzu kom̃t, u. ohne Verletzung der Natur*	red
3	6	47	Gen. 4:4	4*	For zürnete: *zeugete*	red
4	7	91	Gen. 11:10	4	For Cham: *Elam*	red
5	8	99	Gen. 13:4	2	*V. 4. Eben an dem Ort, da er vorhin den Altar gemacht hatte, u. er pre-digte alda den Namen des Herrn.*	black
6	9	162	Gen. 22:13	4*	For Jacobs: *Isaacs*	red
7	10	199	Gen. 26:33	1	*NB. Ungefehr 1 Stunde von Erfurth, ist ein Dorf so diesen Nahmen hat.*	black
8	11	226	Gen. 29:35	4	For Priester: Priester*thum*	black
9	12	230	Gen. 30:14	4	For nichtem: *mit* nichtem	black
10	13	267	Gen. 35 heading	4	For Isaac: *Jacob*	black
11	14	351	Gen. 46:26	1	*NB.*	red
12	15	365	Gen. 48:2	4	For Joseph: *Manasse*	red
13	16	381	Gen. 49:19	4	For Dan: *Gad*	red
14	17	426 (428)	Ex. 5:23 (33)	2	*mit ihm zu reden in deinem Nahmen,*	black
15		427	Ex. 6:3	2	*worden* (?)	black
16		436	Ex. 7:23	2	und nams *nicht* zu Hertzen. (?)	black
17	18	483	Ex. 15:20	1	*NB. Erstes Vorspiel, auf 2 Chören zur Ehre Gottes zu musiciren.*	red
18	20	491	Ex. 16:32	2	*Und Mose sprach:*	black
19	21	541	Ex. 15:10	4	For Länge: *Höhe*	black
20	22	557–58	Ex. 28:17ff.	3	The precious stones are carefully numbered: *(1) (2) (3) (4) (5) (6) (7) (8) (9) (10) (11) (12)*	red
21	23	565	Ex. 29:24	4	For Mittergang: *Nieder*gang	red
22	24	567	Ex. 29:37	2	und ihn *weihen*	red
23	25	599	Ex. 35:30	4	For Levi: *Uri* (?)	black
24	27	610	Ex. 38:29	1,3	*Die sum̃a des freywilligen Opfers beträgt fast in die acht Toñen Goldes.*	red
25	29	702	Lev. 18:16	1	*NB. Scheinet dem Gesetze (so da ordnete, dass ein Bruder seinem verstorbenen Bruder Saamen erwecken solt) contrair zu seyn.*	red
26	30	727	Lev. 23:11	4*	der reiche milde Speise*meister* uns . . .	red
27	31	731	Lev. 23:39	4*	For worden: *werden*	red
28		737	Lev. 25:9	4	*Ta* of Tage written over and himmliche corrected to: himmli*s*che.	red
29	32	870	Num. 19:13	4	so lange er sich *nicht* . . .	black
30	34	1041	Deut. 17:12	4*	Gewalt der *Obrigkeit* . . .	black
31		1068	Deut. 23:4	1	*NB* (?)	black
32		1073	Deut. 24:6	1	*NB.* (?)	black

No.	Facs. No.	Col.	Bibl. Ref.	Type	Entry	Ink Color
33	35	1135	Joshua 1:5	1	*NB.*	black
34	35	1136	Joshua 1:5	1	*NB*	black
35	37	1572	2 Sam. 12:12	1	*NB* (?)	black
36	38	1640	2 Sam. 22:44	2	*und behütest mich zum Haupt unter den Heyden, ein Volk, das ich nicht kañte, dienet mir.*	black
37	40	2047–48	1 Chron. 25 (26)	1	*NB. Dieses Capital ist das wahre Fundament aller gottfälliger Kirchen Music.*	red
38	41	2064	1 Chron. 28 (29):21	1,3	*NB. Ein herrlicher Beweiss, dass neben anderen Anstalten des Gottesdienstes, besonders auch die Musica von Gottes Geist durch David mit angeordnet worden.*	black
39	42	2088	2 Chron. 5:13	1	*NB. Bey einer andächtig Musig ist allezeit Gott mit seiner Gnaden Gegenwart.*	black
	Vol. 1/II					
40		733	Psalm 119:158	1	*NB* (?)	black
41		1046	Prov. Preface	1	*NB* (?)	black
42		1065	Prov. 2:16	1	*NB* (?)	black
43		1091	Prov. 5:16	1	*NB* (?)	black
44		1096	Prov. 6:10	1	*NB* (?)	black
45		1102	Prov. 7:9	1	*NB* (?)	black
46		1103	Prov. 7:9	1	*NB* (?)	black
47		1130	Prov. 10:20	1	*NB* (?)	black
	Vol. 2/III					
48	47	Title page		1	*J S Bach 1733*	black
49	48	81	Is. 15:1	2	*über Ar in Moab: sie ist dahin: das Nachts kömt Zerstörung*	black
50	49	89	Is. 17:10	2	darumb wirstu *lustige* Pflantzen setzen	black
51	50	123	Is. 25:3	4	For ehren dich: *fürchten* dich . . .	black
52	51	982	Dan. 7:25	1	*NB.*	black
53	52	1044–47	Dan. 12:7–12	1,3	Bach repeats in the margin the following numbers, which occur in the text: *1260, 1290, 1335, 1941, 2408.*	black
	Vol. 2/IV					
54		139	Joel 2:2	1	*NB* (?)	black
55	54	214	Amos 6:6	1	*NB.*	red
56		507	Hag. 1:1	1	*NB.* (?)	black

No.	Facs. No.	Col.	Bibl. Ref.	Type	Entry	Ink Color
	Vol. 3/V					
57	55	Title page		1	*J S Bach 1733*	black
58	57	54	Matt. 5:26	1	*NB*	black
59	59	341–42	Mark 6 heading	4	For Fünffte: *Sechste*	black
60	60	351	Mark 8:19	4	hubt *ihr* da auf (?)	black
61	61	365	Mark 10:29–30	2	und Schwester oder *Vatter und* Mutter *oder Weib* und Kinder und Aecker *um meinet Willen, und um des Evangelii Willen. V. 30. Der nicht hundertfältig empfahe, itzt in dieser Zeit, Häuser u. Brüder, u. Schwestern u. Mütter u. Kinder, u Äcker* mit . . .	black
	Vol. 3/VI					
63	66	95	Rom. 8:21	1	*NB* (?)	black
64	73	1420	Rev. 12:14	4	For Prag: *Augsburg*	black

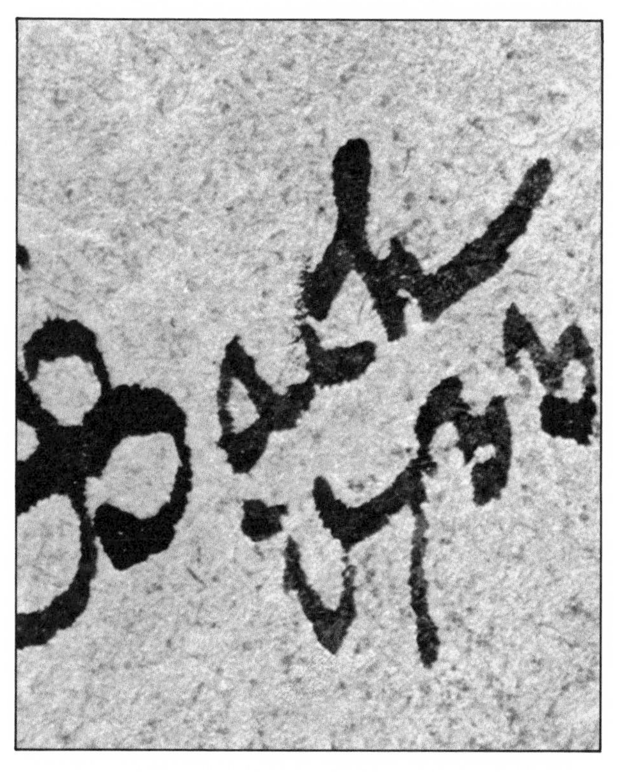

Table 2

Other Markings

Based on Trautmann A, pp. 158–60. The list is not exhaustive. There are other markings and underlinings over which there is some considerable doubt as to their authenticity. Those noted here can, on a conservative estimate, be reasonably linked with Bach. But even here there must be some element of uncertainty, as the list makes clear.

The first column gives the reference in *Die deutsche Bibel;* the second, the number of the facsimile in this volume; and the third, the Biblical reference. Here the numbers in parentheses signify that the marking occurs alongside or within the commentary rather than in the Biblical text itself. The parentheses at 1 Chron. 16 (17) indicate an error in the printed text (see Table 1). The fourth column denotes the type of marking: *a* — underlining; *b* — other marking. The fifth notes the color of the ink used, and the sixth the authenticity of the entry.

Col.	Facs. No.	Bibl. Ref.	Type	Ink Color	Writer
Vol 1/I					
81		Gen. (9.22)	*a*	black	?
82		Gen. (9:25)	*a b*	black	?
195		Gen. (26:20)	*a b*	black	?
197–98		Gen. (26:26)	*a b*	black	?
250		Gen. (32:9–10)	*a b*	black	?
251		Gen. (32:13)	*b*	black	?
257		Gen. (33:10)	*a*	black	?
281		Gen. (36:33,35,39)	*a b*	black	?
342		Gen. (45:16,18)	*a b*	black	?
347		Gen. (46:1)	*b*	black	?
486		Ex. 15:27	*b*	red	Bach
499		Ex. (18:21)	*a b*	black	?
510		Ex. (22:12)	*a*	black	
559		Ex. 28:30	*b*	red	Bach
572–74		Ex. (30:24,34)	*a b*	red	Bach
598		Ex. (35:22)	*a b*	red	Bach
606	26	Ex. 37:24	*a b*	red	Bach
609	27	Ex. 38:24–25	*a b*	red	Bach
612		Ex. (39:21)	*a b*	red	Bach
617		Ex. 40:17	*a b*	red	Bach
619		Ex. 40:34	*a b*	red	Bach
698	28	Lev. 17:11	*a b*	red	Bach
750		Lev. (26:41)	*b*	black	?
766		Num. (1:47)	*a b*	black	Bach ?
793–97		Num. (6:24,26)	*a b*	black	Bach ?
814		Num. (9:23)	*b*	black	?
1052		Deut. (19:15)	*a b*	black	?
1053–54		Deut. (19:21)	*a b*	black	?
1070		Deut. (23:18)	*a*	black	?
1074		Deut. (24:13)	*a*	black	?
1075–76		Deut. (24:17)	*a b*	black	?
1076		Deut. 24:19	*a*	black	?
1076		Deut. (24:20)	*b*	black	?
1439		1 Sam. (15:22)	*a*	black	?
1527–28		2 Sam. 3:1,5	*a*	red	Bach
2015–17	39	1 Chron. 16 (17):4,10	*a b*	red	Bach
Vol. 1/II					
214–15	44	Psalter preface	*a b*	red	Bach
222–23	44	Psalter preface	*a b*	red	Bach
362		Psalm (32:2)	*a*	black	?
468		Psalm (55:23)	*a*	black	?
653–54		Psalm (101:2–3)	*a b*	black	?
655–56		Psalm (101:5,8)	*a b*	black	?
777		Psalm (120:5)	*a*	black	?
1049–50		Prov. (1:2–3)	*a*	black	?
1055–56		Prov. (1:13–14)	*a b*	black	?

Col.	Facs. No.	Bibl. Ref.	Type	Ink Color	Writer
1058		Prov. (1:18)	*a b*	black	?
1059–66		Prov. (2:1,3,6,9, 11,15–17,19)	*a b*	black	?
1069–75		Prov. (3:1,10,17)	*a b*	black	?
1079–83		Prov. (4:5–6,12,14)	*a b*	black	?
1086–91		Prov. (5:2,5–6,8,16)	*a b*	black	?
1093–98		Prov. (6:4–5,7–11)	*a b*	black	?
1099–1109		Prov. (7:1–2,8–9, 11,13–17,19–22, 26,29)	*a b*	black	?
1111–18		Prov. (8:2–4,10,13–17)	*a b*	black	?
1117–22		Prov. (9:1,4,8,11–12)	*a b*	black	?
1123–30		Prov. (10:1–4,8–9, 12,18–20)	*a b*	black	?
1131–34		Prov. (11:1,4,6,9)	*a b*	black	?
1141		Prov. (12:11)	*a*	black	?
Vol. 2/III					
(None)					
Vol. 2/IV					
560		Zech. (4:7)	*a b*	black	?
786		Wisd. (7:6)	*a*	black	?
Vol. 3/V					
34		Matt. (5:2)	*b*	black	?
35		Matt. (5:3)	*a b*	black	?
39		Matt. (5:5)	*a b*	black	?
42		Matt. (5:8)	*a b*	black	?
43		Matt. (5:9)	*a b*	black	?
70		Matt. (6:20)	*b*	black	?
73	58	Matt. (6:25)	*a*	black	?
180		Matt. (18:10)	*a*	black	?
182		Matt. (18:17)	*b*	black	?
187–88		Matt. (18:35)	*b*	black	?
428		Luke (1:74)	*b*	black	Bach ?
643		Luke (23:46)	*b*	black	?
772		John (6:35)	*a b*	black	?
793		John (7:30)	*a b*	black	?
799–800		John (7:46)	*a b*	black	?
919		John (18:17)	*a b*	black	?
947	63	John (19:30)	*a*	black	?
950	63	John (19:34)	*a*	black	?
Vol. 3/VI					
19	65	Rom. (1:17)	*a b*	black	?
96	66	Rom. (8:22)	*a*	black	?
282–83	67	1 Cor. (10:12)	*a b*	black	?
838	70	2 Thess. (3:12)	*a b*	black	?
890–91		1 Tim. (6:16)	*a b*	black	?
1006–07		1 Peter (3:9)	*a b*	black	?

Col.	Facs. No.	Bibl. Ref.	Type	Ink Color	Writer
1037–39	71	1 Peter (5:6)	*a b*	black	?
1040	71	1 Peter (5:7)	*a*	black	?
1092		1 John (1:7)	*b*	black	?
1240–41		Heb. (11:13)	*b*	black	?
1275–76		James (1:6)	*b*	black	?
1298–99		James (3:2)	*a b*	black	?
1300		James (3:6)	*a*	black	?
1306		James (4:15)	*a b*	black	?
Sig. Ddddij recto	77	Druck-Fehler (printing errors)	*a*	red	Bach

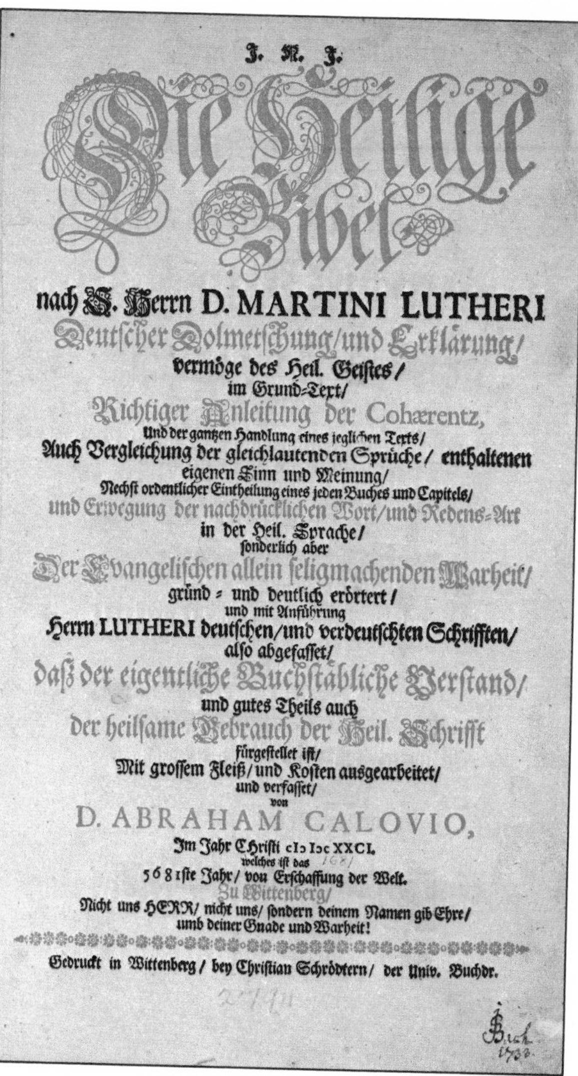

J. N. J.

Die Heilige Bibel

nach S. Herrn D. MARTINI LUTHERI
Deutscher Dolmetschung/und Erklärung/
vermöge des Heil. Geistes/
im Grund-Text/
Richtiger Anleitung der Cohærentz,
Und der gantzen Handlung eines jeglichen Texts/
Auch Vergleichung der gleichlautenden Sprüche/ enthaltenen
eigenen Sinn und Meinung/
Nechst ordentlicher Eintheilung eines jeden Buches und Capitels/
und Erwegung der nachdrücklichen Wort/und Redens-Art
in der Heil. Sprache/
sonderlich aber
Der Evangelischen allein seligmachenden Warheit/
gründ- und deutlich erörtert/
und mit Anführung
Herrn LUTHERI deutschen/und verdeutschten Schrifften/
also abgefasset/
daß der eigentliche Buchstäbliche Verstand/
und gutes Theils auch
der heilsame Gebrauch der Heil. Schrifft
fürgestellet ist/
Mit grossem Fleiß/und Kosten ausgearbeitet/
und verfasset/
von
D. ABRAHAM CALOVIO,
Im Jahr Christi cIↃ IↃc XXCI.
welches ist das 1681
5681ste Jahr/ von Erschaffung der Welt.
Zu Wittenberg/
Nicht uns HERR/ nicht uns/ sondern deinem Namen gib Ehre/
umb deiner Gnade und Warheit!

Gedruckt in Wittenberg/ bey Christian Schrödtern/ der Univ. Buchdr.

JSBach 1733.

Facsimiles with Notes and Commentary

1 The half-title page to vol. 1/I, which is now missing from Bach's copy. The facsimile has been supplied from another copy in Concordia Seminary Library. It reads:

> *J.N.J. The German Bible of Dr. Martin Luther so clearly and thoroughly expounded from the original language, the context, and the parallel passages, with addition of the exposition to be found in Luther's writings, so that, in addition to proper arrangement, everywhere the real literal understanding, and to a considerable extent also the salutary application, of Holy Scripture, especially together with the inspiring words of that man of God, is presented by Dr. Abraham Calov.*

J. N. J.
Die Deutsche Bibel/
D. MARTINI LUTHERI,
Aus der Grund-Sprach/ dem Context,
und parallel-Sprüchen/
Mit Beyfügung der Auslegung/
die in Luthern Schrifften zu finden/
Also
deut- und gründlich erkläret/
daß/ nechst geziemender Eintheilung/
allenthalben
Der eigentliche Buchstäbliche Verstand/
gutes Theils auch
Der heilsame Gebrauch der Heil.
Schrifft/
sonderlich mit des theuren Mannes
GOttes Geistreichen Worten/
fürgestellet ist/
durch
D. ABRAHAM CALOVIUM.

1

J. N. J. is, of course, the abbreviation for *In Nomine Jesu* (or *Im Namen Jesu*, as it is given in no. 4). It was a literary convention, especially in theological works, to begin with the prayer "In the name of Jesus" and can be paralleled in countless books of the period. Calov uses the three letters to introduce every major section of this Bible commentary, and they can be found no less than 85 times throughout the volumes. It was also a convention followed by composers, who used either the three letters or the ascription in full at the head of the manuscript scores of their church music. Bach's predecessor, Johann Kuhnau, used "In Nomine Jesu" (see F. Blume, *Die evangelische Kirchenmusik* [Potsdam, 1931], p. 136), and the two composers who were preferred by the Leipzig town council as Kuhnau's successor rather than Bach, that is, Telemann and Graupner, used the monogram "J. N. J." (see W. Gerstenberg, *Composer's Autographs* [London, 1968], 1:157; *Denkmäler deutscher Tonkunst* 51/52:1, 16, 30, 54, 77, etc.). The manuscripts on which the three letters are found are of church music, cantatas, and passions, but a little later Joseph Haydn was writing *In Nomine Domini* at the head of his symphonies and quartets (see Gerstenberg, plates 89, 90, 93, 94). Bach used J. N. J. in a similar way at the head of the first page of his *Clavier-Büchlein vor Wilhelm Friedemann Bach*, 22 January 1720 (*BD* 4:136). Bach's eldest son seems to have followed his father's example in this manuscript book, for some of his music manuscripts are also headed "J. N. J." (see, for example, the facsimile given at the end of the second volume of C. H. Bitter, *Carl Philipp Emanuel und Wilhelm Friedemann Bach und deren Brüder* [Berlin, 1868]).

There are a number of 18th century manuscript copies of the scores of Bach's cantatas, particularly those transcribed by Penzel, that include the monogram as a heading (e.g. BWV 73, 137, 149—MSS. P664, P1040, P1043), but since these occur in the top left-hand corner of the first leaf, it seems likely that it is a misinterpretation of Bach's usual custom of placing the letters "J. J." (*Jesu Juva*, Jesus help me!) in this position on his scores—even though there is one cantata that is headed "J. N. J. A." (*In Nomine Jesu. Amen;* BWV 16—MS. P45) and another in which the letters "J. J." appear in the center at the top of the first leaf in the customary position of J. N. J. (BWV 57—MS. P144). In another nonautograph manuscript score of a cantata the following monogram is found in place of the usual J. J.: α||ω recalling the words of the risen Christ in Revelation 22:13: "I am the Alpha and the Omega, the First and the Last, the Beginning and the End" (BWV 161—MS. P124). The copyist may well have followed Bach's no longer extant manuscript accurately since there is a testimonial in Bach's hand that is headed by these Greek letters (*BD* 1:127; "Testimonial for Friedrich Gottlieb Wild," Leipzig, 18 May 1727). But Bach's usual practice was to head his manuscripts with J. J. He did so not only on scores of his church music, such as cantatas, motets, passions, *Magnificat, Mass in B Minor,* etc., but also on the scores of so-called "secular" cantatas (for example, BWV 201, 204, 206, 213, 214, 215—MSS. P175, P204, P42, P125, P41, P139). On the cover of one cantata (BWV 71—MS. P45) the dedication is written out in full: "*Jesu Juva.*" Further, at least two organ chorale preludes were headed in this way (BWV 651—MS. P271 and BWV 718, as copied by his pupil Johann Ludwig Krebs; see *NBA* IV/3, p. viii). But Bach put the letters "J. J." not only at the top left-hand corner of the manuscripts of his own music but also on the manuscript copies he made of other composers' works, for example, the anonymous *St. Luke Passion* (BWV 246—MS. 1017) and the cantatas of Johann Ludwig Bach (see W. H. Scheide, "Johann Sebastian Bachs Sammlung von Kantaten seines Vetters Johann Ludwig Bach," *BJ*, 1959, pp. 53–54). In the same way as Calov and other authors began their literary works with the prayer "In the name of Jesus," a prayer that would later reecho in the mind of the reader, Bach began his musical manuscripts with the prayer "Jesus, help me!" which was as much a prayer for a worthy performance of the music as for its composition in the first place. Bach shared with Calov a specifically Christian understanding of human creativity under the grace of God.

The announcement that the work is *Die deutsche Bibel D. Martini Lutheri* (The German Bible of Dr. Martin Luther) has misled many into thinking that the work is simply an edition of the text of Luther's translation of the Bible, rather than a commentary on the whole of Scripture (see further the Introduction, p. 22).

Calov makes clear that he is essentially the editor of the work; the commentary on the Biblical text is taken extensively from the writings of Martin Luther.

2 The main title page in Vol. 1/I:

J. N. J. The Holy Bible according to the blessed Herr Dr. Martin Luther's German translation and exposition on the strength of the Holy Spirit's accurate introduction of the coherence and the total context of each and every passage according to the original language, also containing a comparison of parallel passages, their individual sense and meaning, together with an orderly arrangement of each book and chapter and consideration of the emphatic words and expressions in the sacred language, but especially of the evangelical truth, which alone can save, thoroughly and clearly set forth, with added quotations from Herr Luther's German and translated writings [that is, Latin writings translated into German], *so set forth that the original literal meaning, and to a large extent also the salutary application, of Holy Scripture is presented. Developed with great diligence and expense and drawn up by Dr. Abraham Calov, in the year of Christ 1681, being the year 5681 of the creation of the world. In Wittenberg. "Not to us, O Lord, not to us, but to thy name give glory, for the sake of thy steadfast love and thy faithfulness!"* [Ps. 115:1]. *Printed in Wittenberg by Christian*

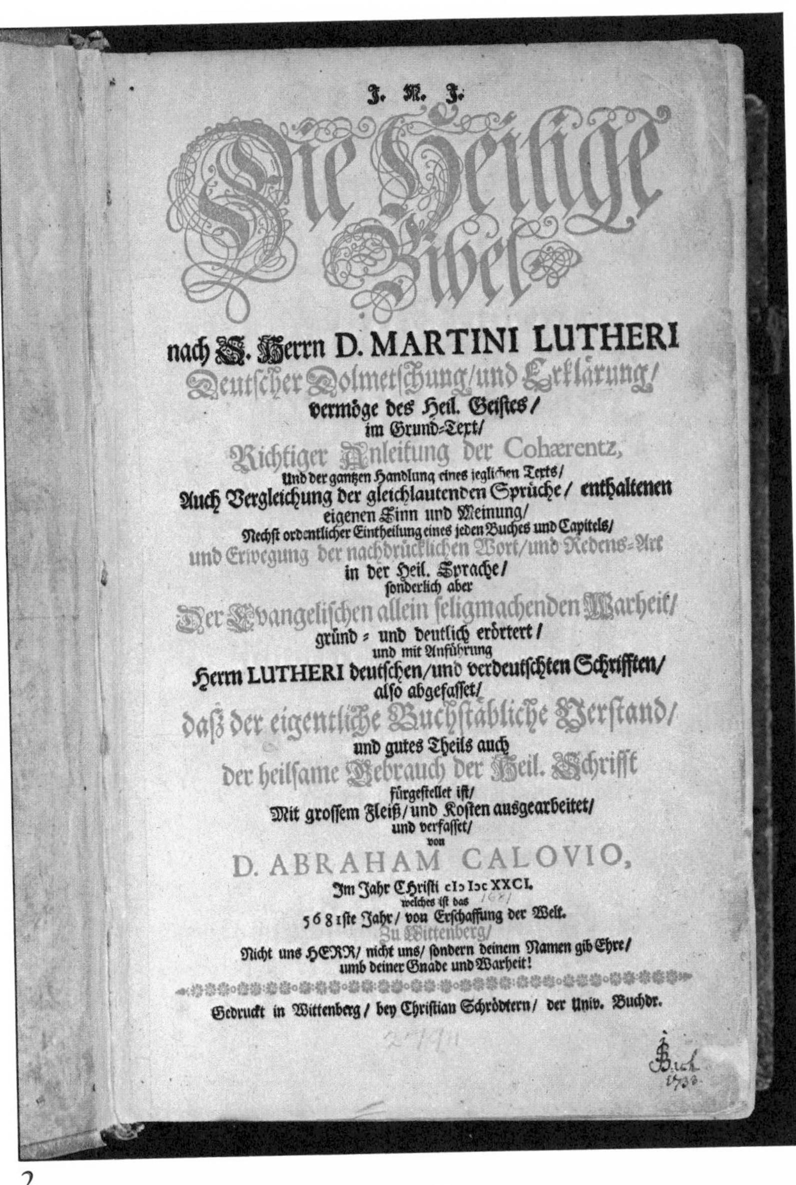

J. N. J.
Die Heilige Bibel
nach S. Herrn D. MARTINI LUTHERI
Deutscher Dolmetschung/ und Erklärung/
vermöge des Heil. Geistes/
im Grund-Text/
Richtiger Anleitung der Cohærentz,
Und der gantzen Handlung eines jeglichen Texts/
Auch Vergleichung der gleichlautenden Sprüche/ enthaltenen
eigenen Sinn und Meinung/
Nechst ordentlicher Eintheilung eines jeden Buches und Capitels/
und Erwegung der nachdrücklichen Wort/ und Redens-Art
in der Heil. Sprache/
sonderlich aber
Der Evangelischen allein seligmachenden Warheit/
gründ- und deutlich erörtert/
und mit Anführung
Herrn LUTHERI deutschen/ und verdeutschten Schrifften/
also abgefasset/
daß der eigentliche Buchstäbliche Verstand/
und gutes Theils auch
der heilsame Gebrauch der Heil. Schrifft
fürgestellet ist/
Mit grossem Fleiß/ und Kosten ausgearbeitet/
und verfasset/
von
D. ABRAHAM CALOVIO,
Im Jahr Christi CIↃ IↃC XXCI.
welches ist das 1681
5681ste Jahr/ von Erschaffung der Welt.
Zu Wittenberg/
Nicht uns HERR/ nicht uns/ sondern deinem Namen gib Ehre/
umb deiner Gnade und Warheit!
Gedruckt in Wittenberg/ bey Christian Schrödtern/ der Univ. Buchdr.

2

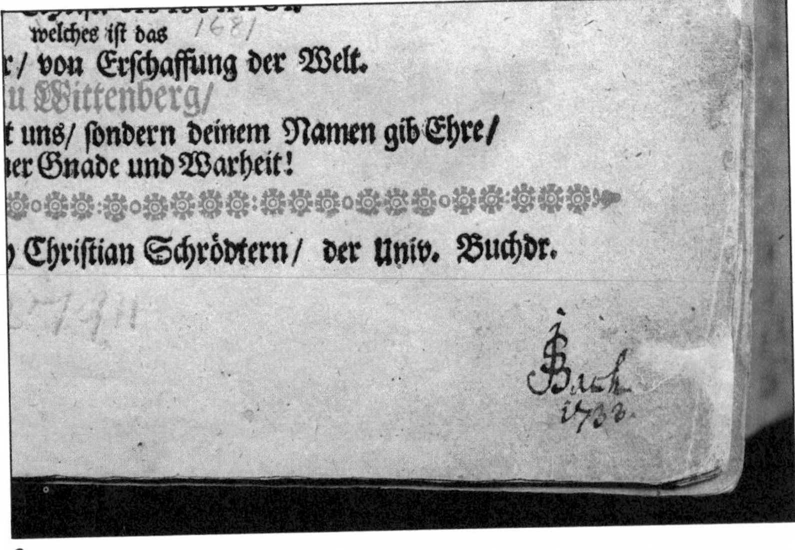

welches ist das 1681
r/ von Erschaffung der Welt.
u Wittenberg/
t uns/ sondern deinem Namen gib Ehre/
er Gnade und Warheit!
Christian Schrödtern/ der Univ. Buchdr.

2a

Schrödter, the university's printer of books.

Here the information on the half-title page (no. 1) is expanded, but again it is emphasized that Calov is the editor; the substance of the commentary is supplied from the writings of Luther.

In the bottom right-hand corner is Bach's monogram and the year "1733" (see the Introduction, p. 26, and nos. 47 and 55).

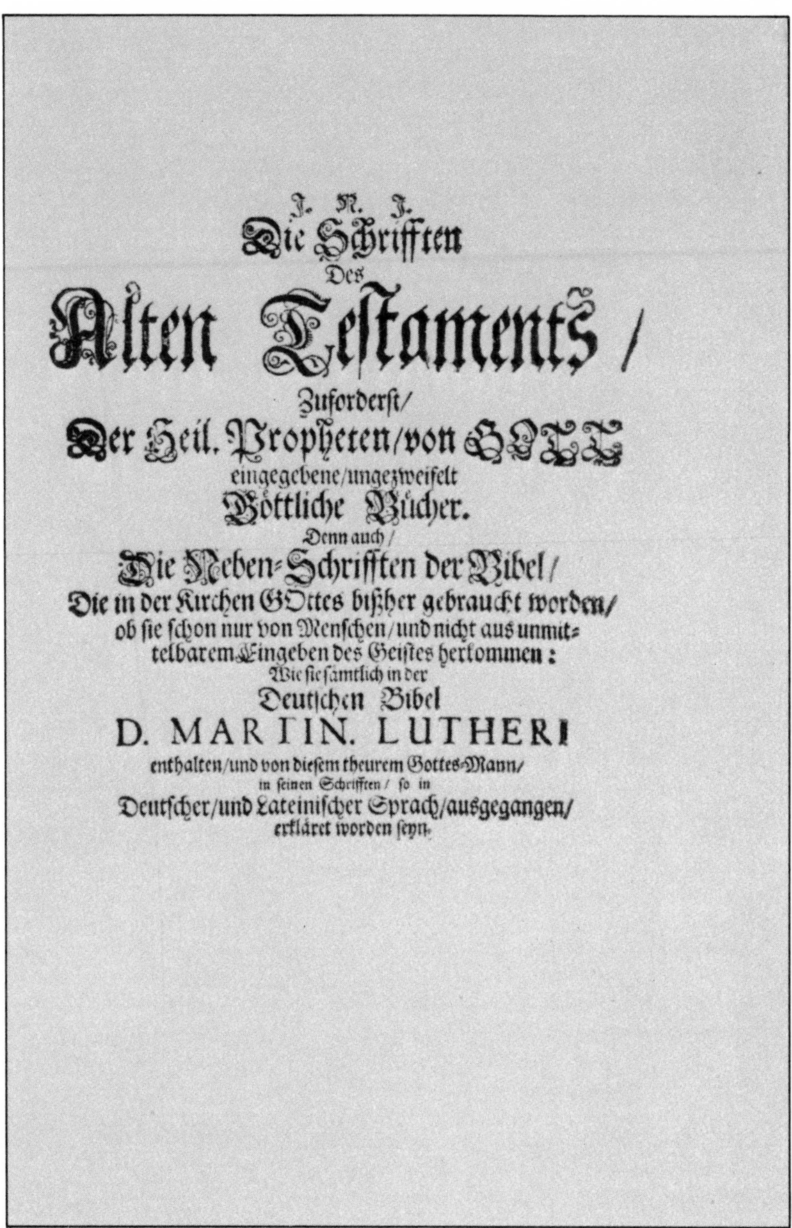

J. N. J.
Die Schrifften
Des
Alten Testaments/
Zuforderst/
Der Heil. Propheten/von GOTT
eingegebene/ungezweifelt
Göttliche Bücher.
Denn auch/
Die Neben-Schrifften der Bibel/
Die in der Kirchen GOttes bißher gebraucht worden/
ob sie schon nur von Menschen/und nicht aus unmit-
telbarem Eingeben des Geistes herkommen:
Wie sie sämtlich in der
Deutschen Bibel
D. MARTIN. LUTHERI
enthalten/und von diesem theurem Gottes-Mann/
in seinen Schrifften/ so in
Deutscher/und Lateinischer Sprach/ausgegangen/
erkläret worden seyn.

3

3 Old Testament section title page, vol. 1/I, sig. ††††††3 recto:

J. N. J. The Scriptures of the Old Testament, in the first place the inspired and incontestable divine books of the holy prophets of God. Then also the secondary writings of the Bible that have been used in the church up to this time, even though they are only of human origin and not of immediate inspiration of the Holy Spirit, as they are all contained in the German Bible of Dr. Martin Luther, and have been expounded in the writings of this dear man of God that have been issued in German and Latin.

This sectional title page follows the introductory material, including the lengthy dedication, which is given here in English translation as appendix 1.

4 The first page of the commentary, vol. 1/I, cols. 1–2. Since this is the beginning of the substance of the work, it is headed by "Jm Namen Jesu!" in full, rather than simply "J. N. J." See no. 1.

1 2

Jm Namen JEsu!

Das Erste Theil

Der Heiligen Göttlichen Schrifft.

Die Fünff Bücher Mosis/

(Des Mannes Gottes 5. Mos. XXXIII, 1. Jos. XIV, 6. Ps. XC, 1. Vergl. 1. Sam. II. 17. c. IX. 6. 7. 8. 10. 1. Kön. XII. 22. c. XIII. 1. 4. folg. 2. Kön. I. 9 folg. c. IV. 7. 9. c. V. 8. 20.)

VOn welchem GOtt selbst zeuget 4. Mos. XII. 6. 7. Ist iemand unter euch ein Prophet des HErrn/ dem wil ich mich kund machen in einem Gesicht/ oder wil mit ihm reden in einem Traum: Aber nicht also mein Knecht Mose/ der in meinem gantzen Hause treu ist. Mündlich rede ich mit ihm, und er sihet den HErrn in seiner Gestalt/ nicht durch dunckele Wort/ oder Gleichnüß. Der von dem Sohn Gottes selbst unmittelbar beruffen/ 2. Mos. III. 2. 6. 10. folg. Von dem er die erste Göttliche Schrifft/ die beyden Taffeln des Gesetzes/ eigenhändig bezeichnet/ empfangen 2. Mos. XXXII. 16. Nach welcher Schrifft er die Zehen Wort auff andere zwey steinerne Taffeln geschrieben 2. Mos. XXXIV. 13. als die Taffeln des Bundes/ und des Zeuanüsses des HErrn 2. Mos. XXXIV. 27. 20. Darin aber der HErr ihm die Hand geführet hat/ wie er andeutet 5. Mos. X. 2. Darumb solche Schrifft Moses dem HErrn als Ober-Schreibern und Urhebern zueignet/ 5. Mos. X. 4. Wie denn Moses darauff alle Wort des Göttlichen Gesetzes auff des HErrn Geboth und Direction, auff grosse mit Kalck getünchte auff dem Berge Ebal auffgerichtete Steine/ zuerst klar/ und deutlich geschrieben 5. Mos. XXVII. 2. 3. 8. wie ihm auch ebenmäßig die Historien seiner Zeit zum Gedächtnüß in ein Buch zu schreiben anbefohlen worden/ 2. Mos. XVII. 14. Daher von ihm David zeuget: Der HErr hat Mose seine Wege wissen lassen/ Ps. CIII. 7. und Jsrael von ihm bekennet: Mose hat uns das Gesetz geboten/ dem Erbe der Gemeine Jacob/ und er verwaltete das Ampt eines Königes/ 5. Mos. XXXIII. 5. Und der H. Geist giebet ihm den Vorzug vor allen Propheten/ 5. Mos. XXXIV. 10. Und es stund hinfort kein Prophet in Jsrael auff/ wie Mose/ den der HErr erkennet hätte von Angesicht. Welchen GOtt würdiget/ daß er ihn mit Christo vergleichet/ 5. Mos. XIIX. 8. 9. Ich wil ihnen einen Propheten/ wie du bist/ erwecken aus ihren Brüdern/ und meine Wort in seinen Mund geben/ der sol zu ihnen reden/ alles was ich ihm gebieten werde/ und wer meine Wort nicht hören wird/ die er in meinem Namen reden wird/ von dem wil ichs fodern. Auff dessen Schrifft der HErr Christus sich selbst beruffen/ Joh. V. 39. 46. Wenn ihr Mose gläubet/ so glaubet ihr auch mir/ denn er hat von mir geschrieben/ und aus seinen Schrifften gegen seine Aposteln dargethan/ wie er leiden/ und zu seiner Herrligkeit eingehen müssen/ Luc. XXIV. 26. 44. massen auch St. Paulus bezeuget/ Er habe nichts gesagt/ ausser dem/ das Moses und die Propheten gesaget haben/ daß es geschehen solt/ Gesch. XXVI. 22. Damit denn Mosis Schrifften als Göttliche von GOtt eingegebene Schrifften 2. Tim. III. 16. gnugsam canonisiret/ und bestätiget seyn. Besiehe auch Luc. XVI. 29. Ebr. III. 5. c. IIX. 5.

A Das

4

5 Vol. 1/I, cols. 31–32, 33–34. On Genesis 3:6–7.

Col. 31. Note the words crossed out in black toward the bottom of the column. They were printed in error, since on later sheets that went through the press they are completely omitted (for example, in the set that was once owned by Ludwig Fuerbringer; see Introduction, p. 19) and were therefore probably struck out by someone working in Schrödter's printing shop.

Col. 32. Marginal addition in Bach's hand: *das von aussen hinzu kömt, u. ohne Verletzung der Natur.* The addition supplies an omission from Calov's quotation from Luther's commentary on the verse, given here in Roman type:

5

> *Luther: The scholastics argue that* [original] *righteousness, when Adam was created, was not part of Adam's nature, but rather like an adornment or gift added to man, as when one places a wreath on a pretty girl, which wreath is not part of the nature of the girl but is something apart from her nature,* which comes from outside and without injuring her nature, *and can be removed again. Therefore they argue about man and about demons that although they have lost their original righteousness, their natural endowments have nevertheless remained pure, just as they were created in the beginning. But this idea must be shunned like poison, for it minimizes original sin.*
>
> *Let us rather maintain that righteousness was not a gift which came from without, separate from man's nature, but that it was truly part of his nature, so that it was Adam's nature to love God, to believe God, to know God, etc. These things were just as natural for Adam as it is natural for the eyes to receive light. But because you may correctly say that nature has been damaged if you render an eye defective by inflicting a wound, so, after man has fallen from righteousness into sin, it is correct and truthful to say that our natural endowments are not perfect but are corrupted by sin. For just as it is the nature of the eye to see, so it was the nature of reason and will in Adam to know God, to trust God, and to fear God. Since it is a fact that this has now*

been lost, who is so foolish as to say that our natural endowments are still perfect? And yet nothing was more common and received more general acceptance in the schools than this thesis.

Therefore let us shun those ravings like real pests and a perversion of the Holy Scriptures, and let us rather follow experience, which shows that we are born from unclean seed and that from the very nature of the seed we acquire ignorance of God, smugness, unbelief, hatred against God, disobedience, impatience, and similar grave faults. These are so widely spread through flesh, body, mind, muscles, and blood, through the bones and the very marrow, in the will, in the intellect, and in reason, that they not only cannot be fully removed but are not even recognized as sin. (Based on LW 1:164–66.)

See further the Introduction, p. 33, and no. 77.

disputiren/ daß die Gerechtigkeit/ darin Adam erschaffen
ist/ nicht sey gewest in Adams Natur/ sondern sey gleich
wie ein Schmuck oder Gabe gewest/ damit der Mensch
erstlich sey gezieret worden / als wenn man einer schönen Jungfrau einen Krantz auffsetzt/ welcher Krantz nicht
ein Theil der Natur ist der Jungfrauen/ sondern ist etwas
sonderliches und abgeschiedenes von der Natur/ wieder
kan abgethan werden. Darumb disputiren sie vom
Menschen und vom Teuffeln/ daß ob sie wol die Gerechtigkeit darin sie geschaffen seyn verlohren haben / so haben sie doch ihre Naturalia, das ist / natürliche Kräfften
rein behalten/ wie sie erstlich seynd geschaffen gewest. A-
ber für solcher Lehre/ weil sie die Erbsünde gering macht/
soll man sich hüten/ wie für einem Gifft. Und wir sollen
vielmehr dafür halten/ daß die Gerechtigkeit nicht gewest
sey eine Gabe/ so von aussen darzu kommen/ und etwas
unterschiedenes von der Natur des Menschen gewest sey/
sondern sey warhafftig natürlich gewest/ also/ daß Adam

5a

33 Das dritte Capitel. 34

5b

6 Vol. 1/I, cols. 47–48. On Genesis 4:4. Simple correction of *zürnete* to *zeugete* in the last line of col. 47, according to the list of typographical errors at the end of vol. 3/VI.

47 Das Erste Buch Mosis/ 48

(*Op*)fersdienst/dieweil beyde Habel und Cain dem HErrn Opffer bringen. Es möchte aber iemand fragen/ was und wovon haben sie ihnen geprediget? Antwort: deß haben sie warlich viel Ursach/ und allerley Materien auß der H. Schrifft gehabt; Sie haben offt zu gedencken gehabt/ ihres ersten Standes/ und des Paradieses/werden ihnen auch ohne Zweiffel denselben Orth/ so von Engeln verwahret worden/ offt geweiset haben/ und sie darbey erinnert/ daß sie sich für der Sünden/dadurch sie so vieler Güter und Gaben jämmerlich beraubet und entblösset waren/ hüten solten/ in Gottesfurcht leben/ und sich seiner Gnaden und Güter trösten/ so würden sie nach diesem Leben ein bessers finden. Darzu werden sie das andere Theil der Lehre auch geführet haben/nemlich von der Verheissung des Samens/ und zukünfftigen Erlösung/ von allem Jammer und Unglück. Von solchen Dingen werden ohne Zweiffel die frommen Eltern ihren Kindern/ an einem gewissen Orth/ und fürnemlich auf den Sabbath/ geprediget haben. Darumb seynd sie auch durch solche Predigten erwecket/und verursacht worden/GOtt zu opffern und zu dienen. Und ist das hier der erste Text in der Schrifft/ darin des Opffers gedacht wird/ darauß zu sehen ist/ daß die Gewohnheit zu opffern nicht neue/sondern von Anfang der Welt gewest ist. Darumb ists kein Wunder/ daß die Weise zu opffern von Adam biß auff Mosen gepflantzet und überreicht / und hernach durch Mosen in eine gewisse Ordnung und Art gefasset/ und gebracht ist/ welcher ohne Zweiffel viel unnutzes Dinges/so von abergläubigen Leuten darzu wird kommen seyn / davon wiederumb abgeschaffet hat / wie man in Exempeln der Heydnischen Opffer/ in dem Poeten Homero und Virgilio/siehet/ welche die Heiden ohne Zweiffel von den Vätern genommen/ und ihnen nachgethan/auch dieselben mit vielen unnützen und gottlosen Dingen gemehret haben. Wiewol aber allhier allein des Opffers/ nicht aber der Predigt gedacht wird / soll man es doch dafür halten/daß sie ohne die Predigt des Worts nicht geopffert haben. Denn GOtt läst ihm mit einem stummen Werck nicht dienen / sondern es muß ein Wort dabey seyn/ welches dem Menschen im Hertzen / und GOtt im Ohren öffentlich schallet / wie denn auch die Anruffung des Namens Gottes zu diesem Opffer kommen ist.)

v. 4. **Und Habel bracht auch von den Erstlingen seiner Heerde / und von ihren Fetten.** (Brachte/ das ist / er opfferte/ welches Opffer Abels gerühmet wird vom Heiligen Geist/ Ebr. XI. 4. Daß er ein besser Opffer dem HErrn gebracht habe: Darumb ist der Mangel nicht an dem gewest/ daß sie geopffert haben/ sondern an der Person / die da geopffert hat. Und ist der Glaube das wichtige gewesen / welches Abels Opffer köstlich und angenehm gemacht hat/ Cains aber unwerth / und falsch. Denn Abel glaubet/ daß GOtt gütig und gnädig sey. Darumb gefället sein Opffer GOtt wol. Cain aber verläst sich auff die Ehre/ daß er der erstgebohrne ist/und achtet gegen ihn seine Bruder als für einen unnützen und untüchtigen Menschen. Wie Herr Lutherus erinnert.) **und der HErr sahe gnädiglich an Habel/** (wegen des Glaubens an den Weibes-Samen/) **und sein Opffer** (dabey er des Versühn-Opffers des unbefleckten Lammes Gottes sich erinnert / und im Glauben auff dessen Versühnung GOtt dem HErrn sein Opffer dargestellet hat / Joh. I. 29. 1. Cor. V. 7. 1. Petr. I. 18. 19. 1. Joh. II. 2. Ebr. VII. 27. c. IX. 26. 27. c. X. 14. Denn durch den Glauben hat Habel Zeugnüß überkommen/ daß er gerecht sey / da GOtt durchs Feuer vom Himmel zürnete von seiner Gabe/ Ebr. XI. 4. Besiehe vom Feuer 3. Mos. IX. 24. 1. Kön. XIIX. 38. 1. Chron. XXII. 26. 2. Chron. VII. 1. Von der Gerechtigkeit Abel Matth. XXIII. 35. Hier observiret Herr Lutherus sehr wol die Ordnung der Rede Mosis/ denn spricht er pag. 123. zeiget nicht Moses mit dem / daß er saget/ GOtt sahe gnädiglich an/ Habel und sein Opffer / klar an/ das GOtt für dem Werck pflege zu sehen auff die Person/ was es für eine sey? So nun dieselbige gut ist / so gefället ihm auch ihr Werck/wo aber die Person nicht gut ist/ so gefället ihm auch ihr Werck nicht. Das ist aber die Summa unserer Lehre/ daß wir lehren und bekennen/ daß GOtt die Person eher annimbt/ denn das Werck / und daß die Person nicht fromm oder gerecht wird/durch ihr gut oder gerecht Werck/ sondern daß das Werck gut und gerecht wird durch die Person/ so gerecht und fromm ist/ wie solches hier der Text beweiset.)

v. 5. **Aber Cain und sein Opffer sahe er nicht gnädig an.** (Cain opfferte auch/sagt Herr Lutherus/und zwar ehe denn Abel. Er opfferte aber also/daß er sich seiner Ehre erhebt/ und hoffet/ GOtt werde ihm das Opffer gefallen lassen / darumb daß es von einem erstgebohrnem gethan wird/kömt also ohne Glauben/ ohne Bekändnüß seiner Sünde/bittet auch nicht umb Gnade oder Vergebung der Sünde / trawet nicht auff Gottes Gnade und Barmhertzigkeit. Dargegen erkennet sich Abel/ daß er ein unwürdiger armer Sünder sey/ darumb hat er Zuflucht zu Gottes Barmhertzigkeit/ und gläubet/ daß GOtt gnädig sey / und sich über uns erbarmen wolle. Also richtet GOtt/der in die Hertzen hinein siehet/ unter diesen beyden Brüdern/ die ihm zugleich opffern/ und verwirfft Cain umbs Opffers willen/ als das nicht gut gewest sey/ (denn so er GOtt eine Nußschale im Glauben geopffert hätte/ so wäre es GOtt angenehm gewesen/) sondern daß die Person böse und ohne Glauben/voll Stoltz und Hoffarth ist. Wiederumb hält er sich zu Habels Opffer/ darumb / daß er an der Person Gefallen hat. Denn wenn einer an der Person Gefallen hat/ so läst er ihm gefallen alles was er thut/ da wiederumb einem alles entgegen und zu wieder ist/ was der thut/ dem man feind ist. Und hier hebet an die Kirche sich zutrennen/ und zu theilen in zweyerley Kirchen/ Eine/ die allein mit dem Namen eine Kirche ist/ am Werck aber ist sie nichts denn eine blutdürstige Kirche / die andere/ so da unfruchtbar / wüste / und unter dem Creutz und Verfolgung ist/ und gegen der heuchlischen Kirchen für der Welt nichts anders ist/ denn Habel/das ist eine eitele Nichtigkeit. Denn Christus nennet Habeln auch gerecht / und macht ihn zum ersten Gliede der Kirchen der Gottfürchtigen / die da bleiben wird/ biß zur Welt Ende. Gleichwie Cain der Anfang ist der Kirchen der Boßhafftigen und Blutdürstigen/ biß ans Ende der Welt/ wie auch Augustinus im Buch de civitate Dei, diese Historien darauff fürhält.) **da ergrimmet Cain sehr / und sein Geberde verstellet sich.** (Er saget nicht von einer Geberde/ oder von einem Stück desselben/ sonder von allen Geberden und Zeichen: wie auch Paulus dieser Ebräischen Art nach geredet hat/ die Liebe stellet sich nicht ungebärdig/ 1. Cor. XIII. 5. das ist/ sie rümpfet sich nicht/ siehet nicht sauer/ siehet nicht rachgierig / sondern führet ein fein/ auffrichtig/ freundlich/ und frölich Gesicht. Denn Zorn und Rachgierigkeit siehet aus allen Gliedern und Geberden / und das ohne Auffhören. Denn der Zorn verschleicht sich nicht mit der Zeit/ oder gehet überhin / wie ein Weltlicher / oder Hauß-Zorn.)

v. 6. Da

6

7 Vol. 1/I, cols. 91–92. On Genesis 11:10. Simple correction of *Cham* to *Elam*. Significantly, the correction occurs in a section of the commentary that includes several numbers; from markings elsewhere in the volumes, Bach appears to have had a special interest in such numbers. See nos. 14, 19, 22, 26, 27, 51, 52.

91 Das Erste Buch Mosis/ 92

die Stadt (und den Thurn) zubauen. (wie sie es etwa bedacht waren/ und angefangen hatten.)

v. 9. Daher heist ihr (derselbigen Stadt) Name Babel/ (Herr Lutherus: *auff deutsch eine Vermischung/ oder Verwirrung*) daß der HErr daselbst verwirret hatte aller Länder Sprache. (aller Menschen aus allen Ländern bißherige einige Sprache/ v. 1.) und sie zerstreuet von dannen in alle Länder/ (nach seinem Göttlichen Willen/ wo er einen iedweden wissen/ und wohnen lassen wolte/ Gesch. XVII. GOtt hat aller Menschen Geschlecht auff dem gantzen Erdboden ein Ziel gesetzt/ und zuvor ersehen/ wie lang und weit sie wohnen solten.)

Der Andere Theil.

Die Nachkommen Sems/ was die Patriarchen/ und ihre Jahr betrifft.

v. 10. Diß sind die Geschlecht (die Nachkommen unter denen die Kirche Gottes ist fortgepflantzet/ und der wahre Gottesdienst erhalten worden/ aus denen auch der gebenedeyete Weibes-Saamen hat entspriessen sollen / Luc. III. 34. 35. 36.) Sem war hundert Jahr alt/ und zeuget Arphaxad/ zwey Jahr nach der Sündfluth. (im 1658. Jahr der Welt/ im 603. Jahr Noah. Vor dem hat er schon/ nach der Sündfluth/ die zwey ältern Söhne/ Elam und Assur gezeuget/ 1. Mos. XI. 12. 1. Chron. I. 17. Darumb müssen schon zwey Jahr völlig verflossen seyn/ nebst etlichen Monaten/ da Arphachsad gebohren ist.)

v. 11. Und lebet darnach fünffhundert Jahr/ und zeuget Söhn und Töchter/ (daß er also alt worden/ 600. Jahr/ und gestorben ist im 2158. Jahr der Welt: nachdem er mit seinem Elter-Vater Methusalem 98. mit seinem Großvater Lamech 43. mit dem Vater Noah 448. Jahr gelebet/ und von ihnen in der waren Religion/ und Gottesdienst unterwiesen war/ solchen auch auff seine Nachkommen nach der Sündfluth allerdinges auff Abraham und Isaac hat fortpflantzen können/ als mit denen er eine ebene Zeit gelebet/ nemlich mit Abraham 150. Jahr/ mit Isaac 50. Jahr.)

v. 12. Arphachsad war fünff und dreißig Jahr alt/ und zeugete Salah. (im 1693. Jahr nach der Welt.)

v. 13. Und lebet darnach vierhundert und drey Jahr/ (die Lateinische Bibel setzet hier 100. Jahr zu wenig/ als hätte er nur 303. Jahr nach selbiger Zeit gelebet/) und zeuget Söhne und Töchter. (und starb also Arphaxad im 438. Jahr seines Alters/ im 2096. Welt-Jahr/ als er gelebet mit seinem Großvater Noah 348. Jahr/ mit dem Vater Sem 436. mit Salah seinem Sohn 405. mit seinem Enckel Eber 373. mit Phaleg/ Regu/ Serug/ Thara/ seinen Nachkommen/ die gantze Lebens-Zeit/ mit Abram 88. Jahr.)

v. 14. Salah war dreißig Jahr alt/ und zeuget Eber/ (im 1723. Jahr der Welt.)

v. 15. Und lebet darnach vierhundert und drey Jahr/ und zeuget Söhne und Töchter. (Starb also der Patriarch Salah im 433. Jahr seines Alters/ im 2126. Jahr der Welt/ hat gelebet mit seinem Vater Arphaxad 403. mit dem Großvater Sem 433. Jahr/ mit seinem Elter-Vater Noah 313. Jahr/ mit seinem Sohn Eber 403. Jahr. Mit denen andern Nachkommenden Patriarchen/ die gantze Zeit ihres Lebens: mit Abraham 118. Jahr/ mit Isaac 18. Jahr.)

v. 16. Eber war vier und dreyßig Jahr alt/ und zeuget Peleg. (im 1757. Welt-Jahr.)

v. 17. Und lebet darnach vierhundert und dreyßig Jahr/ und zeuget Söhne und Töchter. (Derowegen ist dieser Patriarch Eber 464. Jahr alt worden/ welches Alter keiner unter denen/ die nach der Sündfluth gebohren sind/ erreichet hat: und haben zu seiner Zeit gelebet Peleg/ Regu/ Serug/ Nahor/ Thara/ Abraham/ die er alle überlebet hat/ mit Isaac aber hat er 79. Jahr gelebet/ und mit Jacob 19. Jahr.)

v. 18. Peleg war dreyßig Jahr alt/ und zeuget Regu/ (im 1787. Jahr der Welt)

v. 19. Und lebet darnach zweyhundert und neun Jahr/ und zeuget Söhn und Töchter. (Starb also Peleg im Jahr 1996. nach Erschaffung der Welt/ seines Alters im 239. Jahr.)

v. 20. Regu war zwey und dreyßig Jahr alt/ und zeuget Serug. (im 1819. Welt-Jahr.)

v. 21. Und lebet darnach zweyhundert und sieben Jahr/ und zeuget Söhne und Töchter. (Ist gestorben im 2026. Welt-Jahr/ seines Alters im 239. Jahr/ als Abraham 18. Jahr alt war.)

v. 22. Serug war dreyßig Jahr alt/ und zeugete Nahor. (im 1849. Welt-Jahr.)

v. 23. Und lebet darnach zweyhundert Jahr/ und zeuget Söhne und Töchter. (Starb im 230. Jahr seines Alters/ im 2049. Welt-Jahr/ als Abraham alt war 41. Jahr.)

v. 24. Nahor war neun und zwan-

7

8 Vol. 1/I, cols. 99–100. Genesis 13:4. Bach adds the Bible verse that is omitted from Calov's printed text: *V. 4 Eben an dem Ort, da er vorhin den Altar gemacht hatte, u. er predigte alda den Namen des Herrn* (to the place where he had made an altar at the first; and there he called on the name of the Lord). The passage deals with Abram's return from Egypt and his arrival in Bethel. Bach has thought it important to add the omitted verse, which deals with Abram's primary concern to worship the Lord his God.

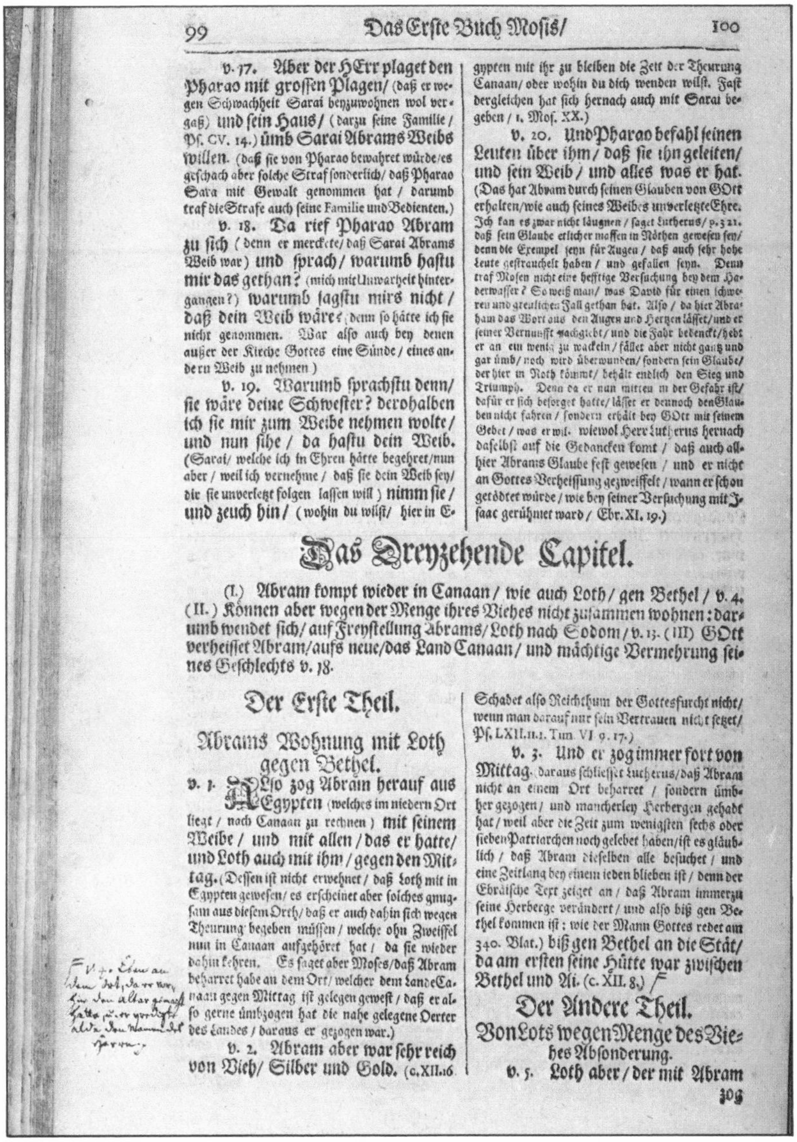

99 Das Erste Buch Mosis/ 100

v. 17. Aber der HErr plaget den Pharao mit grossen Plagen/ (daß er wegen Schwachheit Sarai beyzuwohnen wol vergaß) und sein Haus/ (darzu seine Familie/ Ps. CV. 14.) ümb Sarai Abrams Weibs willen. (daß sie von Pharao bewahret würde/es geschach aber solche Straf sonderlich/ daß Pharao Sara mit Gewalt genommen hat / darumb traf die Strafe auch seine Familie und Bedienten.)

v. 18. Da rief Pharao Abram zu sich (denn er merckete/ daß Sarai Abrams Weib war) und sprach/ warumb hastu mir das gethan? (mich mit Unwarheit hintergangen?) warumb sagstu mirs nicht / daß dein Weib wäre? (denn so hätte ich sie nicht genommen. War also auch bey denen außer der Kirche Gottes eine Sünde / eines andern Weib zu nehmen)

v. 19. Warumb sprachstu denn/ sie wäre deine Schwester? derohalben ich sie mir zum Weibe nehmen wolte/ und nun sihe / da hastu dein Weib. (Sarai/ welche ich in Ehren hätte begehret/nun aber / weil ich vernehme / daß sie dein Weib sey/ dir sie unverletzt folgen lassen will) nimm sie / und zeuch hin / (wohin du wilst/ hier in Egypten mit ihr zu bleiben die Zeit der Theurung Canaan/ oder wohin du dich wenden wilst. Fast dergleichen hat sich hernach auch mit Sarai begeben / 1. Mos. XX.)

v. 20. Und Pharao befahl seinen Leuten über ihm / daß sie ihn geleiten/ und sein Weib / und alles was er hat. (Das hat Abram durch seinen Glauben von GOtt erhalten/wie auch seines Weibes unverletzte Ehre. Ich kan es zwar nicht läugnen / saget Lutherus/ p. 321. daß sein Glaube etlicher massen in Nöthen gewesen sey/ denn die Exempel seyn für Augen / daß auch sehr hohe Leute gestrauchelt haben / und gefallen seyn. Denn traf Mosen nicht eine hefftige Versuchung bey dem Haderwasser? So weiß man/ was David für einen schweren und greulichen Fall gethan hat. Also / da hier Abraham das Wort aus den Augen und Hertzen lässet/und er seiner Vernunfft nachgiebt/ und die Fahr bedenckt/ hebt er an ein wenig zu wackeln / fället aber nicht gantz und gar ümb/ noch wird überwunden/ sondern sein Glaube/ der hier in Noth kömmt/ behält endlich den Sieg und Triumph. Denn da er nun mitten in der Gefahr ist/ dafür er sich besorget hatte/ lässet er dennoch den Glauben nicht fahren / sondern erhält bey GOtt mit seinem Gebet / was er will. wiewol Herr Lutherus hernach daselbst auf die Gedancken komt / daß auch allhier Abrams Glaube fest gewesen / und er nicht an Gottes Verheissung gezweiffelt / wann er schon getödtet würde / wie bey seiner Versuchung mit Isaac gerühmet ward / Ebr. XI. 19.)

Das Dreyzehende Capitel.

(I.) Abram kompt wieder in Canaan / wie auch Loth / gen Bethel / v. 4. (II.) Können aber wegen der Menge ihres Viehes nicht zusammen wohnen: darumb wendet sich/ auf Freystellung Abrams/ Loth nach Sodom / v. 13. (III) GOtt verheisset Abram/ aufs neue/ das Land Canaan / und mächtige Vermehrung seines Geschlechts v. 18.

Der Erste Theil.

Abrams Wohnung mit Loth gegen Bethel.

v. 1. Also zog Abram herauf aus Egypten (welches im niedern Ort liegt / nach Canaan zu rechnen) mit seinem Weibe / und mit allen / das er hatte/ und Loth auch mit ihm / gegen den Mittag. (Dessen ist nicht erwehnet / daß Loth mit in Egypten gewesen/ es erscheinet aber solches gnugsam aus diesem Orth/ daß er auch dahin sich wegen Theurung begeben müssen / welche ohn Zweiffel nun in Canaan aufgehöret hat / da sie wieder dahin kehren. Es saget aber Moses/ daß Abram beharret habe an dem Ort/ welcher dem Lande Canaan gegen Mittag ist gelegen gewest / daß er also gerne ümbzogen hat die nahe gelegene Oerter des Landes / daraus er gezogen war.)

v. 2. Abram aber war sehr reich von Vieh/ Silber und Gold. (c. XII. 16. Schadet also Reichthum der Gottesfurcht nicht/ wenn man darauf nur sein Vertrauen nicht setzet/ Ps. LXII. 11. 1. Tim. VI. 9. 17.)

v. 3. Und er zog immer fort von Mittag. (daraus schliesset Lutherus/ daß Abram nicht an einem Ort beharret / sondern ümbher gezogen / und mancherley Herbergen gehabt hat / weil aber die Zeit zum wenigsten sechs oder sieben Patriarchen noch gelebet haben/ ist es gläublich / daß Abram dieselben alle besuchet / und eine Zeitlang bey einem ieden blieben ist / denn der Ebräische Text zeiget an / daß Abram immerzu seine Herberge verändert / und also biß gen Bethel kommen ist; wie der Mann Gottes redet am 340. Blat.) biß gen Bethel an die Stät/ da am ersten seine Hütte war zwischen Bethel und Ai. (c. XII. 8.) F

F V. 4. Eben an dem Ort, da er vorhin den altar gemacht hatte u. er predigte alda den Namen des Herrn.

Der Andere Theil.

Von Lots wegen Menge des Viehes Absonderung.

v. 5. Loth aber / der mit Abram zog

8

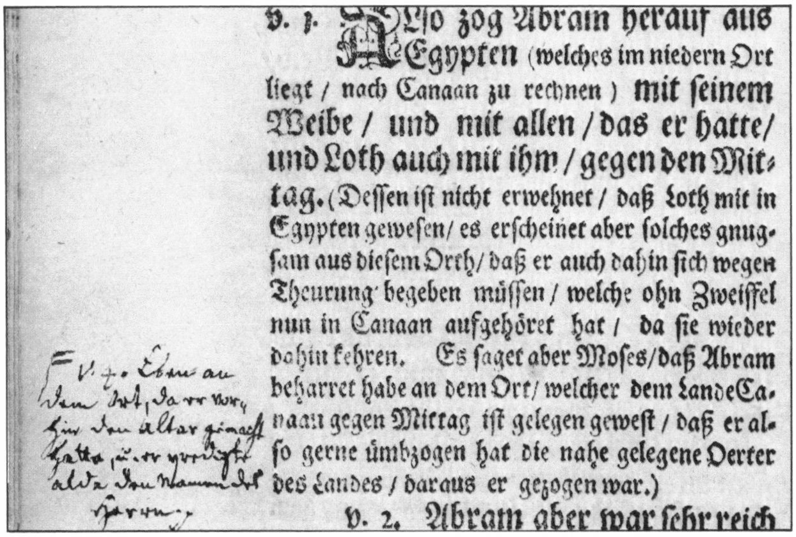

v. 1. Also zog Abram herauf aus Egypten (welches im niedern Ort liegt / nach Canaan zu rechnen) mit seinem Weibe / und mit allen / das er hatte/ und Loth auch mit ihm / gegen den Mittag. (Dessen ist nicht erwehnet / daß Loth mit in Egypten gewesen/ es erscheinet aber solches gnugsam aus diesem Orth/ daß er auch dahin sich wegen Theurung begeben müssen / welche ohn Zweiffel nun in Canaan aufgehöret hat / da sie wieder dahin kehren. Es saget aber Moses/ daß Abram beharret habe an dem Ort/ welcher dem Lande Canaan gegen Mittag ist gelegen gewest / daß er also gerne ümbzogen hat die nahe gelegene Oerter des Landes / daraus er gezogen war.)

F V. 4. Eben an dem Ort, da er vorhin den altar gemacht hatte u. er predigte alda den Namen des Herrn.

v. 2. Abram aber war sehr reich

8a

9 Vol. 1/I, cols. 161–62 (col. 161 misnumbered as 261). On Genesis 22:13. Simple correction of *Jacobs* to *Isaacs,* in col. 162, according to the list of typographical errors at the end of vol. 3/VI.

261 Das Zwey und zwantzigste Capitel. 162

Paulus saget/ 2. Cor. I. wir hoffen und stellen unser Vertrauen auff GOtt/ der die Todten aufferwecket: von dem Glauben haben wir kaum ein kleines Füncklein/ denn so lange gläuben wir/ so lange wir den Todt nicht fühlen/ wo aber derselbige ein wenig herfür blicket/und sich sehen lässet/ da folget alsobald Angst und Schrecken darauff.)

v. 12. Er sprach lege deine Hand nicht an den Knaben/ und thue ihm nichts. (Nun fället hier eine Frage für/ nach Herrn Lutheri Anmerckung/ wie doch Abraham der Stimme des Engels habe gehorchen können/und sich des enthalten/ daß er seinen Sohn nicht geschlachtet hat/ wie wenn er gezweiffelt und gedacht hätte/ es wäre kein Engel/sondern ein Teuffel? Dieweil er je ein ausdrücklich Gebot Gottes gehabt hat/ nemlich/ da GOtt zu ihm gesaget hatte/ schlachte deinen Sohn/ und opffere ihn zum Brandopffer/ wider dies Gebot wird ihm nun vom Engel gebothen/ er sol seines Sohnes verschonen/ und ihm nichts thun. Die erste Anfechtung war wider die Verheissung vom Samen/ da diese Anfechtung vom Samen uberwunden ist/ und er sich nun in seinem Hertzen zum Gehorsam begeben/ und Isaac diesen Trost auch gefast hatte/ wenn er schon würde zu Aschen werden/ so würde doch gleichwol die Verheissung bestehen bleiben/ und würde ihn GOtt wiederumb vom Todt auferwecken: wider solches alles rufft ihm nun der Engel/ und saget/ thue dem Knaben nichts/ solcher Befehl ist ihm stracks eine Anfechtung/ damit/ daß er dem vorigem Geboth zu wider ist/ wie er droben angefochten ward mit dem Gebot so der Verheissung zu wider war. Hierauf antwortet er/ unter andern: Es ist wol gläublich/ dz Abraham aus sonderlicher und heimlicher Bewegung die Hand stille gehalten/ wider das Gebot/ so er zuvor empfangen/ wie im alten Testament die Propheten auch wieder das Wort viel gethan haben/ als da Elias einen Altar bauet auff dem Berge Carmel/ und erwürget die Baals Priester/ dem zu wieder/ das Moses gebothen hatte/ da er sagt im 5. Mos. am XII. an dem Orth/ den der HErr euer GOtt erwehlen wird/ da solt ihr hin kommen und opffern/ rc. solches hat Elia und Elisa nicht gehalten/ Item/ es sind im Volck Israel viel Propheten gewest/ die nicht gen Jerusalem kommen sind/ daselbst zu lehren oder zu predigen. Diese alle haben eine sonderliche Anregung mit einer sonderlichen Freyheit gehabt/ daß sie solches gethan haben. So ist der Engel auch vom Himmel kommen/ und hat sich ohne Zweiffel der Himmel auffgethan/ ein neuer Glantz geleuchtet/ Blitz und Feuer gesehen worden/ und wird zugleich ein Hauff der andern Engel dabey gewest seyn/ für welches Majestät Abraham erschrocken/ und beyde das Messer/ und Gedancken seinen Sohn zuschlachten hat fallen lassen. Zum andern/ so hat Abraham die rechte Regel des Glaubens/ darnach er sich richten kan/ denn der Engel bringt ihm kein Wort/ das der Verheissung zu wider sey/ sondern daß mit dem übereinstimmet, das zu ihm gesagt war/ in Isaac soll dir der Name genennet werden. rc.) **Denn nun weiß ich/ daß du GOtt fürchtest/ und hast deines einigen Sohnes nicht verschonet/ umb meinet willen** (hier sehen wir/ daß dieser Engel niemand anders sey/ als der Engel des Bundes/ der Sohn Gottes/ als der allein ins Hertz siehet/ und den Glauben darin erkennet/ 2. Tim. II. 19. Offenb II. 23. der vom Himmel redet/ und doch auf Erden gehöret wird/ als der zugleich im Himmel und auf Erden ist/ wie denn Abraham seines einigen Sohnes nicht verschonet hat/ sondern ihn schlachten wollen/ nicht umb einiger Creatur willen/ sondern umb des Befehls des einigen Gottes willen/ als der nicht durch einen Engel/ sondern unmittelbahr von GOtt darzu einen Befehl bekommen hat/ (vergl. hiermit v. 16. und wie hätte der Patriarch können gewiß seyn/ GOtt wolle es haben/ daß er seinen einigen Sohn nicht schlachten/ sondern ihm kein Leides thun solle/ wenn er nicht gewiß gewesen wäre/ daß ihm GOtt selbst unmittelbahr contramandire/ daher Nyssenus sagt/ der befohlen hat/ daß er tödten solte/ ruffet ietzo/ daß er schonen soll/ darumb denn Abraham den Engel Jehovam, den HERRN nennet/ wenn er diesem Ort den Namen giebt/ der Berg/ da der HErr siehet.)

v. 13. Da hub Abraham seine Augen auf/ und sahe einen Widder hinter ihm in der Hecken mit seinen Hörnern hangen/ und gieng hin/ und nahm den Widder/ und opffert ihn zum Brand Opffer an seines Sohnes statt. (von diesem Widder saget Augustinus, lib. XVI. de Civ. DEi c. 32. Wer ist anders durch den Widder/ der in den Hecken henget/ abgebildet/ als Christus JEsus/ welcher/ ehe er aufgeopffert worden mit Jüdischen Dornen ist gekrönet worden/ welcher in unsern Sünden/ die ihm auffs Häupt/ wie dem Versühnbock/ und andern Opffern/ geleget worden/ ist verwickelt worden/ aber nach dem Willen Gottes für uns geopffert ist/ an unser statt/ gleich wie hier der Widder an ~~Jacobs~~ *Isaacs* statt geopffert ist.)

v. 14. Und Abraham hieß die Städte/ der HERR siehet (* GOtt sorget für alles/ und wachet*) **daher man noch heutiges Tages saget auf dem Berge/ da der HERR siehet.** (Siehet heist nach Art der hebräischen Sprache/ er hat Vorsorge. Nach den accenten heist es/ auf dem Berge des HErrn wird mans sehen/ oder/ wird Vorsorge geschehen. Etliche erklärens mit R. Sal. Jarchi, auf dem Berge wird der HErr gesehen werden/ welches erfüllet ist/ da GOtt offenbahret im Fleisch/ auf dem Berge gesehen worden/ wie er aufgeopffert/ oder gecreutziget worden. Eigentlich davon zu reden/ so heist es/ in den ersten Worten/ der HErr wird ausersehen ihm ein Schaf zum Opffer. Er wird solches durch seine Göttliche Providentz oder Vorsorge schon schaffen/ wie es denn in Warheit geschehen/ da er einen Widder des Orts plötzlich durch seine Krafft geschaffen/ und dargestellet hat. In den andern Worten da eingeführet/ wie man ein gemein dicterium werde aus dieser Benennung machen/ wird theils in gemein angedeutet/ GOtt werde gesehen/ und erscheine daselbst/ wo es nöthig ist/ daß er mit seiner Hülff erscheine. Darumb nimmt Herr Lutherus hieraus einen Trost/ p. 617. als würde gesaget/ dieser Berg sol nun genennet werden/ Erscheinung des HErrn/ denn GOtt schauet daselbst/

L erschei-

9

10 Vol. 1/I, cols. 199–200. On Genesis 26:33. Bach adds the comment: *NB. Ungefehr 1 Stunde von Erfurth, ist ein Dorf so diesen Nahmen hat* (NB. About one hour from Erfurt there is a village that has this name). Howard H. Cox takes the name to be "Saba" and draws attention to Bach's Epiphany cantata BWV 65: *Sie werden aus Saba alle kommen* (Is. 60:6) ("Bach's Bible," *Bach in Bethlehem Today: A Conference Report* [Bethlehem, 1979], p. 32; cf. M. Geck, "Bachs Schriftverständnis," *Musik und Kirche* 40 [1970]: 10). However, the name to which Bach is referring is *Schwereborn,* which he has underlined. *Schwereborn* (Schwörborn), as Calov points out, means the same as the Hebrew *Beer-Sheba,* that is, "the well of the oath," and is the name of a well near Erfurt. As Calov makes clear, the information is from Luther (Altenburg Edition, 9:807; *LW* 5:88). Bach adds the information, presumably from his own knowledge of the area, that the village is "one hour" from Erfurt. Schwörborn is indeed about eight kilometers north of Erfurt, that is, about one hour's walk away. Erfurt is almost in the center of the triangle enclosed between Meiningen, Mühlhausen, and Jena, within which nearly all of the members of the Bach family lived and worked. It was familiar territory to Bach. Arnstadt was about three hours from Erfurt, and Weimar about three and a half (see the engraved map published by Johann Stridbeck the younger, ca. 1700, reproduced in *BD* 4:149).

199 Das Erste Buch Mosis/ 200

10

v. 33. Und er nennete ihn Saba/ (Hieronymus nimts als einen gemeinen Namen/ Saturitas, eine Fülle. Denn dasselbe heist Saba auch/ daß hier so viel heissen sol/ als wenn man sagt/ puteus Saturitatis, ein Brunn der Fülle/ oder ein voller Brunn. Aber die Rabbini der Ebräer halten hart darüber/ daß mans nach seiner rechten eigentlichen Bedeutung verdolmetschen sol/ daß es heisse/ puteus juramenti, und dasselbe gefält mir auch am besten/ daß ein Brunn des Eydes genant worden/ ein Schwereborn/ welchen Namen man zu Erfurth auch einem Brunn gegeben hat: Herr Lutherus/ p. 807. Und hat der Mann Gottes hier der dreyen Namen der Brunn geistliche Bedeutung hierbey gefüget/ wie folget: Wo iemand ie eine heimliche Deutung haben wolt/ der mag die drey Brunnen ziehen auff die drey Hauptstück der H. Schrifft/ nemlich auff das Gesetz/ auff die Propheten/ und auffs Evangelium. Denn das Gesetz ist Esek/ das ist/ wie man in der deutschen Sprache sagt/ es ist Essig/ ja in der Seele/ oder Gewissen ists Es-

10a

Bach's interest in Biblical topography and distances and their relation to German geography and measurement is confirmed by the presence in his library of Heinrich Bünting, *Itinerarium Sacrae Scripturae, Das ist Ein Reisebuch, Über die gantze heilige Schrifft in zwey Bücher getheilet. Das Erste Theil begreifft aller Reisen der lieben Patriarchen, Richter, Könige, Propheten, Fürsten, etc. Nach deudschen Meilen aufgerechnet . . . Das Ander gehet auff sa Newe Testament und zeiget an wie die Jungfraw Maria, Joseph, die Weisen aus Morgenland, der Herr Jesus Christus, und die lieben Apostel gereiset haben . . .* (*Itinerarium Sacrae Scripturae,* that is, a travel book of the whole of Holy Scripture, divided into two books. The first part details all the travels of the dear patriarchs, judges, kings, prophets, princes, etc., reckoned according to German miles. . . . The second deals with the New Testament, and demonstrates where the Virgin Mary, Joseph, the Wise Men from the East, the Lord Jesus Christ, and the dear apostles traveled . . .). It was first published in Helmstedt, 1581, and was reprinted numerous times in German, as well as being issued in Latin, English, Danish, and Dutch (see Leaver C, no. 11).

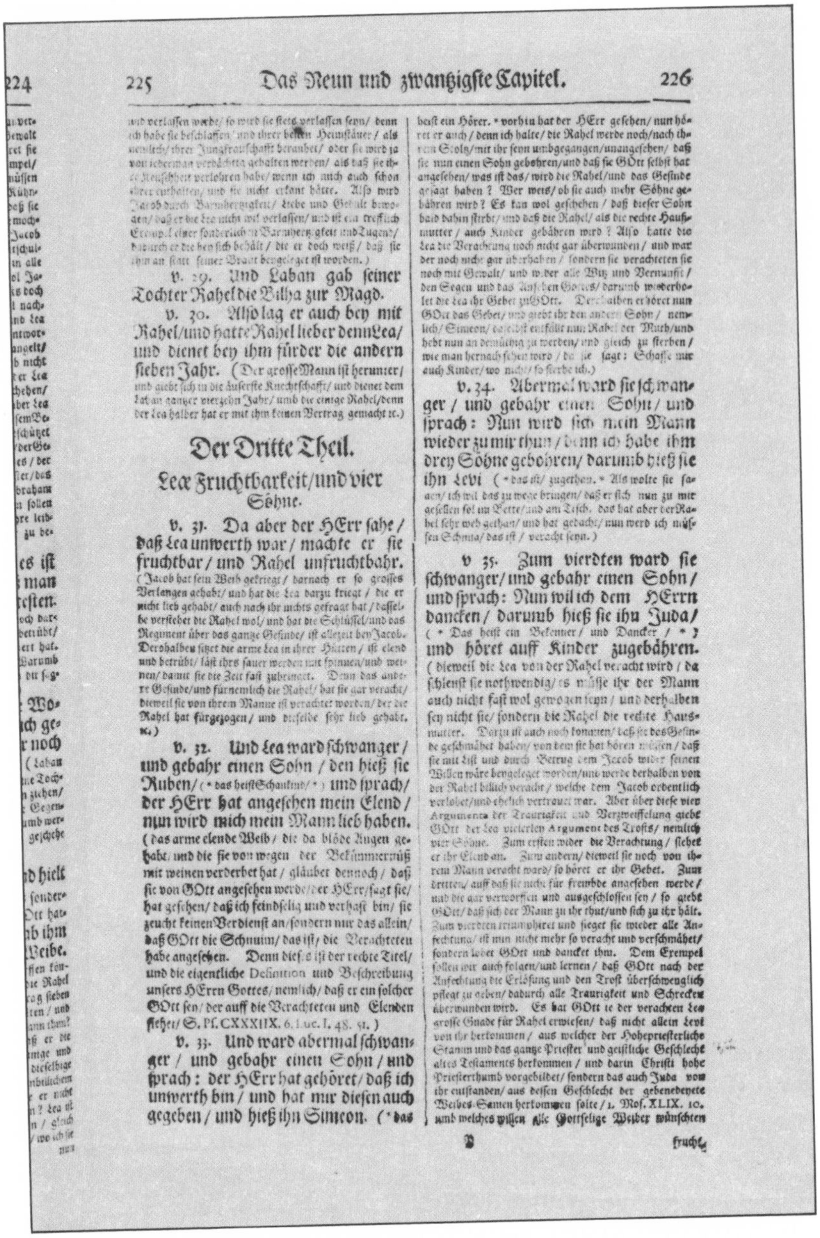
225 Das Neun und zwantzigste Capitel. 226

v. 29. Und Laban gab seiner Tochter Rahel die Bilha zur Magd.

v. 30. Also lag er auch bey mit Rahel/und hatte Rahel lieber denn Lea/ und dienet bey ihm fürder die andern sieben Jahr.

Der Dritte Theil.

Leæ Fruchtbarkeit/und vier Söhne.

v. 31. Da aber der HErr sahe/ daß Lea unwerth war/ machte er sie fruchtbar/ und Rahel unfruchtbahr.

v. 32. Und Lea ward schwanger/ und gebahr einen Sohn/ den hieß sie Ruben/ (* das heist Schaukind/ *) und sprach/ der HErr hat angesehen mein Elend/ nun wird mich mein Mann lieb haben.

v. 33. Und ward abermal schwanger/ und gebahr einen Sohn/ und sprach: der HErr hat gehöret/ daß ich unwerth bin/ und hat mir diesen auch gegeben/ und hieß ihn Simeon.

v. 34. Abermal ward sie schwanger/ und gebahr einen Sohn/ und sprach: Nun wird sich mein Mann wieder zu mir thun/ denn ich habe ihm drey Söhne gebohren/ darumb hieß sie ihn Levi

v. 35. Zum vierdten ward sie schwanger/ und gebahr einen Sohn/ und sprach: Nun wil ich dem HErrn dancken/ darumb hieß sie ihn Juda/ (* Das heist ein Bekenner/ und Dancker/ *) und höret auff Kinder zugebähren.

11

The quotation from Luther is a characteristic statement concerning his understanding of Scripture:

> *If anyone wants an allegorical explanation, let him apply the three wells to the three principal parts of the Holy Scriptures: to the Law, the Prophets, and the Gospel. For the Law is* ʻēseq; *that is, as expressed in German,* es ist Essig; *it is vinegar in the soul, because the Law works wrath [Rom. 4]. The prophets are* sitnāh; *for when they stress the Law, hatred for God arises, not through the fault of the Law but because of the Philistines. Out of good comes evil. But the Gospel is* rehobōth, *which, when it has been published in the entire world, brings its consolation.* (Based on *LW* 5:88)

11 Vol. 1/I, cols. 225–26. On Genesis 29:35. Simple correction of *Priester* to *Priesterthum* in col. 226.

12 Vol. 1/I, cols. 229–30. On Genesis 30:14. Simple correction of *nichtem* to *mit nichtem* in col. 230.

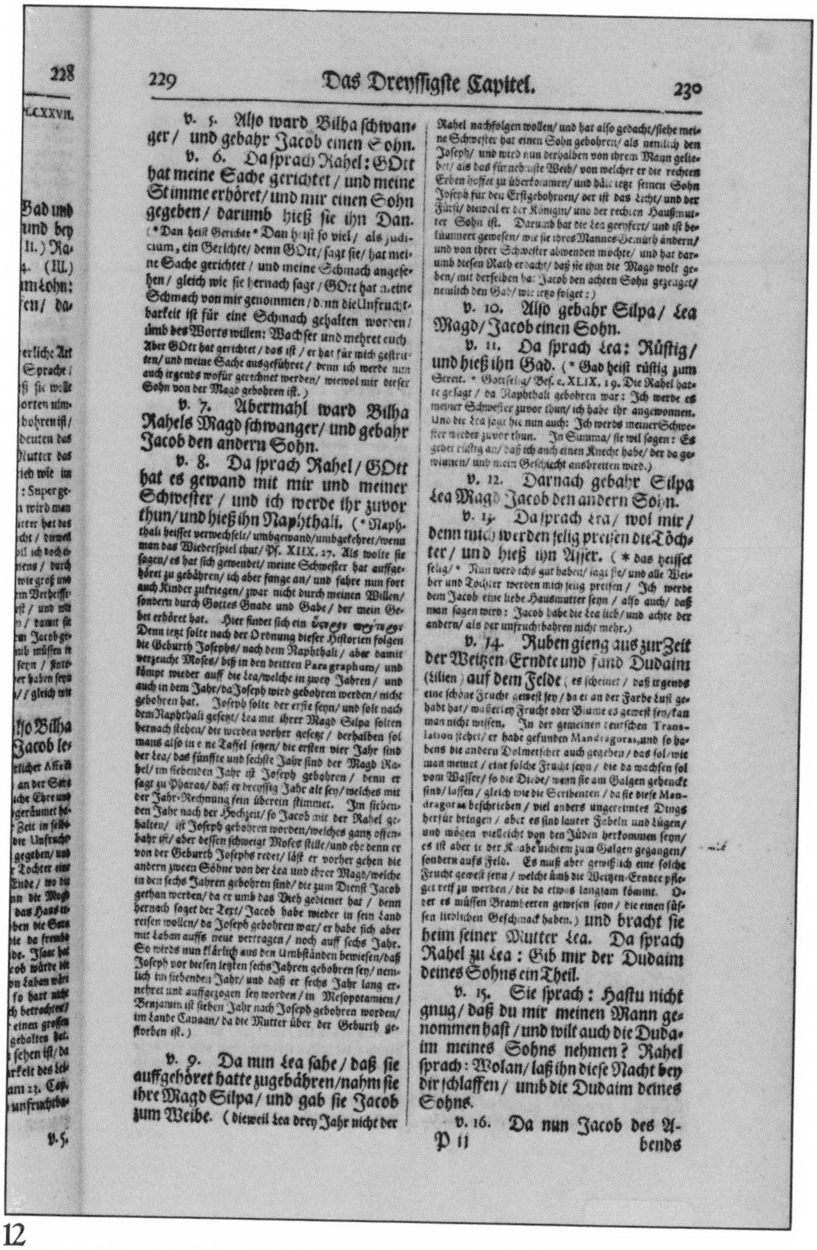

229 Das Dreyssigste Capitel. 230

v. 5. Also ward Bilha schwanger/ und gebahr Jacob einen Sohn.

v. 6. Da sprach Rahel: GOtt hat meine Sache gerichtet/ und meine Stimme erhöret/ und mir einen Sohn gegeben/ darumb hieß sie ihn Dan. (*Dan heist Gerichte* Dan heist so viel/ als judicium, ein Gerichte/ denn GOtt/ sagt sie/ hat meine Sache gerichtet/ und meine Schmach angesehen/ gleich wie sie hernach sagt/ GOtt hat meine Schmach von mir genommen/ denn die Unfruchtbarkeit ist für eine Schmach gehalten worden/ umb des Worts willen: Wachset und mehret euch. Aber GOtt hat gerichtet/ das ist/ er hat für mich gestritten/ und meine Sache ausgeführet/ denn ich werde nun auch irgends wofür gerechnet werden/ wiewol mir dieser Sohn von der Magd gebohren ist.)

v. 7. Abermahl ward Bilha Rahels Magd schwanger/ und gebahr Jacob den andern Sohn.

v. 8. Da sprach Rahel/ GOtt hat es gewand mit mir und meiner Schwester/ und ich werde ihr zuvor thun/ und hieß ihn Naphthali. (*Naphthali heisset verwechselt/ umbgewand/ umbgekehret/ wenn man das Wiederspiel thut/ Ps. XIIX. 27. Als wolte sie sagen/ es hat sich gewendet/ meine Schwester hat auffgehöret zu gebähren/ ich aber fange an/ und fahre nun fort auch Kinder zukriegen/ zwar nicht durch meinen Willen/ sondern durch Gottes Gnade und Gabe/ der mein Gebet erhöret hat. Hier findet sich ein ὕστερον πρότερον Denn jetzt solte nach der Ordnung dieser Historien folgen die Geburth Josephs/ nach dem Naphthali/ aber damit verzeucht Moses/ biß in den dritten Paragraphum/ und kömpt wieder auff die Lea/ welche in zwey Jahren/ und auch in dem Jahr/ da Joseph wird gebohren werden/ nicht gebohren hat. Joseph solte der erste seyn/ und solt nach dem Naphthali gesetzt/ Lea mit ihrer Magd Silpa solten hernach stehen/ die werden vorher gesetzt/ derhalben sol mans also in eine Taffel setzen/ die ersten vier Jahr sind der Lea/ das fünffte und sechste Jahr sind der Magd Rahel/ im siebenden Jahr ist Joseph gebohren/ denn er sagt zu Pharao/ daß er dreyssig Jahr alt sey/ welches mit der Jahr-Rechnung fein überein stimmet. Im siebenden Jahr nach der Hochzeit/ so Jacob mit der Rahel gehalten/ ist Joseph gebohren worden/ welches gantz offenbahr ist/ aber dessen schweigt Moses stille/ und ehe denn er von der Geburth Josephs redet/ läst er vorher gehen die andern zween Söhne von der Lea und ihrer Magd/ welche in den sechs Jahren gebohren sind/ die zum Dienst Jacob gethan werden/ da er umb das Vieh gedienet hat/ denn hernach saget der Text/ Jacob habe wieder in sein Land reisen wollen/ da Joseph gebohren war/ er habe sich aber mit Laban auffs neue vertragen/ noch auff sechs Jahr. So wirds nun klärlich aus den Umbständen bewiesen/ daß Joseph vor diesen letzten sechs Jahren gebohren sey/ nemlich im siebenden Jahr/ und daß er sechs Jahr lang ernehret und auffgezogen sey worden/ in Mesopotamien/ Benjamin ist sieben Jahr nach Joseph gebohren worden/ im Lande Canaan/ da die Mutter über der Geburth gestorben ist.)

v. 9. Da nun Lea sahe/ daß sie auffgehöret hatte zugebähren/ nahm sie ihre Magd Silpa/ und gab sie Jacob zum Weibe. (dieweil Lea drey Jahr nicht der Rahel nachfolgen wollen/ und hat also gedacht/ siehe meine Schwester hat einen Sohn gebohren/ als nemlich den Joseph/ und wird nun derhalben von ihrem Mann geliebet/ als das fürnehmste Weib/ von welcher er die rechten Erben hoffet zu überkommen/ und hält jetzt seinen Sohn Joseph für den Erstgebohrnen/ der ist das Licht/ und der Fürst/ dieweil er der Königin/ und der rechten Haußmutter Sohn ist. Darumb hat die Lea geeyfert/ und ist bekümmert gewesen/ wie sie ihres Mannes Gemüth ändern/ und von ihrer Schwester abwenden möchte/ und hat darumb diesen Rath erdacht/ daß sie ihm die Magd wolt geben/ mit derselben hat Jacob den achten Sohn gezeuget/ nemlich den Gad/ wie jetzo folget:)

v. 10. Also gebahr Silpa/ Lea Magd/ Jacob einen Sohn.

v. 11. Da sprach Lea: Rüstig/ und hieß ihn Gad. (*Gad heist rüstig zum Streit. * Gottselig/ Bes. c. XLIX. 19. Die Rahel hatte gesagt/ da Naphthali gebohren war: Ich werde es meiner Schwester zuvor thun/ ich habe ihr angewonnen. Und die Lea sagt hie nun auch: Ich werds meiner Schwester wieder zuvor thun. In Summa/ sie wil sagen: Es gehet rüstig an/ daß ich auch einen Knecht habe/ der da gewinnen/ und mein Geschlecht ausbreiten wird.)

v. 12. Darnach gebahr Silpa Lea Magd Jacob den andern Sohn.

v. 13. Da sprach Lea/ wol mir/ denn mich werden selig preisen die Töchter/ und hieß ihn Asser. (* das heisset selig/ * Nun werd ichs gut haben/ sagt sie/ und alle Weiber und Töchter werden mich selig preisen/ Ich werde dem Jacob eine liebe Hausmutter seyn/ also auch/ daß man sagen wird: Jacob habe die Lea lieb/ und achte der andern/ als der unfruchtbahren nicht mehr.)

v. 14. Ruben gieng aus zur Zeit der Weitzen-Erndte und fand Dudaim (Lilien) auf dem Felde (es scheinet/ daß irgends eine schöne Frucht gewest sey/ da er an der Farbe Lust gehabt hat/ waserley Frucht oder Blume es gewest sey/ kan man nicht wissen. In der gemeinen teutschen Translation stehet/ er habe gefunden Mandragoras, und so habens die andern Dolmetscher auch gegeben/ das sol/ wie man meinet/ eine solche Frucht seyn/ die da wachsen sol vom Wasser/ so die Diebe/ wenn sie am Galgen gehenckt sind/ lassen/ gleich wie die Scribenten/ da sie diese Mandragoras beschrieben/ viel anders ungereimtes Dings herfür bringen/ aber es sind lauter Fabeln und Lügen/ und mögen vielleicht von den Jüden herkommen seyn/ es ist aber ie der Knabe nichtem zum Galgen gegangen/ sondern aufs Feld. Es muß aber gewißlich eine solche Frucht gewest seyn/ welche umb die Weitzen-Erndte pfleget reif zu werden/ die da etwas langsam kömmt. Oder es müssen Brambeeren gewesen seyn/ die einen süssen lieblichen Geschmack haben.) und bracht sie heim seiner Mutter Lea. Da sprach Rahel zu Lea: Gib mir der Dudaim deines Sohns ein Theil.

v. 15. Sie sprach: Hastu nicht gnug/ daß du mir meinen Mann genommen hast/ und wilt auch die Dudaim meines Sohns nehmen? Rahel sprach: Wolan/ laß ihn diese Nacht bey dir schlaffen/ umb die Dudaim deines Sohns.

v. 16. Da nun Jacob des Abends

P ii

12

13 Vol. 1/I, cols. 267–68. Heading to the first part of Calov's consideration of Genesis 35. Correction of *Isaac* to *Jacob*.

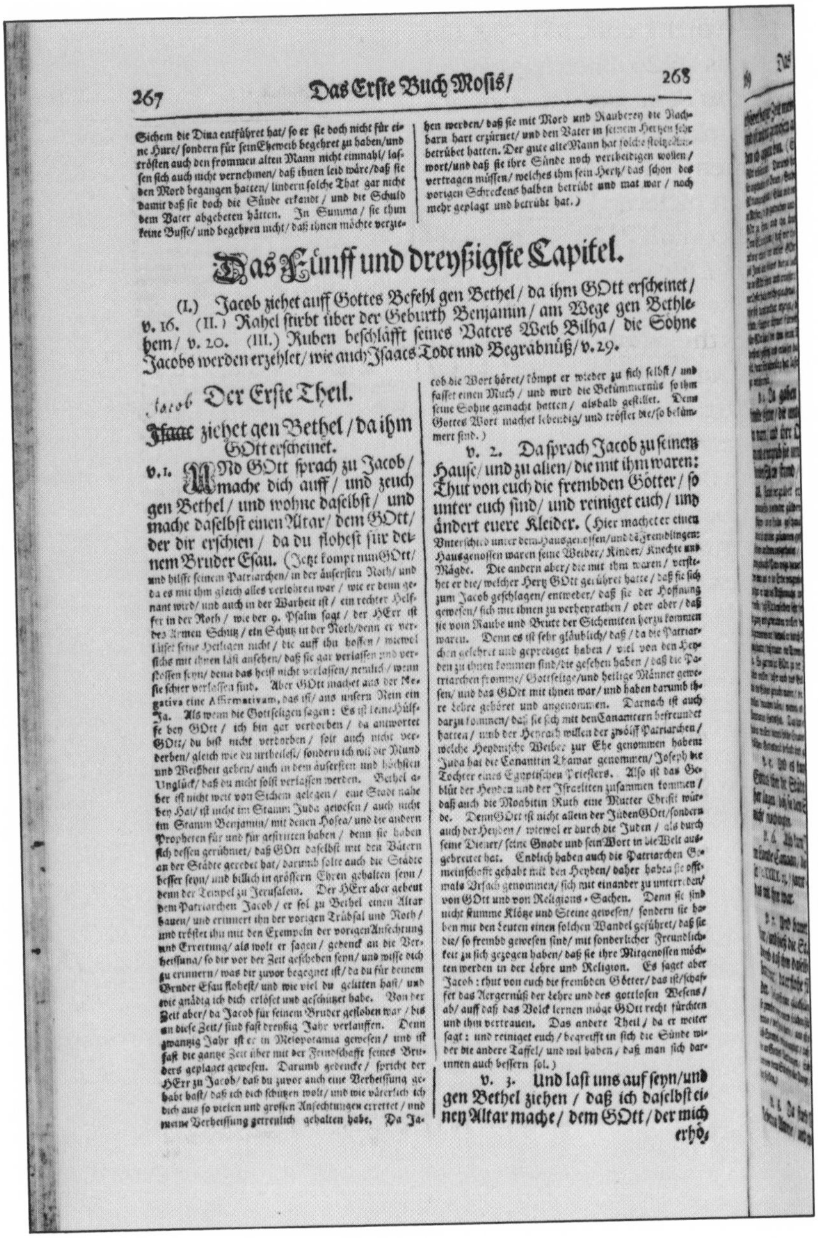

267 Das Erste Buch Mosis/ 268

Sichem die Dina entführet hat/ so er sie doch nicht für ei- ne Hure/ sondern für sein Eheweib begehret zu haben/ und trösten auch den frommen alten Mann nicht einmahl/ las- sen sich auch nicht vernehmen/ daß ihnen leid wäre/ daß sie den Mord begangen hatten/ lindern solche That gar nicht damit daß sie doch die Sünde erkandt/ und die Schuld dem Vater abgebeten hätten. In Summa/ sie thun keine Busse/ und begehren nicht/ daß ihnen möchte verzie- hen werden/ daß sie mit Mord und Rauberey die Nach- barn hart erzürnet/ und den Vater in seinem Hertzen sehr betrübet hatten. Der gute alte Mann hat solche stoltze ... wort/ und daß sie ihre Sünde noch vertheidigen wollen/ vertragen müssen/ welches ihm sein Hertz/ das schon des vorigen Schreckens halben betrübt und mat war/ noch mehr geplagt und betrübt hat.)

Das Fünff und dreyßigste Capitel.

(I.) Jacob ziehet auff Gottes Befehl gen Bethel/ da ihm GOtt erscheinet/ v. 16. (II.) Rahel stirbt über der Geburth Benjamin/ am Wege gen Bethle- hem/ v. 20. (III.) Ruben beschläfft seines Vaters Weib Bilha/ die Söhne Jacobs werden erzehlet/ wie auch Isaacs Todt und Begräbnüß/ v. 29.

Der Erste Theil.

~~Isaac~~ Jacob ziehet gen Bethel/ da ihm GOtt erscheinet.

v. 1. UNd GOtt sprach zu Jacob/ mache dich auff/ und zeuch gen Bethel/ und wohne daselbst/ und mache daselbst einen Altar/ dem GOtt/ der dir erschien/ da du flohest für deinem Bruder Esau. (Jetzt kompt nun GOtt/ und hilfft seinem Patriarchen/ in der äusersten Noth/ und da es mit ihm gleich alles verlohren war/ wie er denn ge- nant wird/ und auch in der Warheit ist/ ein rechter Helf- fer in der Noth/ wie der 9. Psalm sagt/ der HErr ist des Armen Schutz/ ein Schutz in der Noth/ denn er ver- lässet seine Heiligen nicht/ die auff ihn hoffen/ wiewol sichs mit ihnen läst ansehen/ daß sie gar verlassen und ver- stossen seyn/ denn das heist nicht verlassen/ nemlich/ wenn sie schier verlassen sind. Aber GOtt machet aus der Ne- gativa eine Affirmativam, das ist/ aus unserm Nein ein Ja. Als wenn die Gottseligen sagen: Es ist keine Hülf- fe bey GOtt/ ich bin gar verdorben/ da antwortet GOtt/ du bist nicht verdorben/ solt auch nicht ver- derben/ gleich wie du urtheilest/ sondern ich wil dir Mund und Weißheit geben/ auch in dem äusersten und höchsten Unglück/ daß du nicht solst verlassen werden. Bethel a- ber ist nicht weit von Sichem gelegen/ eine Stadt nahe bey Hai/ ist nicht im Stamm Juda gewesen/ auch nicht im Stamm Benjamin/ mit denen Hosea/ und die andern Propheten für und für gestritten haben/ denn sie haben sich dessen gerühmet/ daß GOtt daselbst mit den Vätern an der Städte geredet hat/ darumb solte auch die Städte besser seyn/ und billich in grössern Ehren gehalten seyn/ denn der Tempel zu Jerusalem. Der HErr aber gebeut dem Patriarchen Jacob/ er sol zu Bethel einen Altar bauen/ und erinnert ihn der vorigen Trübsal und Noth/ und tröstet ihn mit den Exempeln der vorigen Anfechtung und Errettung/ als wolt er sagen/ gedenck an die Ver- heissung/ so dir vor der Zeit geschehen seyn/ und wisse dich zu erinnern/ was dir zuvor begegnet ist/ da du für deinem Bruder Esau flohest/ und wie viel du gelitten hast/ und wie gnädig ich dich erlöset und geschützet habe. Von der Zeit aber/ da Jacob für seinem Bruder geflohen war/ bis an diese Zeit/ sind fast dreyßig Jahr verlauffen. Denn zwantzig Jahr ist er in Mesopotamia gewesen/ und ist fast die gantze Zeit über mit der Feindschafft seines Bru- ders geplaget gewesen. Darumb gedencke/ spricht der HErr zu Jacob/ daß du zuvor auch eine Verheissung ge- habt hast/ daß ich dich schützen wolt/ und wie väterlich ich dich aus so vielen und grossen Anfechtungen errettet/ und meine Verheissung getreulich gehalten habe. Da Ja- cob die Wort höret/ kömpt er wieder zu sich selbst/ und fasset einen Muth/ und wird die Bekümmernüs so ihm seine Söhne gemacht hatten/ alsbald gestillet. Denn Gottes Wort machet lebendig/ und tröstet die/ so bekümmert sind.)

v. 2. Da sprach Jacob zu seinem Hause/ und zu allen/ die mit ihm waren: Thut von euch die frembden Götter/ so unter euch sind/ und reiniget euch/ und ändert euere Kleider. (Hier machet er einen Unterschied unter den Hausgenossen/ und den Frembdlingen: Hausgenossen waren seine Weiber/ Kinder/ Knechte und Mägde. Die andern aber/ die mit ihm waren/ verste- het er die/ welcher Hertz GOtt gerühret hatte/ daß sie sich zum Jacob geschlagen/ entweder/ daß sie der Hoffnung gewesen/ sich mit ihnen zu verheyrathen/ oder aber/ daß sie vom Raube und Beute der Sichemiten herzu kommen waren. Denn es ist sehr gläublich/ daß/ da die Patriar- chen gelehret und geprediget haben/ viel von den Hey- den zu ihnen kommen sind/ die gesehen haben/ daß die Pa- triarchen fromme/ Gottseelige/ und heilige Männer gewe- sen/ und daß GOtt mit ihnen war/ und haben darumb ih- re Lehre gehöret und angenommen. Darnach ist auch darzu kommen/ daß sie sich mit den Cananitern befreundet hatten/ umb der Heyrath willen der zwölff Patriarchen/ welche Heydnische Weiber zur Ehe genommen haben: Juda hat die Cananitin Thamar genommen/ Joseph die Tochter eines Egyptischen Priesters. Also ist das Ge- blüt der Heyden und der Israeliten zusammen kommen/ daß auch die Moabitin Ruth eine Mutter Christi wür- de. Denn GOtt ist nicht allein der Jüden GOtt/ sondern auch der Heyden/ wiewol er durch die Juden/ als durch seine Diener/ seine Gnade und sein Wort in die Welt aus- gebreitet hat. Endlich haben auch die Patriarchen Ge- meinschafft gehabt mit den Heyden/ daher haben sie offt- mals Ursach genommen/ sich mit einander zu unterreden/ von GOtt und von Religions-Sachen. Denn sie sind nicht stumme Klötze und Steine gewesen/ sondern sie ha- ben mit den Leuten einen solchen Wandel geführet/ daß sie die/ so frembd gewesen sind/ mit sonderlicher Freundlich- keit zu sich gezogen haben/ daß sie ihre Mitgenossen möch- ten werden in der Lehre und Religion. Es saget aber Jacob: thut von euch die frembden Götter/ das ist/ schaf- fet das Aergernüß der Lehre und des gottlosen Wesens/ ab/ auff daß das Volck lernen möge GOtt recht fürchten und ihm vertrauen. Das andere Theil/ da er weiter sagt: und reiniget euch/ begreifft in sich die Sünde wi- der die andere Taffel/ und wil haben/ daß man sich dar- innen auch bessern sol.)

v. 3. Und last uns auf seyn/ und gen Bethel ziehen/ daß ich daselbst einen Altar mache/ dem GOtt/ der mich erhö-

13

14 Vol. 1/I, cols. 351–52. On Genesis 46:26. Bach has placed his *Nota Bene* and other marks in the margin alongside Calov's comment, which is also underlined. It picks up Luther's point in his commentary on the passage (*LW* 18:91), that the Hebrew word for the *soul* designates the whole person, body and soul. Significantly, these markings occur at this verse that deals with the number of Jacob's descendants, that is, 66, a number that presents certain mathematical problems (see Luther's discussion, *LW* 8:87–90, and cf. the note on no. 7).

351 Das Erste Buch Mosis / 352

v. 24. Die Kinder Naphthali / Jachzeel / Guni / Jezer / und Sillem.

v. 25. Das sind die Kinder Bilha / die Laban seiner Tochter Rahel gab / und gebahr Jacob die sieben Seelen / (das ist Personen.)

N. v. 26. Alle Seelen / die mit Jacob in Egypten kamen / die aus seinen Lenden (sind die Seelen und gantze Personen aus den Lenden entsprossen / so muß ja die Seele von den Eltern mit fortgepflantzet werden / und nicht allein der Leib.) kommen waren / [ausgenommen die Weiber seiner Kinder] sind alle zusammen sechs und sechzig Seelen / (diese Zahl der sechs und sechzig Personen werden also zusammen gebracht / Lea Kinder waren 32. Silpæ 16. Bilhä 7. welche zusammen 55 machen / darzu kamen noch 11. nemlich Benjamin mit seinen zehen Söhnen / thun in Summa 66. Joseph kan hier mit seinen Kindern nicht mit eingerechnet werden / denn der war schon in Egypten / und kam nicht mit Jacob dahin. Jacob kan auch nicht mitgezehlet werden / denn es wird geredet von denen / die mit Jacob kamen / und aus seinen Lenden entsprossen waren / darumb denn auch die Weiber nicht haben können mitgerechnet werden)

v. 27. Und die Kinder Joseph / die in Egypten gebohren sind / waren zwo Seelen / also / daß alle Seelen des Hauses Jacob die in Egypten kamen / waren siebenzig. (Hier wird Joseph mit seinen zween Söhne / Manaß und Ephraim / so mit Jacob mitgerechnet / daher wenn diese vier Personen zu den vorigen 66. hinzugethan werden / werden 70. Personen entstehen. Hier aber muß man sagen / daß die Kinder Josephs / wie auch Peretz / wiewol sie in Egypten gebohren / in Egypten gegangen / und gekommen seyn / in ihren Vätern / als welche aus den Lenden Jacobs entsprossen / und in Egypten Frembdlinge waren / ihrer Eltern und Herkunfft nach. Daher 75. Seelen gezehlet werden / bey den LXX. Dolmetschern / wie auch von S. Luca, Gesch. VII. 14. so haben jene mitgerechnet Manasses Söhne Machir / Galaad; wie auch die Söhne Ephraim / Sutalaam / und Taam / und seinen Enckel Edom / welche sie auch im 20. vers. eingeführet haben / aber zu wider allen Ebräischen / Samaritischen / und Lateinischen Bibeln: der H. Stephan aber / und Lucas berrechnen nicht die Seelen die in Egypten kommen sind / durch welche das Israelitische Geschlecht in Egypten fortgepflantzet ist / sondern iedwede Personen / welche Joseph aus Canaan und seiner gantzen Freundschafft zu sich gefordert hat / wie Gesch. VII. 14. stehet: Joseph lies holen seinen Vater Jacob / und seine gantze Freundschafft / zusammen 75. Seelen / welche also zu berechnen: Lea Kinder waren 30. denn Ger und Onan war getödtet / Hezron und Hamul sind erst in Egypten gezeuget / und konten also nicht von Joseph aus Canaan geholet worden. Silpa hatte 16. Rahel 11. Kinder / weil Joseph mit seinen Söhnen hier nicht gerechnet werden kan / Bilha hat 7. Kinder. Diese machen zusammen 64. Personen. Die übrigen 11. Personen machen die Weiber Jacobs und seine Söhne / die noch im Leben waren / da sie in Egypten zogen. Denn es war nach Rahel auch Lea schon mit Tode abgegangen / und etliche von den Weibern / der Söhne Jacobs.)

Der Dritte Theil.

Jacobs und Josephs freudenreiche Zusammenkunfft.

v. 28. Und er (Jacob /) sandte Juda für ihm hin zu Joseph / daß er ihn anweiset zu Gosen / und kamen in das Land Gosen. (Juda wird von seinem Vater fürhin gesand zu Joseph / welche Ehre billich den ersten drey Söhnen / als Ruben / Simeon / und Levi / gebühret hätte. Aber er zieht diesen (den Juda) herfür / gleich wie er auch droben für Joseph allein den andern das Wort gehalten / und ihre Sache ausgerichtet hat. Darumb ist hieraus zu sehen / daß der Vater viel von ihm gehalten / und ein sonderlich Ansehen bey ihm muß gehabt haben / denn er sich auch mit sonderlichem Fleiß und Geist sein hat angenommen / wie das hernach wird zu sehen seyn / an dem Segen / so der Vater über ihn gesprochen hat / darinnen er weissagen wird / daß Christus von seinem Stamm kommen werde. Juda ist dazumahl 42. Jahr alt gewesen / und ist Vater zu zween Kindes-Kindern / so durch die Blutschande gebohren waren / und ist gleich König und Priester in des Patriarchen Jacobs Hause / wieder die rechte gemeine Ordnung der Geburth / und hat die Kirche oder Gemeine / so in Jacobs Hause versamlet gewesen / gelehret und regiret. Derhalben sendet Jacob den Sohn / so unter den andern der Ehrlichste war / für ihm hin zu Joseph: Lehoroth, wie im Ebräischen stehet / das ist zu unterweisen / denn Jarah auf Ebräisch heist lehren / unterrichten / daher kömt das Wort Morah, ein Lehrer / und Thora, ein Gesetz / daß Juda seinen Bruder berichten sol / und ihm anzeigen / daß sein Vater ietzt daher komme / und ihn vermahne / daß er gen Gosen wolte kommen / denn daselbst wolle der Vater verziehen / und auff seinen Sohn warten. Denn man hat Joseph erinnern müssen der Zukunfft seines Vaters / auf daß er gewisse Oerter bestimmen / und die Herberge bestellen möchte. Wo der Ort gewesen / der hier Gosen genennet wird / davon disputiren die Cosmographi. Es lässet sich aber ansehen / daß er mit den Lande Canaan gegrentzet habe. Hieronymus schreibet / daß dieser Ort zu seiner Zeit sol Ptolomais genennet seyn worden. Es ist aber gewiß / daß er nicht weit von dem Lande Canaan muß gewesen seyn / bey dem Wasser Nilo. Denn sie sind noch nicht in Egypten kommen / sondern sind forn blieben / da man erst hinein zeucht / an dem Ort / da hernach Raemses ist gebauet worden / da man in Palestinam ist gezogen / durchs rothe Meer / und durch die Wüste. Darumb bleiben sie so lange zu Gosen / biß daß Juda in Egypten ist kommen / und hat sich also Jacob durch sonderliche Vorsichtigkeit dafür gehütet / daß er GOtt nicht hat wollen versuchen / daß er sich gefürchtet / es möchte vielleicht etwas durch Unfleiß oder Nachlässigkeit geschehen / das ihm könte Schaden bringen.)

v. 29. Da

14

15 Vol. 1/I, cols. 365–66. On Genesis 48:2. Simple correction of *Joseph* to *Manasse* in col. 365.

365 Das Acht und viertzigste Capitel. 366

nun fort/ daß er auf die Beschreibung komme/ wie Jacob seine Söhne gesegnet habe/ und sagt: Nach etlichen Tagen im selbigem Jahr habe einer dem Joseph verkündiget/ (denn also lautets in dem Ebräischen/) wie daß die Kranckheit und Schwachheit des Leibes mit Jacob immer zunehme/ und grösser werde/ und haben ihm ohn Zweiffel die Ertzte auch angezeiget/ daß ein tödlicher Zufall mit ihm sey zugeschlagen/ davon er noch etwas hefftiger sey geschwächet worden/ und das jetzt fast am Ende mit ihm sey/ auf welches Ende auch Jacob schon vorlängst mit starckem beständigem Muth gewartet und gehoffet hatte/ derohalben befürchtet sich nun Joseph/ es möchte vielleicht der Vater also dahin sterben/ ehe denn er ihn und seine Söhne segnete/ und hatte auch schon zuvor davon mit ihm geredt/ fürnemlich und am allermeisten ümb des Stammes Levi willen/ daß er von den andern abgetheilet/ und abgesondert möchte werden. Darumb bringet er nun seine beyde Söhne mit sich/ daß der Tod ja nicht den Vater übereile/ ehe denn ers nach seiner väterlichen Gewalt mit einem jeglichem Stamm verordne/ wie es damit gehen sol/ entweder nach seinem Willen/ oder aber nach dem Rathschlage/ so sie zuvor darüber mit einander gehalten. Denn diese Ordnung ist gantz hoch von nöthen gewesen/ damit unter den Nachkommen keinerley Zanck/ oder Uneinigkeit erwachsen möchte. Und ist solches aus sonderlichem Rath des H. Geistes geschehen/ daß der Stamm Levi abgesondert/ und zum Priesterthum verordnet würde/ und darumb auch keine eigene Güter oder Acker solt haben/ wie die andern Stämme gehabt. Auff daß aber die Zahl der Zwölff Söhne Jsrael wieder möchte erfüllet werden/ hat Jacob den einigen Joseph in zwey Stämme getheilet/ da er seine zweene Söhne Manasse und Ephraim an Kindesstatt hat angenommen/ welche werden an Josephs und Levi statt gesetzt. Und die H. Schrifft braucht darnach/ ohn Unterscheid/ der zweyer Namen Ephraim und Joseph/ wie das im Propheten Hosea zu sehen ist/ und auch im LXXVIII. Psalm 10. Da aber nun Jacob so viel Krafft und Stärcke nicht gehabt/ daß er hätte können auffstehen/ oder aufn Stuel sitzen/ machet er sich doch starck/ wie er am besten konte/ und sitzet im Bette/ weiß sich zu erinnern/ daß er ihm fürgenommen/ und bey sich beschlossen/ die beyde Söhne seines Sohnes/ an Kindes statt anzunehmen.)

v. 3. **Und sprach zu Joseph: Der allmächtige GOtt erschien mir zu Luß im Lande Canaan und segnete mich/** (c. XXXIX. 12.)

v. 4. **Und sprach zu mir: Siehe ich wil dich wachsen lassen/ und mehren/ und wil dich zum Hauffen Volcks machen/ und wil dies Land zu eigen geben deinem Samen nach dir ewiglich/** (c. XL. 50. c. XLVI. 20.)

v. 5. **So sollen nun deine zween Söhne/ Ephraim und Manasse/ die dir gebohren sind in Egypten Land/ ehe ich herein kommen bin zu dir/ mein seyn/ gleich wie Ruben und Simeon.** (Jos. XIII. 7. c. XVII. 2.)

v. 6. **Welche du aber nach ihnen zeugest/ sollen dein seyn/ und genennet werden/ wie ihre Brüder in ihrem Erbtheil.** (Also fähet Jacob seine Oration an/ die er fast abgebrochen/ und erzehlet/ wie ihm der HErr im Lande Canaan erschienen sey/ und die Verheissung gegeben habe/ daß er seinen Samen mehren wolle: Er wil so viel sagen: Nun erkenne ich erst/ warumb GOtt zu mir gesagt zu Bethel: Sey fruchtbar und mehre dich. Denn da ihm die Verheissung zu Luß geben war/ und da Jacob zu seinen Vater Jsaac zog/ ist ihm unterwegen sein Weib die Rahel gestorben/ von welcher er gehoffet Kinder und Erben zu erlangen/ daß er nun nicht mehr hat Kinder zeugen können/ deßwegen/ daß ihm sein Weib gestorben/ und er auch fast alt war: Derhalben hat er nun also gedacht: Jch sehe/ daß wunderbarlicher Weise noch sol erfüllet werden/ was mir zu Bethel ist verheissen worden. Denn darumb hat GOtt den Joseph sonderlich erhalten/ daß mir noch solten von ihm Erben gebohren werden/ und gleich wie er unter Jacobs Söhnen der gröste gewesen/ also ist der Stamm Ephraim auch ein grosser Königlicher Stamm gewesen/ da er zu Manasse gesetzt worden. Das hat Jacob im Geist gesehen/ und hat daraus geschlossen/ daß die Mehrung/ so ihm verheissen war/ würde in Ephraim geschehen/ des Name herkompt von dem Ebräischen Wort Para, das heist fructificare, Frucht bringen/ wie es Joseph droben auslegt/ im 41. Cap. da der Text sagt: den andern hieß er Ephraim/ denn GOtt/ sagt er/ hat mich lassen wachsen in dem Lande meines Elendes. Und umb der Ursache willen wird er seinem Bruder Manasse fürgezogen werden/ daß er also die Bedeutung seines Namens erfüllen möchte. Darumb hangen die Wort in der Oration, so Jacob alhier gethan/ recht fein an einander. Denn wenn du fragen wilt/ was er darzu für Ursach habe/ daß er Josephs Söhne zu seinen Kindern annimpt? Antwortet er darauff also/ darumb daß der almächtige GOtt mir zu Luß erschienen/ und verheissen hat/ daß ich solte gemehret werden. Also kompts beydes fein mit einander überein/ die Erscheinung und Verheissung Gottes/ mit dem Namen des Sohnes Josephs. Darnach er sie auch auslegt/ als wolt er sagen: du Joseph warest ein verlohrner und verkauffter Sohn/ aber ich habe dich nun durch eine reiche und herrliche Restitution wieder gekriegt/ denn ich wil deine zween Söhne/ so von dir gebohren sind/ annehmen in die Zahl meiner Söhne/ und der zwölff Stämme. Die andern Söhne aber/ die Joseph noch zeugen würde/ saget Jacob/ sollen mit ihrer Brüder Namen genennet werden/ also/ daß sie dieser Vettern seyn/ die er seinen Söhnen gleich machet/ da er sie zu Kindern annimpt/ die solten Kinder Jsrael geschrieben und genennet werden/ und Brüder der andern Söhne Jacobs/ wiewol sie seines Sohnes Kinder waren. Derhalben sind Ephraim und Manasse Brüder Juda/ und ihres Vaters Joseph/ umb der Kindschafft willen/ daß sie Jacob an Kindesstatt angenommen/ welche Kindschafft ihren Grund und Krafft hat von GOtt/ und hat das Zeugnüß der Schrifft und des Heiligen Geistes/ und haben darumb auch mit den andern Stämmen das gelobte Land geerbet und besessen/ und Ephraim hat darzu auch die Königliche Herrligkeit erlangt. Also ehret nun GOtt den frommen heiligen Mann Joseph/ daß seine Söhne nicht geringer geachtet werden/ denn Juda/ und die andern Söhne Jacobs.)

v. 7. **Und da ich aus Mesopotamia kam/ starb mir Rahel im Lande Canaan/ auff dem Wege/ da noch ein Feldweges** (Hier wird von dem Wort Kibrath viel disputirens gemacht/ ist aber nur schlecht und einfältig zu verstehen/ daß es heisse ein Feldweges/ auff lateinisch stadium.) **war gen Ephrath/ und ich begrub sie daselbst an dem Wege Ephrath/ die nun Bethlehem heist.** (Bethlehem oder Ephrat ist nicht weit von Hebron und sind die beyde Städte etwa bey fünff Meilen von einander gelegen. Bethlehem aber ist gleich auff halben Wege der zweyer Orth gelegen/ und

15

16 Vol. 1/I, cols. 381–82. On Genesis 49:19. Simple correction of *Dan* to *Gad.*

381 **Das Neun und viertzigste Capitel.** 382

deons/des Sohnes Joas/ welches ist ein zeitlich Heil/ auch erwarte ich nicht die Erlösung Simsons/ welches ein vergänglich Heil ist: sondern ich erwarte die Erlösung Meßiä/des Sohnes Davids/der da kommen wird/ daß er zu sich bringe die Kinder Israel/dessen Erlösung erwartet meine Seele: dergleichen auch im Jerosolymischen Targum zu finden.)

v. 19. **Gad gerüst/wird das Heer führen/ und wieder herumb führen.** (Gad genennet von Heerweiß ausgehen/ oder überfallen/wird nicht nur seinen Feind Heersweise überfallen/ als/ die von Moab/ und die Kinder Ammon/ sondern er wird ihnen auch immer auff den Fersen seyn/er wird hinter ihnen her seyn/und sich rüstig und glückselig vertheidigen und schützen/ 5. Mos. *XXXIII. 21.* 1. Chron. *V. XIII. 8. Jos. X.* 4. Mos. *XXXII.* die Krieges-Knechte werden sich zusammen werffen/wie es Herr Lutherus in seiner Auslegung p. 1536. erkläret/und einen hauffen Räuber versamlen/un werden diesen Stamm angreiffen/der also gelegen ist/daß ihn die Nachbarn leichtlich beleidigen können/da werden sie ihn berauben/und etliche gefangen nehmen/aber Gad wird ihnen wieder auff den Fersen seyn/ er wird hinter ihnē her seyn/er wird mit göttlicher Hülffe seinen Mördern und Räubern von Moab und Ammon nacheilen.)

v. 20. **Von Asser kömmt sein fett Brod/und er wird den Königen zu Gefallen thun.** (Hiermit wird dem Asser ein fruchtbar Land versprochen/ das fein fett ist/und dem Könige selbst kan niedliche Bissen schaffen/ 5. Mos. *XXXII. 24.* bes. Joh. *XIX. 24.* und ferner. Jacob wil so viel sagen/nach Lutheri Erklärung: Asser sey der allerschönste Stamm/ von wegen der Fruchtbarkeit des Landes/und sonst von Überfluß oder Reichthum der Dinge/ so zu nothdürfftiger Unterhaltung des Lebens gehören/ und daß daselbst sehr guter Wein wachse/ darzu Oel/ und ander Getraide/ als an einem fetten und fruchtbahrem Orth an der Grentze des Meers/ und schier am allerbesten Orth des Galiläischen Landes. Er wird den Königen niedliche Speisen geben/ das ist/ sein Getraide und andere Früchte der Erden werden so gut und köstlich seyn/daß sie auch auf der Könige und Fürsten Tische sollen getragen werden. Es wird warlich der Berg Carmel sehr gerühmet von wegen der grossen Fruchtbarkeit/ welcher nahe bey dem Stamm Asser gelegen hat. Derohalben verkündiget Jacob dem Asser nichts wiederwertiges/ sondern nur das allerbeste/ und saget in Summa/es soll ein gut Land seyn/ daß Könige davon essen möchten.)

v. 21. **Naphthali ist ein schneller Hirsch/und giebt schöne Rede.** (Dieser Stamm ist an der letzten Grentze des heiligen Landes gelegen gegen Mitternacht/ allernechst den Syrern/ und reicht biß an Damascum/und den Berg Libanum. Dieser Stamm wird hoch berühmt/und sehr zart werden/ wie eine Hinde oder Reheböcklein pflegt zu seyn/ nemlich/ das allerschönste und lieblichste unter den andern wilden Thieren/wie Salomo sagt/ Sp. V. 18. 19. Freue dich des Weibes deiner Jugend/ sie ist lieblich wie eine Hinde/und holdselig wie ein Rehe/wie es hier Herr Lutherus erkläret. Daher es auff die Fertigkeit und Hurtigkeit/oder Freudigkeit des Muthes und Hertzens/ so auch an Barack aus diesem Stamm sich erwiesen/ Richt. IV. gehet: dieweil der Stamm Naphthali allernechst Syrien bey Damasco/ und nach dem Berge Libano gelegen gewesen/darumb haben ihn die Nachbaren können angreiffen/ Unrecht und Gewalt zu thun/ gleich wie die Hinde der Jagt unterwarffen ist/ daß sie damit gedrenget wird. Die Könige in Syria haben daselbst Ursach und Gelegenheit gehabt/ ihre Tyranney und Jagt zu üben/ aber es ist gleichwol dieser Stamm durch den Glauben der Väter/ das ist/der gegebenen Verheissung/ und durch den Göttlichen Schutz ausgelassen/ und aus denselbigen Stricken errettet worden/ ist allezeit den Hunden entlauffen/ und für den Spiessen der Jäger hinweg kommen/ daß er gleichwol noch gantz und unverletzt ist blieben. Diese Erklärung gründet der Mann Gottes auff die gemeine Verheissung: Dies Land wil ich deinen Samen geben nach dir. Daraus werden den andern Stämmen die leiblichen Verheissungen fürgehalten/ daß sie sollen geschützt und erhalten werden/ biß auff die Zukunfft Schilo/ als wolte er hier von diesem Stamm so viel sagen: Es werden die Jagthunde den Stamm Naphtali plagen und verfolgen/ man wird ihm mit Spiessen und Netzen nachstellen/ aber er wird genennet werden/ und sol mir heissen eine ausgelassene Hinde die errettet ist. Da sie aber errettet werden/ geben sie schöne Rede: Denn wenn die Leute verjaget oder verfolget werden/fliehen sie zu GOtt/ ruffen ihn an mit beten und dancksagen/ preisen/ loben und rühmen den lieben GOtt/ welches sehr schöne und hübsche Reden sind unsers Mundes/ und ein sehr schönes Lob/ und fürtrefflicher Gottesdienst/ nemlich/ daß wir erstlich unsere Leibe in der Angst und Noth/ darnach aber das Opffer des Lobes GOtt opffern/ wie der L. Psalm lehret/ Opffere GOtt danck. Es gehet aber kurtz vorher/ Ruffe mich an in der Noth. v. 14. 15. Es. *XVI. 16. 17. c. XIIX. 9.*)

v. 22. **Joseph wird wachsen/ er wird wachsen wie an einer Quelle/** (wie 1. Mos. *XLIIX. 3. 6.* GOtt Jacob verheischt/ und daher Ephraim den Namen hat/ filius crescentiæ, ein Sohn der Mehrung/oder des wachsens. Er setzt aber hinzu: Er wird wachsen wie an einer Qvelle. Er wird also wachsen und Frucht bringen/ gleich wie ein Baum/ der bey einem Brunn gepflantzet ist/ und läst sich ansehen/ als habe David im ersten Psalm hierher gesehen/ da er saget/ Er ist wie ein Baum gepflantzt an den Wasserbächen.

Z iv

16

17 Vol. 1/I, cols. 425–26. On Exodus 5:23. The columns are wrongly numbered 427 and 428. As with no. 5 above, there is evidence that the typesetting was corrected while the sheets were going through the press. In the Fuerbringer copy (see Introduction, p. 19) the column numbers, 425 and 426, are printed correctly, even though the wrong verse number (33—should be 23) remains uncorrected.

Bach adds in the margin the words that are necessary to complete the Bible verse: *mit ihm zu reden in deinem Nahmen.* "For since I [Moses] came to Pharaoh *to speak with him in thy Name,* he has done evil to this people, and thou hast not delivered thy people at all." It is interesting that Bach should pick up this prophetic function of declaring the Word of God.

427 Das Fünffte Capitel. 428

wercke / gleich als da ihr Stroh hattet. (das ohn eure Bemühung und Einsamlung euch gereichet wurd.)

v. 14. Und die Amptleute der Kinder Israel / welche die Vögte Pharao über sie gesetzet hatten / wurden geschlagen / und ward zu ihnen gesagt: Warumb habt ihr weder heut noch gestern euer gesetzt Tagwerck gethan / wie vorhin?

Der Andere Theil.

Die Klage bey Pharao / und ferner bey Mose und Aaron / wegen der neuen Bedrängnüß.

v. 15. Da gingen hinnein die Amptleute der Kinder Israel: (welche geplaget waren) und schrien zu Pharao: Warumb wiltu mit deinen Knechten also (hart und tyrannisch) fahren? (oder handeln?)

v. 16. Man giebt deinen Knechten kein Stroh / und sollen die Ziegel machen / die uns bestimmet sind / und siehe deine Knechte werden geschlagen / und dein Volck muß Sünder seyn. (wir sind doch deine getreue Knechte / und dein Volck / und werden so übel geplaget. Sünder d.i. die die Straf der Sünden tragen: deine arme Leute müssen unrecht haben / und Sünder seyn / man suchet Schuld zu deinem Volck.)

v. 17. Pharao sprach (sehr übermütig und gottloß) Ihr seid müßig / müßig seid ihr: darumb sprecht ihr / wir wollen hinziehen / und dem HErrn opffern.

v. 18. So gehet nun hin und frönet / Stroh soll man euch nit geben / aber die Anzahl Ziegel solt ihr reichen.

v. 19. Da sahen die Amptleute der Kinder Israel / daß es ärger war: Weil man sagt ihr solt nichts mindern von dem Tagwerck / an den Ziegeln. (ob ihr schon kein Stroh darzu bekommen werdet: da möget ihr sehen wo ihr es schaffet)

v. 20. Und da sie von Pharao gingen / begegnet sie Mose / und Aaron / und traten gegen sie.

v. 21. Und sprachen zu ihnen (auß grosser Ungedult) der HErr sehe auf euch / und richte es / daß ihr unsern Geruch habt stinckend gemacht für Pharao und seinen Knechten: (daß wir nun so viel mehr einen übeln Stanck müssen erwarten / unser Faulheit und Fürwitzes) und habt ihnen das Schwerd in die Hände gegeben / uns zu tödten. (und hefftiger biß auf den Tod zu plagen.)

Der Dritte Theil.

Mosis Klag für GOtt über des Volcks neue Plage.

v. 22. Mose aber kam zu dem HERRN (im eifrigen Gebet Hos. VI. 1. Ephes. III. 12.) und sprach: HErr warumb thustu so übel an diesem Volck? warumb hastu mich hergesand? (Ihr Elend nur grösser zu machen / ist daß die Erlösung / darauf ich sie habe vertrösten müssen?)

v. 33. Denn sind dem daß ich hinein bin gangen zu Pharao hat er das Volck noch härter geplaget / und du hast dein Volck nicht errettet. (es ist nicht der geringste Schein eines Anfangs der Errettung aufgegangen.)

Das Sechste Capitel.

(I.) GOtt versichert Mosen der Entlassung Pharaonis / iedoch durch eine starcke Hand / da er seinen Namen HErr ihnen erweisen wil / in Erhaltung seines Bundes / und sie hernach erlösen / und zu seinem Volck im gelobten Lande auffnehmen. v. 8. (II) Das Volck höret solches von Mose für seufftzen nicht / es bekompt aber Moses und Aaron deswegen wieder Befehl. v. 13. (III.) Werden die Häupter und Geschlechter dreyer Stämme erzehlet / und Mosi wiederumb von GOtt Befehl ertheilet / der sich abermal wegen seiner Unberedsamkeit entschuldiget / v. 33.

Der Erste Theil.

GOttes Erscheinung / Mosi geschehen.

v. 1. DEr HErr sprach zu Mose: Nun soltu sehen / was ich Pharao thun werde / denn durch eine starcke Hand / (durch meine kräfftige Macht / un derselben mächtige Wunder un Plagen) muß er sie (von sich) lassen ziehen. Er muß sie noch durch eine starcke Hand / aus seinem Lande von sich treiben. (wie solches erfolget ist / c. XI. 1. c. XII. 33. Pharao nam dem

Bb iij

17

HERRN (im eifrigen Gebet Hos. VI. 1. Ephes. III. 12.) und sprach: HErr warumb thustu so übel an diesem Volck? warumb hastu mich hergesand? (Ihr Elend nur grösser zu machen / ist daß die Erlösung / darauf ich sie habe vertrösten müssen?)

v. 33. Denn sind dem daß ich hinein bin gangen zu Pharao hat er das Volck noch härter geplaget / und du hast dein Volck nicht errettet. (es ist nicht der geringste Schein eines Anfangs der Errettung aufgegangen.)

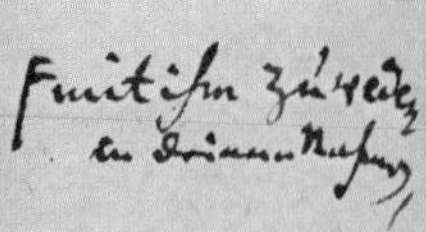

ste Capitel.

17a

18 Vol. 1/I, cols. 483–84. On Exodus 15:20: "Then Miriam the prophetess, the sister of Aaron, took a timbrel in her hand; and all the women went out after her with timbrels and dancing." Alongside the beginning of Calov's comment on this verse Bach has written: *NB. Erstes Vorspiel, auf 2 Chören zur Ehre Gottes zu musiciren* (NB. First prelude, for 2 choirs to be performed for the glory of God). Calov wrote:

18

> *These dances were organized by Miriam as a prophetess in honor of God, their Savior, just as the king and prophet David danced publicly before the ark of the covenant and defended such dancing before mocking Michal, 2 Sam. 6:14; see also 1 Sam. 18:7 and Psalm 68:25. But Miriam and the other Israelite women here did not intone and sing a new song; they performed like an immediate echo to what Moses and the men of Israel had sung to them. This is evident from the responsory at the beginning of their song. And a mightly melody and a tremendous resonance and reverberation there must have been between these two choruses, where so many hundred thousand men, and women and children no less, joined in song. It is also, indeed, not insignificant that such a strong song of joy resounded on earth from the angels of God at the birth of the Messiah, our Savior, Luke 2:13–14.*

The reference to the music of the Christmas angels at the end of Calov's comment might imply that Bach's marginal note refers to settings of the Gloria in excelsis Deo. However, none of his own settings, either of the Latin or German text, is for double chorus (see BWV 110, 191, 197a, 232, 234, 235, 236, 243, 248 II). The unusual feature of the marginal note is the use of the word *Vorspiel.* Trautmann concludes that "Bach is probably not referring to a composition with two preludes or with a prelude in two parts, that is, a prelude in the modern sense, but he is using the word *prelude* in the sense of antiphonal, multichoral performance. In other words, the first prelude is the first part of a composition in several parts or the first of several compositions used in the same service" (Trautmann B, p. 94). Gerhard Herz comes to a similar conclusion but goes further: "The word *Vorspiel* (Prelude) seems puzzling in this context unless Bach intended to refer to the first number, piece, or movement of a multisectional antiphonal work. If we were to look for such a composition, the opening movement for two four-part choruses of the eight-part motet, *Singet dem Herrn ein neues Lied,* comes readily to mind" (G. Herz, "Towards a New Image of Bach," *BACH* 1, no. 4 [Oct. 1970]: 22). Professor Herz also points out that Psalm 149:1–3, the text of the opening movement of Bach's motet BWV 225, is virtually a paraphrase of Exodus 15:20–21 and also that the words of Exodus 15:21, "Lasset uns dem Herrn singen," echo the opening words of the motet, and the words "ein neues lied" occur in Calov's comment (ibid.). There is, however, a problem in that the date that Bach inscribed in the Calov volumes is 1733, whereas the motet dates from 1726/27. However, as Herz points out, 1733 need not necessarily mark the year that Bach purchased them, and he may well have possessed them for some years before this date (Ibid., p. 23; see also C. Trautmann, "Ansätze zu ideell-ideologischen Problemen um Johann Sebastian Bach," *Kerygma und Melos: Christhard Mahrenholz 70. Jahre,* ed. W. Blankenburg, et al [Kassel, 1970], pp. 238–40; R. L. Marshall, *The Compositional Process of J. S. Bach: A Study of the Autograph Scores of the Vocal Works* [Princeton, 1972], 1:40–41; R. A. Leaver, "Bachs Motetten urd das Reformationsfest," *Bach als Ausleger der Bibel: Theologische und musikwissenschaftliche Studien zum Werk Johann Sebastian Bachs,* ed. M. Petzoldt [Berlin; 1984], pp. 39–40. For a discussion of the significance of the year "1733" in these volumes, see the Introduction, p. 26). However, the marginal note may not refer to the motet or any other particular piece of music, but may rather be simply a general comment on the beginning of antiphonal music.

On music to the glory of God, see No. 46.

483 Das Andere Buch Mosis/ 48

alle Weiber folgten ihr nach hinaus mit Paucken und Reigen. (Welche Reigen GOtt ihrem Erlöser zu Ehren angestellet worden von Mirjam als einer Prophetin/ wie auch der König und Prophet David vor der Lade des Bundes offentlich getantzet/und wieder die Spötterin Michal solches vertheidiget hat 2. Sam. VI. 14. Besiehe auch 1. Sam. *XIIX.* 7. Psalm. *LXIIX.* 26. Es haben aber hier Mirjam und die andern Israelitischen Weiber nicht ein neues Lied angestimmet und gesungen/sondern was Moses mit den Israelitischen Männern ihnen vorgesungen / gleich als in einen Echo nachgesungen / wie aus ihrem Responsorio im Anfang des Danckliedes zu sehen; und muß eine gewaltige Weise / und mächtiger Schall und Wiederschall von diesen zweyen Choren gewesen seyn/da so viel hundert tausend Männer/ und nicht minder an der Zahl Weiber und Kinder zusammen gesetzt / und gesungen haben. Wird auch wol nicht leicht jemals ein solcher starcker Freuden-Gesang erschollen seyn / auff Erden/ ohne von den Engeln GOttes bey der Geburth

war/nach dem sie von Raemses außzogen in S
choth/die andere war in Etham/jenseit des Schi
Meers/weil sich die Wüsten Etham/ jen- und d
seit des Meeres erstreckt. Die dritte war
Grunde Hahiroth. Die Vierdte in der Wüs
Etham dißseit des Schilff-Meers zu Sur.)

v. 24. Da murret das Vo
wieder Mosen/und sprach:

v. 25. Was sollen wir trincken
(da war ja gar zu bald vergessen das herrlic
Wunder / daß der HErr bey ihnen/durch sei
Göttliche Allmacht/ in der Durchführung durc
rothe Meer erwiesen hatte / davon Herr Lutheru
gar herrlichen geredet: Allhier ist uns auch ein Exemp
fürgeschrieben und abgemahlet/der jenigen/so GOtte
Wunderwerck sehen/groß halten / loben und rühme
und dennoch balde wieder zurücke fallen/ und aller Wo
thaten GOttes wieder vergessen / in dem daß sie wied
GOtt murreten und ungedultig wurden / daß sie in dre
en Tagen nicht Wasser zu trincken hatten. Kurtz zuvo
hatten sie gesehen und erfahren / das unaußsprechlic
Miracel/wie sie aus Egypten geführet/und durchs roth
Meer gebracht waren/ daß solte in ihren Augen billich ei
groß Ding seyn / denn das rothe Meer ist nicht so schma

18a

19 Vol. 1/I, cols. 485–86. On Exodus 15:27. Bach has put marks in the margin alongside the text: "Then they came to Elim, where there were twelve springs of water and seventy palm trees." Calov's comment draws attention to the parallel numbers—in the Old Testament the 12 tribes of Israel and the 70 elders and in the New Testament the 12 apostles and the 70 disciples. Again we find Bach taking an interest in such symbolic numbers. For Bach's use of the number 12 in the Credo of the *Mass in B Minor,* see R. A. Leaver, "Number Associations in the Structure of Bach's Credo, BWV 232," *BACH* 7, no. 3, pp 20–21. See also no. 22.

485 Das Sechzehende Capitel. 486

und zu Ohren fassen alle seine Geboth und halten seine Gesetz (wie er sie darnach durch Mosen Israeli wird fürtragen lassen / und beschreiben) so wil ich der Kranckheit keine auf dich legen / die ich auff Egypten gelegt habe. Denn ich bin der HErr dein Artzt. (welches Christo imgleichen zugeschrieben wird Matth. IX. 12. dem selbstständigen Worte Gottes / welches alles heilet. Weißh. XVI. 12.)

v. 27. Und sie kamen in Elim / (das war die sechste Station 4. Mos. XXXIII. 9) da waren zwölff Wasserbrunnen / und siebenzig Palmbäume / (wie die Häupter der Stämme Israel und LXX. Räthe in Synedrio und grossen Rath / die hernach erwehlet worden / wie auch im N. Testament vom HErrn Christo XII. Apostel und LXX. Jünger erwehlet und ausgesendet worden sind Matth. X. Luc. X.) und lagerten sich daselbst ans Wasser.

Das Sechzehende Capitel.

(I.) Das Volck murret in der Wüsten Sur / aus Verlangen nach dem

19

20 Vol. 1/I, cols. 491–92. On Exodus 16:32. Bach adds the identity of the speaker by completing the Biblical text of the verse *Und Mose sprach*: (And Moses said).

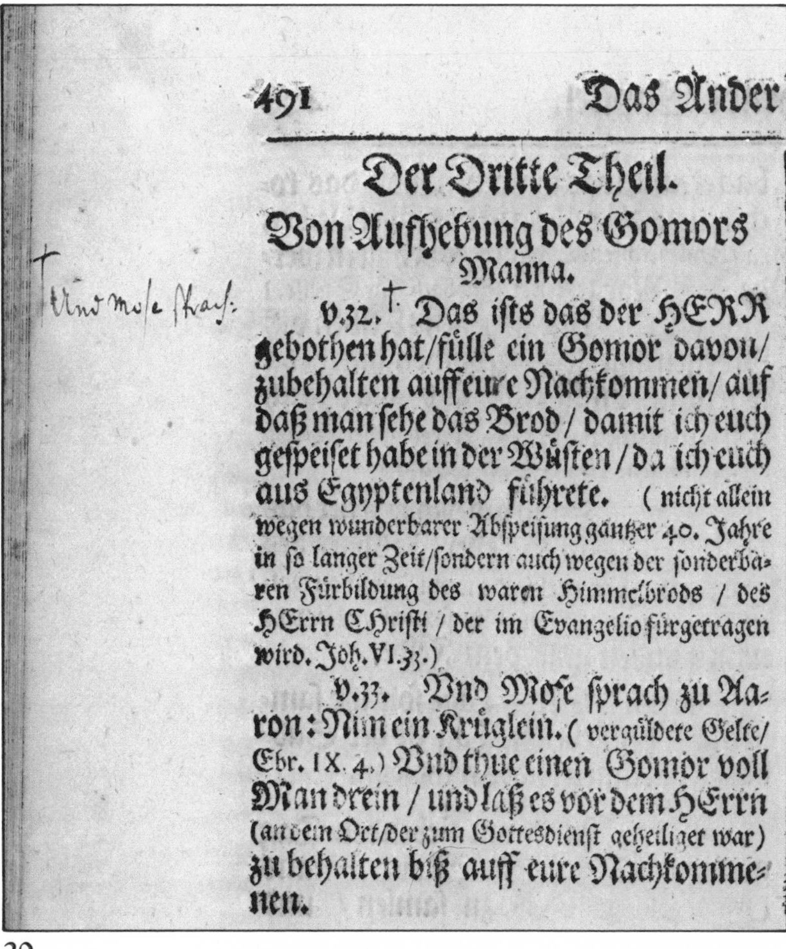

491 Das Ander

Der Dritte Theil.

Von Auffhebung des Gomors Manna.

Und Mose sprach.

v. 32. † Das ists das der HERR gebothen hat / fülle ein Gomor davon / zubehalten auff eure Nachkommen / auf daß man sehe das Brod / damit ich euch gespeiset habe in der Wüsten / da ich euch aus Egyptenland führete. (nicht allein wegen wunderbarer Abspeisung gantzer 40. Jahre in so langer Zeit / sondern auch wegen der sonderbaren Fürbildung des waren Himmelbrods / des HErrn Christi / der im Evangelio fürgetragen wird. Joh. VI. 33.)

v. 33. Und Mose sprach zu Aaron: Nim ein Krüglein. (verguldete Gelte / Ebr. IX. 4.) Und thue einen Gomor voll Man drein / und laß es vor dem HErrn (an dem Ort / der zum Gottesdienst geheiliget war) zu behalten biß auff eure Nachkommenen.

20

21 Vol. 1/I, cols. 541–42. On Exodus 25:10. Simple correction of *Länge* to *Höhe*.

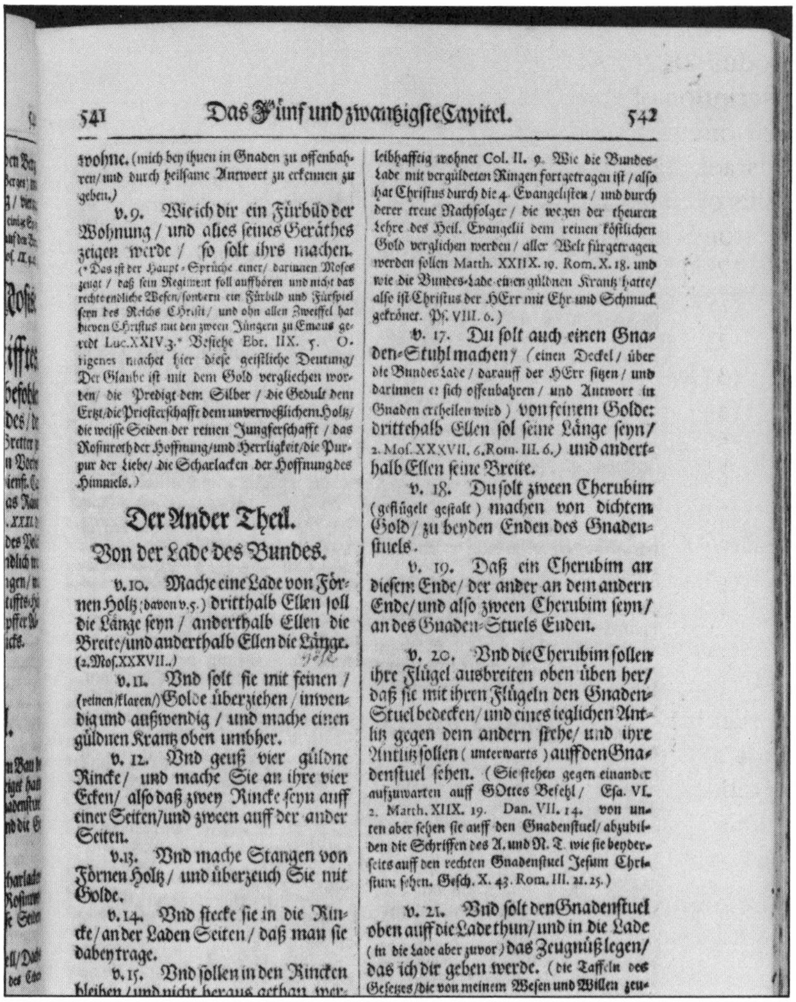

541 Das Fünff und zwantzigste Capitel. 542

wohne. (mich bey ihnen in Gnaden zu offenbahren/ und durch heilsame Antwort zu erkennen zu geben.)

v. 9. Wie ich dir ein Fürbild der Wohnung / und alles seines Geräthes zeigen werde / so solt ihrs machen. (*Das ist der Haupt-Sprüche einer/ darinnen Moses zeugt / daß sein Regiment soll auffhören und nicht das rechte endliche Wesen/ sondern ein Fürbild und Fürspiel seyn des Reichs Christi/ und ohn allen Zweiffel hat hievon Christus mit den zween Jüngern zu Emaus geredt Luc. XXIV. 3.* Besiehe Ebr. IIX. 5. Origenes machet hier diese geistliche Deutung/ Der Glaube ist mit dem Gold vergliechen worden/ die Predigt dem Silber / die Gedult dem Ertzt/ die Priesterschafft dem unverweßlichem Holtz/ die weisse Seiden der reinen Jungferschafft / das Rosinroth der Hoffnung/ und Herrligkeit/ die Purpur der Liebe/ die Scharlacken der Hoffnung des Himmels.)

Der Ander Theil.

Von der Lade des Bundes.

v. 10. Mache eine Lade von Förnen Holtz (davon v. 5.) dritthalb Ellen soll die Länge seyn / anderthalb Ellen die Breite/ und anderthalb Ellen die Länge. (2. Mos. XXXVII.)

v. 11. Und solt sie mit feinen / (reinen/klaren/) Golde überziehen / inwendig und außwendig / und mache einen güldnen Krantz oben umbher.

v. 12. Und geuß vier güldne Rincke/ und mache Sie an ihre vier Ecken/ also daß zwey Rincke seyn auff einer Seiten/ und zween auff der ander Seiten.

v. 13. Und mache Stangen von Förnen Holtz/ und überzeuch Sie mit Golde.

v. 14. Und stecke sie in die Rincke/ an der Laden Seiten / daß man sie dabey trage.

v. 15. Und sollen in den Rincken bleiben / und nicht heraus gethan wer-

leibhafftig wohnet Col. II. 9. Wie die Bundes-Lade mit vergüldeten Ringen fortgetragen ist / also hat Christus durch die 4. Evangelisten / und durch derer treue Nachfolger / die wegen der theuren Lehre des Heil. Evangelii dem reinen köstlichen Gold verglichen werden / aller Welt fürgetragen werden sollen Matth. XXIIX. 19. Rom. X. 18. und wie die Bundes-Lade einen güldnen Krantz hatte/ also ist Christus der HErr mit Ehr und Schmuck gekrönet. Ps. VIII. 6.)

v. 17. Du solt auch einen Gnaden-Stuhl machen / (einen Deckel / über die Bundes-Lade / darauff der HErr sitzen / und darinnen er sich offenbahren / und Antwort in Gnaden ertheilen wird) von feinem Golde: dritthalb Ellen sol seine Länge seyn / 2. Mos. XXXVII. 6. Rom. III. 6.) und anderthalb Ellen seine Breite.

v. 18. Du solt zween Cherubim (geflügelt gestalt) machen von dichtem Gold / zu beyden Enden des Gnadenstuels.

v. 19. Daß ein Cherubim an diesem Ende/ der ander an dem andern Ende/ und also zween Cherubim seyn/ an des Gnaden-Stuels Enden.

v. 20. Und die Cherubim sollen ihre Flügel ausbreiten oben üben her/ daß sie mit ihren Flügeln den Gnaden-Stuel bedecken/ und eines ieglichen Antlitz gegen dem andern stehe/ und ihre Antlitz sollen (unterwarts) auff den Gnadenstuel sehen. (Sie stehen gegen einander aufzuwarten auff GOttes Befehl / Esa. VI. 2. Matth. XIIX. 19. Dan. VII. 14. von unten aber sehen sie auff den Gnadenstuel/ abzubilden die Schrifften des A. und N. T. wie sie beyderseits auff den rechten Gnadenstuel Jesum Christum sehen. Gesch. X. 43. Rom. III. 21. 25.)

v. 21. Und solt den Gnadenstuel oben auff die Lade thun/ und in die Lade (in die Lade aber zuvor) das Zeugnüß legen/ das ich dir geben werde. (die Taffeln des Gesetzes/ die von meinem Wesen und Willen zeu-

21

22 Vol. 1/I, cols. 557–58. Exodus 28:20. Alongside the description of precious stones, each one representing a tribe of Israel, Bach has placed his marks of emphasis, and each of the stones are numbered from 1 to 12:

(1) Sadius . . . ,
(2) Topasius . . . ,
(3) Smaragd . . . ,
(4) Carbunckel . . . ,
(5) Saphir . . . ,
(6) Demant . . . ,
(7) Lyncurer . . . ,
(8) Achat . . . ,
(9) Amethyst . . . ,
(10) Chrysolith . . . ,
(11) Onych . . . ,
(12) Jaspis . . .

In his commentary Calov gives a Christological interpretation to each of the stones. See also no. 19.

22

23 Vol. 1/I, cols. 565–66. On Exodus 29:24. Correction of *Mittergang* to *Niedergang* and marks of emphasis alongside the comment on the verse, in which Calov presents the wave offering as a figure of the overarching effectiveness of the offering of Christ on the cross, which embraces all the people of the world. See no. 63.

23

webe es dem HErrn. (das Ebreische Wor
bedeut eine solche Bewegung / die da geschicht hi
und rückwerts / 2. Mos. XXV. 20. oder vielmeh
hin und her / anzudeuten / die Krafft des Opffer
Christi erstrecke sich vor- und hinwarts / durch all
Menschen der Welt / die gewesen sind / oder di
noch kommen müssen: deßwegen die Opffer ers
in die Höhe gehoben / darnach herunter gezogen
denn nach den Auf- und Mittergang / nach Mit-
ter-Nacht und Mittag beweget worden / dadurch

23a

24 Vol. 1/I, cols. 567–68. On Exodus 29:37. Bach supplies the word *weihen,* which was omitted in Calov's citation of the verse.

24

24a

25 Vol. 1/I, cols. 599–600. On Exodus 35:30. Simple correction of *Levi* to *Uri*.

26 Vol. 1/I, col. 605. On Exodus 37:24. Bach has underlined and marked in the margin that one talent (Centner) is equivalent to 18,000 Reichsthaler. Heinrich Bünting's *Itinerarium Sacrae Scripturae*, which was in Bach's library (see no. 10 above and Leaver C, no. 11), included a third part: *De Monetis et Mensuris Sacrae Scripturae: Das ist Ein eigentliche Ausrechnung und Beschreibung aller Müntz und Masse in heiliger Schrifft . . . mit unser Müntz und Masse Proportionert und vergleichen werden ausgerechnet . . . (De Monetis et Mensuris Sacrae Scripturae,* that is, an accurate calculation and description of all money and measurement in Holy Scripture . . . proportionately and comparatively computed in accordance with our money and measurement . . .). Bach's interest in coins and medals is confirmed by chapter 2 of the *specificatio* of his estate, drawn up after his death (see *BD* 2:491; *BR*, pp. 191–92). See also no. 27.

599 Das Ander Buch Mosis. 600

gebothen hatte durch Mosen daß mans machen solt. (was gemacht werden soll/das war gebeten / was aber dazu gebracht solt werden/ das war ihrer Freywilligkeit übergeben. Davon Paulus ruhmet einen frölichen Geber hat GOTT lieb. 2. Cor. IX. 7. 9. Bes. Psalm CXII. 9. Jer. XXXV. 11.)

Der Dritte Theil.

Die Werckmeister.

v. 30. Und Mose sprach zu den Kindern Israel: Sehet der HErr hat mit Namen beruffen den Bezaleel/den Sohn ~~Levi~~ / des Sohnes Hur/ vom Stamm Juda. 2. Mos. XXX. 2.) *Uri*

v. 31. Und hat ihn erfüllet mit dem Geist Gottes/ (er hat ihn reichlich ausgerüstet mit Gaben des H. Geistes / welcher ein Geist Gottes ist / der vom Vater ausgehet. Joh. XV. 26. Von welchem Erkäntnüß/ Weißheit und Verstand herkompt. 1. Cor. XII. 7. 8. Es. XI. 2.) daß er weise / verständig / geschickt sey zu allerley Werck. (2. Mos. XXXI. 3.)

v. 32. Künstlich zu arbeiten an Gold / Silber / und Ertz.

v. 33. Edelstein schneiden / und einsetzen / Holtzimmern / zu machen allerley künstliche Arbeit.

v. 34. Und hat ihm sein Hertz unterwiesen / samt Achaliab den Sohn Achisamach vom Stamm Dan. (und allerley andern Weisen. wie 2. Mos. XXX. 34. angedeutet.)

v. 35. Er hat ihr Hertz mit Weißheit erfüllet / zu machen allerley Werck/ zu schneiden / Würcken / und zu sticken / mit geler Seiden / Scharlacken/ Rosinroth / und weisser Seiden / und mit Wollen / daß sie machen allerley Werck / und künstliche Arbeit erfinden.

25

605 Das Sieben und Dreyßigste Capitel/ 606

breit hoch / und machet einen güldnen Krantz umb die Leisten her.

v. 13. Und goß dazu vier güldene Ringe / (c. XXV. 26.) und thät sie an die vier Ort / an seinen vier Füssen.

v. 14. Hart an der Leisten / daß die Stangen drinnen weren / damit man den Tisch trüge. (Ebr. Gegen über der Leisten waren vier Beine zu örtern für die Stangen/ da man nemlich die Stangen hinein steckt den Tisch zu tragen. c. XXV. 28.)

v. 15. Und macht die Stangen von Föern Holtz / und überzog sie mit Golde / daß man den Tisch damit trüge.

v. 16. Und macht auch von feinem Golde daß Geräth auf den Tisch/ Schüsseln/Becher/Kannen/und Schalen/ damit man aus und einschencket. (Andere: damit sie bedecket worden. Das Ebr. Wort heisset beydes bedecken / und ausgiessen / nemlich die Schau-Brod zu bedecken / oder das Trinck-Opffer auszugiessen.)

v. 17. Und macht den Leuchter von feinem dichtem Golde / daran waren die Schafft mit Rören / Schalen Knäuffen / und Blumen. (c. XXV. 31.)

v. 18. Sechs Rören giengen zu seinen Seiten aus / zu ieglicher Seiten drey Röhren. (c. XXV. 32.)

v. 19. Drey Schalen waren an ieglichen Rohr / mit Knäuffen / und Blumen. (c. XXV. 33.)

v. 20. An dem Leuchter aber / (an dem Schafft des Leuchters) waren vier Schalen mit Knäuffen / und Blumen.

v. 22. Und ihre Knäuffe / und Röhren dran / und war alles aus dichtem feinem Golde. (c. XXV. 36.)

v. 23. Und macht die sieben Lampen mit ihren Lichtschneutzen / und Leschnäpffen von feinem Golde. (c. XXV. 37. 38.)

v. 24. Aus einem Centner feines Goldes / (das macht 18000. Rthr.) machte er ihn / und alle sein Geräthe (c. XXV. 39.)

Der Dritte Theil.

Der Räuch-Altar.

v. 25. Er macht auch den Räuch-Altar von Föern Holtz / ein Ellen lang/ und breit/ gleich vierecket / und zwo Ellen hoch / mit seinen Hörnern. (2. Mos. XXX. 1.)

v. 26. Und überzog ihn mit feinem Golde / sein Dach und seine Wände rings umbher / und seine Hörner: Und macht ihm einen Krantz umbher von Golde. (c. XX. 3.)

v. 27. Und zween gülden Rincken / unter dem Krantz / zu beyden Seiten / daß man Stangen drein thät / und ihn damit trüge. (c. XXX. 4.)

v. 28. Aber die Stangen macht er von Föern Holtz / und überzog sie mit Golde. (c. XXX. 4.)

v. 29. Und macht die heilige Salbe und Räuchwerck von reiner Specerey / nach Apotecker Kunst. (2. Mos. XXX. 23. 34. 35. Aller dieser Sachen wird stückweise ge-

26

27 Vol. 1/I, col. 609–10. On Exodus 38:24–29. Bach has underlined and marked the value and weight of the various metals used for the artifacts in the Tabernacle. Alongside verse 29 he adds the marginal summary: *Die suṁma des freywilligen Opfers beträgt fast in die acht Toñen Goldes* (The sum of the freewill offering amounts to almost eight tons of gold). The third part of Bünting's book *Itinerarium Sacrae Scripturae, De Monetis et Mensuris Sacrae Scripturae* (see No. 26 above), also included information on weights and measures, as well as linear measurements.

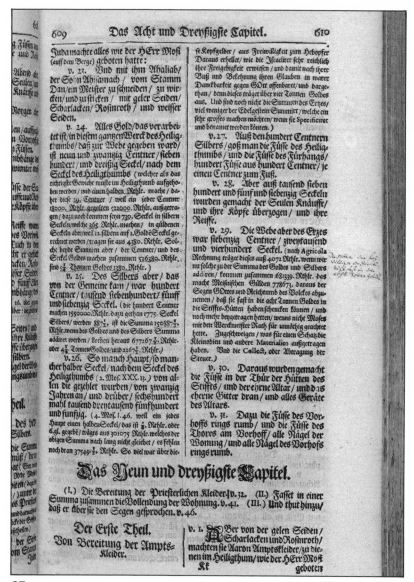

609 Das Acht und Dreyßigste Capitel. 610

Juda machte alles wie der HErr Mosi (auff dem Berge) geboten hatte:

v. 23. Und mit ihm Ahaliab/ der Sohn Ahisamach/ vom Stamm Dan/ein Meister zu schneiden/ zu wircken/und zu sticken/ mit geler Seiden/ Scharlacken/ Rosinroth/ und weisser Seiden.

v. 24. Alles Gold/das verarbeitet ist/in diesem gantzen Werck des Heiligthumbs/ daß zur Webe gegeben ward/ ist neun und zwantzig Centner/sieben hundert/ und dreißig Seckel/ nach dem Seckel des Heiligthumbs (welcher als das richtigste Gewicht muste im Heiligthumb aufgehoben werden/ und einen halben Rthlr. machet/ daher diese 29. Centner/ weil ein jeder Centner 18000. Rthlr. gegolten 522000. Rthlr. außgetragen/ dazu noch kommen seyn 730. Seckel in silbern Seckeln/welche 365. Rthlr. machen/ in güldenen Seckeln aber/weil 12. silbern auf 1. Goldē Seckel gerechnet werden/tragen sie aus 4380. Rthlr. Solche beyde Summen aber/ der Centner/ und des Seckel Goldes machen zusammen 526380. Rthlr. sind $5\frac{1}{4}$. Thonnen Goldes 1380. Rthlr.)

v. 25. Des Silbers aber/ das von der Gemeine kam/ war hundert Centner/ tausend siebenhundert/ fünff und siebenzig Seckel. (die hundert Centner machen 1550000. Rthlr. dazu gethan 1775. Seckel Silbers/ werden $887\frac{1}{2}$. ist die Summa $150887\frac{1}{2}$. Rthlr. wenn des Goldes und des Silbers Summa addiret werden/ komen heraus $677267\frac{1}{2}$. Rthlr. oder $4\frac{3}{4}$. Tonnen Goldes/und $2267\frac{1}{2}$. Rthlr.)

v. 26. So manch Haupt/so mancher halber Seckel/ nach dem Seckel des Heiligthumbs (2. Mos. XXX. 13.) von allen die gezehlet wurden/ von zwanzig Jahren an/ und drüber/ sechshundert mahl tausend dreytausend fünfhundert und funfzig. (4. Mos. 1. 46. weil ein jedes Haupt einen halben Seckel/ das ist $\frac{1}{2}$. Rthlr. oder 6. gl. gegebē/ trägts aus 301075 Rthlr. welches der obigen Summa nach lang nicht gleichet/ es fehlen noch dran $37549\frac{1}{2}$. Rthlr. So viel war über diese Kopfgelder/ aus Freiwilligkeit zum Hebopfer Daraus erhellet/ wie die Israeliter sehr reichlich ihre Freigebigkeit erwiesen/ und damit nach ihrer Buß und Bekehrung ihren Glauben in warer Danckbarkeit gegen GOtt offenbaret/ und dargethan/ denn dieses träget über vier Tonnen Goldes aus. Und sind noch nicht die Summen des Ertzes/ viel weniger der Edelgestein Summirt/ welche ein sehr grosses machen möchten/ wenn sie Specificiret und benamet werden könten.)

v. 27. Auß den hundert Centnern Silbers/ goß man die Füsse des Heiligthumbs/ und die Füsse des Fürhangs/ hundert Füsse aus hundert Centner/ je einen Centner zum Fuß.

v. 28. Aber auß tausend sieben hundert und fünf und siebenzig Seckeln wurden gemacht der Seulen Knäuffe/ und ihre Köpfe überzogen/ und ihre Reiffe.

v. 29. Die Webe aber des Erzes war siebenzig Centner/ zweytausend und vierhundert Seckel. (nach Agricola Rechnung träget dieses auß 4072 Rthlr. wenn wir nu solche zu der Summa des Goldes und Silbers addiren/ kommen zusammen 681339. Rthlr. das macht Meißnischen Gülden 778673. daraus der Segen GOttes und Reichtumb des Volckes abzunemen/ daß sie fast in die acht Tonnen Goldes in die Stiffts-Hütten haben schencken können/ und noch mehr beygetragen hetten/ wenns nicht Moses mit den Werckmeister Rath für unnöthig geachtet hette. Zugeschweigen/ was für einen Schatz die Kleinodien und andere Materialien außgetragen haben. Und die Collect, oder Abtragung der Steuer.)

v. 30. Daraus wurden gemacht die Füsse in der Thür der Hütten des Stiffts/ und der ehrne Altar/ und das eherne Gitter dran/ und alles Geräte des Altars.

v. 31. Dazu die Füsse des Vorhoffs rings rumb/ und die Füsse des Thores am Vorhoff/ alle Nägel der Wonung/ und alle Nägel des Vorhofs rings rumb.

Das Neun und dreyßigste Capitel.

(I.) Die Bereitung der Priesterlichen Kleider. v. 32. (II.) Fasset in einer Summa zusammen die Vollendung der Wohnung. v. 41. (III.) Und thut hinzu/ daß er über sie den Segen gesprochen. v. 46.

Der Erste Theil.
Von Bereitung der Ampts-Kleider.

v. 1. ABer von der gelen Seiden/ Scharlacken und Rosinroth/ machten sie Aaron Amptskleider/ zu dienen im Heiligthum/ wie der HErr Mose geboten

27

v. 29. Die Webe aber des Erzes war siebenzig Centner/ zweytausend und vierhundert Seckel. (nach Agricola Rechnung träget dieses auß 4072 Rthlr. wenn wir nu solche zu der Summa des Goldes und Silbers addiren/ kommen zusammen 681339. Rthlr. das macht Meißnischen Gülden 778673. daraus der Segen GOttes und Reichtumb des Volckes abzunemen/ daß sie fast in die acht Tonnen Goldes in die Stiffts-Hütten haben schencken können/ und noch mehr beygetragen hetten/ wenns nicht Moses mit den Werckmeister Rath für unnöthig geachtet hette. Zugeschweigen/ was für einen Schatz die Kleinodien und andere Materialien außgetragen haben. Und die Collect, oder Abtragung der Steuer.)

v. 30. Daraus wurden gemacht die Füsse in der Thür der Hütten des

27a

28 Vol. 1/I, col. 697–98. On Leviticus 17:11. Bach has put his marks of emphasis alongside the first part of the verse and Calov's comment on it, as well as underlining it all:

> v. 11. For the life of the body is in the blood *(Not only the life of mankind but also the life of animals has its nature and being in blood, so that the tyrannical view is that whoever eats the blood of the animal will certainly swallow its life. However, such a Levitical commandment does not bind the Christian, even though in the early church it was forbidden for a while so that the Jews would not be offended, Acts 15:29.)*

28

(alß ein Feind ihn mit zornigen Antlitz anzusehen/)
und wil ihn mitten aus seinem Volck
rotten/ (daß er keinen Platz unterm Volck Gottes habe/3. Mos. III. 17. c. VII, 16. 5 Mos. XII 23.)
v. 11. Denn des Leibes Leben ist im
Blut (das Leben nicht nur des Menschen/sondern
der Thiere hat sein Wesen und Auffenthalt im Blut/
daß es das Ansehen hat / wer das Blut der Thiere
isset / wolle ihr Leben gar verschlingen / welches tyrannisch / doch bindet die Christen solches Levitisch
Gebot nicht/ungeachtet in der ersten Kirchen/ damit die Jüden nicht geärgert werden/auff eine Zeitlang das Blut zu essen /verboten worden ist/ Gesch.
XV. 29.) und ich habs euch zum Altar
gegeben / daß eure Seelen damit (durch
das Blut der Thiere) versünet werden/denn

28a

29 Vol. 1/I, col. 701–02. On Leviticus 18:16. The verse and the commentary appear thus:

> v. 16. You shall not uncover the sexuality of the wife of your brother *(should he die or divorce her)* for it is your brother's sexuality.

To this Bach adds the marginal note: *NB. Scheinet dem Gesetze (so da ordnete, dass ein Bruder seinem verstorbenen Bruder Saamen erwecken solt) contrair zu seyn* (NB. The Law [since it orders that a brother shall raise up his deceased brother's offspring] appears to be against this). Here Bach is referring to Deuteronomy 25:5–10, which provides an exception to the statement in Leviticus: "If brothers dwell together, and one of them dies and has no son, the wife of the dead shall not be married outside the family to a stranger; her husband's brother shall go in to her, and take her as his wife . . . .And the first son whom she bears shall succeed to the name of his brother who is dead . . . ." Here is a clear indication that Bach was a careful student of the Bible.

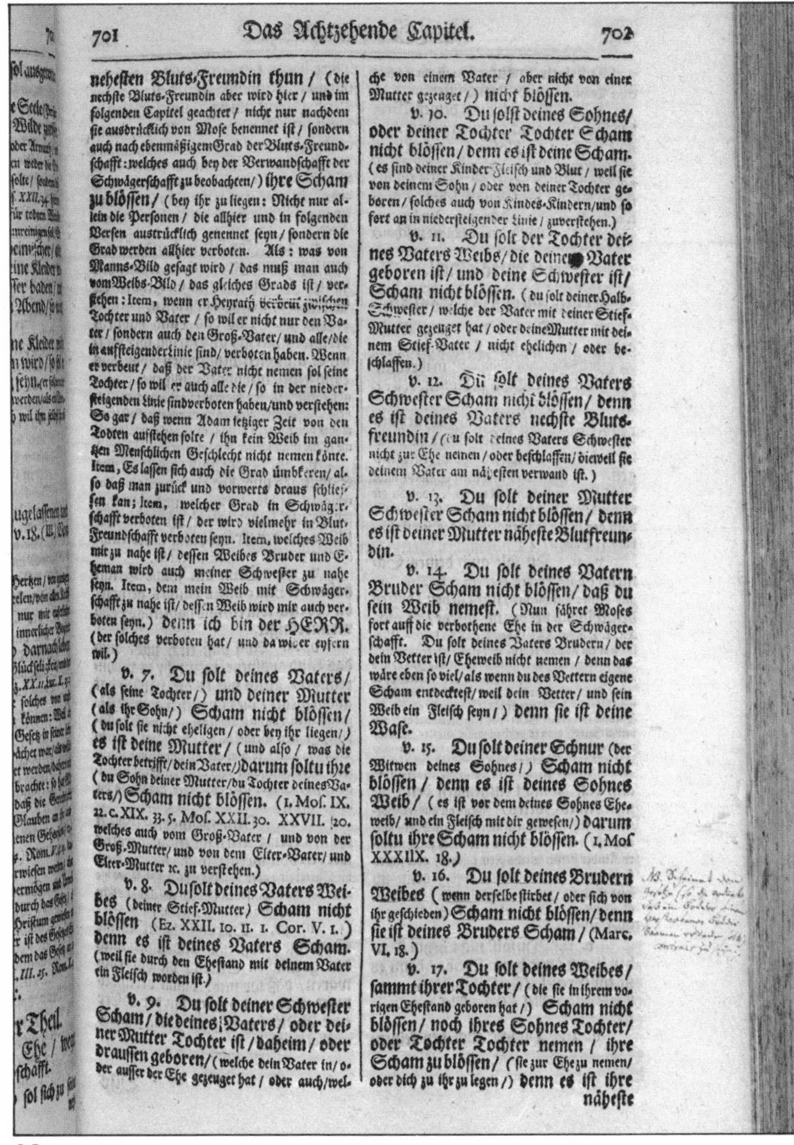

701 Das Achtzehende Capitel. 702

nehesten Bluts-Freundin thun / (die nechste Bluts-Freundin aber wird hier / und im folgenden Capitel geachtet / nicht nur nachdem sie ausdrücklich von Mose benennet ist / sondern auch nach ebenmäßigem Grad der Bluts-Freundschafft: welches auch bey der Verwandschafft der Schwägerschafft zu beobachten/) ihre Scham zu blössen / (bey ihr zu liegen: Nicht nur allein die Personen / die allhier und in folgenden Versen austrücklich genennet seyn / sondern die Grad werden allhier verboten. Als: was von Manns-Bild gesagt wird / das muß man auch vom Weibs-Bild / das gleiches Grads ist / verstehen: Item, wenn er Heyrath verbeut zwischen Tochter und Vater / so wil er nicht nur den Vater / sondern auch den Groß-Vater / und alle / die in auffsteigender Linie sind / verboten haben. Wenn er verbeut / daß der Vater nicht nemen sol seine Tochter / so wil er auch alle die / so in der niedersteigenden Linie sind verboten haben / und verstehen: So gar / daß wenn Adam jetziger Zeit von den Todten auffstehen solte / ihn kein Weib im gantzen Menschlichen Geschlecht nicht nemen könte. Item, Es lassen sich auch die Grad ümbkeren / also daß man zurück und vorwerts draus schliessen kan; Item, welcher Grad in Schwägerschafft verboten ist / der wird vielmehr in Blut-Freundschafft verboten seyn. Item, welches Weib mir zu nahe ist / dessen Weibes Bruder und Eheman wird auch meiner Schwester zu nahe seyn. Item, dem mein Weib mit Schwägerschafft zu nahe ist / dessen Weib wird mir auch verboten seyn.) denn ich bin der HERR. (der solches verboten hat / und dawider eyfern wil.)

v. 7. Du solt deines Vaters / (als seine Tochter /) und deiner Mutter (als ihr Sohn /) Scham nicht blössen / (du solt sie nicht ehelichen / oder bey ihr liegen /) es ist deine Mutter / (und also / was die Tochter betrifft / dein Vater /) darum soltu ihre (du Sohn deiner Mutter / du Tochter deines Vaters /) Scham nicht blössen. (1. Mos. IX. 22. c. XIX. 33. 5. Mos. XXII. 30. XXVII. 20. welches auch vom Groß-Vater / und von der Groß-Mutter / und von dem Elter-Vater / und Elter-Mutter rc. zu verstehen.)

v. 8. Du solt deines Vaters Weibes (deiner Stief-Mutter) Scham nicht blössen (Ez. XXII. 10. 11. 1. Cor. V. 1.) denn es ist deines Vaters Scham. (weil sie durch den Ehestand mit deinem Vater ein Fleisch worden ist.)

v. 9. Du solt deiner Schwester Scham / die deines Vaters / oder deiner Mutter Tochter ist / daheim / oder draussen geboren / (welche dein Vater in / oder ausser der Ehe gezeuget hat / oder auch / welche von einem Vater / aber nicht von einer Mutter gezeuget /) nicht blössen.

v. 10. Du solst deines Sohnes / oder deiner Tochter Tochter Scham nicht blössen / denn es ist deine Scham. (es sind deiner Kinder Fleisch und Blut / weil sie von deinem Sohn / oder von deiner Tochter geboren / solches auch von Kindes-Kindern / und so fort an in niedersteigender Linie / zuverstehen.)

v. 11. Du solt der Tochter deines Vaters Weibs / die deinem Vater geboren ist / und deine Schwester ist / Scham nicht blössen. (du solt deiner Halb-Schwester / welche der Vater mit deiner Stief-Mutter gezeuget hat / oder deine Mutter mit deinem Stief-Vater / nicht ehelichen / oder beschlaffen.)

v. 12. Du solt deines Vaters Schwester Scham nicht blössen / denn es ist deines Vaters nechste Bluts-freundin / (du solt deines Vaters Schwester nicht zur Ehe nemen / oder beschlaffen / dieweil sie deinem Vater am nähesten verwand ist.)

v. 13. Du solt deiner Mutter Schwester Scham nicht blössen / denn es ist deiner Mutter näheste Blutfreundin.

v. 14. Du solt deines Vatern Bruder Scham nicht blössen / daß du sein Weib nemest. (Nun fähret Moses fort auff die verbothene Ehe in der Schwägerschafft. Du solt deines Vaters Brudern / der dein Vetter ist / Eheweib nicht nemen / denn das wäre eben so viel / als wenn du des Vettern eigene Scham entdecktest / weil dein Vetter / und sein Weib ein Fleisch seyn /) denn sie ist deine Wase.

v. 15. Du solt deiner Schnur (der Witwen deines Sohnes /) Scham nicht blössen / denn es ist deines Sohnes Weib / (es ist vor dem deines Sohnes Eheweib / und ein Fleisch mit dir gewesen /) darum soltu ihre Scham nicht blössen. (1. Mos. XXXIIX. 18.)

v. 16. Du solt deines Brudern Weibes (wenn derselbe stirbet / oder sich von ihr geschieden) Scham nicht blössen / denn sie ist deines Bruders Scham / (Marc. VI. 18.)

v. 17. Du solt deines Weibes / sammt ihrer Tochter / (die sie in ihrem vorigen Ehestand geboren hat /) Scham nicht blössen / noch ihres Sohnes Tochter / oder Tochter Tochter nemen / ihre Scham zu blössen / (sie zur Ehe zu nemen / oder dich zu ihr zu legen /) denn es ist ihre näheste

29

blössen / denn es ist deines Sohnes Weib / (es ist vor dem deines Sohnes Eheweib / und ein Fleisch mit dir gewesen /) darum soltu ihre Scham nicht blössen. (1. Mos. XXXIIX. 18.)

v. 16. Du solt deines Brudern Weibes (wenn derselbe stirbet / oder sich von ihr geschieden) Scham nicht blössen / denn sie ist deines Bruders Scham / (Marc. VI. 18.)

v. 17. Du solt deines Weibes / sammt ihrer Tochter / (die sie in ihrem vorigen Ehestand geboren hat /) Scham nicht blössen / noch ihres Sohnes Tochter / oder Tochter Tochter nemen / ihre

29a

30 Vol. 1/I, col. 727–28. On Leviticus 23:11. Simple correction of *Speise* to *Speisemeister* in line 7 of col. 727, according to the list of typographical errors at the end of Vol. 3/VI.

727 Das Dritte Buch Moſis/ 728

opffert worden/) ſol die Garbe gewebet werden für dem HErrn/ (das iſt gewendet gegen die vier Oerter der Welt/) das von euch angeneme ſey/ (daß GOtt ſolche Erſtlinge gefällig ſey/ und er forthin euch ferner mit euren Getraidig ſegne/ die er als der reiche milde Speiſe uns ausſpendet/ das alle lebhaffte leibliche Creaturen geſättiget werden.) ſolches ſol aber der Prieſter thun/des andern Tages nach dem Sabbath. (des andern Tages im Oſter-Feſt.)

v. 12. Und ſolt des Tages/ da euer Garbe gewebet wird/ ein Brand-Opffer dem HErrn thun/ von einem Lamm/ das ohne Wandel und Jährig ſey. (eure Sünden in Krafft des Lammes Gottes/ das da zu tragen hat die Sünde der Welt/ Joh. I. 29. durch den Glauben an daſſelbige zuverſühnen)

v. 13. Sampt dem Speißoffer (davon c. II. 6.) zwo zehenden (nemlich von

den Oſtern geſchach das Speißopffer von Korn-Ehern/ welches ſelbiger Zeit begunte reif zu werden im Jüdiſchen Lande/ da es heiſſer iſt/ als bey uns und alles ward eher zeitig; in Pfingſten aber von Weitzenbrodt/ Beſ. 2. Moſ. c. XXXIV. 22.)

v. 18. Und ſolt herzu bringen neben euerm Brod ſieben Jährige Lämmer ohne Wandel/ und einen Jungen Farren/ und zwey Widder/ (im Namen des Volcks/) das ſol des HErrn Brandopffer/ Speißopffer/ und Tranckopffer ſeyn. (zu einem iedern Brandopffer des erwachſenen Viehes ſollen hinzugethan werden/ die gebührende Speiß- und Tranckopffer/ v. 13.) das iſt ein Opffer eines ſüſſen Geruchs dem HErrn. (theils wegen Anſehung des Brandopffers Chriſti/ theils wegen der geiſtlichen Opffer/ die zur Danckbarkeit dem HErrn durch Chriſtum gebracht worden/ und daher angenehm waren/ weil ſolches im Glauben geſchach/ Ebr. XI. 6.)

v. 19. Darzu ſolt ihr machen

30

31 Vol. 1/I, col. 731–32. On Leviticus 23:39. Simple correction of *worden* to *werden* in col. 731, according to the list of typographical errors at the end of Vol. 3/VI.

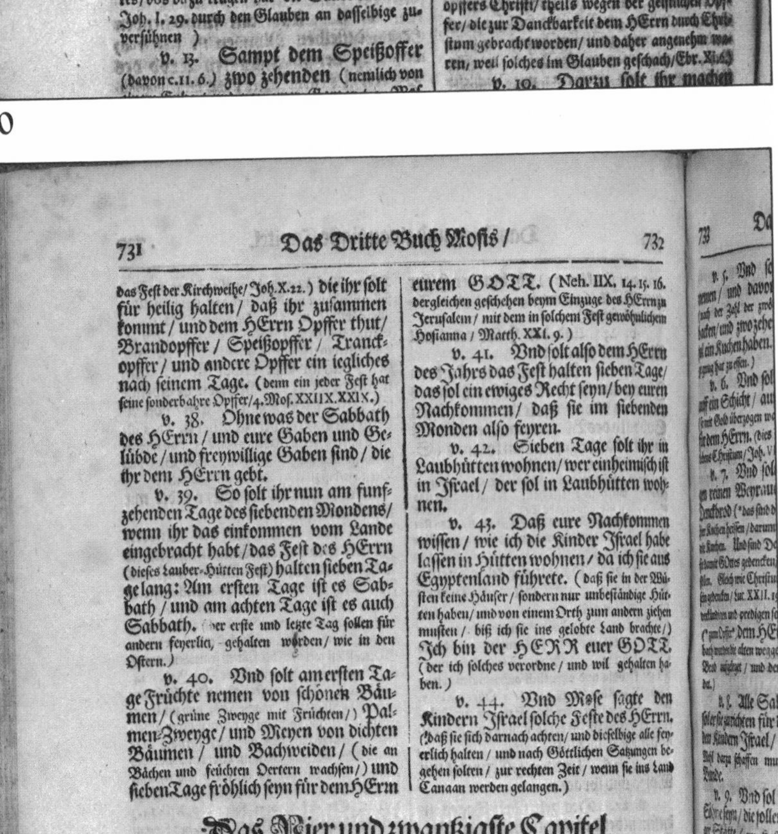

731 Das Dritte Buch Moſis/ 732

das Feſt der Kirchweihe/ Joh. X. 22.) die ihr ſolt für heilig halten/ daß ihr zuſammen kommt/ und dem HErrn Opffer thut/ Brandopffer/ Speißopffer/ Tranckopffer/ und andere Opffer ein iegliches nach ſeinem Tage. (denn ein jeder Feſt hat ſeine ſonderbahre Opffer/ 4. Moſ. XXIIX. XXIX.)

v. 38. Ohne was der Sabbath des HErrn/ und eure Gaben und Gelübde/ und freywillige Gaben ſind/ die ihr dem HErrn gebt.

v. 39. So ſolt ihr nun am funfzehenden Tage des ſiebenden Mondens/ wenn ihr das einkommen vom Lande eingebracht habt/ das Feſt des HErrn (dieſes Lauber-Hütten Feſt) halten ſieben Tage lang: Am erſten Tage iſt es Sabbath/ und am achten Tage iſt es auch Sabbath. (der erſte und letzte Tag ſollen für andern feyerlich gehalten worden/ wie in den Oſtern.)

v. 40. Und ſolt am erſten Tage Früchte nemen von ſchönen Bäumen/ (grüne Zweyge mit Früchten/) Palmen-Zweyge/ und Meyen von dichten Bäumen/ und Bachweiden/ (die an Bächen und feuchten Oertern wachſen/) und ſieben Tage fröhlich ſeyn für dem HErrn

eurem GOTT. (Neh. IIX. 14. 15. 16. dergleichen geſchehen beym Einzuge des HErrn zu Jeruſalem/ mit dem in ſolchem Feſt gewöhnlichem Hoſianna/ Matth. XXI. 9.)

v. 41. Und ſolt alſo dem HErrn des Jahrs das Feſt halten ſieben Tage/ das ſol ein ewiges Recht ſeyn/ bey euren Nachkommen/ daß ſie im ſiebenden Monden alſo feyren.

v. 42. Sieben Tage ſolt ihr in Laubhütten wohnen/ wer einheimiſch iſt in Jſrael/ der ſol in Laubhütten wohnen.

v. 43. Daß eure Nachkommen wiſſen/ wie ich die Kinder Jſrael habe laſſen in Hütten wohnen/ da ich ſie aus Egyptenland führete. (daß ſie in der Wüſten keine Häuſer/ ſondern nur unbeſtändige Hütten haben/ und von einem Orth zum andern ziehen muſten/ biß ich ſie ins gelobte Land brachte/) Jch bin der HERR euer GOTT. (der ich ſolches verordne/ und wil gehalten haben.)

v. 44. Und Moſe ſagte den Kindern Jſrael ſolche Feſte des HErrn. (daß ſie ſich darnach achten/ und dieſelbige alle feyerlich halten/ und nach Göttlichen Satzungen begehen ſolten/ zur rechten Zeit/ wenn ſie ins Land Canaan werden gelangen.)

Das Vier und zwantzigſte Capitel.

31

32 Vol. 1/I, col. 869–70. Numbers 19:9, 13. Two corrections to the Biblical text. The first, in the final line of col. 869, is the crossing out of the duplicated *dass sie*. The second is the addition of the word *nicht*, which was omitted from verse 13.

869 **Das Neunzehende Capitel.** 870

und auff die noch nie kein Joch kommen ist. (Hier ist der HErr Christus fürgebildet / röthlich durch sein Blut / in seinem besten Wandel geschlachtet / Ebr. IX. 13. 14. in welchem keine Sünde war / 2. Cor. V. 21. der auch von selbsten dem Joch des Gesetzes nicht unterworffen war / als der der HErr des Gesetzes war / Matth. XII. 8. sondern freywillig demselben umb unsert willen sich unterworffen / Gal. IV. 4.)

v. 3. Und gebet sie dem Priester Eleasar / (der der Oberste nach Aaron war / 4. Mos. III. 3.) der sol sie hinaus für das Lager führen / und daselbst für ihm schlachten lassen / (damit fürgebildet ist / Christus werde für dem Thor getödtet werden / Ebr. XIII. 12.)

v. 4. Und Eleasar der Priester sol ihres Bluts mit seinem Finger nemen / und stracks gegen die Hütten des Stiffts sieben mal sprengen. (damit gedeutet ist auff des Bluts Christi / das für uns vergossen ist / Sprengung / Ebr. IX. 14. c. XII. 24. 1. Petr. I. 2.)

v. 5. Und die Kuh für ihnen verbrennen lassen / beyde ihr Fell / und ihr Fleisch / darzu ihr Blut sampt ihren Mist. (4. Mos. XIV. 4.)

v. 6. Und der Priester sol Cedern Holtz / und Isopen / und rosinrothe Wollen nemen / und auff die brennende Kuh werffen. (daß es zugleich mit verbrenne.)

v. 7. Und sol sein Kleid waschen / und seinen Leib mit Wasser baden / und darnach ins Lager gehen / und unrein seyn biß an den Abend. (Weil der Priester selber sich verunreinigte / und waschens von nöthen hatte / eben in dem er das Volck entsündigte / so kan hieraus leicht die Unvollkommenheit des Levitischen Priesterthumbs abgenommen werden / Vergl. Hebr. VII. 27. 28.)

v. 8. Und der sie verbrand hat / sol auch seine Kleider mit Wasser waschen / und seinen Leib in Wasser baden / und unrein seyn biß an den Abend. (auch die Christum gecreutziget und getödtet haben / können gereiniget werden von ihren Sünden / Gesch. II. 23. 30.)

Der Andere Theil.

Vom Sprengwasser.

v. 9. Und ein reiner Mann sol die Aschen von der Kuh auffraffen / und sie schütten ausser dem Läger an eine reine Stätte / daß sie ~~daß sie~~ daselbst verwahret werde für die Gemeine der Kinder Israel zum Sprengwasser. (Auf die Asche ward Wasser gegossen / und durchgeseiget / daß es wie eine Lauge ward / und ward Sprengwasser / und das Wasser der Absonderung genand / weil die unreine abgesonderte damit zu ihrer Reinigung besprenget worden. Dieses Fürbild ist Ebr. IX. 13. erkläret.) denn es ist ein Sündopffer / (den Sündopffern gleich / dienend zu reinigen von der Levitischen Unreinigkeit.)

v. 10. Derselbe / der die Asche der Kuh auffgeraffet hat / sol seine Kleider waschen / und unrein seyn biß an den Abend. Das sol ein ewig Recht seyn / den Kindern Israel / und den Frembdlingen / die unter euch wohnen. (Jedoch / da sie die Jüdische Religion und Beschneidung angenommen haben.)

Der Dritte Theil.

Nutz des Sprengwassers.

v. 11. Wer nun irgend einen todten Menschen anrühret / der wird sieben Tage unrein seyn. (Hiermit wird angedeutet / daß die / so mit todten Wercken ihr Gewissen verunreiniget / Ebr. IX. 14 keinen Zugang in das Himmlische Heiligthum haben / Offenb. XXI. 26. 2. Cor. VI. 27. 1. Tim. V. 22.)

v. 12. Der sol sich hiermit entsündigen am dritten Tage / und am siebenden Tage / so wird er rein / und wo er sich nicht am dritten Tage und am siebenden Tage entsündiget so wird er unrein seyn. (Weil er meine Ordnung verwerffend / sich nach derselbigen nicht zu reinigen begehret / darumb er mehr mit Unreinigkeit der Sünden sich durch Ungehorsam besudelt.)

v. 13. Wenn aber iemand irgend einen todten Menschen anrühret / und sich nicht entsündigen wolt / der verunreiniget die Wohnung des HERRN. (Wenn er zu derselben mit andern reinen kommt /) und solche Seele (solcher Mensch) sol ausgerottet werden aus Israel / darumb / daß das Sprengwasser nicht über ihn gesprenget ist: so ist er unrein / so lange er sich davon reinigen läst. (darin er endlich sterben muß / wegen schnöder und beharrlicher Verachtung meines Gesetzes / ja als ein Verächter dessen / das hier abgebildet war / der Reinigung des Bluts Christi / Ebr VI. 5. 6. c. X. 25. folg.) + nicht

v. 14. Das ist dis Gesetz / wenn ein Mensch in der Hütten stirbt / (wer bey seinem Todt zugegen ist in der Hütten / und ehe der Verstorbene begraben ist /) wer in die Hütten

32

33 Vol. 1/I, col. 901–02. On Numbers 25:1. There is no marginal comment or underlining here, but the quotation from Luther deals with the question of apostasy, falling away from the true faith. In "Das Andere Register" (the second index) at the end of Vol. 3/VI, this passage is the only one listed under *Abfall* (Apostasy) (see no. 76). The subject matter links with a book in Bach's library that is discussed under no. 69. Luther's comment is taken from his *Commentary on Hosea* (9:10):

> *Here it is useful to observe how easily a person can fall away from the true religion and how wicked and powerful the devil is. For it is highly significant that God compares the people of Israel, as it was led out of Egypt, to a grape and to the season's first fig. By this comparison he shows that this people received God's Word with enthusiasm and walked in the fear of God so that God delighted in this people and took special pleasure in its worship, godliness, faith, and adoration, for the first grape and the first fig delight the gardener most. But the people that walked so well in the fear of God and in faith was deluded by the devil and fell into shameful idolatry, and that idolatry turned into a cause of shameful lust, even as the story tells us, that they were invited to the sacrifice, that they ate, and that they worshiped the idol.*

901 Das Fünff und zwanzigste Capitel. 902

Das Fünff und zwantzigste Capitel.

(I.) Der Israeliten Hurererey/und Abgötterey mit den Moabitern/ v. 5.
(II.) Pineä Eyver/wider die Ehebrecher/und Gottes Wolgefallen darüber/ v.15.
(III.) Gottes Befehl die Midianiter zu schlagen. v.18.

Der Erste Theil.

Israels Unzucht / und Moabitische Abgötterey.

v.1. UNd Israel wohnet in Sittim/ (denn sie waren nun aus der Wüsten heraus kommen/und hatten sich im weiten Felde am lustigen Orth von Beth Jesimoth / biß an die Breite Sittim/ des Gefildes der Moabiter gelägert/ c. XXXIII. 49. welcher Orth vers. 49. Abel Sittim heisset/ woselbst Israel geblieben / biß nach Mosis Todt Josua sie nach Gilgal geführet/ Jos. I. 3. c. II. 1.) und das Volck hub an zu huren. (da sie kaum freye Lufft bekommen hatten: War eine schöne Danckbarkeit zu GOtt!) mit der Moabiter Töchter. (nach dem Rath Bileams/c. XXIV. 13. gereitzet durch die Schönheit des Moabitischen Frauenzimmers. H. Luth. T. IIX. Alt. p. 678. Es ist alhier sehr nützlich zu betrachten/ wie leichtlich einer von der waren Religion fallen kan/ und wie böse und gewaltig der Teuffel ist/ denn es ist nicht ein geringes/ daß GOtt das Volck Israel/ wie es aus Egypten geführet ist/ einer Trauben unn ersten Feigen vergleichet. Denn er zeiget damit an/ daß dis Volck das Wort Gottes mit Fleiß angenommen / und in Gottesfurcht gewendet habe/ also / daß GOtt seine Lust an ihm gehabt/ und an dieses Volcks Dienst / Gottesfürchtigkeit/ Glauben und Anruffung einen sonderlichen Wolgefallen getragen hat/ denn die erste Traube und die erste Feige die belustigen den Gärtner am sehrsten. Aber daß Volck/ das so fein in Gottesfurcht und Glauben daher gehet/wird vom Teuffel bethöret/und fället in schändliche Abgötterey/ welche darnach auch eine Ursach ist der schändliche Lust/ wie denn die Historie anzeigt / daß sie zum Opffer geladen sind/daß sie gegessen/ und den Abgot angebetet haben.)

v. 2. Welche (viel unterm Volck/ 1. Cor. X. 8. da gleichwol andere noch beständig geblieben sind/5. Mos. IV. 3. 4. Wir sehen aber/ ...

v. 4. Und sprach zu Mose: Nimb alle Obersten des Volcks / (die sich an den Baal Peor gehengt / und geistliche Hurerey getrieben haben/) und henge sie dem HErrn an die Sonne/(an den Galgen/) auff daß der grimmige Zorn des HErrn von Israel gewendet werde. (Vergl. 2. Sam. XXI. 6. 9. Wenn die Herren durch die Finger sehen/ und lassen frey Schande und Sünde im vollem Schwang gehen/so wil GOtt auch der Unterthanen Sünden an ihnen rechen und straffen/und das Blut von ihren Händen fordern/Ez. XXXIII. 8. Weißh. VI. 5 und da müssen denn die Fürsten in der Straff vorn an gehen.)

v. 5. Und Mose sprach zu den Richtern Israel: (nach dem die Obersten auffgehenget waren/) Erwürge ein ieglicher seine Leute / (die unter seinem Gericht seyn/ vermöge der im 4. Mos. XIIX. 25. gemachten Ordnung/) die sich an den Baal Peor gehenget haben.

Der Ander Theil.

Pineä Eyver.

v. 6. Und siehe ein Mann aus den Kindern Israel/ (ein Fürst/ davon v. 14. zu lesen/ der Gottes Straffe / die schon zum Theil ergangen war/ aus den Augen setzete/) kam/ und brachte unter seine Brüder eine Midianitin/ (eines Midianitischen Fürsten Tochter/ v. 15. mit ihr Unzucht im Lager zu treiben/) und ließ Mose zu sehen / (wie er sie führete) und die gantze Gemeine der Kinder Israel/ die da weineten ...

33

34 Vol. 1/I, col. 1041. On Deuteronomy 17:12. Simple insertion of the word *Obrigkeit,* which was omitted from the printed text, according to the list of typographical errors at the end of Vol. 3/VI.

1041 Das Fünffte Buch Mosis / 1042

dem sie dir sagen / an der Stäte / die der HErr erwehlet hat: und solt halten / daß du thust nach allem / das sie dich lehren werden.

v. 11. Nach dem Gesetz / das sie dich lehren / (nach der Erklärung des Gesetzes des HErrn / wie dasselbe durch den eigentlichen Verstand der Wort / und nach andern über einstimmenden Orten / muß gedeutet werden / damit nicht aus eignen Gutdüncken / sondern Schrifft durch Schrifft erkläret werde / 2. Petr. I. 20. 21.) und nach dem Recht / das sie dir sagen / soltu dich halten / daß du von denselben nicht abweichest / weder zur Rechten / noch zur Lincken.

v. 12. Und wo iemand vermessen handeln würde / daß er dem Priester nicht gehorchet / der daselbst in des HErrn deines GOttes Ammt stehet / (c. X. 8.) oder dem Richter / der sol sterben / (so ernstlich wil GOtt über die Hoheit und Gewalt der gehalten wissen.) und solt den Bösen aus Israel thun (wie v. 7.)

v. 13. Das alles Volck höre / und fürchte sich / und nicht mehr vermessen sey.

Der Dritte Theil.

Vom Könige in Israel.

v. 14. Wenn du in das Land kommest / das dir der HErr dein GOtt geben wird / und nimmest es ein / und wonest darinnen / und wirst sagen: (durch einen ordentlichen Gottseligen / und mit des HErrn willen gemachtē Schlus / dergleichen 1. Sam. IIX. 5. folg. nicht zu finden / darumb solcher von GOtt nicht gelobet worden ist / und GOtt gab ihnen einen König in seinem Zorn. Hos. XIII. 11.) ich wil einen König über mich setzen / wie alle Völcker umb mich her haben. (mir zu Schutz / aber nicht aus Mistrauen gegen GOtt / sondern daß sie sich Göttlichen Schutzes

nicht frembde Religion / Satzungen und Weisen auff dich ziehest.)

v. 16. Allein daß er nicht viel Rosse halte / (damit gar zu grosse Macht zu treiben / oder auf die Menge der Pferde und Wagen sich zu verlassen / wie von den Egyptern geschach / immassen sich Salomo wider dieses Gesetz versündiget hat / 1. Kön. IV. 25. X. 26.) und führe das Volck nicht wieder in Egypten / (weil daselbst grosse Menge der Roß waren / 1. Kön. X. 28. 2. Mos. XIV. XV. Es. XXXI. 1. 3. Ez. XVII. 15.) umb der Rösser menge willen (mit ihnen einen Bund zu machen / oder sich bey ihnen einzulassen / und in ihre Gemeinschafft zu treten / viel weniger sich gar dahin zu wenden /) weil der HErr euch gesagt hat / daß ihr fort nicht wieder durch diesen Weg kommen solt.

v. 17. Er sol auch nicht viel Weiber nemen / daß sein Hertz nicht abgewendet werde / (von dem HErrn / welches durch ausländische Weiber gar leicht geschehen konte / 1. Kön. XI. 4.) und sol auch nicht viel Silber und Gold samlen. (sein Hertz daran zu hangen / und sich darauf zu verlassen / Ps. LXII. 11. oder also / daß das Volck mit schweren Schatzungen beleget werde.)

v. 18. Und wenn er nun sitzen wird auf dem Stuel seines Königreichs / sol er dieses ander Gesetz (dieses fünfften Buchs Mosis /) von den Priestern und Leviten nemen / (in dem Haupt- und Grundtext / so von ihnen bewaret worden / 2. Kön. XXII. 8.) und auf ein Buch schreiben lassen.

v. 19. Das sol bey ihm seyn / und sol darinnen lesen sein lebenlang / auff daß er lerne fürchten den HErrn seinen GOtt / daß er halte alle Worte dieses Gesetzes / und diese Rechte / daß er darnach thue.

v. 20. Er sol sein Hertz nicht erheben über seine Brüder

34

35 Vol. 1/I, col. 1135–36. On Joshua 1:5. Similar words from Joshua 1:5 and Hebrews 13:5 are underlined and marked with "NB.": *I will not fail you or forsake you—I will never fail you nor forsake you.* Bach set the words from Hebrews on two occasions: in the second movements of Cantatas BWV 56 and 58.

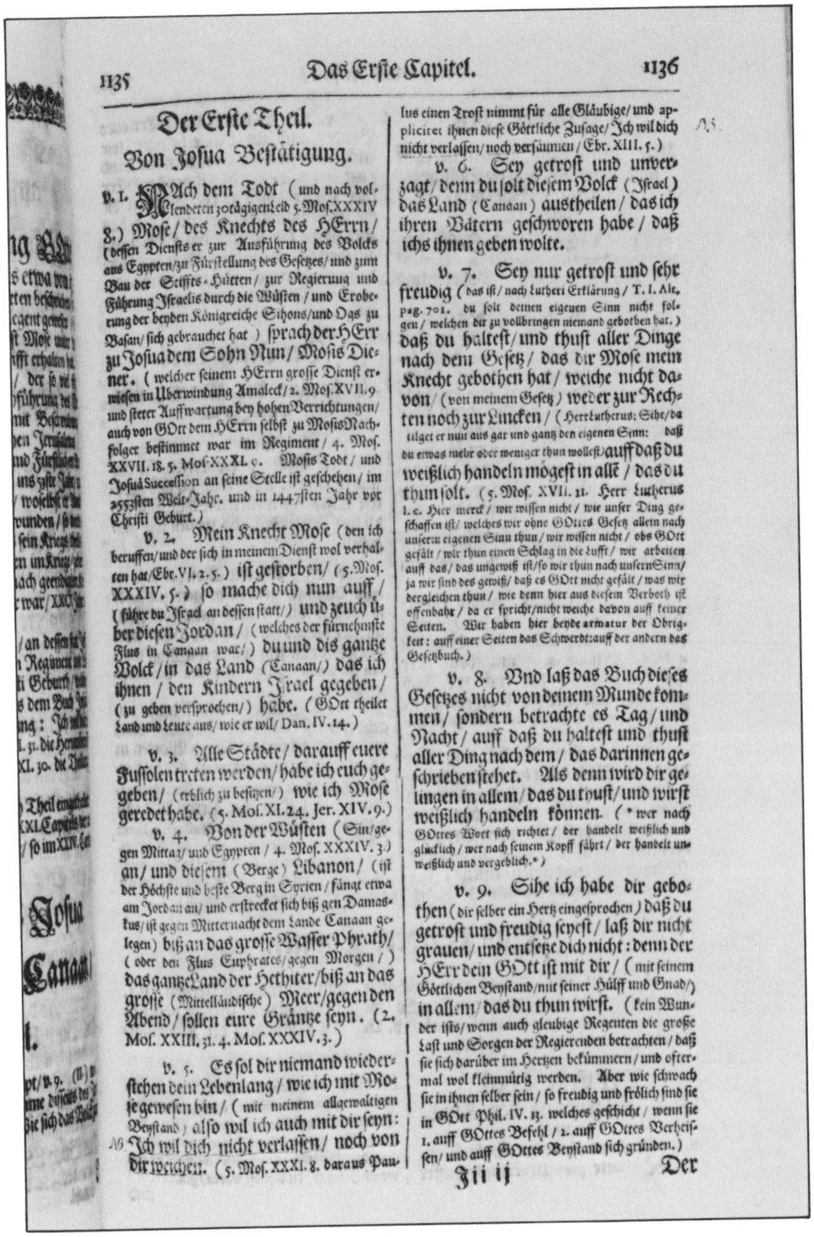

1135 Das Erste Capitel. 1136

Der Erste Theil.

Von Josua Bestätigung.

v. 1. NAch dem Todt (und nach vollendeten 30tägigen Leid 5. Mos. XXXIV 8.) Mose/ des Knechts des HErrn/ (dessen Diensts er zur Ausführung des Volcks aus Egypten/ zu Fürstellung des Gesetzes/ und zum Bau der Stiffts-Hütten/ zur Regierung und Führung Israelis durch die Wüsten/ und Eroberung der beyden Königreiche Sihons/ und Ogs zu Basan/ sich gebrauchet hat) sprach der HErr zu Josua dem Sohn Nun/ Mosis Diener. (welcher seinem HErrn grosse Dienst erwiesen in Uberwindung Amaleck/ 2. Mos. XVII. 9. und steter Auffwartung bey hohen Verrichtungen/ auch von GOtt dem HErrn selbst zu Mosis Nachfolger bestimmet war im Regiment/ 4. Mos. XXVII. 18. 5. Mos. XXXI. 9. Mosis Todt/ und Josuä Succession an seine Stelle ist geschehen/ im 2553sten Welt-Jahr. und in 1447sten Jahr vor Christi Geburt.)

v. 2. Mein Knecht Mose (den ich beruffen/ und der sich in meinem Dienst wol verhalten hat/ Ebr. VI. 2. 5.) ist gestorben/ (5. Mos. XXXIV. 5.) so mache dich nun auff/ (führe du Israel an dessen statt/) und zeuch über diesen Jordan/ (welches der fürnehmste Flus in Canaan war/) du und dis gantze Volck/ in das Land (Canaan/) das ich ihnen/ den Kindern Israel gegeben/ (zu geben versprochen/) habe. (GOtt theilet Land und Leute aus/ wie er wil/ Dan. IV. 14.)

v. 3. Alle Städte/ darauff euere Fussolen treten werden/ habe ich euch gegeben/ (erblich zu besitzen/) wie ich Mose geredet habe. (5. Mos. XI. 24. Jer. XIV. 9.)

v. 4. Von der Wüsten (Sin/ gegen Mittag/ und Egypten/ 4. Mos. XXXIV. 3.) an/ und diesem (Berge) Libanon/ (ist der Höchste und beste Berg in Syrien/ fängt etwa am Jordan an/ und erstrecket sich biß gen Damaskus/ ist gegen Mitternacht dem Lande Canaan gelegen) biß an das grosse Wasser Phrath/ (oder den Flus Euphrates/ gegen Morgen/) das gantze Land der Hethiter/ biß an das grosse (Mittelländische) Meer/ gegen den Abend/ sollen eure Gräntze seyn. (2. Mos. XXIII. 31. 4. Mos. XXXIV. 3.)

v. 5. Es sol dir niemand wiederstehen dein Lebenlang/ wie ich mit Mose gewesen bin/ (mit meinem allgewaltigen Beystand) also wil ich auch mit dir seyn: Ich wil dich nicht verlassen/ noch von dir weichen. (5. Mos. XXXI. 8. daraus Paulus einen Trost nimmt für alle Gläubige/ und appliciret ihnen diese Göttliche Zusage/ Ich wil dich nicht verlassen/ noch versäumen/ Ebr. XIII. 5.)

v. 6. Sey getrost und unverzagt/ denn du solt diesem Volck (Israel) das Land (Canaan) austheilen/ das ich ihren Vätern geschworen habe/ daß ichs ihnen geben wolte.

v. 7. Sey nur getrost und sehr freudig (das ist/ nach Lutheri Erklärung/ T. I. Alt. pag. 701. du solt deinen eigenen Sinn nicht folgen/ welchen dir zu vollbringen niemand gebothen hat.) daß du haltest/ und thust aller Dinge nach dem Gesetz/ das dir Mose mein Knecht gebothen hat/ weiche nicht davon/ (von meinem Gesetz) weder zur Rechten noch zur Lincken/ (Herr Lutherus: Sihe/ da tilget er nun aus gar und gantz den eigenen Sinn: daß du etwas mehr oder weniger thun wollest) auff daß du weißlich handeln mögest in allē/ das du thun solt. (5. Mos. XVII. 11. Herr Lutherus l. c. Hier merck/ wir wissen nicht/ wie unser Ding geschaffen ist/ welches wir ohne GOttes Gesetz allein nach unserm eigenen Sinn thun/ wir wissen nicht/ obs GOtt gefält/ wir thun einen Schlag in die Lufft/ wir arbeiten auff das/ das ungewiß ist/ so wir thun nach unsern Sinn/ ja wir sind des gewiß/ daß es GOtt nicht gefält/ was wir dergleichen thun/ wie denn hier aus diesem Verboth ist offenbahr/ da er spricht/ nicht weiche davon auff keiner Seiten. Wir haben hier beyde armatur der Obrigkeit: auff einer Seiten das Schwerdt: auff der andern das Gesetzbuch.)

v. 8. Und laß das Buch dieses Gesetzes nicht von deinem Munde kommen/ sondern betrachte es Tag/ und Nacht/ auff daß du haltest und thust aller Ding nach dem/ das darinnen geschrieben stehet. Als denn wird dir gelingen in allem/ das du thust/ und wirst weißlich handeln können. (* wer nach GOttes Wort sich richtet/ der handelt weißlich und glücklich/ wer nach seinem Kopff fährt/ der handelt unweißlich und vergeblich.*)

v. 9. Sihe ich habe dir gebothen (dir selber ein Hertz eingesprochen) daß du getrost und freudig seyest/ laß dir nicht grauen/ und entsetze dich nicht: denn der HErr dein GOtt ist mit dir/ (mit seinem Göttlichen Beystand/ mit seiner Hülff und Gnad/) in allem/ das du thun wirst. (kein Wunder ists/ wenn auch gleubige Regenten die große Last und Sorgen der Regierenden betrachten/ daß sie sich darüber im Hertzen bekümmern/ und offtermal wol kleinmütig werden. Aber wie schwach sie in ihnen selber sein/ so freudig und frölich sind sie in GOtt Phil. IV. 13. welches geschicht/ wenn sie 1. auff GOttes Befehl/ 2. auff GOttes Verheissen/ und auff GOttes Beystand sich gründen.)

Jii ij Der

35

kus/ ist gegen Mitternacht dem Lande Canaan gelegen) biß an das grosse Wasser Phrath/
(oder den Flus Euphrates/ gegen Morgen /)
das gantze Land der Hethiter/ biß an das
grosse (Mittelländische) Meer/ gegen den
Abend/ sollen eure Gräntze seyn. (2.
Mos. XXIII. 31. 4. Mos. XXXIV. 3.)

v. 5. Es sol dir niemand wiederstehen dein Lebenlang / wie ich mit Mose gewesen bin/ (mit meinem allgewaltigen
Beystand) also wil ich auch mit dir seyn:
NB. Ich wil dich nicht verlassen/ noch von
dir weichen. (5. Mos. XXXI. 8. daraus Pau-

35a

te Capitel. 1136

lus einen Trost nimmt für alle Gläubige/ und appliciret ihnen diese Göttliche Zusage/ Ich wil dich NB.
nicht verlassen/ noch versäumen / Ebr. XIII. 5.)

v. 6. Sey getrost und unver-
zagt/ denn du solt diesem Volck (Israel)
das Land (Canaan) austheilen / das ich
ihren Vätern geschworen habe / daß
ichs ihnen geben wolte.

v. 7. Sey nur getrost und sehr
freudig (das ist/ nach Lutheri Erklärung / T. I. Alt.
pag. 701. du solt deinen eigeuen Sinn nicht folgen / welchen dir zu vollbringen niemand gebothen hat.)
daß du haltest/ und thust aller Dinge
nach dem Gesetz/ das dir Mose mein

35b

36 Vol. 1/I, col. 1443–44, 1445–46. On 1 Samuel 16:14–23, the passage dealing with David's music that soothed Saul. There is no annotation or underlining here, but the passage is listed under *Musica* in the subject index at the end of Vol. 3/VI. It is clearly a passage that Bach must have referred to at some time or other. Indeed, at the end of the quotation from Luther at verse 23, the reference to "Syr. XI. 27" has been carefully changed to "Syr. XI. 26," although at the first attempt the 2 was changed into a 6. However, "27" is the correct reference. The quotation from Luther is taken from *Operationes in psalmos* on Psalm 5:12:

> *Therefore, as I have often said, our Saul, when he was troubled by the evil spirit from the Lord, had no easier or better medicine than that David should take the harp or psaltery and strike it with his hand; that is, when your soul is in distress, take and sing some psalm or else a spiritual song of your God and reflect upon it. You will soon feel relief and refreshment, and discover that the counsel of the wise man is good, when he says, Ecclesiasticus 11:27* [25 in English usage], *"In the day of prosperity . . . "*

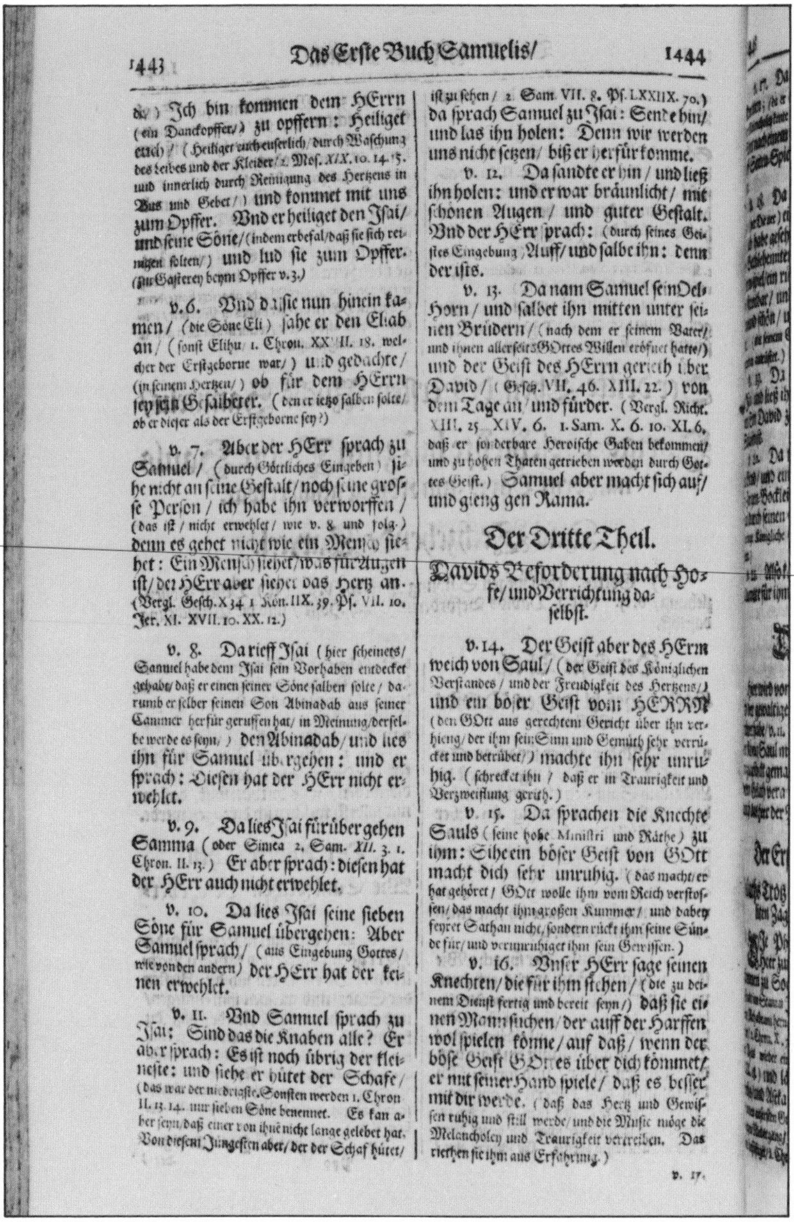

1443 Das Erste Buch Samuelis/ 1444

de/) Ich bin kommen dem HErrn (ein Danckopffer/) zu opffern: Heiliget euch/ (Heiliget euch euserlich/ durch Waschung des Leibes und der Kleider/ 2. Mos. XIX. 10. 14. 15. und innerlich durch Reinigung des Hertzens in Bus und Gebet/) und kommet mit uns zum Opffer. Und er heiliget den Isai/ und seine Söne/ (indem er befal/ daß sie sich reinigen solten/) und lud sie zum Opffer. (zu Gasterey beym Opffer v. 3.)

v. 6. Und da sie nun hinein kamen/ (die Söne Eli) sahe er den Eliab an/ (sonst Elihu 1. Chron. XXVII. 18. welcher der Erstgeborne war/) und gedachte/ (in seinem Hertzen/) ob für dem HErrn sey sein Gesalbeter. (den er ietzo salben solte/ ob er dieser als der Erstgeborne sey?)

v. 7. Aber der HErr sprach zu Samuel/ (durch Göttliches Eingeben) sihe nicht an seine Gestalt/ noch seine grosse Person/ ich habe ihn verworffen/ (das ist/ nicht erwehlet/ wie v. 8. und folg.) denn es gehet nicht wie ein Mensch siehet: Ein Mensch siehet/ was für Augen ist/ der HErr aber siehet das Hertz an. (Vergl. Gesch. X. 34. 1 Kön. IIX. 39. Ps. VII. 10. Jer. XI. XVII. 10. XX. 12.)

v. 8. Da rieff Isai (hier scheinets/ Samuel habe dem Isai sein Vorhaben entdecket gehabt/ daß er einen seiner Söne salben solte/ darumb er selber seinen Son Abinadab aus seiner Cammer herfür geruffen hat/ in Meinung/ derselbe werde es seyn/) den Abinadab/ und lies ihn für Samuel übergehen: und er sprach: Diesen hat der HErr nicht erwehlet.

v. 9. Da lies Isai fürüber gehen Samma (oder Simea 2. Sam. XII. 3. 1. Chron. II. 13.) Er aber sprach: diesen hat der HErr auch nicht erwehlet.

v. 10. Da lies Isai seine sieben Söne für Samuel übergehen: Aber Samuel sprach/ (aus Eingebung Gottes/ wie von den andern) der HErr hat der keinen erwehlet.

v. 11. Und Samuel sprach zu Isai: Sind das die Knaben alle? Er aber sprach: Es ist noch übrig der kleineste: und siehe er hütet der Schafe/ (das war der niedrigste. Sonsten werden 1. Chron. II. 13. 14. nur sieben Söne benennet. Es kan aber seyn/ daß einer von ihnē nicht lange gelebet hat. Von diesem Jüngesten aber/ der der Schaf hütet/ ist zu sehen/ 2. Sam. VII. 8. Ps. LXXIIX. 70.) da sprach Samuel zu Isai: Sende hin/ und las ihn holen: Denn wir werden uns nicht setzen/ biß er herfür komme.

v. 12. Da sandte er hin/ und ließ ihn holen: und er war bräunlicht/ mit schönen Augen/ und guter Gestalt. Und der HErr sprach: (durch seines Geistes Eingebung) Auff/ und salbe ihn: denn der ists.

v. 13. Da nam Samuel sein Oelhorn/ und salbet ihn mitten unter seinen Brüdern/ (nach dem er seinem Vater/ und ihnen allerseits GOttes Willen eröfnet hatte/) und der Geist des HErrn gerieth über David/ (Gesch. VII. 46. XIII. 22.) von dem Tage an und fürder. (Vergl. Richt. XIII. 25. XIV. 6. 1. Sam. X. 6. 10. XI. 6. daß er sonderbare Heroische Gaben bekommen/ und zu hohen Thaten getrieben werden durch Gottes Geist.) Samuel aber macht sich auf/ und gieng gen Rama.

Der Dritte Theil.

Davids Beforderung nach Hofe/ und Verrichtung daselbst.

v. 14. Der Geist aber des HErrn weich von Saul/ (der Geist des Königlichen Verstandes/ und der Freudigkeit des Hertzens/) und ein böser Geist vom HERRN (den GOtt aus gerechtem Gericht über ihn verhieng/ der ihm sein Sinn und Gemüth sehr verrücket und betrübet/) machte ihn sehr unruhig. (schrecket ihn/ daß er in Traurigkeit und Verzweiflung gerith.)

v. 15. Da sprachen die Knechte Sauls (seine hohe Ministri und Räthe) zu ihm: Sihe ein böser Geist von GOtt macht dich sehr unruhig. (das macht/ er hat gehöret/ GOtt wolle ihn vom Reich verstossen/ das macht ihm grossen Kummer/ und dabey feyret Sathan nicht/ sondern rückt ihm seine Sünde für/ und verunruhiget ihm sein Gewissen.)

v. 16. Unser HErr sage seinen Knechten/ die für ihm stehen/ (die zu deinem Dienst fertig und bereit seyn/) daß sie einen Mann suchen/ der auff der Harffen wol spielen könne/ auf daß/ wenn der böse Geist GOttes über dich kömmet/ er mit seiner Hand spiele/ daß es besser mit dir werde. (daß das Hertz und Gewissen ruhig und still werde/ und die Music möge die Melancholey und Traurigkeit vertreiben. Das riethen sie ihm aus Erfahrung.)

v. 17.

36

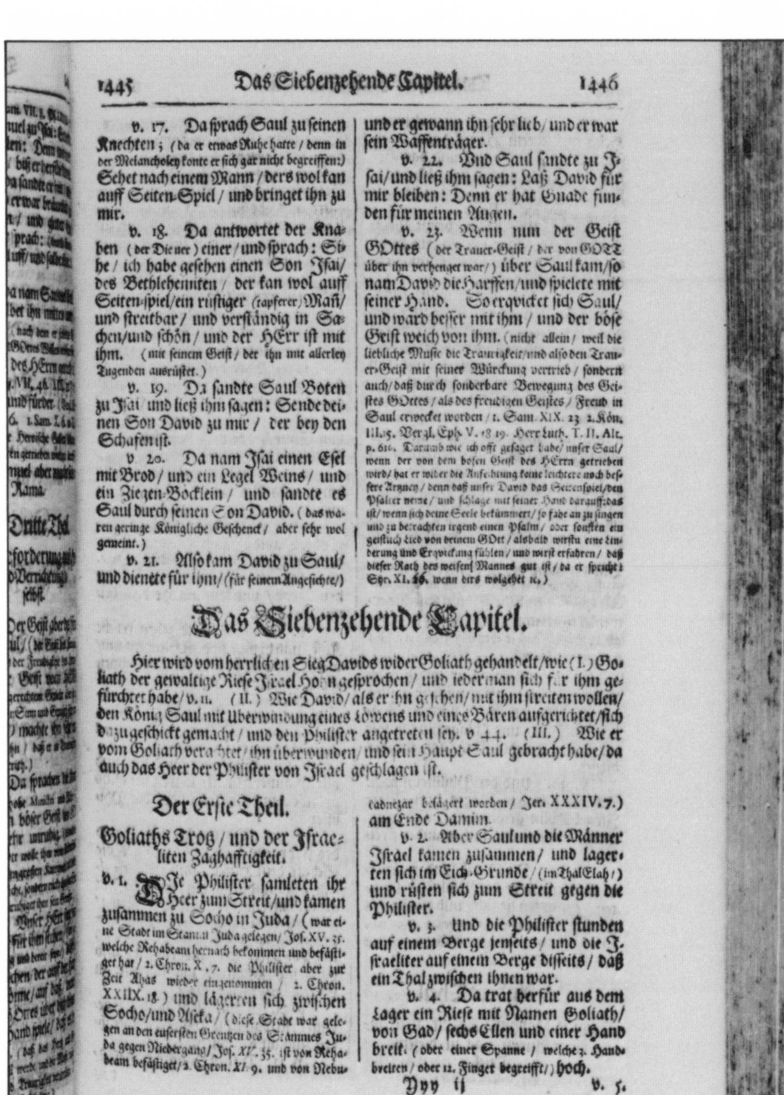

1445 Das Siebenzehende Capitel. 1446

v. 17. Da sprach Saul zu seinen
Knechten; (da er etwas Ruhe hatte / denn in
der Melancholey konte er sich gar nicht begreiffen:)
Sehet nach einem Mann / ders wol kan
auff Seiten-Spiel / und bringet ihn zu
mir.
v. 18. Da antwortet der Kna-
ben (der Diener) einer / und sprach: Sihe / ich habe gesehen einen Son Jsai /
des Bethlehemiten / der kan wol auff
Seiten-spiel / ein rüstiger (tapferer) Man /
und streitbar / und verständig in Sachen / und schön / und der HErr ist mit
ihm. (mit seinem Geist / der ihn mit allerley
Tugenden ausrüstet.)
v. 19. Da sandte Saul Boten
zu Jsai und ließ ihm sagen: Sende deinen Son David zu mir / der bey den
Schafen ist.
v. 20. Da nam Jsai einen Esel
mit Brod / und ein Legel Weins / und
ein Ziegen-Böcklein / und sandte es
Saul durch seinen Son David. (das waren geringe Königliche Geschenck / aber sehr wol
gemeint.)
v. 21. Also kam David zu Saul /
und dienete für ihm / (für seinem Angesichte /)
und er gewann ihn sehr lieb / und er war
sein Waffenträger.
v. 22. Und Saul sandte zu J-
sai / und ließ ihm sagen: Laß David für
mir bleiben: Denn er hat Gnade fun-
den für meinen Augen.
v. 23. Wenn nun der Geist
GOttes (der Trauer-Geist / der von GOTT
über ihn verhenget war /) über Saul kam / so
nam David die Harffen / und spielete mit
seiner Hand. So erqvicket sich Saul /
und ward besser mit ihm / und der böse
Geist weich von ihm. (nicht allein / weil die
liebliche Music die Traurigkeit / und also den Trauer-Geist mit seiner Würckung vertrieb / sondern
auch / daß durch sonderbare Bewegung des Geistes GOttes / als des freudigen Geistes / Freud in
Saul erwecket worden / 1. Sam. XIX. 23. 2. Kön.
III. 15. Vergl. Eph. V. 18. 19. Herr Luth. T. II. Alt.
p. 616. Darumb wie ich offt gesaget habe / unser Saul /
wenn der von dem bösen Geist des HErrn getrieben
wird / hat er wider die Anfechtung keine leichtere noch bes-
sere Artzney / denn daß unser David das Seitenspiel / den
Psalter neme / und schlage mit seiner Hand darauff: das
ist / wenn sich deine Seele bekümmert / so fahe an zu singen
und zu betrachten irgend einen Psalm / oder sonsten ein
geistlich Lied von deinem GOtt / alsbald wirstu eine Lin-
derung und Erqvickung fühlen / und wirst erfahren / daß
dieser Rath des weisen Mannes gut ist / da er spricht:
Syr. XI. 26. wenn dirs wolgehet rc.)

Das Siebenzehende Capitel.

Hier wird vom herrlichen Sieg Davids wider Goliath gehandelt / wie (I.) Goliath der gewaltige Riese Jsrael Hohn gesprochen / und iederman sich für ihm gefürchtet habe / v. 11. (II.) Wie David / als er ihn gesehen / mit ihm streiten wollen /
den König Saul mit Überwindung eines Löwens und eines Bären aufgerichtet / sich
dazu geschickt gemacht / und den Philister angetreten sey. v. 44. (III.) Wie er
vom Goliath verachtet / ihn überwunden / und sein Haupt Saul gebracht habe / da
auch das Heer der Philister von Jsrael geschlagen ist.

Der Erste Theil.

Goliaths Trotz / und der Jsraeliten Zaghafftigkeit.

v. 1. DJe Philister samleten ihr
Heer zum Streit / und kamen
zusammen zu Socho in Juda / (war eine Stadt im Stamm Juda gelegen / Jos. XV. 35.
welche Rehabeam hernach bekommen und befästiget hat / 2. Chron. XI. 7. die Philister aber zur
Zeit Ahas wieder eingenommen / 2. Chron.
XXIIX. 18.) und lägerten sich zwischen
Socho / und Aseka / (diese Stadt war gelegen an den eusersten Grentzen des Stammes Juda gegen Niedergang / Jos. XV. 35. ist von Rehabeam befästiget / 2. Chron. XI. 9. und von Nebu-
cadnezar belägert worden / Jer. XXXIV. 7.)
am Ende Damim.
v. 2. Aber Saul und die Männer
Jsrael kamen zusammen / und lagerten sich im Eich-Grunde / (im Thal Elah /)
und rüsten sich zum Streit gegen die
Philister.
v. 3. Und die Philister stunden
auf einem Berge jenseits / und die J-
sraeliter auf einem Berge disseits / daß
ein Thal zwischen ihnen war.
v. 4. Da trat herfür aus dem
Lager ein Riese mit Namen Goliath /
von Gad / sechs Ellen und einer Hand
breit. (oder einer Spanne / welche 3. Hand-
breiten / oder 12. Finger begreifft /) hoch.

Yyy ij v. 5.

36a

und ward besser mit ihm / und der böse
Geist weich von ihm. (nicht allein / weil die
liebliche Music die Traurigkeit / und also den Trauer-Geist mit seiner Würckung vertrieb / sondern
auch / daß durch sonderbare Bewegung des Geistes GOttes / als des freudigen Geistes / Freud in
Saul erwecket worden / 1. Sam. XIX. 23. 2. Kön.
III. 15. Vergl. Eph. V. 18. 19. Herr Luth. T. II. Alt.
p. 616. Darumb wie ich offt gesaget habe / unser Saul /
wenn der von dem bösen Geist des HErrn getrieben
wird / hat er wider die Anfechtung keine leichtere noch bes-
sere Artzney / denn daß unser David das Seitenspiel / den
Psalter neme / und schlage mit seiner Hand darauff: das
ist / wenn sich deine Seele bekümmert / so fahe an zu singen
und zu betrachten irgend einen Psalm / oder sonsten ein
geistlich Lied von deinem GOtt / alsbald wirstu eine Lin-
derung und Erqvickung fühlen / und wirst erfahren / daß
dieser Rath des weisen Mannes gut ist / da er spricht:
Syr. XI. 26. wenn dirs wolgehet rc.)

36b

37 Vol. 1/I, col. 1571–72. On 2 Samuel 12:12. By Calov's comment on the verse there is "NB" alongside the words "sie in der Pfalzischen Bibel," which are also underlined. Calov is taking contemporary Reformed theologians, the followers of Zwingli and Calvin, to task for misunderstanding Scripture in a gloss added in the margin of an edition of Luther's German translation of the Bible. This "Pfalzischen Bibel" is *Biblia . . . durch D. Martin Luther verteutscht. In dieser newen Edition . . . ist der Text . . . am rande . . . erklärt* (Heidelberg, 1617–18), which was often reprinted. It was the work of Paul Tossanus and was frequently attacked by Lutherans for its Calvinistic tendencies. This *Nota Bene* and the underlining links with the note that Bach added to the title page of his *Clavier-Büchlein vor Anna Magdalena Bachin Anno 1722* [MS. P224]:

Ante Calvinismus und
Christen Schule item
Anti Melancholicy } von D. Pfeifern

See *BD* 1:268; 4:142; *NBA* V/4 *KB,* pp. 22–23. The reference is to three titles by August Pfeiffer, which were in Bach's library at his death (see Leaver C, nos. 37, 36, 39). The manuscript book for his wife was begun by Bach during his service at the Calvinist court of Köthen. However, during this time he and his family attended the local Lutheran Agnuskirche, and he was concerned that his wife should be aware of the differences between Lutherans and Calvinists. The title page of the first of the three titles that Bach inscribed on the *Clavier-Büchlein* includes the statement that the book is a "report and instruction on Reformed religion, showing how far the Reformed, generally known as Calvinists, have departed from us Evangelicals [i.e., Lutherans] in their faith and doctrine."

See also no. 44.

37

38 Vol. 1/I, col. 1639–40. 2 Samuel 22:44. Bach completes the Bible verse with his marginal addition: ***und behütest mich zum Haupt unter den Heyden, ein Volk, das ich nicht kañte, dienet mir*** (thou didst keep me as the head of the nations; people whom I had not known served me).

38

Der Lobgesang des HErrn Messiä nach seiner Erhöhung/ sonderlich unter den Heyden.

v. 44. Du hilffest mir von dem zänckischen Volck. (das ist von den abtrünnigen Juden/die meine Ertzfeinde worden sind: davon werde ich erlöset/ die werden gar von dir verstossen S. Ps. II. 1. 2. 3. 4. Ps. XXII. 17. Ps. LXIX. 19. 25. Ps. XXXV. 19. 25. 26. Ps. CIX. 29. 30. 31. Matth. XXI. 42. 43.) F

F und behütest mich zum Haupt unter den Heyden ein Volk, das ich nicht kante, dienet mir.

v. 45. Den frembden Kindern hats wider mich gefehlet: (über diese

38a

39 Vol. 1/I, col. 2015–16. 1 Chronicles 16:4–34. Various underlinings of the Biblical text, which is headed "The Appointment of the Singers and the Singing of a Psalm of Thanksgiving." Since Bach was responsible for the appointment of the singers for the worship of the churches in which he was responsible for the music, this passage had a particular interest for him. It is connected with the later passage, 1 Chronicles 25, to which he has added a significant marginal comment (see no. 40). Note that the chapter is wrongly given as 17. The error is to be traced back to col. 1971–72, where the fifth chapter is headed: "Das Sechste Capitel."

2015 Das Siebenzehende Capitel. 2016

man ꝛc. Sie haben aber alle sechs Schritte stil gehalten / und alsdenn hat man einen Ochsen und ein Fett Schaf geopffert / 2. Sam. *VI.* 13.) sieben Farren und sieben Widder. (weil sie nicht nur still gehalten / sondern auch die Lade abgeladen und andere an ihre Stelle getreten / haben sie sieben Farren und sieben Widder geopffert.)

v. 27. Und David hatte einen leinen Rock an / (weil er sich mit den Leviten vermenget für dem HErrn / der bey der Lade des Bundes zu gegen war / sich demütigend /) dazu alle Leviten / die die Lade trugen / und die Sänger / und Chenanja der Sangmeister mit den Sängern. Auch hatte David einen leinen Leibrock. (ein Ephod. 1. Sam. II. 18.) an.

v. 28. Also brachte das gantze Israel die Lade des Bundes des HErren hinauff / mit jauchtzen / Posaunen / Drommeten / und hellen Cymbeln / mit Psalter und mit Harffen.

Der Dritte Theil.

Michal verachtung über diesem Proceß.

v. 29. Da nun die Lade des Bundes des HErrn in die Stadt David kam / sahe Michal / die Tochter Saul / zum Fenster aus / (2. Sam. VI. 16.) und da sie den König David (ihren Herrn und Gemahl) sahe hüpfen und spielen / verachtete sie ihn in ihrem Hertzen. (ja auch hernach mit spöttischen Worten wie 2. Sam. VI. 19. stehet / wie herrlich ist heute der König von Israel gewesen / der sich vor den Mägden seiner Knechte entblöset hat / wie sich die losen Leute entblösen: Aber der HErr hat sie darüber gestrafft / daß sie unfruchtbar worden ihr Lebenlang.)

Das Siebenzehende Capitel.

(I.) Die Lade des Bundes wird mit Opfern und Einsegnung des Volckes nieder gesetzet v. 3. (II.) Die Sänger werden bestellet / und wird durch Assaph ein Dancklied gesungen v. 26. (III.) Anordnung der Dienst im Heiligthum. v. 48.

Der Erste Theil.

Die Niedersetzung der Bundes-Lade zu Jerusalem.

v. 1. Und da sie die Lade GOttes hinein (in Davids Hauß) brachten / satztē sie sie in die Hütten / die ihr David auffgerichtet hatte / und opfferten Brandtopfer / (zur Versöhnung GOttes) und Danckopffer. (GOtt dem HErrn zu dancken für Erhöhung der Lade des Bundes.)

v. 2. Und da David die Brandtopffer und Danckopffer ausgerichtet hatte / segnet er das Volck im Namen des HErrn.

v. 3. Und theilet aus iederman in Israel beyde Mann und Weibern ein Laib Brodts / ein Stück Fleisches / und ein Nösel Weins. (*diese drey Ebreische Wörter / Cicar / Espar / Asisa / heissen nicht allein die Materia / als Brodt / Fleisch / Wein / sondern auch das Maaß und Gewichte / als so ich auff deutsch sprech / er gab ein Loth Brodts / ein Pfund Fleisch / ein Nössel Weins.*)

Der Andere Theil.

Bestellung der Sänger und Absingung eines Danck-Psalms.

v. 4. Und er stellete für die Lade des HErrn etliche Leviten zu dienen / daß sie preiseten / danckten / und lobeten den HErrn / den GOtt Israel.

v. 5. Nemlich Assaph den ersten / Sacharja den andern / Jejel / Semiramoth / Jehiel / Mathithja / Eliab / Benaja / ObedEdom / und Jejel / mit Psaltern / und Harffen / Assaph aber mit hellen Cymbeln.

v. 6. Benaja aber und Jehasiel die Priester mit Drommen allezeit / (alle Tage zu gewissen Stunden /) für der Laden des Bundes Gottes.

v. 7. Zu der Zeit bestellet David zum ersten dem HErrn zu dancken durch Assaph und seine Brüder. (Verwandten. Es scheinet als weñ sie bey diesem dancksagendem Chor bestellet / und in einen jeden sonderbare Directores und Sangmeister gewesen. Zuletzt aber habe das Volck mit dem Amē beschlossen v. 36.)

v. 8. Dancket dem HErrn / prediget seinen Namen / thut kund unter den Völckern alle sein Thun. (das ist ein Stück des CV. Psalms.)

v. 9. Singet / spielet / und tichtet ihm von allen seinen Wundern.

v. 10. Rühmet seinen heiligen Namen;

39

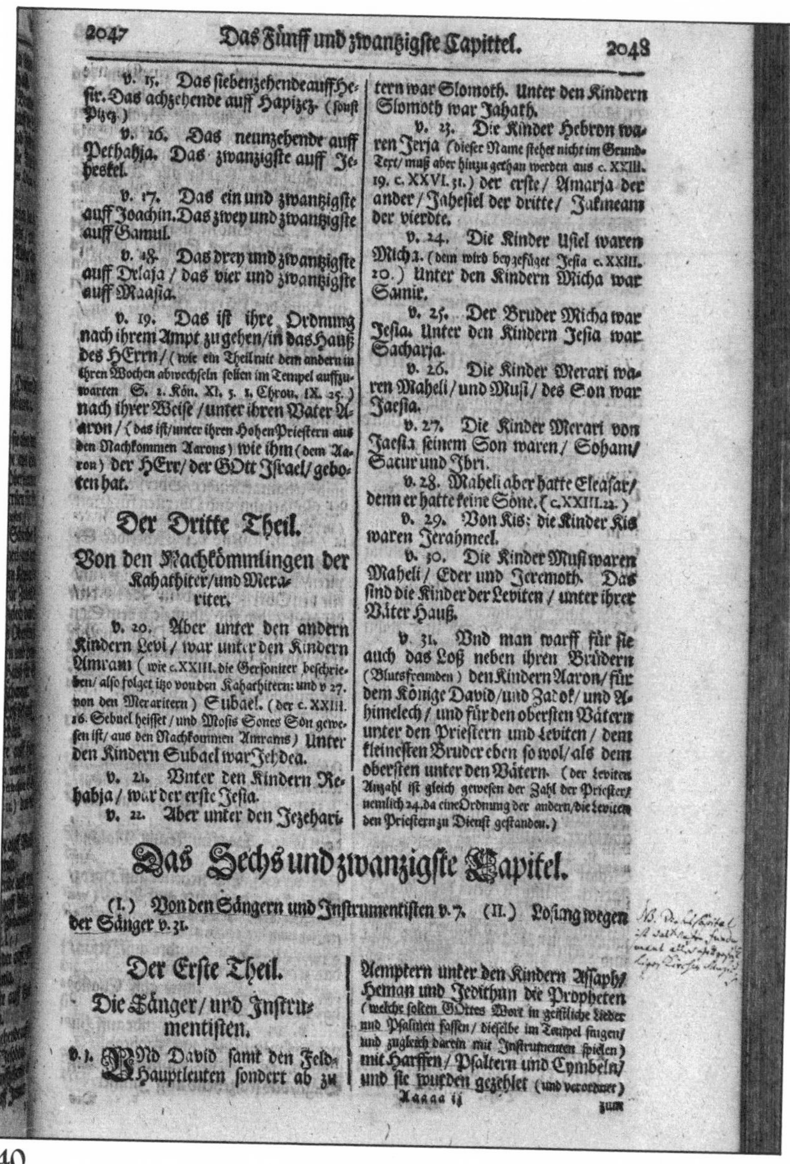

2047 Das Fünff und zwantzigste Capittel. 2048

v. 15. Das siebenzehende auff Hesir. Das achzehende auff Hapizez. (sonst Pizez.)

v. 16. Das neunzehende auff Pethahja. Das zwanzigste auff Jeheskel.

v. 17. Das ein und zwantzigste auff Joachin. Das zwey und zwantzigste auff Gamul.

v. 18. Das drey und zwantzigste auff Delaja / das vier und zwantzigste auff Maasia.

v. 19. Das ist ihre Ordnung nach ihrem Ampt zu gehen / in das Hauß des HErrn / (wie ein Theil mit dem andern in ihren Wochen abwechseln sollen im Tempel auffzuwarten S. 1. Kön. XI, 5. 1. Chron. IX. 25.) nach ihrer Weise / unter ihren Vater Aaron / (das ist / unter ihren Hohen Priestern aus den Nachkommen Aarons) wie ihm (dem Aaron) der HErr / der GOtt Israel / geboten hat.

Der Dritte Theil.

Von den Nachkömmlingen der Kahathiter / und Merariter.

v. 20. Aber unter den andern Kindern Levi / war unter den Kindern Amram (wie c. XXIII. die Gersoniter beschrieben / also folget itzo von den Kahathitern: und v. 27. von den Meraritern) Subael. (der c. XXIII. 16. Sebuel heisset / und Mosis Sones Sön gewesen ist / aus den Nachkommen Amrams) Unter den Kindern Subael war Jehdea.

v. 21. Unter den Kindern Rehabja / war der erste Jesia.

v. 22. Aber unter den Jezeharitern war Slomoth. Unter den Kindern Slomoth war Jahath.

v. 23. Die Kinder Hebron waren Jerja (dieser Name stehet nicht im Grund-Text / muß aber hinzu gethan werden aus c. XXIII. 19. c. XXVI. 31.) der erste / Amarja der ander / Jahesiel der dritte / Jakmeam der vierdte.

v. 24. Die Kinder Usiel waren Micha. (dem wird beygefüget Jesia c. XXIII. 20.) Unter den Kindern Micha war Samir.

v. 25. Der Bruder Micha war Jesia. Unter den Kindern Jesia war Sacharja.

v. 26. Die Kinder Merari waren Maheli / und Musi / des Son war Jaesia.

v. 27. Die Kinder Merari von Jaesia seinem Son waren / Soham / Sacur und Ibri.

v. 28. Maheli aber hatte Eleasar / denn er hatte keine Söne. (c. XXIII. 22.)

v. 29. Von Kis: die Kinder Kis waren Jerahmeel.

v. 30. Die Kinder Musi waren Maheli / Eder und Jeremoth. Das sind die Kinder der Leviten / unter ihrer Väter Hauß.

v. 31. Und man warff für sie auch das Loß neben ihren Brüdern (Blutsfreunden) den Kindern Aaron / für dem Könige David / und Zadok / und Ahimelech / und für den obersten Vätern unter den Priestern und Leviten / dem kleinesten Bruder eben so wol / als dem obersten unter den Vätern. (der Leviten Anzahl ist gleich gewesen der Zahl der Priester / nemlich 24. da eine Ordnung der andern / die Leviten den Priestern zu Dienst gestanden.)

Das Sechs und zwanzigste Capitel.

(I.) Von den Sängern und Instrumentisten v. 7. (II.) Losung wegen der Sänger v. 31.

Der Erste Theil.

Die Sänger / und Instrumentisten.

v. 1. Und David samt den Feld-Hauptleuten sondert ab zu Aemptern unter den Kindern Assaph / Heman und Jedithun die Propheten (welche solten GOttes Wort in geistliche Lieder und Psalmen fassen / dieselbe im Tempel singen / und zugleich darein mit Instrumenten spielen) mit Harffen / Psaltern und Cymbeln / und sie wurden gezehlet (und verordnet)

Aaaaa ij zum

40

40 Vol. 1/I, col. 2047–48. On 1 Chronicles 25. Bach adds various underlinings and the significant marginal comment: *NB. Dieses Capital ist das wahre Fundament aller gottfälliger Kirchen Music* (NB. This chapter is the true foundation of all God-pleasing church music). The comment links with two of Bach's letters in which he expresses his concern to compose and direct "God-pleasing church music." The first is dated 25 June 1708 and is his request for dismissal from the post of organist of the Blasiuskirche, Mühlhausen. In it he speaks of his concern for "eine regulirte kirchen music zu Gottes Ehren" (a well-regulated church music to the glory of God—*BD* 1:19; *BR,* p. 60). The second is dated 23 August 1730 and is a memorandum rather than a personal letter. It is addressed to the Leipzig Town Council and headed: "Kurtzer, iedoch höchstnöthiger Entwurff einer wohlbestallten Kirchen Music; nebst einigem unvorgreiflichen Bedencken von dem Verfall derselben" (Short but most necessary draft for a well-appointed church music; with certain modest reflections on the decline of the same—*BD* 1:60ff.; *BR,* p. 120ff.). Bach complains about the lack of adequate resources for the church music in Leipzig and asks the town council to improve the situation. Here in the Bible commentary, presumably only a few years later, Bach adds his comment and underlining to this important chapter, which has to do with the establishment of choral and instrumental worship for the people of God under the old covenant. King David had nearly 300 musicians; Bach had barely 30, and some of these were liabilities rather than assets!

In addition to the marginal comment there is also the underlining of the summary of the chapter: "(I.) Of the Singers and Instrumentalists. (II.) Appointment of the singers by lot." Also underlined is Calov's comment on verse 1 that the musicians are to "express the Word of God in spiritual songs and psalms, sing them in the temple, and at the same time to play with instruments: (cf. the underlinings of no. 39). These words of commentary make it clear that composition as well as performance should be the concern of the musicians who provide music for worship. Taken with Bach's marginal note, this underlining indicates that Bach understood his art in terms of the proclamation of the Word of God and his profession as a church musician in terms of divine order. "In this testimony Bach was deeply conscious of his own office as a church musician, ordained for him by God through David. Accordingly, the office was in his view not merely the name of a calling or the description of a sphere of activity, but on the basis of Biblical authority he identified himself as a called and ordained servant of the church" (Trautmann B, p. 94). Further, the chapter makes it clear that not only vocal music but also instrumental music has its place in the worship of the people of God. Pietists in Bach's day wanted to restrict church music to simple congregational song, but the Leipzig cantor did not agree with them. Significantly, in Mühlhausen the pastor of the Blasiuskirche was a pietist, Johann Adolph Frohne, and that may have been a factor in Bach's seeking "a well-regulated church music to the glory of God" elsewhere.

Note that the chapter is wrongly identified as 26, for the same reason as noted at no. 39. See no. 44; see also M. Petzoldt, "Bibel, Gesangbuch, Katechismus: Johann Sebastian Bachs theologische Welt," *Cantate: Eine Handreichung für Pfarrer und Kirchenmusiker zum Schütz- und Bach-Gedenkjahr* 1985 (Kassel, 1984), pp. 33–34.

See also no. 44.

zwanzigste Capitel.

Instrumentisten v. 7. (II.) Losung wegen

Aemptern unter den Kindern Assaph/ Heman und Jedithun die Propheten (welche solten GOttes Wort in geistliche Lieder und Psalmen fassen/ dieselbe im Tempel singen/ und zugleich darein mit Instrumenten spielen) mit Harffen/ Psaltern und Cymbeln/ und sie wurden gezehlet (und verordnet)

Aaaaa ij zum

40a

41 Vol. 1/I, col. 2063–64. On 1 Chronicles 28:21. Alongside Calov's commentary on the verse Bach has added: *NB. Ein herrlicher Beweiss, dass neben anderen Anstalten des Gottesdienstes, besonders auch die Musica von Gottes Geist durch David mit angeordnet worden* (NB. Splendid proof that, besides other arrangements of the service of worship, music too was instituted by the Spirit of God through David). Verse 21 reads: "Behold the divisions of the priests and the Levites for all the service of the house of God; and with you in all the work will be every willing man who has skill for any kind of service; also the officers and all the people will be wholly at your command." Calov's commentary, which Bach marked for emphasis in the margin, runs:

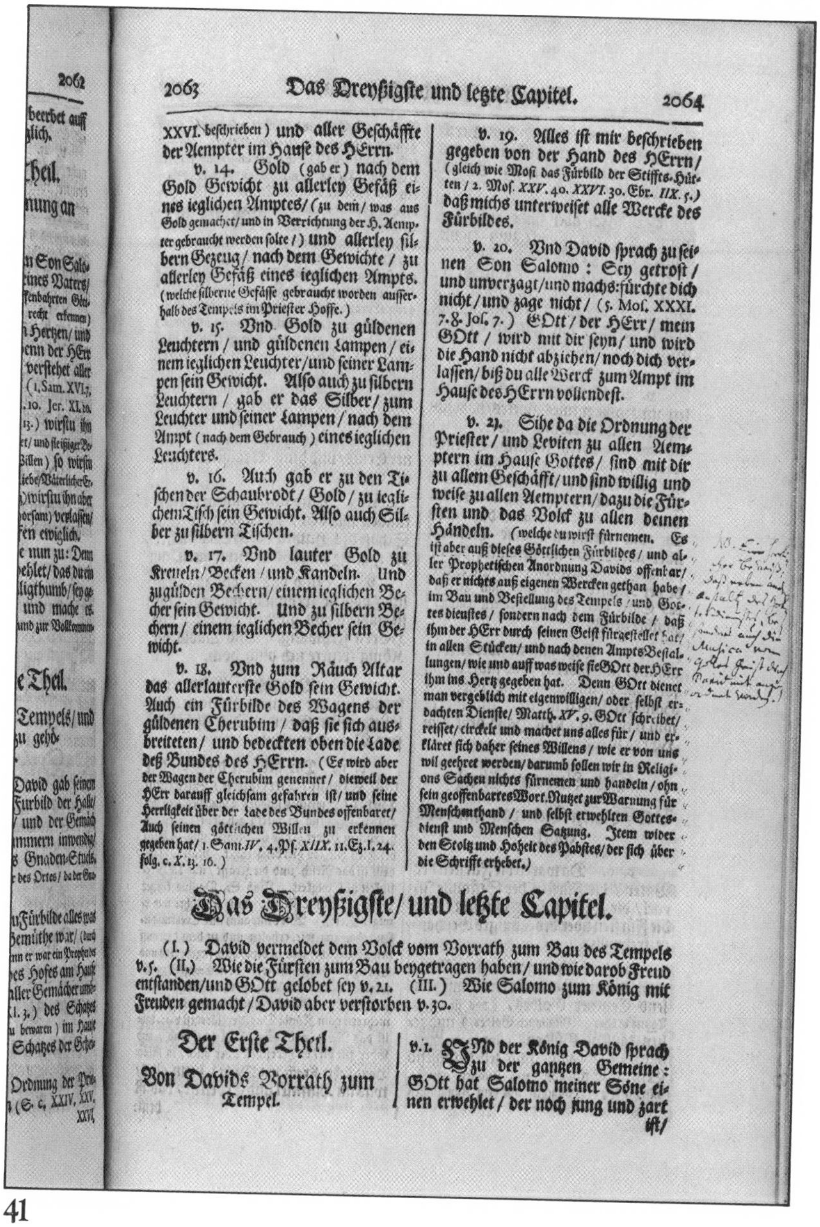

> *Now it is clear from this divine example and all the prophetic institutions of David that he did nothing on his own initiative in connection with the building of the temple and arranging the service but that he in all things acted according to the plan which the Lord through His Spirit communicated to him and according to those institutions and offices, exactly as the Lord God had instructed his heart. For we serve God in vain when we insist on our will and on services we dream up ourselves, Matt. 15:9. God prescribes, outlines, encircles, and shows us all things and therefore reveals His will, how He wishes to be honored by us. Therefore in matters of religion we should not plan and do anything without His revealed Word. Use this as a warning against human deception, self-chosen worship, and man-made rules. Similarly, it is contrary to the arrogance and haughtiness of the papists who raise themselves above Scripture.*

41

Here Bach goes further than his marginal note on 1 Chron. 25 (no. 40) and explicitly states that music in the liturgy is a Spirit-given institution. It needs to be remembered that the musicians of the old covenant were a division of the Levites and were thus "ordained" to their office. Thus music, and those who perform it, are not to be regarded as optional extras that can easily be dispensed with; they are essentials in the worship of the people of God. Although in theory orthodox Lutheran theologians regarded music in worship as being among the *adiaphora* (things indifferent), in practice they regarded it as indispensable (see J. Irwin, "Music and the Doctrine of Adiaphora in Orthodox Lutheran Theology," *The Sixteenth Century Journal* 14 [1983]: 157–72). Thus we find Bach accepting and endorsing the orthodox point of view rather than that of the Pietists (cf. the note on no. 40).

As with nos. 39 and 40, the chapter number has been increased in error by one and appears as 29 instead of 28.

See no. 44; see also M. Petzoldt, "Bibel, Gesangbuch, Katechismus: Johann Sebastian Bachs theologische Welt," *Cantate: Eine Hardreichung für Pfarrer und Kirchenmusiker zum Schütz- und Bach-Gedenkjahr 1985* (Kassel, 1984), pp. 34–36.

v. 21. Sihe da die Ordnung der
ter / und Leviten zu allen Aem-
im Hause Gottes / sind mit dir
em Geschäfft / und sind willig und
zu allen Aemptern / dazu die Für-
nd das Volck zu allen deinen
eln. (welche du wirst fürnemen. Es
auß dieses Göttlichen Fürbildes / und al-
phetischen Anordnung Davids offenbar /
ichts auß eigenen Wercken gethan habe /
u und Bestellung des Tempels / und Got-
stes / sondern nach dem Fürbilde / daß
HErr durch seinen Geist fürgestellet hat /
Stücken / und nach denen AmptsBestal-
wie und auff was weise sie GOtt der HErr
Hertz gegeben hat. Denn GOtt dienet
rgeblich mit eigenwilligen / oder selbst er-
Dienste / Matth. XV. 9. GOtt schreibet /
irckelt und machet uns alles für / und er-

41a

42 Vol. 1/I, col. 2087–88. On 2 Chronicles 5:13. Bach adds the marginal note: *NB. Bey einer andächtig Musig ist allezeit Gott mit seiner Gnaden Gegenwart* (NB. Where there is devotional music, God with His grace is always present). This entry is in black ink, but there are also a few underlings in red in verses 12 and 13, as well as the words "Beautiful Music" in the subtitle at the top of col. 2088: "How the Glory of the Lord Appeared After Beautiful Music." The Bible verse reads:

> *And it was the duty of the trumpeters and singers to make themselves heard in unison in praise and thanksgiving to the Lord, and when the song was raised, with trumpets and cymbals and other musical instruments, in praise to the Lord, "For He is good, for His steadfast love endures for ever," the house, the house of the Lord was filled with a cloud.*

In his comment Bach has beautifully summed up the conviction that through appropriate music in the service of worship the worshipers become aware of the presence and grace of God. Trautmann concludes, "In the future this sentence may well be listed among the classic aphorisms of great musicians" (Trautmann B, p. 95). Although it is not a verbatim quotation, Bach's statement is reminiscent of some of Luther's thoughts on music that occur in his *Tischreden,* a volume Bach had in his own per-

42

42a

sonal library (Leaver C, no. 4). For example, "Die Musica ist eine schöne herrliche Gabe Gottes . . . .Die Noten machen den Text lebendig" (Music is a beautiful and glorious gift of God . . . .The notes make the text live—*Tischreden Oder Colloquia Doct. Mart: Luthers* . . . [Eisleben, 1566], fols. 578 recto and 577 verso).

See M. Petzoldt, "Bibel, Gesangbuch, Katechismus: Johann Sebastian Bachs theologische Welt," *Cantate: Eine Handreichung für Pfarrer und Kirchenmusiker zum Schütz- und Bach-Gedenkjahr 1985* (Kassel, 1984), pp. 40–41. The libretto of Cantata 194, written for the dedication of the church and new organ in Störmthal, picks up imagery from Solomon's dedication of the temple.

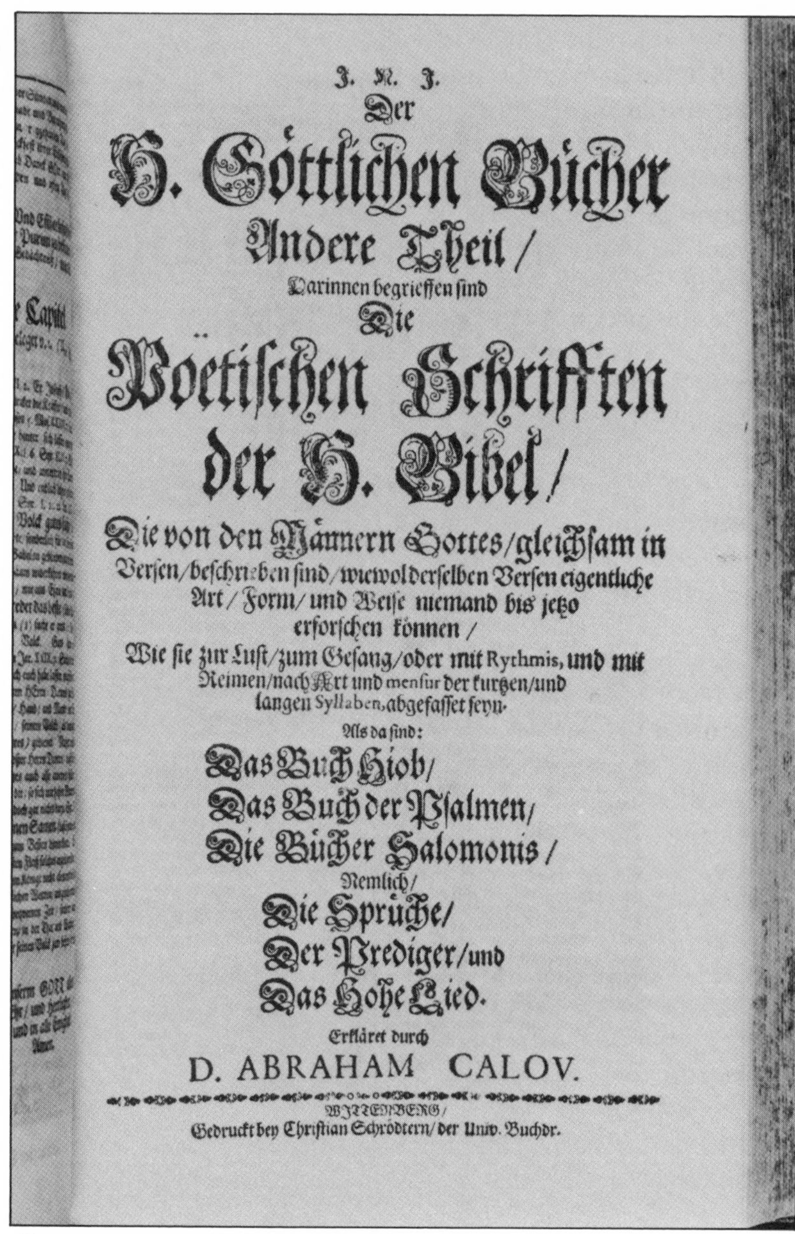

J. N. J.
Der
H. Göttlichen Bücher
Andere Theil/
Darinnen begrieffen sind
Die
Poetischen Schrifften
der H. Bibel/
Die von den Männern Gottes/gleichsam in Versen/beschrieben sind/wiewol derselben Versen eigentliche Art/Form/und Weise niemand bis jetzo erforschen können/
Wie sie zur Lust/zum Gesang/oder mit Rythmis, und mit Reimen/nach Art und mensur der kurtzen/und langen Syllaben, abgefasset seyn.
Als da sind:
Das Buch Hiob/
Das Buch der Psalmen/
Die Bücher Salomonis/
Nemlich/
Die Sprüche/
Der Prediger/und
Das Hohe Lied.
Erkläret durch
D. ABRAHAM CALOV.
WITTENBERG/
Gedruckt bey Christian Schrödtern/der Univ. Buchdr.

43

43 Vol. 1/II, title page:

J. N. J. The holy and divine books part two, in which are contained the poetical writings of the Holy Bible written in verse form, so to speak, by men of God, although no one has been able to fathom their peculiar character, form, and manner up to the present time, as they have been formulated for enjoyable singing or with rhythms and rhymes according to the measure of their short and long syllables. These are: The Book of Job, The Book of Psalms, The Books of Solomon, namely, Proverbs, Ecclesiastes, and the Song of Solomon. Expounded by Dr. Abraham Calov. Wittenberg. Printed by Christian Schrödter, the university's printer of books.

44 Vol. 1/II, cols. 213–14 to 224–25. Calov's preface to the psalter, which includes substantial quotations from Luther, is given in a complete English translation as Appendix 2.

Bach has underlined various words in red in two sections of the preface. First, in col. 217–18 (misnumbered 214–15) Bach has underlined thus (given here in Roman type):

> *Therefore the whole book is* called Psalterium, after the name of a musical instrument on which psalms, hymns, and songs of thanksgiving are accompanied. ***Many beautiful names have been given to it. Basil the Great called it a rich, common storehouse . . . of all good teaching, in which one can find . . . all the medicines to counteract the poison of souls,*** . . . to voice all kinds of beautiful melodies and arrange angelic songs. ***Athanasius calls the psalter*** . . .

213 214

J. N. J.

Das heilige Psalm-Buch.

VORREDE

über den

Psalter Davids.

Dieses H. Buch des Königs / und Propheten Davids bestätiget recht den Göttlichen Ausspruch Es. XXXII. 8. Fürsten werden Fürstliche Gedancken haben: als welches von dem Fürsten-Geist / wie David den Heiligen Geist Ps. LI. 14. nennet / eingegeben ist: immaßen David mit voller Feder bezeuget 2. Sam. XXIII. 2. 3. der Geist des HErrn hat durch mich geredet / und seine Rede ist durch meine Zunge geschehen: Es hat der GOtt Israel (GOtt der ewige Vater) zu mir gesprochen / (was ich durch seinen Geist ausgesprochen habe / Gesch. I. 4. wie es mir von GOtt eingegeben war / 2. Tim. III. 16. 2. Petr. I. 21. denn meine Zunge ist ein Griffel eines guten Schreibers / des werthen Heil. Geistes / Ps. XLV. 2.) der Hort Israel hat (in mir / und durch mich) geredet / der gerechte Herrscher unter den Menschen / (der Son Gottes / der da Recht und Gerechtigkeit auf Erden anrichtet / und der HErr / der unsere Gerechtigkeit ist / Jer. XXIII. 5. 6. c. XXXIII. 15. 16. den David für seinen Herrn erkennet / Ps. CX. 1. und als dem Herrscher des gantzen Erdbodens einführet / Ps. XCVII. 5. und von ihm v. 2. daselbst singet: Gerechtigkeit / und Gericht ist seines Stuels Festung / und v. 6. Die Himmel verkündigen seine Gerechtigkeit / und alle Völcker sehen seine Ehre /) der Herrscher in der Furcht Gottes / (wie denn auch auf ihm / da er als eine Ruthe von dem Stamm Isai aufgegangen / der Geist des HErrn / als der Geist der Erkäntnüß / und der Furcht des HErrn / geruhet hat / und sein Riechen gewesen ist in der Furcht des HErrn / Es. XI. 1. 2. 3.) und daher wird David von S. Paulo gepriesen / daß er den Geist des Glaubens gehabt / 2. Cor. IV. 13. dessen Psalmen der HErr Christus selbst / der grosse Prophet des HErrn / die selbständige ewige Weißheit / seinen Jüngern und Aposteln / den Lehrern der gantzen Welt / fürgetragen / erkläret / und nebenst den Schrifften Mosis / und der Propheten / als die einige von GOtt eingegebene Canonische Schrifft des A. Testaments / die Regel des Glaubens und Lebens des Israelis Gottes / commendiret Luc. XXIV. 44. 45. Gal. VI. 16. und daraus die hohe Glaubens Artickel von seiner Göttlichen Natur / und Erhöhung zur Rechten Gottes / nach der Menschlichen Natur / behauptet hat / Luc. XX. 42. weil David im Psalm-Buch davon gezeuget / Ps. CX. 1. 2. da er durch den H. Geist gesprochen: Der HErr hat gesagt zu meinen Herrn / setze dich zu meiner Rechten / Marc. XII. 36. Matth. XXII. 44. dessen Psalm-Buch S. Petrus für den ersten Jüngern n. 2. in öffentlicher Gemeine aus dem LXIX. Ps. v. 26. und abermal aus dem CIX. Ps. v. 8. eingeführet hat / Gesch. I. 20 folg. Gesch. II. 25. 35. aus dẽ XVI. Ps. v. 8. folg. und aus dem ietzt angezogenen CX. Ps. v. 2. und unser Himmlischer Meister / Rabbi / und Lehrer / der von GOtt kommen / Joh. III. 2. mehrmals dieses H. Psalm-Buch / als eine Göttliche Canonische Schrifft zur Erweisung der Glaubens-Stück gebraucht hat / so wol in den Tagen seines Fleisches / als Matth. XXI. 16. den IIX. Ps. v. 3. und Joh. X. 11. aus den XXIII. Ps. v. 1. und Joh. XIII. 18. den 10. vers. des XLI. Ps. Joh. XV. 25. den XXXV. Ps. v. 19. so wol Joh. X. 34. aus dem XXCII. Ps. v. 6. ingleichen Joh. XVII. 12. aus dem CIX. Ps. v. 8. und aus dem CXIIX. Ps. v. 22. Matth. XXI. 42. Marc. XII. 10. Luc. XX. 17. und am Stamm des Creutzes den XXII. Ps. v. 1. bey Matth. XXVII. 46. Marc. XV. 34. den LXIX. Ps. v. 22. bey Joh. XIX. 28. Item den XXXI. Ps. v. 6. beym Luc. XXIII. 46. als auch nach seiner Er-

44

One would expect Bach to notice the thought that the whole psalter is, as it were, a musical instrument on which to play the praise and thanksgiving of God, especially as the psalms were a constant source of inspiration to him. Again and again he set words from the psalms in his choral works. The following is a list of the principal settings:

Psalm	*BWV*
3:7	149:3
6:5	135:3
16:11	70:10, 140:6
19:1, 3	76:1
19:5	17:2
19:6	62:3
22:26	75:1
23:1–3	104:6
23:1–6	112
23:4	184:1
25:1–2	150:2
25:5	150:4
25:15	150:6
26:8	51:2
29:2	148
31:5	106:6
34:8	19:3, 149:3
34:20	245:64
37:20	64:5
38:3	25:1
40:7–8	182:3
40:11	52:6
42:1	148:3
42:3	138:2
42:5, 11	21:6
46:1	58:3
47:5–6	43:1
48:10	171:1
50:23	17:1
51:13	33:4, 105:2
57:10	17:3
65:1	120:1
65:3	193:2
66:1	51:1
68:19	43:2

Psalm	*BWV*
68:20	244a:5
72:1–2	Anh. 3
73:26	156:5
74:12	71:1
74:16–17	71:4
74:19	71:6
75:1	29:2
80:1	104:1
84:1–2	32:4
84:11	79:1, 2
85:10	29:4
85:11	119:2, 120:4, 190:6
87:2	193:1
88:1	98:2
88:10	48:5
90:12	106:3
94:19	21:2
96:8	148:1
97:11–12	195:1
98:1	16:2
103:1–6	28:2
103:2	69:1
103:13	17:7
103:13–16	225
103:21	Anh. 5:1
104:27–28	187:1
110:1	162:2
115:12–15	196
116:7	21:9
117	230
118:15	149:1
118:23	34:3
118:24	122:5
118:25	18:2
119:105	186:9
119:166	60:1
119:175	Anh. 5:1
120:5	30:10
121:4–5	193:2
122:6	34:5
122:6–7	Anh. 4:1
124	178
124:1–2	14:1
124:7–8	14:5
126:2	110:1
128:4–6	34a:3
130:1–2	131:1
130:1–3	38:1
130:3–4	131:2
130:5	131:3
130:6	131:4
130:7	131:5
138:2	51:2
138:7	103:4
139:7–10	55:2
139:23	136:1
142:12–14	119:1
143:2	105:1
145:15	23:3
146:1	143:1
146:5	143:3
146:10	143:5
147:9	138:3
149:1	190
149:1–3	225
150:2	225
150:4, 6	190:1
150:6	225

214 Vorrede. 215

auch die Griechische Kirche es genennet ein Buch der Hymnorum / und Lobgesänge / weil darinn viel geistreiche herrliche Lob- und Danckpsalmen zu finden: daher das gantze Buch Psalterium genennet wird / von einem Musicalischen Instrument / damit die Psalmen / Hymni / und Dancklieder gespielet werden. Und sind demselben viel schöne Namen gegeben worden: Es heisset dasselbe beym Basilio M. ein reiches gemeines promptuarium aller guten Lehre / darinn zu finden / was zu eines jedweden Heil dienlich ist / darin ein Schatz der volkommenen Theologi / und aller guter Vorrath verborgen ist / da alle Artzney der Seelen Gifft / und die böse Geister zu vertreiben / und den Englischen Schutz zu erhalten: alle Mittel / und herrliche Feyer- und Freuden-Tage anzurichten: allerley geistliche Opffer herfür zubringen / allerley schöne Melodeyen / anzustimmen / und Engliche Gesänge einzurichten. Athanasius heisset den Psalter einen kurtzen Begriff der gantzen H. Schrifft. Augustinus der Knaben Schutz / der Jugend Zierde / der Alten Trost / ein Register und Summarischen Inhalt des alten Testaments / Herr Lutherus ein Epitomen und kurtzen Auszug der gantzen Bibel. Andere gottselige Theologi nennen es einen Schauplatz der göttlichen Wercke / einen schönen Rosengarten / und liebliche Wiese aller schönen Blumen / einen anmuthigen Paradies / da nicht nur wolriechende Blumen / sondern auch angeneme Früchte zu finden: Ein weites Meer / darinn köstliche Perlen liegen / welche aber allein von denen gefunden werden / die die Sturmwinde der Anfechtung ausstehen: eine Himmlische Schule / darin wir GOtt den HErrn anreden: einen klaren Spiegel der göttlichen Gnade / darin das allerfreundlichste Antlitz des

44a

(Compare with the briefer listings in W. H. Scheide, *Johann Sebastian Bach as a Biblical Interpreter* [Princeton, 1952], pp. 37–38; W. G. Whittaker, *The Cantatas of Johann Sebastian Bach Sacred and Secular* [London, 1959] 2:498–99; M. Gorali, B. Hirshowitz, and T. Turel, *The Old Testament in the Works of Johann Sebastian Bach* [Haifa, 1979] passim; see further C. Wetzel, "Die Psalmen in Bachs Kantaten im Detempore der Leipziger Schaffensperiode," *Bach als Ausleger der Bibel: Theologische und musikwissenschaftliche Studien zum Werk Johann Sebastian Bachs,* ed. M. Petzoldt (Berlin, 1985), pp. 131–50.)

The second group of underlinings is to be found at col. 222–23:

> *According to their titles, the remaining 27* [Psalms] belong to the following . . . twelve . . . to the prophet Asaph, King David's Capellmeister. . . . *For even though Heman and Jeduthun were prophets (1 Chron. 25:1), as* Heman *is called a seer, that is, a prophet of the king "in the words of God, to lift up the horn" (1 Chron. 25:5; 2 Chron. 35:15), and* Jeduthun *is called a seer of King Josiah,* yet they served in instrumental music making as they had been

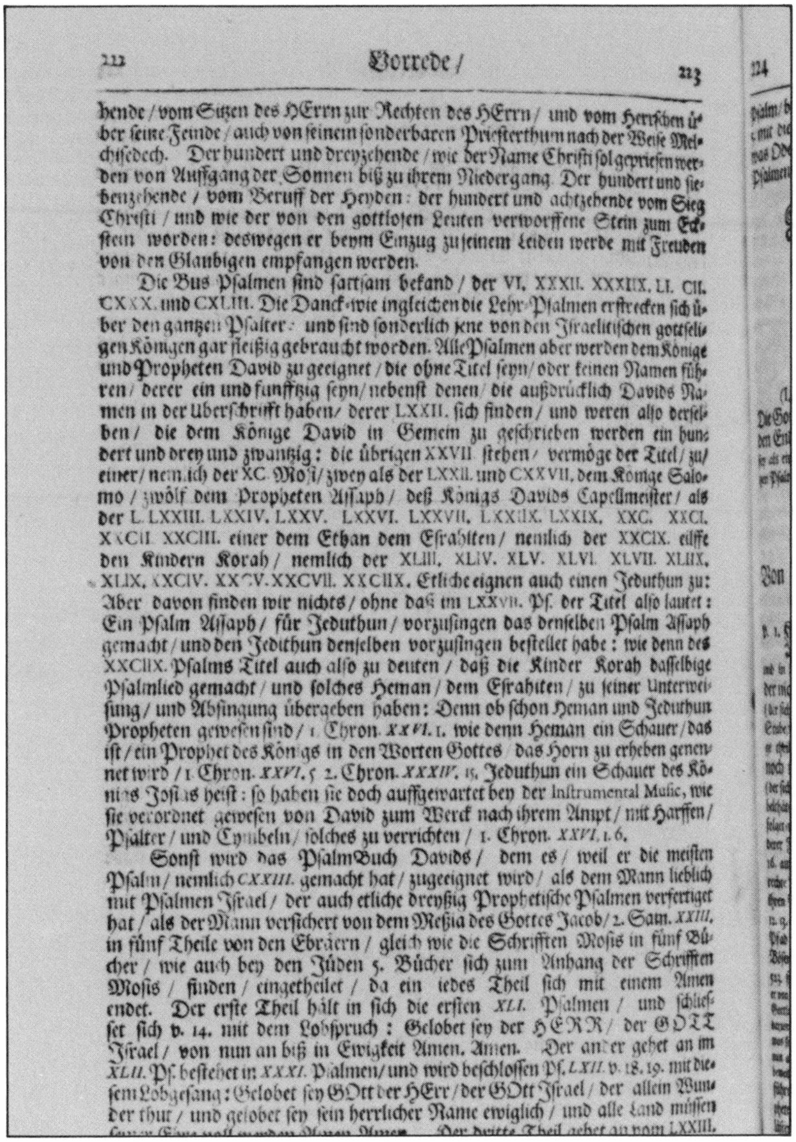

ordered by David for the work of their office to perform this "with harps, with psalteries, and with cymbals" *(1 Chron. 25:1, 6).*

That Bach should underline the statement that Asaph was the Capellmeister to the court of King David is hardly surprising since it was a title he himself had carried for a good many years. In 1717 he was appointed Capellmeister to the court of Prince Leopold of Anhalt-Köthen, and even though his employment at the court ceased in 1723 when he moved on to Leipzig, he continued to hold the title until the prince's death in 1728. The following year, 1729, he was awarded the courtesy title of Capellmeister to the court of Duke Christian of Sachsen-Weissenfels, which was terminated in 1736 on the duke's death. On 19 November 1736, Bach was appointed "Compositeur bey der Königlichlichen Hof-Capelle" (*BD* 2:278; *BR*, p. 151), that is, composer to the royal court *Capelle* of Friedrich Augustus II, elector of Saxony and king of Poland (Augustus III). Although the term *Capellmeister* was not included in the official title, it seems that Bach understood it that way. On 27 July 1733 he had petitioned the elector of Saxony, who had just succeeded to the title on the death of his father, for "ein Praedicat von Dero Hoff-Capelle" (a title of your Highness's Court Capelle—*BD* 1:74; *BR*, p. 128) in the letter he sent with the Kyrie and Gloria of the *Mass in B Minor* (BWV 232). The same letter also reveals that the Leipzig cantor made no artificial division between sacred and secular music. He writes of his energies "in Componirung der Kirchen Musique sowohl als zum Ochestre" (in the composition of church music as well as for the orchestra—*BD* 1:74; *BR*, p. 129). There is the temptation to see the work of a cantor in religious terms and that of a Capellmeister in secular terms. For Bach there was no such distinction. To be a Capellmeister is to be involved in the music making of both the court and the sanctuary, as the Biblical example of Asaph demonstrates.

This underlining links with the marginal comment alongside 1 Chron. 25:1: "NB. This chapter is the true foundation of all God-pleasing church music" (see no. 40). Within the area of the underlining there are no less than three references to that chapter. (Note that the references are to chapter "26" rather than "25" in the printed text. This was neces-

222 Vorrede / 223

hende / vom Sitzen des HErrn zur Rechten des HErrn / und vom Herrschen über seine Feinde / auch von seinem sonderbaren Priesterthum nach der Weise Melchisedech. Der hundert und dreyzehende / wie der Name Christi sol gepriesen werden von Auffgang der Sonnen biß zu ihrem Niedergang. Der hundert und siebenzehende / vom Beruff der Heyden: der hundert und achtzehende vom Sieg Christi / und wie der von den gottlosen Leuten verworffene Stein zum Eckstein worden: deswegen er beym Einzug zu seinem Leiden werde mit Freuden von den Glaubigen empfangen werden.

Die Bus Psalmen sind sattsam bekand / der VI. XXXII. XXXIIX. LI. CII. CXXX. und CXLIII. Die Danck- wie ingleichen die Lehr-Psalmen erstrecken sich über den gantzen Psalter: und sind sonderlich jene von den Israelitischen gottseligen Königen gar fleißig gebraucht worden. Alle Psalmen aber werden dem Könige und Propheten David zugeeignet / die ohne Titel seyn / oder keinen Namen führen / derer ein und funfftzig seyn / nebenst denen / die außdrücklich Davids Namen in der Uberschrifft haben / derer LXXII. sich finden / und weren also derselben / die dem Könige David in Gemein zu geschrieben werden ein hundert und drey und zwantzig: die übrigen XXVII. stehen / vermöge der Titel / zu / einer / nemlich der XC. Mosi / zwey als der LXXII. und CXXVII. dem Könige Salomo / zwölf dem Propheten Assaph / deß Königs Davids Capellmeister / als der L. LXXIII. LXXIV. LXXV. LXXVI. LXXVII. LXXIIX. LXXIX. XXC. XXCI. XXCII. XXCIII. einer dem Ethan dem Esrahiten / nemlich der XXCIX. eilffe den Kindern Korah / nemlich der XLIII. XLIV. XLV. XLVI. XLVII. XLIIX. XLIX. XXCIV. XXCV. XXCVII. XXCIIX. Etliche eignen auch einen Jeduthun zu: Aber davon finden wir nichts / ohne daß im LXXVII. Ps. der Titel also lautet: Ein Psalm Assaph / für Jeduthun / vorzusingen das denselben Psalm Assaph gemacht / und den Jedithun denselben vorzusingen bestellet habe: wie denn des XXCIIX. Psalms Titel auch also zu deuten / daß die Kinder Korah dasselbige Psalmlied gemacht / und solches Heman / dem Esrahiten / zu seiner Unterweisung / und Absingung übergeben haben: Denn ob schon Heman und Jeduthun Propheten gewesen sind / 1. Chron. XXVI. 1. wie denn Heman ein Schauer / das ist / ein Prophet des Königs in den Worten Gottes das Horn zu erheben genennet wird / 1. Chron. XXVI. 5. 2. Chron. XXXIV. 15. Jeduthun ein Schauer des Königs Josias heist: so haben sie doch auffgewartet bey der Instrumental Music, wie sie verordnet gewesen von David zum Werck nach ihrem Ampt / mit Harffen / Psalter / und Cymbeln / solches zu verrichten / 1. Chron. XXVI. 1. 6.

Sonst wird das PsalmBuch Davids / dem es / weil er die meisten Psalm / nemlich CXXIII. gemacht hat / zugeeignet wird / als dem Mann lieblich mit Psalmen Israel / der auch etliche dreyßig Prophetische Psalmen verfertiget hat / als der Mann versichert von dem Meßia des Gottes Jacob / 2. Sam. XXIII. in fünf Theile von den Ebräern / gleich wie die Schrifften Mosis in fünf Bücher / wie auch bey den Jüden 5. Bücher sich zum Anhang der Schrifften Mosis / finden / eingetheilet / da ein iedes Theil sich mit einem Amen endet. Der erste Theil hält in sich die ersten XLI. Psalmen / und schliesset sich v. 14. mit dem Lobspruch: Gelobet sey der HERR / der GOTT Israel / von nun an biß in Ewigkeit Amen. Amen. Der ander gehet an im XLII. Ps. bestehet in XXXI. Psalmen / und wird beschlossen Ps. LXII. v. 18. 19. mit diesem Lobgesang: Gelobet sey GOtt der HErr / der GOtt Israel / der allein Wunder thut / und gelobet sey sein herrlicher Name ewiglich / und alle Land müssen [...] Der dritte Theil gehet an vom LXXIII.

44b

sary since a whole sequence of chapter numbers in 1 Chronicles was misnumbered in the commentary; see on nos. 39, 40, 41.) Since both the underlining here and the marginal note alongside 1 Chron. 25:1 are in red ink, it is possible that they were written at about the same time. Indeed, it is quite possible that Bach was directed to that passage by this section; on reading this passage, Bach underlined what was important to him and then turned to look up the 1 Chron. 25 passage and was moved to add his marginal comment. Both here and in 1 Chron. 25 the musicians Asaph, Heman, and Jeduthun are referred to as prophets, which is revealing in this context. Prophecy, as the proclamation of the Word of God, is seen as having a musical dimension, and these men were given this task of "musical prophecy" by King David. By his underlining Bach appears to have endorsed this proclamatory function of church music. Calov, in his commentary on 1 Chron. 28:21, speaks of "all the prophetic institutions of David" in connection

und Propheten David zugeeignet / die ohne Titel seyn / oder keinen Namen führen / derer ein und funfftzig seyn / nebenst denen / die außdrücklich Davids Namen in der Uberschrifft haben / derer LXXII. sich finden / und weren also derselben / die dem Könige David in Gemein zu geschrieben werden ein hundert und drey und zwantzig: die übrigen XXVII. stehen / vermöge der Titel / zu / einer / nemlich der XC. Mosi / zwey als der LXXII. und CXXVII. dem Könige Salomo / zwölf dem Propheten Assaph / deß Königs Davids Capellmeister / als der L. LXXIII. LXXIV. LXXV. LXXVI. LXXVII. LXXIIX. LXXIX. XXC. XXCI. XXCII. XXCIII. einer dem Ethan dem Esrahiten / nemlich der XXCIX. eilffe den Kindern Korah / nemlich der XLIII. XLIV. XLV. XLVI. XLVII. XLIIX. XLIX. XXCIV. XXCV. XXCVII. XXCIIX. Etliche eignen auch einen Jeduthun zu: Aber davon finden wir nichts / ohne daß im LXXVII. Ps. der Titel also lautet: Ein Psalm Assaph / für Jeduthun / vorzusingen das denselben Psalm Assaph gemacht / und den Jedithun denselben vorzusingen bestellet habe: wie denn des XXCIIX. Psalms Titel auch also zu deuten / daß die Kinder Korah dasselbige Psalmlied gemacht / und solches Heman / dem Esrahiten / zu seiner Unterweisung / und Absingung übergeben haben: Denn ob schon Heman und Jeduthun Propheten gewesen sind / 1. Chron. *XXVI.* 1. wie denn Heman ein Schauer / das ist / ein Prophet des Königs in den Worten Gottes / das Horn zu erheben genennet wird / 1. Chron. *XXVI.* 5. 2. Chron. *XXXIV.* 15. Jeduthun ein Schauer des Königs Josias heist: so haben sie doch auffgewartet bey der Instrumental Music, wie sie verordnet gewesen von David zum Werck nach ihrem Ampt / mit Harffen / Psalter / und Cymbeln / solches zu verrichten / 1. Chron. *XXVI.* 1. 6.

Sonst wird das PsalmBuch Davids / dem es / weil er die meisten Psalm / nemlich *CXXIII.* gemacht hat / zugeeignet wird / als dem Mann lieblich

44c

with the worship of the people of God as being "Spirit communicated," and Bach added alongside: "Splendid proof that, besides other arrangements of the service of worship, music too was instituted by the Spirit of God" (see no. 41). Church music was therefore a "prophetic institution," a means whereby God's Word is proclaimed and applied; see also Bach's comment on 2 Chron. 5:13: "NB. Where there is devotional music, God with His grace is always present" (no. 42).

See no. 68.

45 Vol. 1/II, col. 871–72, 873–74. Psalm 148:14 and commentary on Psalms 149 and 150.

In col. 872 the word *erhöret* has been corrected to *erhöhet* in Psalm 148:14.

Col. 873 is referred to under *Musica* in the subject index at the end of Vol. 3/VI. Various verses from Psalms 149 and 150 were set by Bach in BWV 190 and 225. Calov comments on Psalm 149:1 that the new song sung to the Lord is, "as Herr Luther teaches, actually heard in the New Testament"; in other words, the "new song" is the message of the Gospel. On Psalm 150:3 Calov states: "This and the following two verses deal with instrumental music, which is improperly forbidden in the congregation of the saints by the Zwinglians. The last verse [v. 6] deals with vocal music" (see nos. 37, 42, 44). Calov's commentary on verse 6 runs thus:

871 Der Hundert und neun und vierzigste Psalm. 872

Stimmen/ so wol mit Instrumenten/ Ps. CXLIX. 3. Ps. CL. 3. 4. 5.) den Namen (die Ehre und Herrligkeit) des HErrn: denn sein Name allein ist hoch/ (so hoch/ daß er nach der ersten Taffel des Gesetzes soll geehret/ gelobet/ und gepreisen werden/ welche Ehre keiner blossen Creatur zustehet/ 2. Mos. XX. 3. Es. XLII. 8.) sein Lob gehet so weit Himmel und Erden ist. (er wird beyde im Himmel und auff Erden gepriesen.)

v. 14. Und er erhöhet das Horn seines Volcks/ (den HErrn Christum/ der das Horn Israelis und Davids ist/ Ps. XXCIX. 18. 25. Ps. CXXXII. 17. das Horn des Heils/ Luc. I. 69. von dessen Erhöhung Phil. II. 9. folg.) alle seine Heiligen sollen loben/ die Kinder Israel/ das Volck/ das ihm dienet/ (Altes und Neues Testaments/) Hallelujah. (lobet den HErrn.)

Der Hundert und neun und viertzigste Psalm.

(I.) Wie Israel den HErrn loben sol/ v. 3. (II.) Wie die Heiligen ihn preisen sollen wegen seiner gnädigen Hülffe/ v. 5. (III.) Wie sie ihn erhöhen sollen/ wegen Erlegung ihrer Feinde/ v. 9.

Der Erste Theil.

Wie Israel den HErrn loben soll.

v. 1. Hallelujah. Singet dem HERRN ein neues Lied/ (welches/ wie es Herr Lutherus lehret/ eigentlich ins Neue Testament gehöret/ vergl. Ps. XXXIII. 3. Ps. XCVI. 1. XCIIX. 1.) die Gemeine der Heiligen (die Kirche GOttes) sol ihn loben.

v. 2. Israel (die Gläubige Christenheit/ Gal. VI. 16.) freue sich/ (das ist das erste/ daß das Lob mit Freuden geschehen soll/ Rom. XIV. 17.) denn der ihn gemacht hat/ (Ebr. denen die ihn gemacht haben/ in der Schöpffung/ 1. Mos. I. 26. c. XX. 13. Job. XXV. 10. Pred. XII. 1. Es. LIV. 10. und erneuert zu seinem Volck/ 1. Petr. II. 9. und zu einer neuen Creatur 1. Cor. V. 17. Eph. II. 10. S. auch Ps. C. 3.) die Kinder Zion (die geistlichen Einwohner Zion/ oder Jerusalem/ Ebr. XII. 22.) seyn frölich über ihrem Könige. (das ist eine Freude in dem HErrn/ Phil. IV. 4. Luc. I. 32. 33.)

v. 3. Sie sollen loben seinen Namen mit Reigen (S. Ps. XXCVII. 7. Ps. LXIIX. 26. daß es also in Zusamenkunfften geschehe in ordentlichen Reigen/ 2. Mos. XV. 20. 2. Sam. VI. 14.) mit Paucken/ und Harffen/ (mit Musicalischen Instrumenten/) sollen sie ihm spielen. (S. Ps. XXX. 12. CL. 4. Jer. XXXI. 4. 13.)

Der Andere Theil.

Wie die Heiligen ihn preisen sollen/ wegen seiner gnädigen Hülffe.

v. 4. Denn der HErr hat Wolgefallen an seinem Volck/ er hilfft den Elenden herrlich. (Ps. CXLVII. 3. 6. Ebr. Er zieret die Armen mit Heil/ mit dem Schmuck JEsu/ Es. LXI. 10.)

v. 5. Die Heiligen sollen frölich seyn/ und preisen/ und rühmen auff ihren Lägern (oder beten/ auch in Trübsal und Kranckheit/ Rom. V. 3. Jac. I. 2. 3.)

Der Dritte Theil.

Wie GOtt zu erhöhen sey/ wegen seiner Gerichte.

v. 6. Ihr Mund soll GOtt erhöhen/ und (oder denn/ wie das Ebräische Vav offt so gebrauchet wird/) sollen scharffe Schwerdter in ihren Händen haben. (das erklären etliche von leiblichen Schwerdtern der Israeliten/ mit welchen die Richter offt gesieget haben wider die Feinde. Andere aber verstehen es vielmehr vom Schwerdt des Geistes/ dem Wort GOttes/ Eph. VI. 17. 1. Cor. X. 4. 2. Thess. II. 8.)

v. 7. Daß sie Rache üben unter den Heyden/ (sie wegen ihrer Abgötterey dämpfend/ aus GOttes Wort/ Joh. XVI. 4. 2. Cor. X. 4. 5. 1. Thess. II. 8. Ebr. IV. 12. Offenb. I. 16.) Strafe unter den Völckern. (sie zu überführen von der Göttlichen Warheit/ Offenb. XXI. 24. oder zu züchtigen/ wegen ihrer beharrlichen Verstockung/ wie Es. VI. 10. c. XLV. 14. Ps. II. 3. Gesch. XXIV. 25.)

v. 8. Ihre Könige zu binden mit Ketten/ und ihre Edlen mit eisernen Fesseln. (Es. XLI. 25. Mich. IV. 13. vergl. Offenb. II. 27.)

v. 9. Daß sie ihnen thun das Recht/ davon geschrieben ist/ (entweder sie von Sünden frey sprechen/ oder wegen des Unglaubens verdammen/ Joh. XX. 23.) solche Ehre werden alle Heiligen haben/ (daß sie das Wort

45

> Let everything that hath breath, praise the Lord *(this means the praise of the mouth, that is, from mankind on earth in whom is spirit and breath. The Lord God is to be honored and praised with instruments and voices in the temple and in the sanctuary where he dwells, and also in your prayers to heaven, for the Lord's throne is heaven and the earth is His footstool, Isaiah 66:1.)* Alleluia. *(that is, Praise the Lord. This praise goes from us now on earth, but it will be fulfilled in eternity. The prophet shows us this by the way he ends his fifth book of the psalter, and thereby the whole psalter, as St. Augustine says. St. John heard it in the voice of the great multitude in heaven, Rev. 19:1. It says: "Alleluia! Salvation and glory, honor and power be unto our God." Again it says: v. 3. "Alleluia! . . . v.4. And the four and twenty elders and the four beasts fell down and worshiped God that sat on the throne, saying, Amen! Alleluia!" Then St. John heard the voice of a great multitude: v.6. "as a voice of mighty thunderings, saying, Alleluia! . . . v.7. Let us be glad and rejoice and give Him honor.")*
>
> May the same true

and living God bestow his blessing on this exposition of the little Bible of the holy Psalter and receive from us this acclamation: Salvation and glory, honor and power throughout eternity.

Alleluia!
Amen!
Alleluia!

This eschatological aspect of church music was consistently expounded by Lutheran theologians and musicians; see, for example, the woodcut block that appears in Michael Praetorius's *Syntagma Musicum,* 3 vols. (Wittenberg and Wolfenbüttel, 1614/15–20), and *Musae Sionae,* 9 vols. (Magdeburg, 1605–10) (reproduced in C. Schalk, ed., *Key Words in Church Music: Definition Essays on Concepts, Practices, and Movements of Thought in Church Music* [St. Louis, 1978], p. 311). The woodcut clearly takes its imagery from the book of Revelation. It depicts three vocal and instrumental groups of the church on earth, which anticipate the antiphonal and instrumental music of heaven, and both the music of earth and the music of heaven are directed to the Lamb (see Rev. 4). Significantly, BWV 50, of which only a single movement exists, a setting of Rev. 12:10, is an antiphonal piece for double chorus (the movement probably comes from a no longer extant cantata for the Michaelsfest, possibly written in 1723; see W. H. Scheide, 'Nun ist das Heil und die Kraft' BWV 50: Doppelchörigkeit, Datierung und Bestimmung," *BJ,* 1982, pp. 90ff.).

873 Der Hundert und funfzigste Psalm. 874

das Wort GOttes/ haben daraus Weißheit und Verstand daß sie erhalten werden zur Seligkeit / 5. Mos. IV. 6. 2. Tim. III. 15. Jac. I. 21.) Hallelujah.

Der Hundert und funfftzigste / und letzte Psalm.

(I.) Wo der HErr zu loben/ v. 1. (II.) Warumb? v. 2. (III.) Womit / v. 6.

Der Erste Theil.

Wo der HErr zu loben sey.

v. 1. HAllelujah. Lobet den HErrn in seinem Heiligthum. (das ist/ in seinem Tempel / Es. III. 1. Vergl. Ps. LX. 8. CIIX 8. XX. 3. Es. LVII. 15. 1. Kön. XIX. 13 49. Andere/ wegen seiner Heiligkeit) lobet ihn in der Fäste seiner Macht. (das ist/ im Himmel / Matth. VI. 9. Ps. CXV. 16.)

Der Andere Theil.

Warumb der HERR zu loben sey.

v. 2. Lobet ihn in seinen Thaten (wegen seiner herrlichen Göttlichen Werck/ Ps. CXLV. 4.) lobet ihn in seiner grossen Herrligkeit. (das ist/ wegen seiner Grösse und Majestät / weil dieselbige es werth ist / Vergl. 5. Mos. V. 24. c. XXXII. 3.)

Der Dritte Theil.

Womit der HErr zu loben sey.

v. 3. Lobet ihn mit Posaunen/ lobet ihn mit Psalter und Harffen. (vergl. Ps. CXLIX. 3. diese und die zwey folgende Vers gehen auff die Instrumental-Music: Darumb denn solche in der Gemeine der Heiligen zur Ungebühr von den Zwinglianern verboten wird. Der letzte Vers gehet auff die Vocal-Music.)

v. 4. Lobet ihn mit Paucken/ (Ps. LXLIX. 3.) und Reigen/ (welches hier untern Instrumenten stehet/) lobet ihn mit Seiten und Pfeiffen. (S. 1. Mos. IV. 21. Job. XXI. 12. CXXX. 31.)

v. 5. Lobet ihn mit hellen Cymbeln/ (2. Sam. VII. 5. 1. Chron. XV. 16. 19. c. XVI. 42. Neh. XII. 27.) lobet ihn mit wolklingenden Cymbeln. (oder Cymbeln des Freuden-Schalls. Die Rede steiget/ Darumb ist dieses was mehrers/ als das vorhergehende/ S. Ps. XXVII. 6. Ps. XXXIII. 3. Ps. XXCIX. 16 hier erwehnet R. Ar. ms: daß die Posaune zum Neumonden / die Paucke zum Buß Tagen / der Psalter und Cither zum zehenden Tag des zehenden Monden / die Orgel zum Lauber-Hütten Fest/ die Cymbeln zum grossen Hosianna gebraucht seyn.)

v. 6. Alles was Othem hat/ lobe den HErrn/ (das gehet auff das Lob / so mit dem Mund geschicht / und zwar auff Erden von den Menschen / darzu Geist / und Othem gehöret: die GOtt dem HErrn beydes mit Instrumenten / und mit dem Loben im Tempel/ und im Heiligthum / da er wohnet / ehren / erheben/ auch ihre Andacht gen Himmel / denn des HErrn Stuel ist der Himmel / und die Erde seine Fußbanck / Es. LXVI. 1.) Hallelujah. (das ist / Lobet den HErrn. Dieses gehet hier auff Erden bey uns an / aber es wird vollenzogen in Ewigkeit: Dahin uns der Prophet weiset / wenn er sein fünfftes Buch des Psalters / und also den gantzen Psalter / damit beschliesset / wie denn zu jenem Loben das ewige Hallelujah gehöret/ wie der H. Augustinus davon redet. Davon hörete der H. Johannes eine Stimme grosser Scharen im Himmel / Offenb. XIX. 1. Die sprachen: Hallelujah / Heil / und Preiß/ Ehr und Krafft/ sey GOtt unserm HErrn: und sie sprachen abermal / v. 3. Hallelujah: Und die vier und zwanzig Eltesten/ und die vier Thiere fielen nieder / und beteten an GOtt/ der auff dem Stuel saß/ und sprachen: Amen / Hallelujah / v. 4. Da eine Stimme einer grossen Schaar gehöret ward / von S. Johanne/ v. 6. und als eine Stimme grosser Wasser / und als eine Stimme starcker Donner/ die sprachen: Hallelujah / lasset uns freuen und frölich seyn/ und ihm die Ehre geben.)

Demselbigen waren lebendigen GOTT sey wegen verliehenen Segen zu dieser Erklärung der kleinen Bibel/ des H. Psalters/ von uns gesagt/ Heil und Preiß/ Ehre und Krafft/ in alle Ewigkeit/

Hallelujah!
Amen!
Hallelujah!

Oo ij J.N.J.

45a

ihnen beydes die Gaben und Güter der Heiligung / und denn die Gaben / die zu ihrem Dienst und Ampt von nöthen ertheilet werden in diesem Leben / und sie dennoch nach diesem Leben / zur gnädigen Vergeltung / ein jeder zweyhundert Silberling zu erwarten haben.)

Der Dritte Theil.

Das Beschluß-Gespräch des Bräutigams / der seiner Liebsten lieblichen Stimme / und der Braut / die ihres Bräutigams Flucht / auf die Würtz-Berge / begierig ist.

v. 13. (O du allgemeine Apostolische Kirche /) Die du wonest in den Garten / (saget der himmlische Seelen-Bräutigam / die du in den vielen Versammlungen auf Erden / in aller Welt deine Wonung hast / welche mir eitel Lustgärten / wegen des lieblichen Geruchs / und der unterschiedenen schönen Verrichtungen seyn / von meinen Aposteln / und derer Nachfolger / aus allerley Völckern / Juden / und Heyden versamlet / Ps. LXIIX. 23. Matth. XXIIX. 19. Eph. IV. 11. S. dr. c. IV. 12. 16. VI. 1.) laß mich deine Stimme (die liebliche Stimme deines glaubigen Bekändtniß / deines inbrünstigen Gebets / deines hertzlichen Lobes / und deiner freudenreichen Dancksagung) hören: Die Gesellschafften mercken drauf. (die fromme heilige Geister und himmlische Gesellschafft hören mit Freuden zu.)

v. 14. Fleuch / mein Freund / (saget die geistliche Braut / eile und säume nicht lang / mein liebster Hertzens-Freund) und sey gleich einem Rehe / oder jungen Hirschen (c. II. 17. komm bald / und nimb mich zu dir / da du bist / auf daß ich deine Herrlichkeit sehe / Joh. XVII. 24.) auf den Würtz-Bergen. (auf den Bergen / und geistlichem Garten der Kirchen in dieser Welt / darin du mir beyzuwonen verheissen biß an der Welt Ende / Matth. XXIIX. 20. wenn auch nur zwey / oder drey in deinem Namen etwa versamlet wären c. XIIX. 20. da du alles erfüllest Eph. IV. 10. auf die himmlische Würtzberge / in das himmlische Jerusalem / Offenb. XXI. 10. woselbsten alle Pilgrims / und sehr unbeständige / offt unanmuthige Scheideberge zu beharrlichen / anmuthigen / wolriechenden Würtzbergen verkehret werden sollen / und alles Leid in Freud verwandelt werden wird Joh. XVI. 20. in jener Welt / und in den herrlichen Paradiß-Garten des ewigen Lebens / Offenb. XXI. 10. folg. daß ich nun erhaben werde / in deines Vaters Haus / da viel Wonungen seyn / Joh. XIV. 2. da die Scheideberge ein Ende haben / dr. c. II. 17. da werden wir allezeit bey einander seyn / 1. Thess. IV. 17. u. da alsdenn wird Freude die Fülle / und lieblich Wesen seyn immer und ewiglich / Ps. XVI. 11. da wird kein Sünden-Stanck mehr statt haben / Offenb. XXI. 4. sondern eitel lieblicher Geruch / dadurch Seel und Leib in Ewigkeit erfreuet wird. Ey so eile doch du mein Hertzens-Freund / und komme / uns zu dir anheim einzuholen. Gleich wie die Geistliche Braut im Anfang nach seiner ersten Ankunfft in diese irrdische Welt / zur Erlösung des Menschlichen Geschlechts / ein hertzliches Verlangen trug / c. I. 1. II. 8. 9. 17. also ist sie von Hertzen begierig / nach dem sie seine herrliche Gestalt im Glauben ersehen / auch seiner andern Zukunfft / zur völligen Seligkeit / da sie in ewiger Freud und Herrligkeit / bey und mit ihm / ungetrennet leben und schweben wird. Ach! da wird es gut seyn zu bleiben auf diesen Würtzbergen / wie S. Petrus Matth. XVII. 4. vom Berge darauf die Verklärung Christi / wie im Schatten und Fürbild fürgestellet ward / zeugete. Ach! komm doch mein werthester Hertzens-Schatz meine schönste Freuden-Krone / komm doch / und bleib nicht lange / deiner wart ich mit Verlangen! Ja komm! O JEsu / komm / AMEN!)

ENDE des Hohenliedes Salomonis / und des gantzen Ersten TOMI der Biblischen Erklärung.

GOTT allein die Ehre!

46

46 Vol. 1/II, col. 1201–02. The final page of the first (double) volume, which deals with the final chapter of the Song of Solomon. The imagery of the bride and the bridegroom from this book, which was interpreted in terms of the soul of the believer and the Savior, Jesus Christ, is taken up in a number of Bach's choral works (for example, BWV 27; 36; 49; 154; 244:1, 30; 248/I and IV, etc.). The final prayer of col. 1202 is taken up in a variety of forms in choral works that have to do with Advent or funerals (see BWV 21:8, 61:3, 106:2, 140:3, and 229:1).

Gott allein die Ehre is the German equivalent of the Latin *Soli Deo Gloria* (To God alone be glory). In the same way that it was literary custom to begin with a prayer expressed in the monogram "J. N. J." (In Nomine Jesu—see no. 1), so it was customary to end with an ascription of praise: *Soli Deo Gloria* or the abbreviation "S. D. G." Although he is not as consistent in his use of *Gott allein die Ehre* as he is with "J. N. J.," Calov nevertheless always completes a Biblical book with an expanded offering of praise. However, *Gott allein die Ehre* occurs nine times throughout the three double volumes, including here at the end of vol. 1/II and at the end of vol. 2/IV. At the end of vol. 3/VI (col. 1501–02) there is an expanded ascription of glory. The convention is not only found in literary works but also at the end of musical manuscripts. For example, all of the extant scores, numbering about 1,400, of Christoph Graupner's cantatas in the Hessische Landes- und Hochschulbibliothek, Darmstadt, have *Soli Deo Gloria* in full at the end (information from Dr. Oswald Bill, Darmstadt), and Bach's pupil Johann Ludwig Krebs did the same (see R. Sietz, "Die Orgelkompositionen des Schülerkreise um Johann Sebastian Bach," *BJ*, 1935, p. 41). Another pupil of Bach, Johann Peter Kellner, used the ascription in French: *La gloire au Dieu!* (ibid.). Bach himself tended to use the abbreviation "S. D. G." at the end of his manuscripts. However, when these manuscripts are investigated it is found that he used a variety of forms for the ascription. The following is a sample based on an examination of copies of most but not all of Bach's holograph full scores:

Form	*BWV and Manuscript Details*
S D G	13 (P45), 16 (P45), 19 (P45), 20 (PRudorff), 26 (P47a), 27 (P164), 32 (P126), 35 (P86), 36 (P45), 41 (P874), 43 (P44), 45 (P80), 47 (P163), 51 (P104), 52 (P85), 57 (P144), 58 (P866), 62 (P877), 76 (P67), 79 (P98), 82 (P114), 84 (P108), 85 (P106), 86 (P157), 88 (P145), 91 (P869), 92 (P873), 96 (P179), 98 (P160), 99 (P647), 102 (P97), 114 (PRudorff), 116 (PParisBN), 121 (P867), 122 (P868), 124 (P876), 127 (P872), 130 (PPrivate), 151 (PCoburg), 169 (P93), 175 (P75), 176 (P81), 180 (PStuttgart), 187 (P84), 197a (PNew York), 198 (P41), 207 (P174)
S D G1	14 (P879), 28 (P92), 66 (P73), 94 (P47), 97 (PNew York), 100 (P159), 103 (P122), 109 (P112), 110 (P153), 118 (Princeton), 133 (P1215), 134 (P44), 147 (P102), 171 (PKoch), 174 (P115), 177 (P116), 243 (P39), 244 (P25), 247, 248/I-IV, VI (P32), the anonymous *Lucaspassion* (BWV 247), and five cantatas by J. L. Bach: Nos. 1–4, 9 (see W. H. Scheide, "Johann Sebastian Bachs Sammlung von Kantaten seines Vetters Johann Ludwig Bach," *BJ*, 1959, pp. 53–54).
D S G	56 (P118), 128 (PWinterthur), 168 (P152), 170 (P154), 173a (P42)
D S G1	9 (PWashington), 112 (PPrivate), 120a (P670), 191 (P870), 213 (P125), 214 (P41), 232 at the end of the *Missa* and *Ossana* (P180), 248/V (P32)
D G S	11 (P44)
Laus Deo	67 (St377), at the end of the organ obbligato part.
Solio Deo Sit Gloria	(New Haven) at the end of the *Claview-Büchlein vor Wilhelm Friedemann Bach*, 22 January 1720 (*NBA* V/5 *KB*, p. 32).

At the end of the *Johannespassion* (BWV 245[P28]) are the letters "D. J. C. C. Gl." (*Domine Jesu Christe, Christo Gloria* [?]); however, they are of doubtful authenticity (see *NBA* II/4 *KB*, p. 21). At the end of his copy of J. L. Bach's Cantata No. 11 Bach has written "S. D. Gloria" (see Scheide, pp. 53–54). Copies of Bach's scores made by his pupils have the ascription *Soli Deo Gloria* in full (BWV 148 [P46 in Gottlob Harrer's hand] and 244b [PAm.B.6/7 in Johann Christoph Altnickol's hand]). It is therefore clear that Bach stood in the same tradition as Calov in dedicating his creative work, both its composition and performance—since he included the ascription on copies he made of other composers' music—to the greater glory of God.

In the subject index at the end of Vol. 3/VI, under "Ehre Gottes," a number of passages that contain quotations from Luther are referred to, including the following:

Vol. 1/II, col. 1015, on Proverbs 27:21:

> *Those men must be few and very highly spiritual who through honor and praise alike remain indifferent and unchanged, so that they do not care for it or take pride and pleasure in it, but remain utterly free and unconcerned, ascribe all their honor and good name to God alone, offer it to Him alone, and use it to no purpose other than the glory of God and the benefit of their neighbors and in no way to their own benefit or advantage. Men like this trust not in their own honor, nor exalt themselves above the most useless and despised man on earth, but acknowledge themselves as servants of God, who has given them the honor in order to serve God and neighbor, just as if He had commanded them to distribute gulden to the poor for His sake.* ("Treatise on Good Works," *LW* 44:44–45)

Vol. 2/IV, col. 448, on Habakkuk 2:14:

> *The prophets borrowed this verse from Moses, who says of king Pharoah in Ex. 9:16: "For this purpose I have let you live, to show you My power, so that My name may be declared throughout all the earth," that is, "You despise Me as an inept God of a wretched nation and as having no great reputation. All right, I shall make an example of you, so that I will no longer be so condemned and despised. On the contrary, all the lands shall sing and speak of My power." Also Num. 14:21: "Truly, as I live, all the earth shall be filled with the glory of the Lord," that is, "You tempt Me and dishonor Me, but I shall manifest Myself on you and assail you so that the earth will be filled with My glory; that is, people will sing and speak of Me, praise, honor, and fear Me everywhere when they hear what I did to you who tempt Me so." Thus Is. 11:9 also says of Christ's kingdom: "The earth shall be full of the knowledge of the Lord, as the waters cover the sea," that is, that the whole*

> *world is hearing the Gospel of Christ richly and is learning to know God in it. We must get accustomed to this manner of speech. For to sing, preach, and speak about God is termed "to be filled with glory." . . . the honor and the glory of the Lord shall prevail in all countries, so that no one can silence or hinder it.* ("Lectures on Habakkuk," *LW* 19:217–18)

For Bach, the ascription "S. D. G" at the end of his manuscripts was no empty formality; it was an aim he pursued throughout his life, as can be documented from his own writing, in which he echoes some of the concerns Luther expresses in the quotations given above. As was noted under no. 40, his request for dismissal from the post of organist of the Blasiuskirche, dated 25 June 1708, included the statement that his aim in life was to compose and direct "regulirte kirchen music zu Gottes Ehren" well-regulated church music to the glory of God—*BD* 1:19; *BR,* p. 60). The title page of his *Orgelbüchlein* (BWV 599–644 [P283], dating from 1713, although the title page itself probably dates from some time after 1720) contains the following dedication:

> *Dem Höchsten Gott allein zu Ehren, Dem Nechsten, draus sich zu belehren. (*BD *1:214)*
>
> *(To the highest God alone be glory And to my neighbor's instruction.)*

Alongside Exodus 15:20 (no. 18), Bach wrote the marginal note: "NB. First prelude, for 2 choirs to be performed for the glory of God." Later in life, as part of the teaching he gave his pupils, he endorsed the opinion of Friedrich Ehrhard Niedt:

> *Der General Bass ist das vollkommste Fundament der Music . . . .darzu greift damit dieses eine wohlklingende Harmonie gebe zur Ehre Gottes und zulässiger Ergötzung des Gemüths wie aller Music, also auch des General Basses Finis und End Uhrsache anders nicht, als nur zu Gottes Ehre und Recreation des Gemüths seyn. Wo dieses nicht in Acht genommen wird da ists keine eigentliche Music sondern ein Teuflisches Geplerr und Geleyer (Figured Bass is the whole foundation of music . . . .the result is a well-sounding harmony to the glory of God and justifiable gratification of the senses; for the sole end and aim of all music, as well as that of the Figured Bass, should be nothing else than for the glory of God and pleasant recreations. Where this object is not kept in view there can be no true music but only an infernal scraping and bawling—P. Spitta,* Johann Sebastian Bach *[Wiesbaden, 1964], 2:915–16; translation based on P.Spitta,* Johann Sebastian Bach: His Work and Influence on the Music of Germany, 1685–1750, *trans. C. Bell and J. A. Fuller-Maitland [New York, 1951], 3:318).*

47 The main title page of the second double volume, that is, Vol. 2/III:

J.N.J. The second volume of the divine writings of the Old Testament, in which are contained the prophets, both major and minor, according to the German Bible of Dr. Luther, including summaries, drawn up in correct arrangement and order and so expounded from the original text, context, and the parallel passages according to the intention of the Holy Spirit and the analogy of faith, that not only the real, literal meaning of the words and expressions of Holy Scripture is thoroughly interpreted, but also the salutary application, especially from the writings of the German prophet Luther in his inspiring manner and lively and edifying interpretation, is presented. Done with painstaking diligence by Dr. Abraham Calov, public professor, chairman of the theological faculty, and senior pastor of the church consistory, as well as general superintendent of Electoral Saxony in Wittenberg. In the year of Christ 1682. Printed in Wittenberg by Christian Schrödter, the university's printer of books.

Again there is the insistence that the commentary is essentially taken from the writings of Martin Luther, arranged

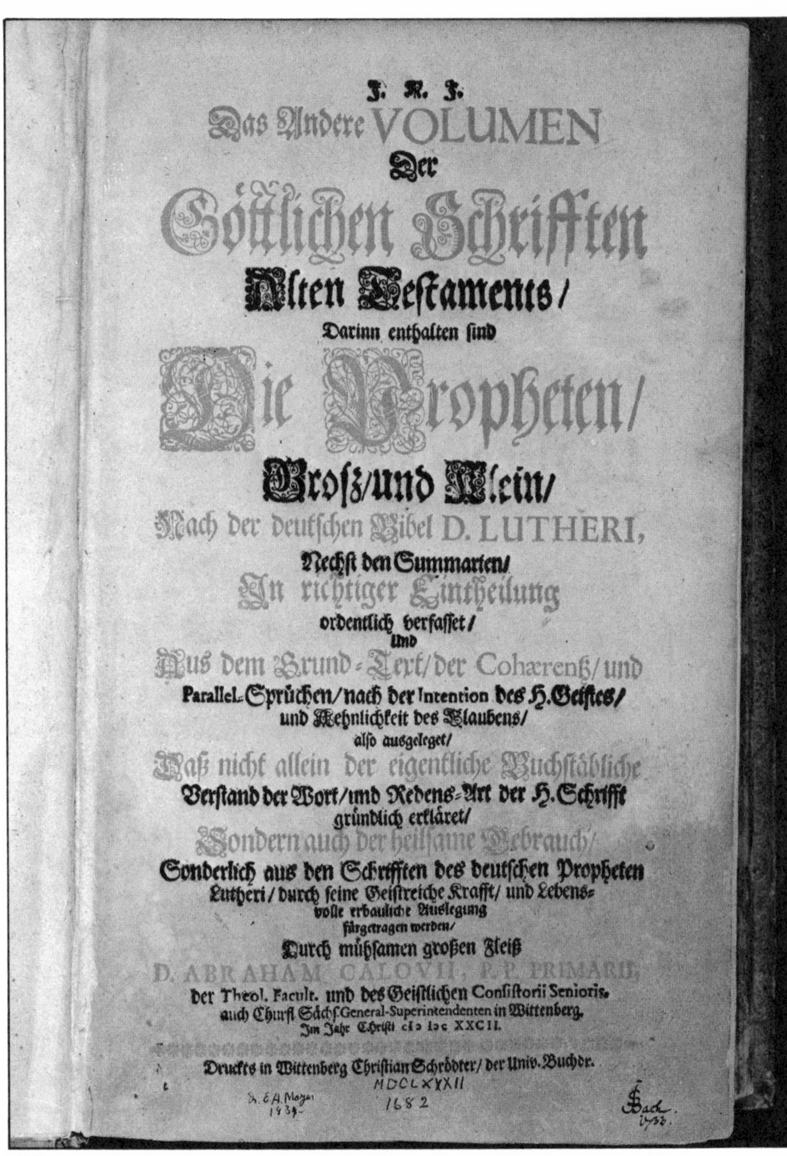
J. N. J.
Das Andere VOLUMEN
Der
Göttlichen Schrifften
Alten Testaments/
Darinn enthalten sind
Die Propheten/
Groß/und Klein/
Nach der deutschen Bibel D. LUTHERI,
Nechst den Summarien/
In richtiger Eintheilung
ordentlich verfasset/
und
Aus dem Grund-Text/der Cohærentz/und
Parallel-Sprüchen/nach der Intention des H. Geistes/
und Aehnlichkeit des Glaubens/
also ausgeleget/
Daß nicht allein der eigentliche Buchstäbliche
Verstand der Wort/und Redens-Art der H. Schrifft
gründlich erkläret/
Sondern auch der heilsame Gebrauch/
Sonderlich aus den Schrifften des deutschen Propheten
Lutheri/durch seine Geistreiche Krafft/ und Lebens-
volle erbauliche Auslegung
fürgetragen werden/
Durch mühsamen großen Fleiß
D. ABRAHAM CALOVII, P.P. PRIMARII,
der Theol. Facult. und des Geistlichen Consistorii Senioris.
auch Churf. Sächs. General-Superintendenten in Wittenberg.
Im Jahr Christi clɔ Iɔc XXCII.
Druckts in Wittenberg Christian Schrödter/ der Univ. Buchdr.
MDCLXXXII
1682
JSBach. 1733.

47

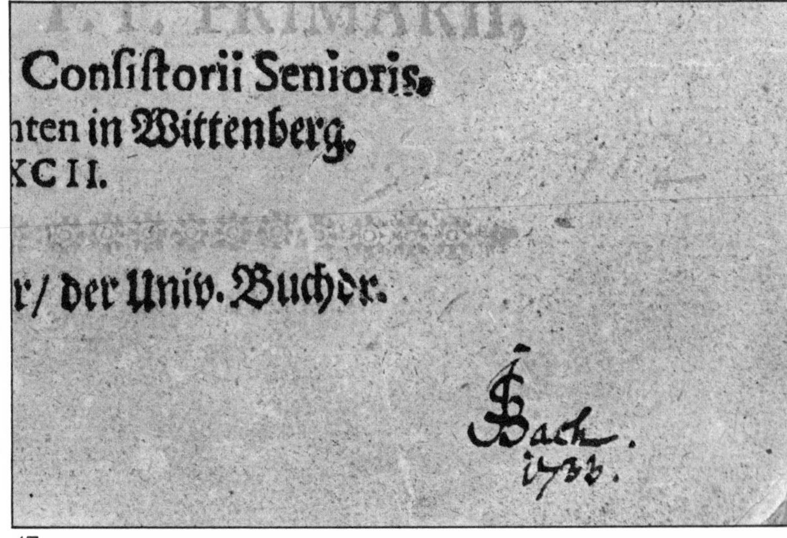
Consistorii Senioris.
nten in Wittenberg.
XCII.
r/ der Univ. Buchdr.
JSBach. 1733.

47a

and edited by Calov.

In the bottom right-hand corner is Bach's monogram and the year "1733"; see the Introduction, p. 26, and nos. 2 and 55.

48 Vol. 2/III, col. 81–82. Isaiah 15:1. Bach completes the Biblical text in the opposite margin and also repeats some of the words: *über Ar in Moab: sie ist dahin: das Nachts kömt Zerstörung.*

81 Das Funffzehende Capitel. 82

(*Es kömt ein Rauch / ein gantzes Heer / und zeucht nicht einzelen/sondern mit Hauffen.*)

v. 32. Und was werden die Boten der Heiden hin und wider sagen? (von diesem Kriegs-Zuge Hiskiä wider die Philister werden die Feinde des Volckes Gottes / die ehe über selbiges gefrolocket haben sich über Hiskiä Macht entsetzen / und fürchten / es werde die Ordnung auch bald an sie kommen) nemlich: (sie werden sagen / daß ist die Antwort auff die Frage) Zion hat der HErr gegründet / (diese Burg / der Berg des HErren / und die gantze Stadt / so daran hänget / wird wol bleiben S. Psalm XXCVII. 5. CIII. 17.) und daselbst werden die Elenden seines Volckes (zur Zeit der Noth) Zuversicht haben. (und ihre Zuflucht dahin nemen. GOtt wird seinem Volck Gnade geben/ daß sie Glück und Segen wider ihre Feind haben / daß ihnen weder Philister noch Assyrier was anhaben werden/nach ihrem Willen.)

Das Funffzehende Capitel.

(I.) Die Last der Moabiter v. 4. (II.) Derowegen wird von ihren Flüchten gen Moab geruffen: und vom Raub/ und von der Grausamkeit der Feinde. v. 9.

Der Erste Theil.

Die Last der Moabiter.

v. 1. DJß ist die Last (die schwere Strafe) über Moab (derer Hoffarth groß war wegen der Fruchtbarkeit ihrer Länder und anderer Gaben / die den Juden sehr gefährlich fielen) des Nachts kömt Zerstörung (durch den Sennacherib S. Es. XVI. 14. Vergl. Jer. XLIIX. 1. Ez. XXV. 8. Am. II. 1. Ebr. in der Nacht / des Verstörens) über Kir in Moab: sie ist dahin. (die Meinung ist / die Moabiter sind auff einmahl zu Grunde gegangen / in der Nacht / da ihre beyde fürnemste Städte sind verstöret worden. Von Ar der Hauptstadt in Moab ist zu lesen 4 Mos. XXI. 28. 5. Mos. II. 18. 29. Kir heisset sonsten Kirhares c. XVI. 11. Jer. XLIIX. 31. auch Kirharaseth Es. XVI. 7. und war eine von den fürnemsten Städten der Moabiter.)

v. 2. Sie gehen hinauff (nemlich die Moabiter) gen Baith und Dibon zun Altaren (oder zu den Höhen) daß sie weinen und heulen (in ihren Götzenhäusern / und für ihren Götzen. Baith erklären etliche von einer Stadt genandt Beon / Baal-Meon und Beth-Baal Meon 4. Mos. XXXII. 3. 38. Jos. XIII. 17. die wegen der Abgötterey sehr berühmt gewesen. Dibon war eine Stadt / die den Rubenitern zugetheilet war S. Jos. XIII. 17. und wird hier v. 9. Dimon genennet) über Nebo (die auch den Rubenitern zugetheilet war. 4 Mos. XXXII. 38.) und Medba (welches eine Stadt war in der Moabiter Land) in Moab. Aller Häupt ist beschoren / (dieß war die Weise in Moab im Trauren / daß sie ihre Haar abschnitten / und ihr Häupt kahl machten Jer. XLIIX. 37. Ez. VII. 18. dergleichen aber dem Volck Gottes verboten war 3. Mos. XIX. 27. 5. Mos. XIV. 1. dieweil GOtt alle unsere Haar gezehlet hat Matth. X. 30.) aller Bart ist abgeschnitten.

v. 3. Auff ihren Gassen gehen sie mit Säcken umbgürtet: (das ist / mit Trauerkleidern) auf ihren Dächern (wenn sie beten wollen / gehen sie auf ihren Dächern Zeph. I. 5.) und Strassen heulen sie alle / und gehen weinend herab. (wie sie weinend auf ihre Dächer steigen / also gehen sie auch weinend wider herab / weil sie nirgends einen Trost finden.)

v. 4. Hesbon / und Eleale (dieß waren auch Städte in Moab S. 4. Mos. XXXII. 30. Jos. XIII. 17.) schreien / daß mans zu Jahza (so ein Land war / daß an Moab gräntzet / 4. Mos. XXI.) höret. Darumb wehklagen die Gerüsteten in Moab / (die Soldaten werden drüber furchtsam und zaghaffte gemacht) denn es gehet ihrer Seelen (der Moabiter Leben) sehr übel.

Der Andere Theil.

Der Prophet schreyet von ihrer Flucht von der Feinde Raub / und Tyranney.

v. 5. Mein Hertz schreyet zu Moab / (über Moab. Ich kan mich selbst des Klagens nicht enthalten / wegen des so grossen Jammers / so in Moab entstehet S. Es. XVI. 11. XXI. 3. Jer. XLIIX. 5. 31. folg.) Ihre flüchtige fliehen von der drey Jährigen Kuhe (von Moab / so starck und geil ist wie eine drey

F Jährige

48

XLIIX. 37. Ez. VII. 18. dergleichen aber dem Volck Gottes verboten war 3. Mos. XIX. 27. Mos. XIV. 1. dieweil GOtt alle unsere Haar gezehlet hat Matth. X. 30.) aller Bart ist bgeschnitten.

v. 3. Auff ihren Gassen gehen e mit Säcken umbgürtet: (das ist / mit rauerkleidern) auf ihren Dächern (wenn beten wollen / gehen sie auf ihren Dächern Zeph. 5.) und Strassen heulen sie alle / und ehen weinend herab. (wie sie weinend auf re Dächer steigen / also gehen sie auch weinend ider herab / weil sie nirgends einen Trost finn.)

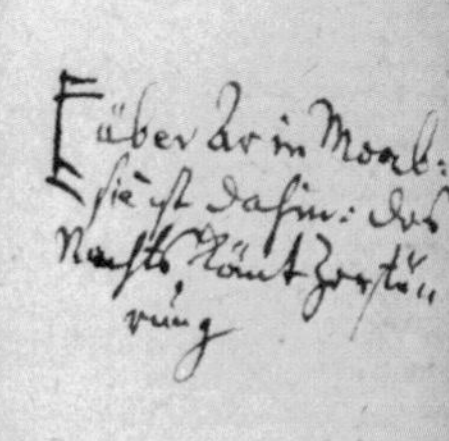

48a

49 Vol. 2/III, col. 89–90. Isaiah 17:10. The word *lustige*, which is omitted from Calov's citation of the Biblical text, is supplied in the margin.

89 Das Siebenzehende Capitel. 90

Der Andere Theil.

Wie etliche von den Israeliten noch solten bekehret werden.

v. 7. Zu der Zeit wird sich der Mensch halten zu dem / der ihn gemacht hat / (nach dem die schwere Plage über Israel werden fürüber sein / sonderlich wenn der verheissene Meßias kommen wird / so werden die übrigen sich zu GOTT halten /) und seine Augen / werden auff den Heiligen in Israel schauen. (die Gläubigen werden auff den Heiligen in Israel den HERRN Meßiam Es. LIV. 5. Dan. IX. 24. mit Glaubens Augen schauen / und auff ihn allein ihr Vertrauen stellen.)

v. 8. Und wird sich nicht halten zu den (abgöttischen) Altaren / die seine Hände gemacht haben / und nicht schauen auff das / das seine Finger gemacht haben / weder auff Hayne (die Wälder der Abgötter) noch Bilder. (die ihren Göttern geheiliget waren / oder Sonnen Bilder 3. Mos. XXVI. 30.)

v. 9. Zu der Zeit werden die Städte ihrer Stärcke sein (* daß sind die Städte / darinnen ihre Götzen und Gottesdienst war / darauf sie sich verliessen / * wie ein verlassen Ast / und Zweig / so verlassen wird / welchen man stehen lässet / wenn man die Bäume umbhäuet /) so verlassen ward für den Kindern Israel / (oder / von wegen der Kinder Israel / dieweil der HErr etlicher der Kinder Israel schonen wolte / und sie erhalten,) und werden wüste sein. (* denn wie die Kinder Israel kaum einen Ast und Zweig liessen / das ist / wenig Volckes / da sie das Land der Cananiter einnamen / also sols ihnen auch ergehen. *)

v. 10. Denn du hast vergessen Gottes deines Heils / und nicht gedacht an den Felsen deiner Stärcke. (an GOtt den HERRN auff denn du allein deine Hoffnung hast stellen sollen /) darumb wirstu
lustige Pflantzen (in den Weinbergen und Gärten) setzen / aber du wirst damit den Frembden die Feser gelegt haben. (den Assyriern / sie werden ihrer geniessen.)

v. 11. Zur Zeit des Pflantzens wirstu sein wol warten / daß dein Same zeitlich wachse: Aber in der Erndten / wenn du die Mandeln (oder Trauben) solt erben / wirstu dafür Schmertzen eines Betrübten haben. (weil es die Feinde rauben / und verheeren werden.)

Der Dritte Theil.

Klage über die Assyrier / und derselben Strafe.

v. 12. O wehe der Menge so großes Volckes (* daß sind die Assyrer / welchen er verkündigt ihr Verderben / zu Trost dem Volck Israel /) wie das Meer wird es brausen / und das Getümmel der Leute wird wüten / wie große Wasser wüten. (wegen der großen Menge der Völcker / die dem Assyrier wider die Jüden dienen werden / sonderlich in Belagerung der Stadt Jerusalem.)

v. 14. Ja wie große Wasser wüten / so werden die Leute wüten: Aber er wird sie schelten / so werden sie ferne weg fliehen / (wie er mit Schelten die Wasser hat fliehend gemacht 2. Mos. XIV.) und wird sie verfolgen / wie dem Staube auff den Bergen vom Winde geschicht / und wie einem Windwirbel vom Ungewitter geschicht. (S. 2. Kön. XIX. 36. Vergl. Job. XXI. 18. Ps. I. 4. XXXV. 5. XXCIII. 14. Hos. XIII. 8)

v. 14. Umb den Abend / sihe / so ist Schrecken da / und ehe es Morgen wird / sind sie nimmer da. (denn sie sind in der Nacht durch den Engel des HErrn erleget Es. XXXVII. 36.) Daß ist der Lohn (oder / die Strafe / Job. XX. 19.) unsere Räuber / und das Erbe derer / die uns das unser nemen. (oder / die uns zertreten.)

Das Achzehende Capitel.

(I.) Weissagung wider Morenland und die Völcker / so am rothen Meer liegen v. 2. (II.) Weissagung wider die Assyrer. v. 6. (III.) Trost / daß etliche hirvon dermaleins zum Erkentnüß des Evangelii kommen werden. v. 7.

F iij Der

49

50 Vol. 2/III, col. 123–24. Isaiah 25:2, 3. There are two corrections here of the Biblical text, either by different hands or at least written at different times. The first corrects *so* to *sie* in verse 2 and may have been written by someone other than Bach. The second, which is almost certainly Bach's, corrects *ehren* to *fürchten*. Note the end of the quotation from Luther: "New Testament worship is not sacrifice, not the building of the temple, not masses, etc., but rather the praise and fear of God without hypocrisy."

123 **Der Prophet Jesaia/** 124

deinen Namen/ denn du thust Wunder/ (die Wunder und Gedancken saget „Herr Lutherus/ sein die Verheissungen und „Prophecenungen/ so den Vätern geschehen „sind vom künfftigen Reich Christi und Er„lösung vom Tode/ und von der Sünden: de„rowegen jauchzet und freuet sich die Kirche/ „daß dieselbe so reichlich durch Christum erfül„let sein/ nach der Verkündigung des Evange„lii/ und Ertheilung des Heiligen Geistes/) deine Fürnemen von alten her sind treu und warhafftig. (Vergl. 2. Mos. XV. 1. 2. 3. Ps. XXCIX. 3.)

v. 2. Denn du machest die Stadt (Jerusalem) zum Steinhauffen/ (Vergl. c. XXI. 9. XXIII. 13. Offenbar. XIV. 8. XIII. 3.) die feste Stadt/ (Luth: so „wird Jerusalem genennet wegen ihrer Vermes„senheit über dem Tempel/ das Gesetz/ und den „Dienst GOttes/ so bey ihnen waren/) daß sie auff einem Hauffen liegt/ der frembden (Luth. Er nennet sie Frembde wegen des „unglaubens/ es muß eine gewaltige Blindheit „der Jüden sein/ daß sie diesen so klaren Text „nicht betrachten.) Pallast/ daß nicht mehr eine Stadt sey/ und nimmermehr gebauet werde.

v. 3. Darumb ehret dich (O HErr der Herrligkeit) ein mächtig Volck/ (das aus aller Welt zu dir versamlet ist/) die Städte gewaltiger Heyden ehren dich. (weil die Heyden aus aller Welt zu dir bekehret/ und zu deines Namens Erkentnüß gebracht sind Es. XI. 9. Bißhieher/ sagt Herr Luth. „hat dich ein klein und hartes und leicht Volck im „Winckel des Jüdischen Landes geehret/ an des„sen statt mustu haben ein großes gewaltiges „Volck/ nemlich alle Heyden/ und mercket hier „an/ welches der Gottesdienst sey des Neuen Te„staments/ nicht Opffer/ nicht Erbauung der „Tempel/ nicht messen ꝛc. sondern das Lob und „Furcht Gottes/ ohne Heucheley.)

v. 4. Denn du (o GOtt) bist der Geringen Stärcke/ der Armen Stärcke in Trübsal/ eine Zuflucht für dem Ungewitter/ ein Schatten für der Hitze/ wenn die Tyrannen wüten/ wie ein Ungewitter wider eine Wand. (Vergl. Es. LXI. 1. Ps. XC. 1. folg. Matth. XI. „27. Herr Lutherus/ du bist die Zuversicht derer „die getrieben werden vom Sturm und Unge„witter/ das ist die Verfolgung leiden wegen „des Wortes GOttes/ die gedruckt werden von „der Sünden/ und ihrem eigenen Fleisch und Satan. In allen diesen Gefährligkeiten haben wir keine andere Zuflucht ohne allein Christum/ wenn wir zu dem fliehen/ sind wir sicher wider Anfall alles bösen Matth. VII. 25 da haben wir einen Schatten wider die Hitze/ wenn der Grimm der Tyrannen auff uns zustößt/ wie ein Ungewitter an die Wand. Ist eine schöne Figur. In Trübsal und Ungewitter können wir nicht erkennen/ daß die Hülffe und das Heil uns so viel nahe sey/ denn wir urtheilen nur nach dem wirs empfinden/ oder/ nach dem Sinn der durchs Ubel afficiret und bewogen wird/ und nicht siehet auff die Errettung/ da empfinden wir in Warheit/ daß wir nur eine elende Wand sein/ so einem Sturm nicht kan widerstehen.)

v. 5. Du demüthigest der Frembden (der Ungläubigen und Feinde deiner Kirchen v. 2.) Ungestüm/ wie die Hitze an einem dürren Ort/ (wie die Hitze durch den Regen bald gedämpfet wird: also wird durch die Wolcken der Gnaden bald der Feinde Zorn und Ungestüm geleget/) daß die Hitze den Reben der Tyrannen verderbe/ und die Wolcke dennoch Schatten gebe. (Ebr. Gleich wie die Hitze: durch den Schatten einer Wolcken wird der Gesang der Tyrannen fallen/ das ist/ ihre Freude und ihr Triumph/ so sie über die Frommen pflegen zuführen sol ihnen geleget werden. Herr Lutherus: Er nennet einen „Schatten der Wolcken/ was wir auff deutsch „Meelthau/ dadurch die Saat verbrennet wird/ „und die Blätter der Bäume/ und Weinreben „verwelcken/ und umbkommen: deutet also an/ die „Tyrannen werden müssen durch sich selbst umb„kommen/ wenn GOtt nicht einem fruchtbaren „Regen/ sondern einen schädlichen Meelthau „giebt.)

Der Andere Theil.

Weissagung von der Kirchen neuen Testaments/ und Wolthaten/ und Verdienst Christi.

v. 6. Und der HERR Zebaoth wird allen Völckern (so wol Heyden/ als Juden) machen auff diesem Berge ein fett Mahl/ ein Mahl von reinem Wein/ von Fett/ von Marck/ (von wolgemesten fetten Vieh/) von Wein/ darinne keine Hefen ist. (Verg. Psalm. XXII. 27. 30 Ps. XXXVI. 9. Spr. IX. 1. folg. Es. LV. 1. folg. Matth. VIII. 11. XXII. 2. folg. Luc. XIV. 16. folg. da von diesem geistlichen Mahl/ das die Gläubigen geniessen ebenmäßig geredet wird.)

v. 2. Denn

50

51 Vol. 2/III, col. 981–82. On Daniel 7:25. *NB.* and marks of emphasis occur in the margin alongside part of Calov's commentary on the verse in col. 982:

> They shall be given into his hand (*see above v. 21*) for a time (*one year*) two times (*two years*) and half a time (*half a year, cf. chap. 4:13; a duration to be understood as the Angelic Year, which is 1,277½ years and follows the Mohammedan kingdom that came to an end in the year of Christ 613, so that there are yet 211 years remaining after this 1,679th year of Christ: thus there are still a few years before the elect shall be gathered in. Ah, come Lord Jesus, come, Rev. 22:20*).

The Angelic Year is calculated on the basis of a *time* being equivalent to one year, and one day equivalent to one year, that is, 3½ × 365 = 1,277½. However, it was customary to do the calculation according to the "moon-year," that is, 3½ × 360 = 1,260, as given in Rev. 11:3. This is taken up by Calov in his commentary on Dan. 12:7 (col. 1044; see no. 52). It is also discussed at some length in an important book in Bach's personal library (Leaver C, no. 33): *Haupt-Schlüssel über die hohe Offenbarung S. Johannis* . . . [mit] *Erklärung aller und jeder Zahlen* . . . (The main key to the great Revelation of St. John with an explanation of each and every number). In the first edition

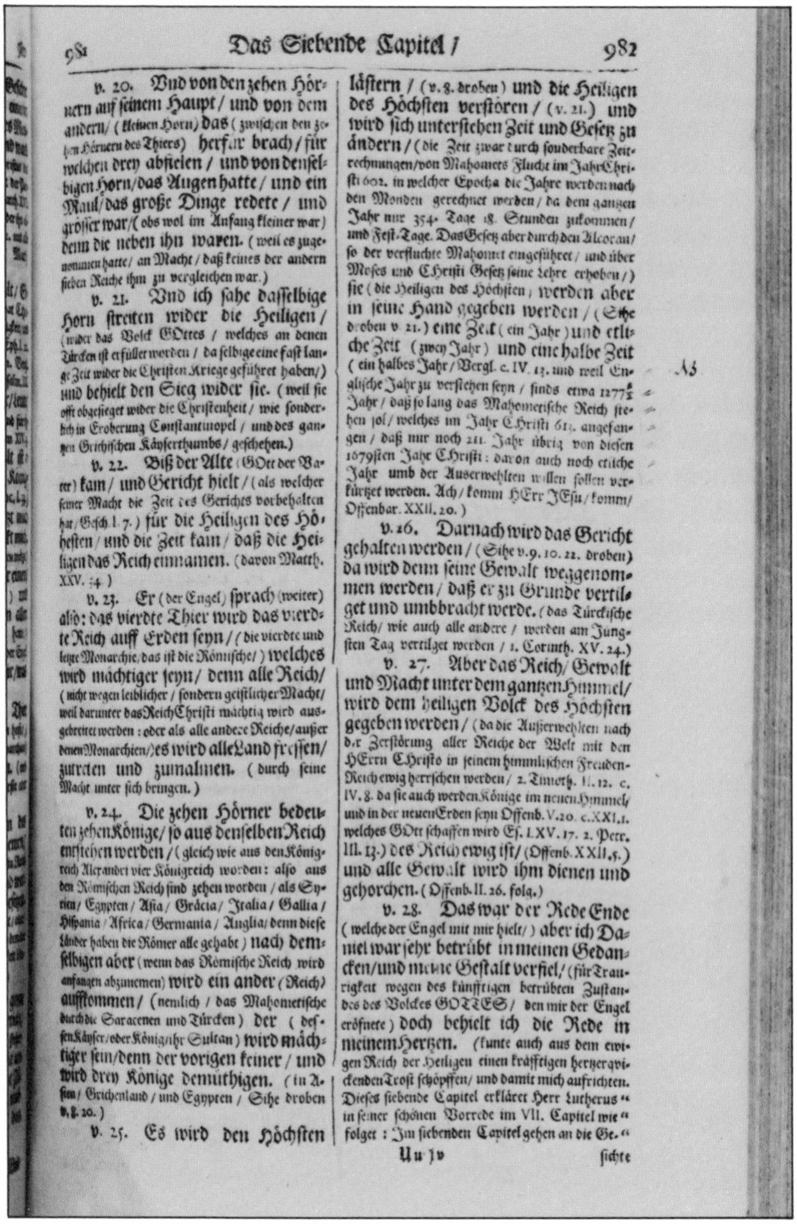
981 Das Siebende Capitel / 982

v. 20. Und von den zehen Hörnern auf seinem Haupt / und von dem andern / (kleinen Horn) das (zwischen den zehen Hörnern des Thiers) herfür brach / für welchen drey abfielen / und von denselbigen Horn / das Augen hatte / und ein Maul / das große Dinge redete / und grösser war / (obs wol im Anfang kleiner war) denn die neben ihm waren. (weil es zugenommen hatte / an Macht / daß keines der andern sieben Reiche ihm zu vergleichen war.)

v. 21. Und ich sahe dasselbige Horn streiten wider die Heiligen / (wider das Volck GOttes / welches an denen Türcken ist erfüllet worden / da selbige eine fast lange Zeit wider die Christen Kriege geführet haben /) und behielt den Sieg wider sie. (weil sie offt obgesieget wider die Christenheit / wie sonderlich in Eroberung Constantinopel / und des gantzen Grichischen Käyserthumbs / geschehen.)

v. 22. Biß der Alte (GOtt der Vater) kam / und Gericht hielt / (als welcher seiner Macht die Zeit des Gerichtes vorbehalten hat / Gesch. I. 7.) für die Heiligen des Höhesten / und die Zeit kam / daß die Heiligen das Reich einnamen. (davon Matth. XXV. 34.)

v. 23. Er (der Engel) sprach (weiter) also: das vierdte Thier wird das vierdte Reich auff Erden seyn / (die vierdte und letzte Monarchie / das ist die Römische /) welches wird mächtiger seyn / denn alle Reich / (nicht wegen leiblicher / sondern geistlicher Macht / weil darunter das Reich Christi mächtig wird ausgebreitet werden: oder als alle andere Reiche / außer denen Monarchien /) es wird alle Land fressen / zutreten und zumalmen. (durch seine Macht unter sich bringen.)

v. 24. Die zehen Hörner bedeuten zehen Könige / so aus denselben Reich entstehen werden / (gleich wie aus den Königreich Alexandri vier Königreich worden: also aus den Römischen Reich sind zehen worden / als Syrien / Egypten / Asia / Grácia / Italia / Gallia / Hispania / Africa / Germania / Anglia / denn diese Länder haben die Römer alle gehabt) nach demselbigen aber (wenn das Römische Reich wird anfangen abzunemen) wird ein ander (Reich) aufkommen / (nemlich / das Mahometische durch die Saracenen und Türcken) der (dessen Käyser / oder König / ihr Sultan) wird mächtiger sein / denn der vorigen keiner / und wird drey Könige demüthigen. (in Asien / Grichenland / und Egypten / Sihe droben v. 8. 20.)

v. 25. Es wird den Höchsten lästern / (v. 8. droben) und die Heiligen des Höchsten verstören / (v. 21.) und wird sich unterstehen Zeit und Gesetz zu ändern / (die Zeit zwar durch sonderbare Zeitrechnungen / von Mahomets Flucht im Jahr Christi 602. in welcher Epocha die Jahre werden nach den Monden gerechnet werden / da dem gantzen Jahr nur 354. Tage 18. Stunden zukommen / und Fest-Tage. Das Gesetz aber durch den Alcoran / so der verfluchte Mahomet eingeführet / und über Moses und Christi Gesetz seine Lehre erhoben /) sie (die Heiligen des Höchsten) werden aber in seine Hand gegeben werden / (Sihe droben v. 21.) eine Zeit (ein Jahr) und etliche Zeit (zwey Jahr) und eine halbe Zeit (ein halbes Jahr / Vergl. c. IV. 13. und weil Englische Jahr zu verstehen seyn / finds etwa 1277½ Jahr / daß so lang das Mahometische Reich stehen sol / welches im Jahr Christi 613. angefangen / daß nur noch 211. Jahr übrig von diesen 1679sten Jahr Christi: davon auch noch etliche Jahr umb der Auserwehlten willen sollen verkürtzet werden. Ach / komm HErr JEsu / komm / Offenbar. XXII. 20.)

v. 26. Darnach wird das Gericht gehalten werden / (Sihe v. 9. 10. 22. droben) da wird denn seine Gewalt weggenommen werden / daß er zu Grunde vertilget und umbbracht werde. (das Türckische Reich / wie auch alle andere / werden am Jüngsten Tag vertilget werden / 1. Corinth. XV. 24.)

v. 27. Aber das Reich / Gewalt und Macht unter dem gantzen Himmel / wird dem heiligen Volck des Höchsten gegeben werden / (da die Außerwehlten nach der Zerstörung aller Reiche der Welt mit den HErrn Christo in seinem himmlischen Freuden-Reich ewig herrschen werden / 2. Timoth. II. 12. c. IV. 8. da sie auch werden Könige im neuen Himmel / und in der neuen Erden seyn Offenb. V. 20. c. XXI. 1. welches GOtt schaffen wird Es. LXV. 17. 2. Petr. III. 13.) des Reich ewig ist / (Offenb. XXII. 5.) und alle Gewalt wird ihm dienen und gehorchen. (Offenb. II. 26. folg.)

v. 28. Das war der Rede Ende (welche der Engel mit mir hielt /) aber ich Daniel war sehr betrübt in meinen Gedancken / und meine Gestalt verfiel / (für Traurigkeit wegen des künfftigen betrübten Zustandes des Volckes GOTTES / den mir der Engel eröfnete) doch behielt ich die Rede in meinem Hertzen. (kunte auch aus dem ewigen Reich der Heiligen einen kräfftigen hertzerqvickenden Trost schöpffen / und damit mich aufrichten. Dieses siebende Capitel erkläret Herr Lutherus " in seiner schönen Vorrede im VII. Capitel wie " folget: Im siebenden Capitel gehen an die Ge- "

Uu iv sichte

51

(Schleusingen, 1684; facsimile, Basel, 1981), there is a section devoted to a discussion of the Angelic Year and the number 1,260 (pp. 14ff.). Here is another indication that Bach had an interest in symbolic numbers, and especially in their eschatological aspects (see also nos. 14, 19, 22, 26, 27, 52). Perhaps Bach noted the passage since, by the time he was reading about the calculations, the 211 remaining years had been further reduced by between 50 and 60.

On *Ach, komm Herr Jesu, komm,* cf. the note on eschatology at no. 46.

The mention of the year 1679 gives some insight into the time it took for Calov to complete this project. The dedication to the third double volume, presumably written after the commentary was complete, is dated 31 October 1682 (see no. 56). This means that it took him about three years to compile the sections from Daniel to Revelation. Therefore, allowing for the same rate of progress, the whole work must have taken something like six years or more to complete.

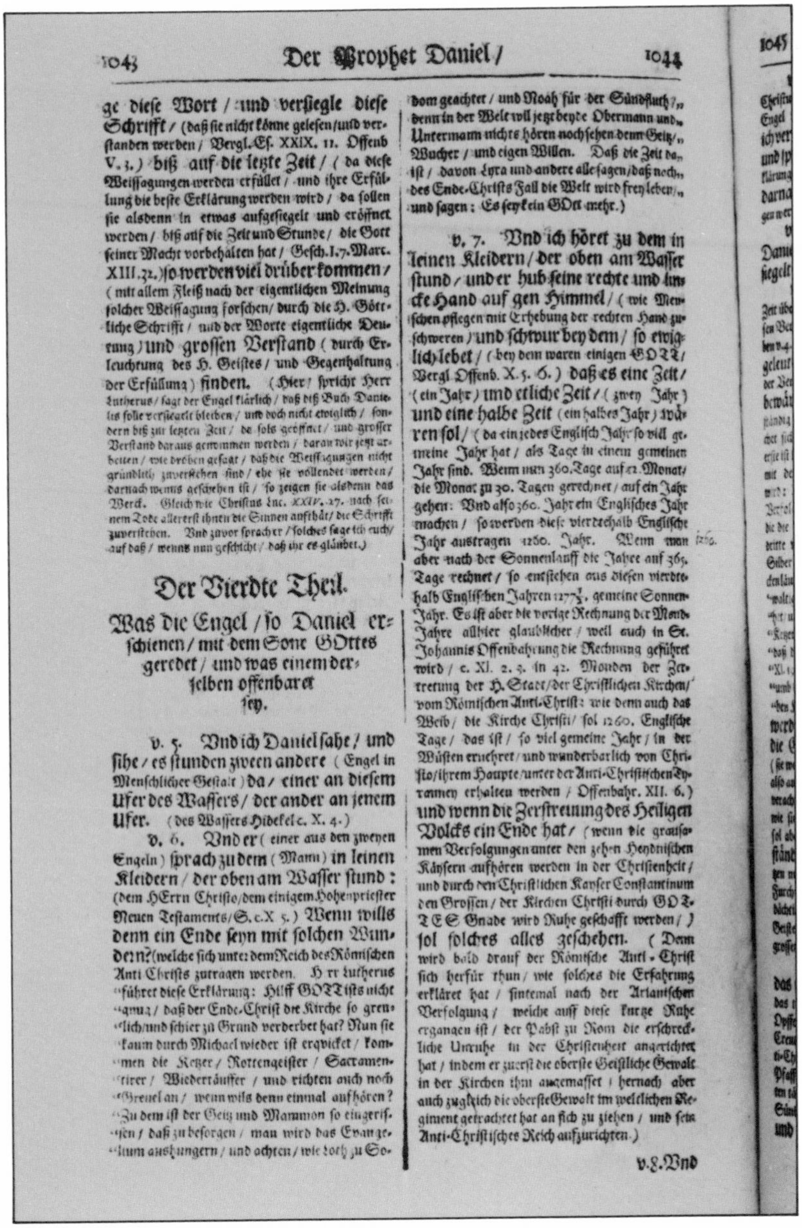

1043 Der Prophet Daniel / 1044

ge diese Wort / und versiegle diese Schrifft / (daß sie nicht könne gelesen/und verstanden werden / Vergl. Es. XXIX. 11. Offenb V. 3.) biß auf die letzte Zeit / (da diese Weissagungen werden erfüllet / und ihre Erfüllung die beste Erklärung werden wird / da sollen sie alsdenn in etwas aufgesiegelt und eröffnet werden / biß auf die Zeit und Stunde / die Gott seiner Macht vorbehalten hat / Gesch. I. 7. Marc. XIII. 32.) so werden viel drüber kommen / (mit allem Fleiß nach der eigentlichen Meinung solcher Weissagung forschen / durch die H. Göttliche Schrifft / und der Worte eigentliche Deutung) und grossen Verstand (durch Erleuchtung des H. Geistes / und Gegenhaltung der Erfüllung) finden. (Hier / spricht Herr Lutherus / sagt der Engel klärlich / daß diß Buch Daniels solle versiegelt bleiben / und doch nicht ewiglich / sondern biß zur letzten Zeit / da sols geöffnet / und grosser Verstand daraus gewonnen werden / daran wir jetzt arbeiten / wie droben gesagt / daß die Weissagungen nicht gründlich zuverstehen sind / ehe sie vollendet werden / darnach wenns geschehen ist / so zeigen sie alsdenn das Werck. Gleich wie Christus Luc. XXIV. 27. nach seinem Tode allererst ihnen die Sinnen aufthät / die Schrifft zuverstehen. Und zuvor sprach er / solches sage ich euch / auf daß / wenns nun geschicht / daß ihr es gläubet.)

Der Vierdte Theil.

Was die Engel / so Daniel erschienen / mit dem Sone GOttes geredet / und was einem derselben offenbaret sey.

v. 5. Vnd ich Daniel sahe / und sihe / es stunden zween andere (Engel in Menschlicher Gestalt) da / einer an diesem Ufer des Wassers / der ander an jenem Ufer. (des Wassers Hidekel c. X. 4.)

v. 6. Vnd er (einer aus den zweyen Engeln) sprach zu dem (Mann) in leinen Kleidern / der oben am Wasser stund: (dem HErrn Christo / dem einigem Hohenpriester Neuen Testaments / S. c. X 5.) Wenn wills denn ein Ende seyn mit solchen Wundern? (welche sich unter dem Reich des Römischen Anti Christs zutragen werden. Herr Lutherus führet diese Erklärung: Hilff GOTT ists nicht gnug / daß der Ende-Christ die Kirche so greulich / und schier zu Grund verderbet hat? Nun sie kaum durch Michael wieder ist erqvicket / kommen die Ketzer / Rottengeister / Sacramentirer / Wiedertäuffer / und richten auch noch Greuel an / wenn wils denn einmal aufhören? Zu dem ist der Geitz und Mammon so eingerissen / daß zu besorgen / man wird das Evangelium aushungern / und achten / wie Loth zu Sodom geachtet / und Noah für der Sündfluth / denn in der Welt will jetzt beyde Obermann und Untermann nichts hören noch sehen denn Geitz / Wucher / und eigen Willen. Daß die Zeit da ist / davon Lyra und andere alle sagen / daß nach des Ende-Christs Fall die Welt wird frey leben / und sagen: Es sey kein GOtt mehr.)

v. 7. Vnd ich höret zu dem in leinen Kleidern / der oben am Wasser stund / und er hub seine rechte und lincke Hand auf gen Himmel / (wie Menschen pflegen mit Erhebung der rechten Hand zu schweren) und schwur bey dem / so ewiglich lebet / (bey dem waren einigen GOTT / Vergl. Offenb. X. 5. 6.) daß es eine Zeit / (ein Jahr) und etliche Zeit / (zwey Jahr) und eine halbe Zeit (ein halbes Jahr) wären sol / (da ein jedes Englisch Jahr so viel gemeine Jahr hat / als Tage in einem gemeinen Jahr sind. Wenn nun 360. Tage auf 12. Monat / die Monat zu 30. Tagen gerechnet / auf ein Jahr gehen: Vnd also 360. Jahr ein Englisches Jahr machen / so werden diese vierdtehalb Englische Jahr austragen 1260. Jahr. Wenn man aber nach der Sonnenlauff die Jahre auf 365. Tage rechnet / so entstehen aus diesen vierdtehalb Englischen Jahren 1277½. gemeine Sonnen-Jahr. Es ist aber die vorige Rechnung der Mond-Jahre allhier glaublicher / weil auch in St. Johannis Offenbahrung die Rechnung geführet wird / c. XI. 2. 3. in 42. Monden der Zertretung der H. Stadt / der Christlichen Kirchen / vom Römischen Anti-Christ: wie denn auch das Weib / die Kirche Christi / sol 1260. Englische Tage / das ist / so viel gemeine Jahr / in der Wüsten ernehret / und wunderbarlich von Christo / ihrem Haupte / unter der Anti-Christischen Tyranney erhalten werden / Offenbahr. XII. 6.) und wenn die Zerstreuung des Heiligen Volcks ein Ende hat / (wenn die grausamen Verfolgungen unter den zehen Heydnischen Käysern aufhören werden in der Christenheit / und durch den Christlichen Kayser Constantinum den Grossen / der Kirchen Christi durch GOTTES Gnade wird Ruhe geschafft werden /) sol solches alles geschehen. (Denn wird bald drauf der Römische Anti-Christ sich herfür thun / wie solches die Erfahrung erkläret hat / sintemal nach der Arianischen Verfolgung / welche auff diese kurtze Ruhe ergangen ist / der Pabst zu Rom die erschreckliche Unruhe in der Christenheit angerichtet hat / indem er zuerst die oberste Geistliche Gewalt in der Kirchen ihm angemasset / hernach aber auch zugleich die oberste Gewolt im weltlichen Regiment getrachtet hat an sich zu ziehen / und sein Anti-Christisches Reich aufzurichten.)

v. 8. Vnd

52

52 Vol. 2/III, cols. 1043–44, 1045–46, 1047–48. On Daniel 12:7-13. Bach repeats in the margin the following numbers, which occur in the text:

col. 1044 — *1260*
col. 1046 — *1290, 1335*
col. 1047 — *1941, 2408*

The numbers represent the calculations based on the chronology that the book of Daniel suggests for the epochs and periods of the end-time. Again, they underline Bach's concern for and interest in such eschatological numbers (see also no. 51).

On the quotation from Rev. 22:20, "Surely I come quickly! Even so come, Lord Jesus! Amen," see BWV 140:3 and the notes on nos. 46 and 51.

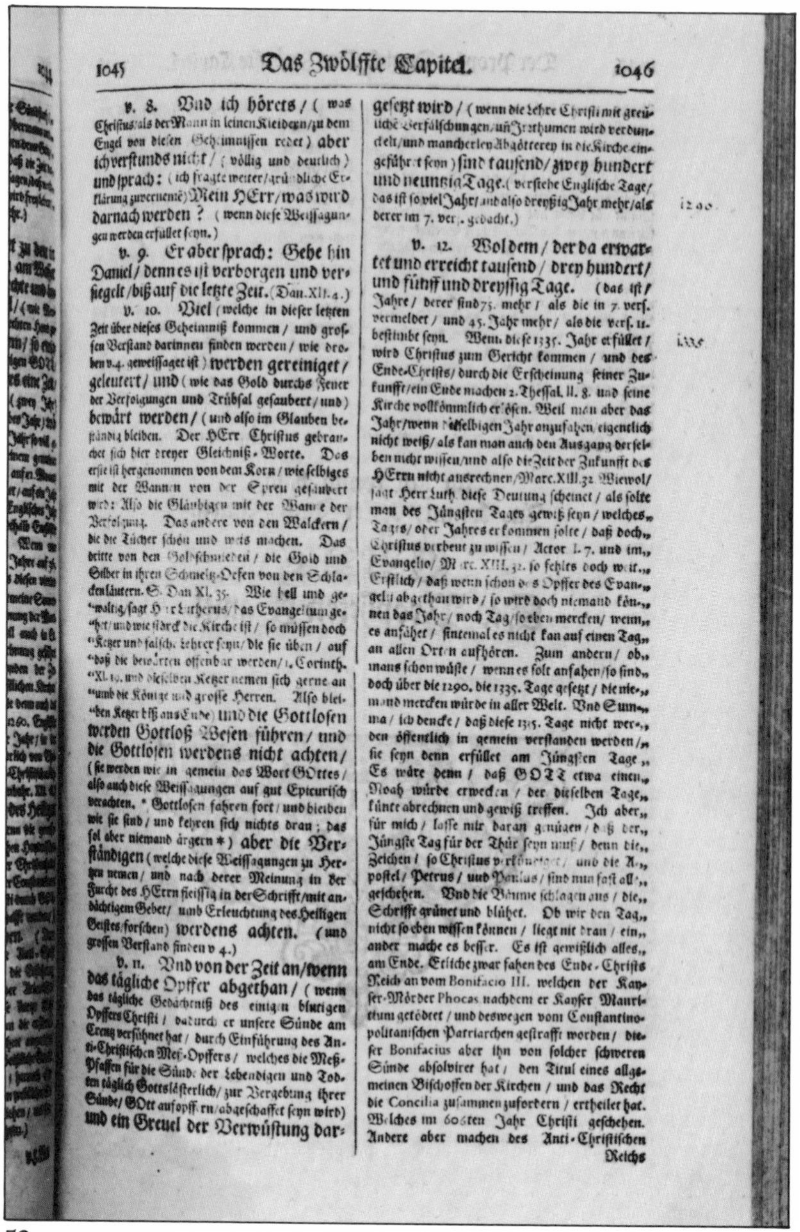

1045 Das Zwölffte Capitel. 1046

v. 8. Und ich hörets / (was Christus/als der Mann in leinen Kleidern/zu dem Engel von diesen Geheimnissen redet) aber ich verstunds nicht / (völlig und deutlich) und sprach: (ich fragte weiter/gründliche Erklärung zuvernemē) Mein HErr/was wird darnach werden? (wenn diese Weissagungen werden erfüllet seyn.)

v. 9. Er aber sprach: Gehe hin Daniel/ denn es ist verborgen und versiegelt/biß auf die letzte Zeit. (Dan. XII. 4.)

v. 10. Viel (welche in dieser letzten Zeit über dieses Geheimniß kommen / und grossen Verstand darinnen finden werden / wie droben v. 4. geweissaget ist) werden gereiniget / geleutert / und (wie das Gold durchs Feuer der Verfolgungen und Trübsal gesaubert / und) bewärt werden / (und also im Glauben beständig bleiben. Der HErr Christus gebrauchet sich hier dreyer Gleichniß-Worte. Das erste ist hergenommen von dem Korn / wie selbiges mit der Wannen von der Spreu gesaubert wird: Also die Gläubigen mit der Wanne der Verfolgung. Das andere von den Walckern / die die Tücher schön und weis machen. Das dritte von den Goldschmieden / die Gold und Silber in ihren Schmeltz-Oefen von den Schlacken läutern. S. Dan XI. 35. Wie hell und ge"waltig / sagt Herr Lutherus/ das Evangelium ge"het/ und wie starck die Kirche ist / so müssen doch "Ketzer und falsche Lehrer seyn/ die sie üben / auf "daß die bewärten offenbar werden/ 1. Corinth. "XI. 19. und dieselben Ketzer nemen sich gerne an "umb die Könige und grosse Herren. Also blei"ben Ketzer biß ans Ende) und die Gottlosen werden Gottloß Wesen führen / und die Gottlosen werdens nicht achten / (sie werden wie in gemein das Wort GOttes / also auch diese Weissagungen auf gut Epicurisch verachten. * Gottlosen fahren fort / und bleiben wie sie sind / und kehren sich nichts dran; das sol aber niemand ärgern *) aber die Verständigen (welche diese Weissagungen zu Hertzen nemen / und nach derer Meinung in der Furcht des HErrn fleissig in der Schrifft/mit andächtigem Gebet/ umb Erleuchtung des Heiligen Geistes/forschen) werdens achten. (und grossen Verstand finden v 4.)

v. 11. Und von der Zeit an/wenn das tägliche Opffer abgethan / (wenn das tägliche Gedächtniß des einigen blutigen Opffers Christi / dadurch er unsere Sünde am Creutz versühnet hat / durch Einführung des Anti-Christischen Meß-Opffers / welches die Meß-Pfaffen für die Sünde der Lebendigen und Todten täglich Gotteslästerlich/ zur Vergebung ihrer Sünde/ GOtt aufopffern/abgeschaffet seyn wird) und ein Greuel der Verwüstung dargesetzt wird / (wenn die Lehre Christi mit greulichē Verfälschungen/ uñ Irrthumen wird verdunckelt/und mancherley Abgötterey in die Kirche eingeführet seyn) sind tausend/ zwey hundert und neuntzig Tage. (verstehe Englische Tage/ das ist so viel Jahr/ und also dreyßig Jahr mehr/als 1290
derer im 7. vers. gedacht.)

v. 12. Wol dem / der da erwartet und erreicht tausend / drey hundert/ und fünff und dreyssig Tage. (das ist / Jahre / derer sind 75. mehr / als die in 7. vers. vermeldet / und 45. Jahr mehr / als die vers. 11. bestimbt seyn. Wenn diese 1335. Jahr erfüllet / 1335
wird Christus zum Gericht kommen / und des Ende-Christs/ durch die Erscheinung seiner Zukunfft/ein Ende machen 2. Thessal. II. 8. und seine Kirche vollkömmlich erlösen. Weil man aber das Jahr/wenn dieselbigen Jahr anzufahen eigentlich nicht weiß/ als kan man auch den Ausgang derselben nicht wissen/und also die Zeit der Zukunfft des HErrn nicht ausrechnen/Marc. XIII. 32. Wiewol/ sagt Herr Luth. diese Deutung scheinet / als solte man des Jüngsten Tages gewiß seyn / welches" Tages/ oder Jahres er kommen solte / daß doch" Christus verbeut zu wissen / Actor I. 7. und im" Evangelio/ Marc. XIII. 32. so fehlts doch weit." Erstlich / daß wenn schon das Opffer des Evan" gelii abgethan wird / so wird doch niemand kön" nen das Jahr / noch Tag/so eben mercken/ wenn" es anfähet / sintemal es nicht kan auf einen Tag" an allen Orten aufhören. Zum andern / ob" mans schon wüste / wenn es solt anfahen/so sind" doch über die 1290. die 1335. Tage gesetzt / die nie" mand mercken würde in aller Welt. Und Sum" ma / ich dencke / daß diese 1335. Tage nicht wer" den öffentlich in gemein verstanden werden /" sie seyn denn erfüllet am Jüngsten Tage" Es wäre denn / daß GOTT etwa einen" Noah würde erwecken / der dieselben Tage" künte abrechnen und gewiß treffen. Ich aber" für mich / lasse mir daran genügen / daß der" Jüngste Tag für der Thür seyn muß / denn die" Zeichen / so Christus verkündiget / und die A" postel/ Petrus / und Paulus / sind nun fast all" geschehen. Und die Bäume schlagen aus / die" Schrifft grünet und blühet. Ob wir den Tag" nicht so eben wissen können / liegt nit dran / ein" ander mache es besser. Es ist gewißlich alles" am Ende. Etliche zwar fahen des Ende-Christs Reich an vom Bonifacio III. welchen der Kayser-Mörder Phocas nachdem er Kayser Mauritium getödtet / und deswegen vom Constantinopolitanischen Patriarchen gestrafft worden / dieser Bonifacius aber ihn von solcher schweren Sünde absolviret hat / den Titul eines allgemeinen Bischoffen der Kirchen / und das Recht die Concilia zusammen zufordern / ertheilet hat. Welches im 606ten Jahr Christi geschehen. Andere aber machen des Anti-Christischen Reichs

52a

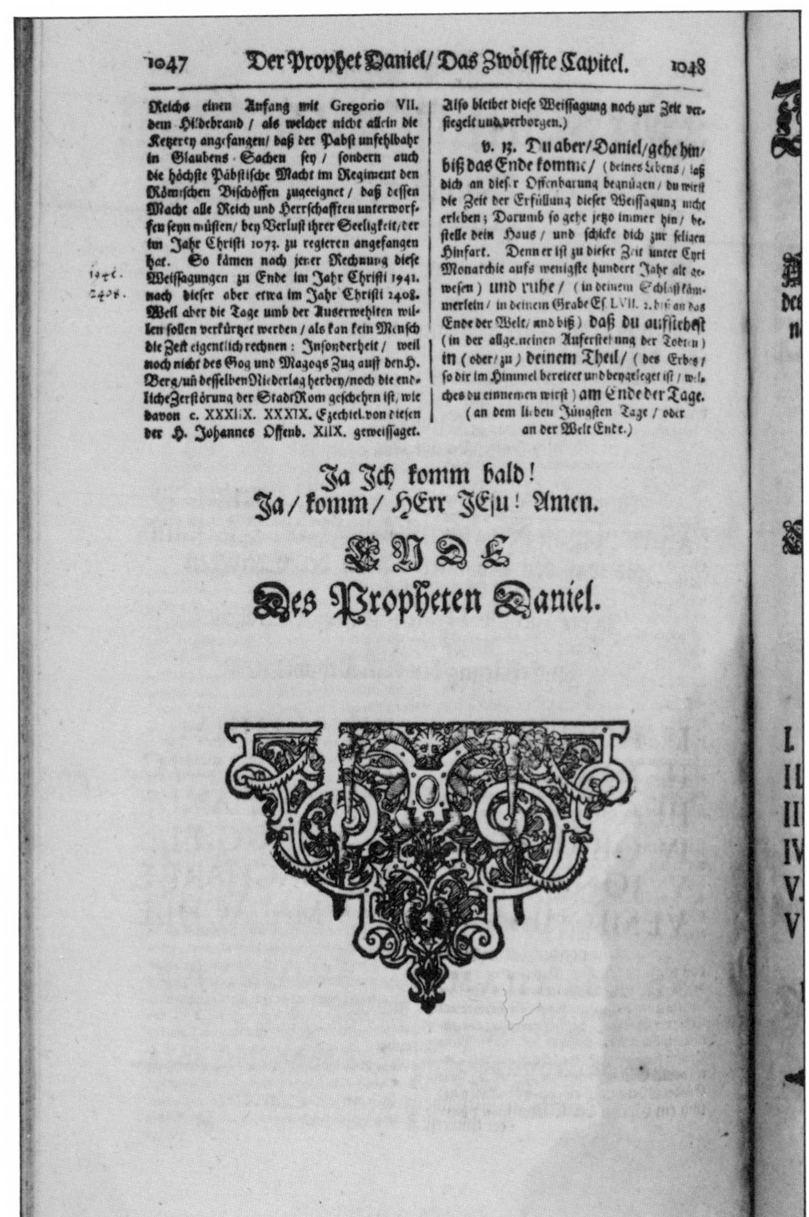

1047 Der Prophet Daniel/ Das Zwölffte Capitel. 1048

Reichs einen Anfang mit Gregorio VII. dem Hildebrand / als welcher nicht allein die Ketzerey angefangen/ daß der Pabst unfehlbahr in Glaubens-Sachen sey / sondern auch die höchste Päbstische Macht im Regiment den Römischen Bischöffen zugeeignet / daß dessen Macht alle Reich und Herrschafften unterworffen seyn müsten/ bey Verlust ihrer Seeligkeit/ der im Jahr Christi 1073. zu regieren angefangen hat. So kämen nach jener Rechnung diese Weissagungen zu Ende im Jahr Christi 1941. nach dieser aber etwa im Jahr Christi 2408. Weil aber die Tage umb der Auserwehlten willen sollen verkürtzet werden / als kan kein Mensch die Zeit eigentlich rechnen: Insonderheit / weil noch nicht des Gog und Magogs Zug auff den H. Berg/ uñ desselben Niederlag herbey/ noch die endliche Zerstörung der Stadt Rom geschehen ist, wie davon c. XXXIIX. XXXIX. Ezechiel. von diesen der H. Johannes Offenb. XIIX. geweissaget. Also bleibet diese Weissagung noch zur Zeit versiegelt und verborgen.)

v. 13. Du aber/ Daniel/ gehe hin/ biß das Ende komme/ (deines Lebens / laß dich an dieser Offenbarung begnügen / du wirst die Zeit der Erfüllung dieser Weissagung nicht erleben; Darumb so gehe jetzo immer hin/ bestelle dein Haus / und schicke dich zur seligen Hinfart. Denn er ist zu dieser Zeit unter Cyri Monarchie aufs wenigste hundert Jahr alt gewesen) und ruhe / (in deinem Schlaffkämmerlein / in deinem Grabe Es. LVII. 2. biß an das Ende der Welt/ und biß) daß du auffstehest (in der allgemeinen Aufferstehung der Todten) in (oder/ zu) deinem Theil/ (des Erbes / so dir im Himmel bereitet und beygeleget ist / welches du einnemen wirst) am Ende der Tage. (an dem lieben Jüngsten Tage / oder an der Welt Ende.)

Ja Ich komm bald!
Ja / komm / HErr JEsu! Amen.

ENDE
Des Propheten Daniel.

52b

53 The title page for the remainder of the commentary on the Old Testament, that is, Vol. 2/IV:

J.N.J. The Minor Prophets according to the German translation of blessed Dr. Martin Luther, diligently examined in the original text and according to the phraseology of the Holy Spirit, in words and expressions, following the real meaning and intention according to the whole context and the parallel passages of Holy Scripture, the elucidation of the New Testament, and the analogy of faith, and compiled from the valuable writings of Luther, in the interest of both the real literal meaning and of the salutary application of divine Scripture, and in the fear of the Lord, the 12 prophets are expounded, namely:

I.	Hosea	VII.	Nahum
II.	Joel	VIII.	Habakkuk
III.	Amos	IX.	Zephaniah
IV.	Obadiah	X.	Haggai
V.	Jonah	XI.	Zechariah
VI.	Micah	XII.	Malachi

by Dr. Abraham Calov, public professor, chairman of the theological faculty, senior pastor of the church consistory, pastor and general superintendent at Wittenberg. In the year of Christ 1682. printed at Wittenberg by Christian Schrödter, the university's printer of books.

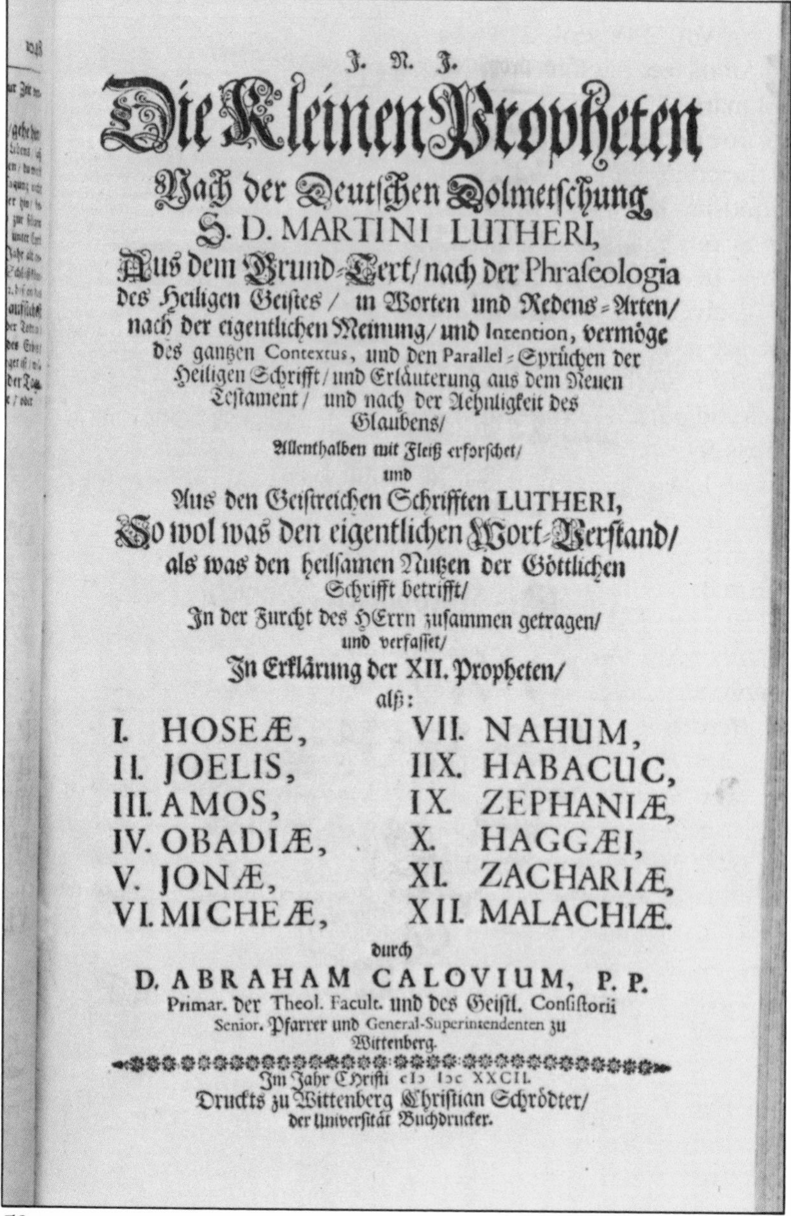

J. N. J.

Die Kleinen Propheten

Nach der Deutschen Dolmetschung

S. D. MARTINI LUTHERI,

Aus dem Grund-Text/ nach der Phraseologia des Heiligen Geistes / in Worten und Redens-Arten/ nach der eigentlichen Meinung/ und Intention, vermöge des gantzen Contextus, und den Parallel-Sprüchen der Heiligen Schrifft/ und Erläuterung aus dem Neuen Testament/ und nach der Aehnligkeit des Glaubens/

Allenthalben mit Fleiß erforschet/

und

Aus den Geistreichen Schrifften LUTHERI,

So wol was den eigentlichen Wort-Verstand/ als was den heilsamen Nutzen der Göttlichen Schrifft betrifft/

In der Furcht des HErrn zusammen getragen/ und verfasset/

In Erklärung der XII. Propheten/

alß:

I. HOSEÆ,	VII. NAHUM,
II. JOELIS,	IIX. HABACUC,
III. AMOS,	IX. ZEPHANIÆ,
IV. OBADIÆ,	X. HAGGÆI,
V. JONÆ,	XI. ZACHARIÆ,
VI. MICHEÆ,	XII. MALACHIÆ.

durch

D. ABRAHAM CALOVIUM, P. P.

Primar. der Theol. Facult. und des Geistl. Consistorii Senior. Pfarrer und General-Superintendenten zu Wittenberg.

Im Jahr Christi cIↄ Iↄc XXCII.

Druckts zu Wittenberg Christian Schrödter/ der Universität Buchdrucker.

53

54 Vol. 2/IV, col. 213–14. On Amos 6:6. Bach has put *NB.* and marks of emphasis, as well as some underlining of the text, by the commentary on the verse and has done so in red ink. Amos 6:6 reads: "Who drink wine in bowls, and anoint themselves with the finest oils, but are not grieved over the ruin of Joseph!" Bach underlines and puts *NB* alongside the words *Schaden Joseph* (ruin of Joseph). As Christoph Trautmann has pointed out (Trautmann B, p. 96), this recalls a title in Bach's library (Leaver C, no. 19): *Evangelisches Praeservative wider den Schaden Josephs in allen dreyen Ständen, Herausgezogen Auss den Sonn-und Fest-Tags Evangelein . . . von Heinrich Müllern . . .* [herausgegeben von] *Samuele Christiano Mummio . . .* (Evangelical preservative against the ruin of Joseph in all three estates, extracted from the Gospels for the Sundays and festivals . . . by Heinrich Müller . . . [edited by] Samuel Christian Mummius) (Frankfurt, 1681). The volume also contains, as an appendix, a series of sermons on the Passion of Jesus that influenced the libretto of Bach's *Matthäuspassion,* BWV 244 (see E. Axmacher, "Ein Quellenfund zum Text der Matthäus-Passion," *BJ,* 1978, pp. 181–91; E. Axmacher, *"Aus Liebe will mein Heyland sterben": Untersuchungen zum Wandel des Passionsverständnisses im frühen 18. Jahrhundert* [Stuttgart, 1984], pp. 28–52, 170–85).

Calov's commentary on the verse, which includes a substantial quotation from

54

Luther, is as follows (the words in Roman type are those underlined in red by Bach):

> *Or, they have no sorrow and pain over the miserable* condition of the kingdom of Israel, *in the family of* Ephraim and Joseph, *neither in religious nor secular life, see Isaiah 5:12. Similarly, the brothers of Joseph, after they had cast their brother into the pit to die of thirst, sat down to eat, Gen. 37:24, and were unconcerned about his wailing and cries for help: consequently, they live in sensual pleasures, without censure, while the religious and secular life of the kingdom of Israel was in such a distress and miserable condition, and*

> *their brothers of the tribe of Manasseh, on the other side of the Jordan, suffered such great ruin from the Syrians, as it is given in the marginal note in the Weimar Bible. Herr Luther: "God does not condemn the possession of wealth and goods but rather the evil use of them, that is, solely for one's own amusement and pleasure instead of helping the poor, and more than that, so that he is no true benefactor and dispenser of what the dear God has given and presented to us. Here he is condemning the impure and ungodly way that they are not grieved over the ruin of Joseph, that is, over the poor and afflicted people in the kingdom of Israel, that they did not administer rightful justice, but oppressed, devoured, and plagued the poor in their deliberations, as I have said before."*

The "Weimar Bible" was issued under the auspices of Duke Ernst of Sachsen-Weimar, with notes by Johann Gerhard, Solomon Glass, Johann Michael Dilherr, and others: *Biblia . . . Teutsch D. Martin Luthers . . . Von etlichen reinen Theologen . . . erkläret . . .* (Nürnberg, 1641), with frequent reprints (on another Bible edition referred to by Calov, see no. 37). The marks of emphasis alongside this passage, which deals with one's responsibilities to the poor, link with some underlining in black in at Deut. 24:17 (Vol. 1/I, col. 1075), which reads: "This law stands over all duty and right, the one owes nourishment and clothing to the poor . . . the lender should bestow and give to that the poor may live."

The commentary on the previous verse, Amos 6:5 (col. 213), has a particular significance for Bach, and it may have been his concern for this verse that led him to the commentary on the following verse (6):

> *That is, in imitation of David, but not with David's spirit. Herr Luther: "That is, they would do the same as David and also sing and play the psaltery. But David used his psaltery to praise God, and to kindle his heart towards God, and to stir up the spirit through the Word of God: but they misuse it for entertainment, to satisfy their own ears."*

55 The main title page of the third double volume, that is, Vol. 3/V:

> *J.N.J. The New Testament as translated into German by Dr. Martin Luther, presented according to the real intention and meaning of the Holy Spirit from the words of the original texts, as well as from the context, and parallel passages, and from the writings of the dear man of God, Luther, in the single, true literal sense, for the wholesome use in education, refutation, exhortation, and consolation, by Abraham Calov, public professor, chairman of the theological faculty, senior pastor of the church consistory, and general superintendent of Electoral Saxony in Wittenberg. Wittenberg, printed by Christian Schrödter, the university's printer of books.*

As on the half-title and main title pages there is the statement that the commentary is essentially taken from the writings of Luther.

In the bottom right-hand corner is Bach's monogram and the year "1733"; see the Introduction, p. 26, and nos. 2 and 47.

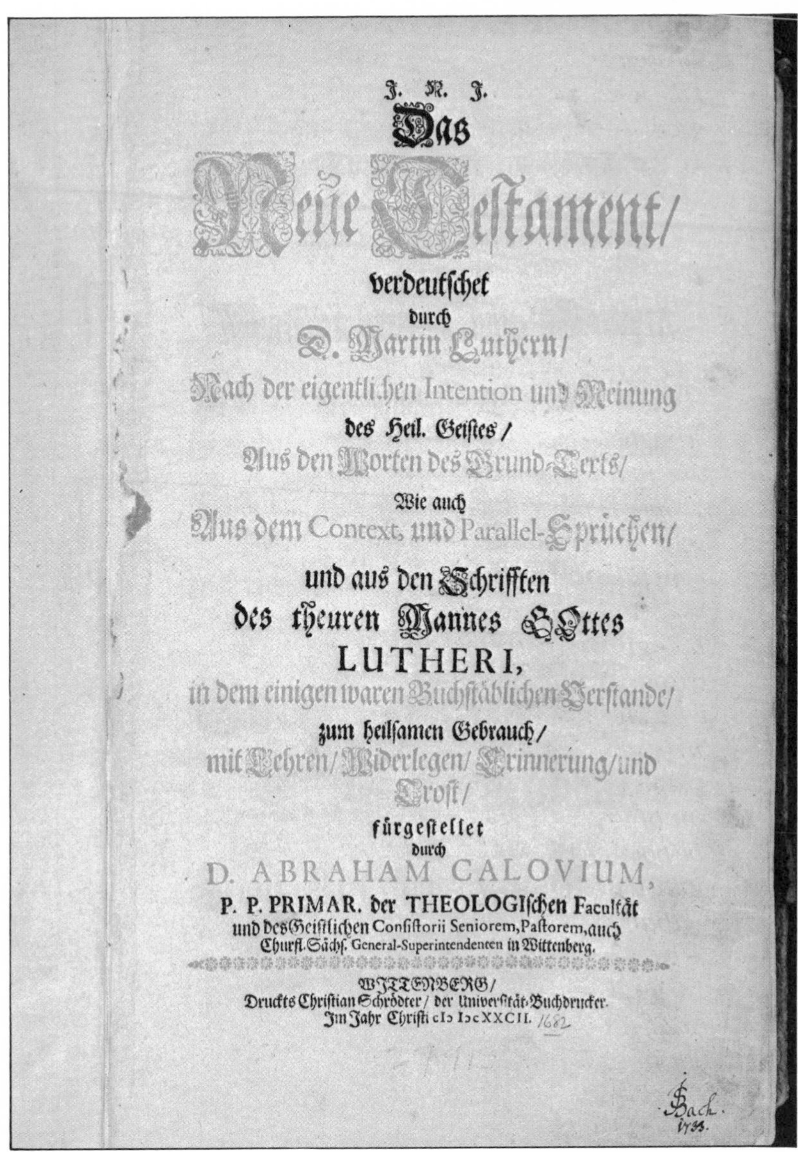

J. N. J.
Das
Neüe Testament/
verdeutschet
durch
D. Martin Luthern/
Nach der eigentlichen Intention und Meinung
des Heil. Geistes/
Aus den Worten des Grund-Texts/
Wie auch
Aus dem Context, und Parallel-Sprüchen/
und aus den Schrifften
des theuren Mannes GOttes
LUTHERI,
in dem einigen waren Buchstäblichen Verstande/
zum heilsamen Gebrauch/
mit Lehren/ Widerlegen/ Erinnerung/ und
Trost/
fürgestellet
durch
D. ABRAHAM CALOVIUM,
P. P. PRIMAR. der THEOLOGIschen Facultät
und des Geistlichen Consistorii Seniorem, Pastorem, auch
Churfl. Sächs. General-Superintendenten in Wittenberg.
WITTENBERG/
Druckts Christian Schrödter/ der Universität-Buchdrucker.
Im Jahr Christi CIↃ IↃCXXCII. 1682

Bach
1733.

55

tät-Buchdrucker.
CII. 1682

Bach
1733.

55a

56 Vol. 3/V, sig. †††††2 recto. The final page of the dedication of this third double volume, which marks the completion of the project. Calov writes:

> *Wittenberg on 31 October (on which Herr Luther, the angel with the eternal Gospel, who rose up in the heaven of the church* [see Rev. 14:6], *on the Eve of All Saints, placarded on the door of the Castle Church here, also known as the Church of All Saints, the first disputation against the papacy on indulgences* [the *95 Theses or Disputation on the Power and Efficacy of Indulgences,* 1517], *by which the Roman Anti-Christ was given a great jolt, and the light of the Gospel was spread throughout all the world) in the year from the birth of Christ our Savior 1682, from the creation of the world 5682.*

By this time 31 October was celebrated as the Reformation Festival in Lutheran Germany, and the Gospel for the day was Rev. 14:6–8. Since Calov finished, or contrived to finish, on this significant date, it is not surprising to find him referring to it and its significance. See further the notes on nos. 51, 69, 74.

Dedication-Schrifft/

zogen werden / welches der allerhöchste GOtt in Gnaden also dirigiren und zu Ende bringen wolle/daß an dem Ort/ da das ewige Evangelium durch seine überschwengliche Gnade wieder herfür gebracht/ und in andere Länder und Königreiche fortgepflantzet ist / auch solche theure Lutherische Beylage anietzo durch die Schrifft-mäßige Erklärung und Vertretung solcher heilsamen Lehre/auß dem eigentlichen buchstäblichen Verstande des Wortes Gottes / propagiret / und in die werthe Christenheit ausgebreitet werden möge.

Derselbe verleihe gnädiglich / daß auch dieselbige allhier und allenthalben / wo sie geleuchtet hat / immerdar biß an den Tag der Zukunfft und herrlichen Erscheinung des grossen Gottes und unsers Heylandes Christi JEsu / hell und klar leuchten möge/ ohn einige Verdunckelung / daß dafür die Heilige Hochgelobte Drey-Einigkeit gepriesen werde.

Wittenberg/ am XXXI. Octobris, (da Herr LUTHERUS/ der Engel mit dem ewigen Evangelio/ durch den Kirchen-Himmel anfahen zu fliegen/ in Vigilia omnium Sanctorum, an das Thor der Schloß-Kirchen allhier/ die auch Templum omnium Sanctorum heißet / die erste Disputation wider das Pabstthum / de Indulgentiis, anschlagend/ dadurch dem Römischen Anti-Christ ein grosser Stoß gegeben/und das Liecht des Evangelii in aller Welt ausgebreitet worden /) im Jahr von der Geburt CHristi unsers Heylandes cIↄ Iↄc LXXXII. von Erschaffung der Welt 5682.

††††† 2 F. R. J.

56

57 Vol. 3/V, col. 53–54. On Matthew 5:26. Bach has placed "NB" and marks of emphasis alongside Luther's commentary on the verse and has also underlined a number of phrases. Matt. 5:25–26: "Make friends quickly with your accuser, while you are going with him to court, lest your accuser hand you over to the judge, and the judge to the guard, and you be put in prison; truly, I say to you, you will never get out till you have paid the last penny." Luther's comment, taken from vol. 5 of the Altenburg edition, fol. 842, which begins towards the end of col. 53, is as follows (the passage Bach has marked out in the margin is given within the signs < >, and the words he has underlined are given in Roman type):

53 Das Fünffte Capitel. 54

er über dich seufftzen muß / daß du nicht deinen Zorn wilt sincken lassen /) **und der Richter** (GOtt der dich zur Versöhnung anmahnet / und dir fürschreibet / du solt deinem Nechsten seine Fehle und Schuld vergeben / Matth. VI. 12. c. XIIX. 35.) **überantworte dich dem Diener / und werdest in den Kercker geworffen.** (des höllischen Feuers / dahin die Unversöhnliche gehören / die Greulichen und Todschläger Offenb. XXI. 8. XXII. 15. Denn Feindschafft / Hader / Neid / Zorn Zanck / Zwietracht sind die Wercke des Fleisches und die solches thun / werden das Reich Gottes nicht ererben / Galat. V. 20. 21. Darumb ermahnet der H. Geist / daß wir untereinander freundlich und hertzlich seyn sollen / und vergeben einer dem andern / gleich wie GOtt uns vergeben hat in Christo Eph. IV. 32. und die Sonne nicht lassen über unserm Zorn untergehen / v. 26. Sondern in der Liebe wandeln / wie Christus uns geliebet hat / Eph. V. 2. Col. III. 13.)

v. 26. **Ich sage dir warlich / du wirst nicht von dannen herauß kommen / biß du auch den letzten Heller bezahlest.** (das ist / nimmer / in alle Ewigkeit / denn in der Hölle geschicht keine Bezahlung. Hier alle Sünde vergeben werden: in diesem Leben / nicht aber nach diesem Leben / da kan nicht der geringste Heller bezahlet werden / so wenig als einige Hoffnung der Erlösung ist aus der Höllen. Darumb spricht er nun / sagt Herr Lutherus l. c. p. 842. Wilt du GOtt dienen und opffern / und hast iemand beleidiget / oder einen Zorn wider deinen Nechsten / so wisse kurtz umb / daß GOtt deines Opffers nicht haben wil / sondern lege es schlecht nieder / und laß alles anstehen / und gehe vorhin / und versöhne dich mit deinem Bruder. Damit meinet er nun alle Wercke / so man thun kan / GOtt zu Dienst oder Lob (denn zu der Zeit war kein besser Werck / denn opffern) und verwirffts doch gar / heissets schlecht lassen liegen. Es sey denn / daß dir dein Hertz vorhin sage / du seyst versühnt mit deinem Nechsten / und keinen Zorn bey dir wissest. Wenn das geschehen ist / so komme denn / (sagt er /) und bringe dein Opffer. Das setzt er dennoch darzu / daß man nicht dencke / er wolle solch Opffer verwerffen / oder verachten / denn es ist nicht ein böß Werck gewesen / sondern von GOTT geordnet und geboten. Aber das ist böse / und verderbt es gar / daß sie die andern höhern Gebot in Wind schlagen / und dagegen verachten. Das heist des Opffers mißbraucht wider den Nechsten. Und ferner über den 25. Vers. Sey willfärtig / schreibt Herr Lutherus p. 842. Im vorigen Text hat er dem geprediget / der dem Nechsten beleidiget oder erzürnet hat: Hie aber sagt er / wie sich der soll halten / der da beleidiget ist. Und führet noch das Gleichniß / als er hat angefangen / wie es für Gericht gehet / da zwey Theil gegen einander stehen / und einer klagt / der andere beklagt wird / und der Richter das Urtheil spricht / und das Theil / so schuldig ist / straffet. Und ist nichts anders / denn so viel gesagt: Daß wer den andern beleidiget / soll sich freundlich mit ihm versühnen: der andere aber soll sich versühnen lassen / und gerne vergeben: Das ist nun auch ein subtil Stück / und können hie auch viel Leute den Schalck aus dermassen fein decken und schmücken / damit daß sie sagen: Sie wollens gerne vergeben / aber nicht vergessen. Wahr ist es / wie gesagt / daß Zorn muß und soll seyn / aber da siehe zu / daß er gehe / wie er gehen soll / und dir befohlen sey / daß du nicht von deinet wegen / sondern von Ampts und Gottes wegen müssest zürnen / und nicht die zwey / deine Person und Ampt in einander mengest. Für deine Person solt du mit niemand zürnen / wie hoch du beleidiget bist / wo es aber dein Ampt fordert / da must du zürnen / ob dir wol für deine Person kein Leid geschehen ist. Wenn aber dein Bruder etwas wider dich gethan / und dich erzürnet hat / und bittet dirs abe / und legt das böse Werck abe / so soll auch der Zorn weggehen. Woher kömpt denn der heimliche Groll / den du gleichwol im Hertzen behältest / so doch das Werck und Ursach des Zorns hinweg ist / und er dafür nun ander Werck erzeigt / als der sich bekehrt / und nun gar ein ander Mensch / und ein neuer Baum ist worden mit neuen Früchten / der dich nun liebet und ehret auffs allerhöchste. Damit daß er sich gegen dir beschuldiget / und selbsten strafft / und must für GOtt und aller Welt ein verzweiffelter Mensch seyn / wo du nicht wiederumb dich gegen ihm so erzeigest / und von Hertzen vergiebest / daß dir billich solch Urtheil wiederfähret / wie Christus hier dräuet. Vergleiche auch Tom. IIX. Altenburg. p. 884. da Herr Lutherus saget: GOtt wil keinem gnädig seyn / noch seine Sünde vergeben / er vergebe denn seinem Nechsten auch. So kan auch der Glaube nicht rechtschaffen seyn / er bringe denn diese Frucht / daß er dem Nechsten vergebe / und umb Vergebung bitte. Sonst darff der Mensch für GOtt nicht kommen / ist diese Frucht nicht da / so ist der Glaube und die erste Beichte auch nicht rechtschaffen.)

v. 27. **Ihr habt gehöret / daß zu den Alten gesaget ist: du solt nicht Ehebrechen.** (2. Mos. XX. 18.)

v. 28. **Ich aber sage euch: wer ein Weib ansiehet ihr zu begehren / der hat schon mit ihr die Ehe gebrochen in seinen Hertzen.** (5. Mos. V. 18. das verstehet Moses nicht allein / von einem Eheweib / sondern wie Christus es deutet von einer ieglichen Weibes Personen / Vergl. Jer. III. 9. Os. IV. 3. Job. XXIV. 35. S. auch 3. Mos. XIX. 29. c. XXI. 7. 5. Mos. XXII. 20. 21. c. XXIII. 2. 12. 13. 17. 18. Ez. XVI. 15. item Job XXXI. 9. Sprüchw. VI. 24. c. XXIII. 11. Jer. V. 8. Ez. VI. 9. c. XXIII. 6. Die Ehe wird nicht allein mit Wercken / oder Geberden / sondern auch mit bösen Begierden / und Gedancken des Hertzens gebrochen / Matth. XV. 19. Von Ehebruch / sagt Herr Lutherus / hatten die Pharisæer es gedeutet / es wäre nicht mehr verboten / denn wo ein Ehebruch mit der That geschehe / und hieltens nicht für Sünde / ob sie gleich im Hertzen entbrand wären mit böser Lust und Liebe / gegen einer andern / und auch außwendig mit hübschen Worten / und schandbaren Geberden sich erzeigten / und schadet ihnen nichts an ihrer Heiligkeit / wenn sie nur sonst gute Wercke thäten / fleissig opfferten und beteten. Das heist nicht Gottes Gebot gelehret / sondern gar verkehret / und nicht die Leute fromm gemacht sondern nur ärger / und nur Raum und Urlaub gegeben / zu allerley Sünde und Unzucht. Aber hie hörest du einen andern Meister / der solche ihre Heiligkeit zu Sünden und Schanden machet / und recht in dis Gebot leuchtet / und schleust / daß Ehebruch auch wol mit Augen / Ohren / Mund / ja allermeist mit dem Hertzen geschicht / als wenn ein Mann ein Weib ansiehet / oder mit ihr schertzet / ja an sie gedencket mit böser Lust. etc.)

v. 29. **Ergert dich aber dein rechtes Auge / so reiß es aus und wirffs von dir.** (* Geistliches außreissen ist hier geboten / das ist / wenn der Augen-Lust getödtet wird im Hertzen und abgethan

D y

57

In the preceding verses He [Christ] *was preaching against the man who injured his neighbor or became angry with him. Now He talks about how the injured party should behave. He stays with the analogy He had used earlier, that is, the procedure in a courtroom with two parties opposed to each other, one party as the accuser and the other party as the accused, and with the judge pronouncing sentence and punishing the guilty party. What He wants to say is that while a man who injures another should in a friendly way become reconciled with him, the injured party should also be willing to be reconciled and to forgive. This, too, is a delicate problem, where it is easy for many people to cover up and decorate their malice by saying that they are willing to forgive but not to forget . . . Of course, as we have said, anger is sometimes necessary and proper. But be sure that you use it correctly. You are commanded to get angry, not on your own behalf, <but on behalf of your office and of God; you must not confuse the two, your person and your office. As far as your person is concerned, you must not get angry with anyone regardless of the injury he may have done to you.* But where your office requires it, there you must get angry, *even*

> *though* no injury has been done to you personally. . . . But if your *brother has* done something *against* you *and* angered you, and then begs your pardon *and stops doing wrong, your anger, too, should disappear. Where does the secret spite come from which you continue to keep in your heart?> The deed that caused your anger is gone, and in its place have come other deeds, which show that the man is converted and has become a completely different person, a new tree with new fruits. Now he gives you his love and his highest esteem, he blames and reproaches himself on your account. If you do not give him another chance and cordially forgive him, you must really be a scoundrel before both God and all the world; and you deserve the sentence which Christ threatens here.* ("Sermon on the Mount," *LW* 21:82–83)

Gerhard Herz, who also gives an alternative translation of part of the passage quoted above, concludes that Bach's underlining shows that "the composer found in this remarkable passage an answer, even a God-given justification, for his own pugnacious nature in professional matters" (G. Herz, "Toward a New Image of Bach," *BACH* 1, no. 4 [Oct. 1970]: 26). There is no doubt that Bach could be stubborn, irascible, and impatient, as can be seen in his brawl with one Geyersbach, whom he called a nanny goat bassoonist [Zippelfaggottist] in Arnstadt, August 1705 (see BD 2:15–18; *BR,* p. 51), or in the almost continous disputes of one kind or another he had in Leipzig (see R. A. Leaver, "Leipzig's Rejection of J. S. Bach," *BACH* 3, no. 3 [July 1972]: 27–29, and no. 4 [Oct. 1972]: 3–7). But the major disputes were professional rather than personal, or at least they were on the surface. His conflict over the question of the provision of music for the official occasions of the university, 1725–26, was one that concerned his professional office; his predecessor Kuhnau had done so, so why not Bach? A similar case was the conflict in 1728 over who should choose the hymns for the services; Bach argued that it was his function by virtue of the practice of his predecessors (see *BD* 1:54–55; *BR,* p. 114–15). And his petition to the town council of 1730, in which he asked for more adequate musical resources, and the long-running battle with the rector of the Thomasschule, Johann August Ernesti, 1736–37, over the question of the appointment of prefects, were both matters that touched his office and calling as cantor and director of music in Leipzig. If the town council would not pay for good instrumentalists, and if Ernesti persisted in downgrading the practice of music and singing in the Thomasschule, then there could not be the "God-pleasing music" in the churches of Leipzig that it was his prime function to provide. It is clear, especially from this passage with Bach's markings, that the Thomascantor saw these as professional rather than personal disputes. But notice that the element of forgiveness is also noted by Bach; where forgiveness and reconciliation are requested, they should never be withheld.

58 Vol. 3/V, col. 73–74. On Matthew 6:25. A portion of the commentary on the verse is underlined, and *wenn* is corrected to *wer.* The verse reads: "Therefore I tell you, do not be concerned about your life, what you shall eat or what you shall drink, not about your body, what you shall put on." Although it is not identified as such, the commentary on these words is taken almost verbatim from Luther (the words underlined are given here in Roman type):

> *Christ is not talking here about the concerns of vocation, which must be sharply distinguished from greed. It is not concerned for its own sake but for the neighbor's sake. It does not seek its own interests but even neglects them, in order to serve somebody else, which is called a concern of love, something divine and Christian, not a concern devoted to its own advantage or to Mammon, which is against both faith and love, and even hinders the concerns of vocation.* The one who loves money and looks out for his own advantage will not have much regard for his neighbor nor his neighbor's vocation. (based on *LW* 21:194).

On the concern for the poor and the neighbor's needs, see the note on no. 54.

73 Das Sechste Capitel. 74

58

v. 25. Darumb sag ich euch/sorget nicht für euer Leben/was ihr essen/ und trincken werdet / auch nicht für euren Leib/womit ihr euch kleiden werdet. (Hier redet Christus nicht von der Amptsorge / die weit zu scheiden ist von dem Geitz. Denn sie sorget nicht umb ihren/sondern umb des Nechsten willen. Suchet nicht das ihre/ja läst wol dasselbe anstehen/ und fahren / und dienet einem andern/daß es heist / eine Sorge der Liebe/ die da Göttlich und Christlich ist/nicht des Eigen Nutzes oder Mammons / welche ist beyde wider den Glauben/ und Liebe / und eben die/ die da hindert die Sorge des Ampts. Denn wer das Geld liebet / und nach seinen Nutzen trachtet / der wird sich des Nechsten oder seines Amptes gegen den Nechsten gerichtet / nicht groß annehmen. rc.) Ist nicht das Leben mehr/denn die Speise / und der Leib mehr / denn die Kleidung. (Herr Lutherus : Das ist/ Könnt ihr/und müst GOtt euer Leben / Leib und Seele

58a

59 Vol. 3/V, col. 341–42. At the top of the page the heading to this chapter 6 of St. Mark's gospel is given as "Das Fünffte Capitel"; *Fünffte* has been corrected to *Sechste.*

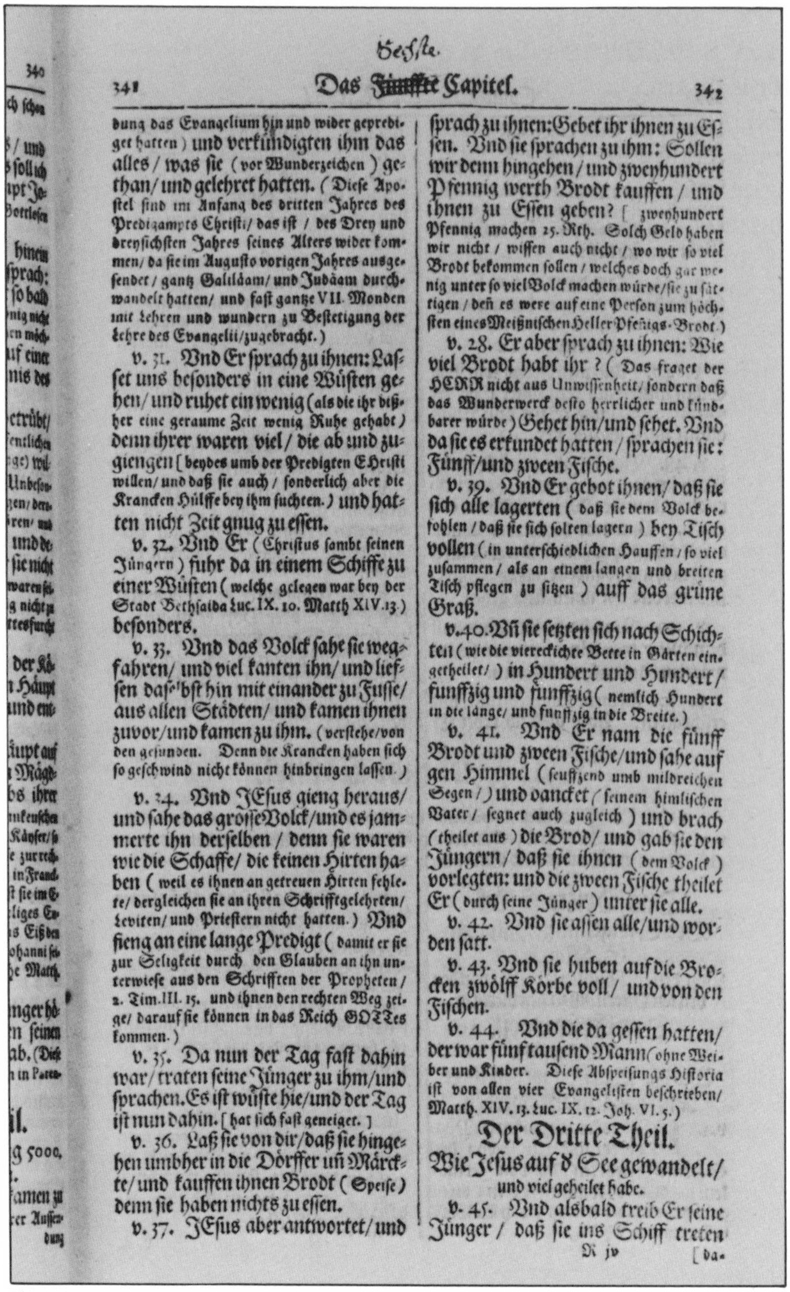
Sechste.

341 Das ~~Fünffte~~ Capitel. 342

dung das Evangelium hin und wider geprediget hatten) und verkündigten ihm das alles / was sie (vor Wunderzeichen) gethan/ und gelehret hatten. (Diese Apostel sind im Anfang des dritten Jahres des Predigampts Christi/ das ist / des Drey und dreysichsten Jahres seines Alters wider kommen/ da sie im Augusto vorigen Jahres ausgesendet / gantz Galiläam/ und Judäam durchwandelt hatten/ und fast gantze VII. Monden mit Lehren und wundern zu Bestetigung der Lehre des Evangelii/zugebracht.)
v. 31. Und Er sprach zu ihnen: Lasset uns besonders in eine Wüsten gehen/ und ruhet ein wenig (als die ihr bißher eine geraume Zeit wenig Ruhe gehabt) denn ihrer waren viel/ die ab und zugiengen [beydes umb der Predigten Christi willen/ und daß sie auch / sonderlich aber die Krancken Hülffe bey ihm suchten.) und hatten nicht Zeit gnug zu essen.
v. 32. Und Er (Christus sambt seinen Jüngern) fuhr da in einem Schiffe zu einer Wüsten (welche gelegen war bey der Stadt Bethsaida Luc. IX. 10. Matth XIV. 13.) besonders.
v. 33. Und das Volck sahe sie wegfahren/ und viel kanten ihn/ und liessen daselbst hin mit einander zu Fusse/ aus allen Städten/ und kamen ihnen zuvor/ und kamen zu ihm. (verstehe/von den gesunden. Denn die Krancken haben sich so geschwind nicht können hinbringen lassen.)
v. 34. Und JEsus gieng heraus/ und sahe das grosse Volck/ und es jammerte ihn derselben / denn sie waren wie die Schaffe/ die keinen Hirten haben (weil es ihnen an getreuen Hirten fehlete/ dergleichen sie an ihren Schrifftgelehrten/ Leviten/ und Priestern nicht hatten.) Und fieng an eine lange Predigt (damit er sie zur Seligkeit durch den Glauben an ihn unterwiese aus den Schrifften der Propheten / 2. Tim. III. 15. und ihnen den rechten Weg zeige/ darauf sie können in das Reich GOTTes kommen.)
v. 35. Da nun der Tag fast dahin war/ traten seine Jünger zu ihm/ und sprachen. Es ist wüste hie/ und der Tag ist nun dahin. [hat sich fast geneiget.]
v. 36. Laß sie von dir/ daß sie hingehen umbher in die Dörffer und Märckte/ und kauffen ihnen Brodt (Speise) denn sie haben nichts zu essen.
v. 37. JEsus aber antwortet/ und sprach zu ihnen: Gebet ihr ihnen zu Essen. Und sie sprachen zu ihm: Sollen wir denn hingehen / und zweyhundert Pfennig werth Brodt kauffen / und ihnen zu Essen geben? [zweyhundert Pfennig machen 25. Rth. Solch Geld haben wir nicht / wissen auch nicht / wo wir so viel Brodt bekommen sollen / welches doch gar wenig unter so viel Volck machen würde/ sie zu sättigen / denn es were auf eine Person zum höchsten eines Meißnischen Heller Pfennigs-Brodt.)
v. 38. Er aber sprach zu ihnen: Wie viel Brodt habt ihr? (Das fraget der HERR nicht aus Unwissenheit/ sondern daß das Wunderwerck desto herrlicher und kündbarer würde) Gehet hin/ und sehet. Und da sie es erkundet hatten / sprachen sie: Fünff/ und zween Fische.
v. 39. Und Er gebot ihnen/ daß sie sich alle lagerten (daß sie dem Volck befohlen / daß sie sich solten lagern) bey Tisch vollen (in unterschiedlichen Hauffen / so viel zusammen / als an einem langen und breiten Tisch pflegen zu sitzen) auff das grüne Graß.
v. 40. Und sie setzten sich nach Schichten (wie die viereckichte Bette in Gärten eingetheilet/) in Hundert und Hundert/ funffzig und funffzig (nemlich Hundert in die länge/ und funffzig in die Breite.)
v. 41. Und Er nam die fünff Brodt und zween Fische/ und sahe auf gen Himmel (seuffzend umb mildreichen Segen/) und dancket (seinem himlischen Vater/ segnet auch zugleich) und brach (theilet aus) die Brod/ und gab sie den Jüngern/ daß sie ihnen (dem Volck) vorlegten: und die zween Fische theilet Er (durch seine Jünger) unter sie alle.
v. 42. Und sie assen alle/ und worden satt.
v. 43. Und sie huben auf die Brocken zwölff Körbe voll/ und von den Fischen.
v. 44. Und die da gessen hatten/ der war fünf tausend Mann (ohne Weiber und Kinder. Diese Abspeisungs Historia ist von allen vier Evangelisten beschrieben/ Matth. XIV. 13. Luc. IX. 12. Joh. VI. 5.)

Der Dritte Theil.
Wie Jesus auf d' See gewandelt/ und viel geheilet habe.

v. 45. Und alsbald treib Er seine Jünger / daß sie ins Schiff treten

R iv [da-

59

60 Vol. 3/V, col. 351–52. Mark 8:19. The missing word *ihr* is inserted into the Biblical text. However, there must be some doublt over the authenticity of the entry; the shape of the letters is not characteristic of Bach's hand. But since it occurs in the margin nearest the spine it would have been difficult to have written with normal fluency.

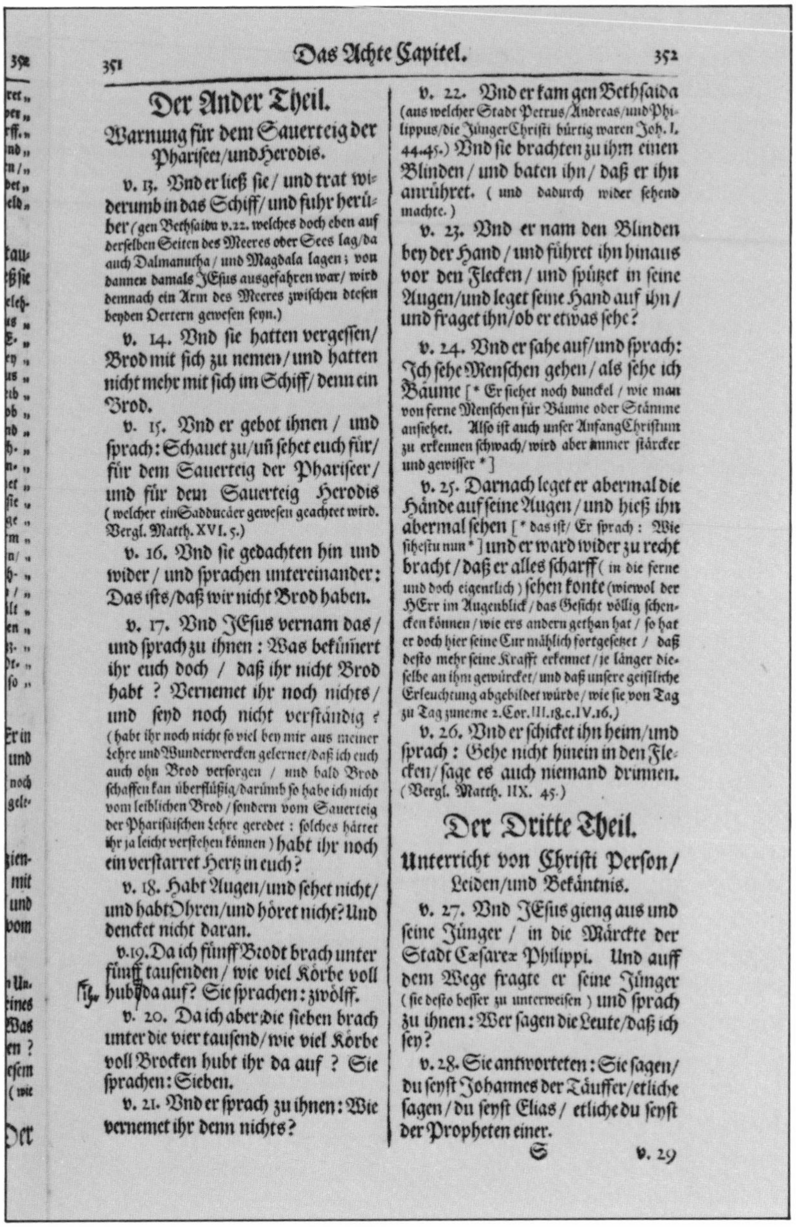

351 Das Achte Capitel. 352

Der Ander Theil.

Warnung für dem Sauerteig der Phariseer/und Herodis.

v. 13. Vnd er ließ sie/ und trat widerumb in das Schiff/ und fuhr herüber (gen Bethsaida v.22. welches doch eben auf derselben Seiten des Meeres oder Sees lag/da auch Dalmanutha/ und Magdala lagen; von dannen damals JEsus ausgefahren war/ wird demnach ein Arm des Meeres zwischen diesen beyden Oertern gewesen seyn.)

v. 14. Vnd sie hatten vergessen/ Brod mit sich zu nemen/und hatten nicht mehr mit sich im Schiff/ denn ein Brod.

v. 15. Vnd er gebot ihnen/ und sprach: Schauet zu/und sehet euch für/ für dem Sauerteig der Phariseer/ und für dem Sauerteig Herodis (welcher ein Sadducäer gewesen geachtet wird. Vergl. Matth. XVI. 5.)

v. 16. Vnd sie gedachten hin und wider/ und sprachen untereinander: Das ists/daß wir nicht Brod haben.

v. 17. Vnd JEsus vernam das/ und sprach zu ihnen: Was bekümmert ihr euch doch/ daß ihr nicht Brod habt? Vernemet ihr noch nichts/ und seyd noch nicht verständig? (habt ihr noch nicht so viel bey mir aus meiner Lehre und Wunderwercken gelernet/daß ich euch auch ohn Brod versorgen/ und bald Brod schaffen kan überflüßig/darümb so habe ich nicht vom leiblichen Brod/sondern vom Sauerteig der Pharisäischen Lehre geredet: solches hättet ihr ja leicht verstehen können) habt ihr noch ein verstarret Hertz in euch?

v. 18. Habt Augen/und sehet nicht/ und habt Ohren/und höret nicht? Und dencket nicht daran.

v. 19. Da ich fünff Brodt brach unter fünff tausenden/ wie viel Körbe voll hubt ihr da auf? Sie sprachen: zwölff.

v. 20. Da ich aber die sieben brach unter die vier tausend/ wie viel Körbe voll Brocken hubt ihr da auf? Sie sprachen: Sieben.

v. 21. Vnd er sprach zu ihnen: Wie vernemet ihr denn nichts?

v. 22. Vnd er kam gen Bethsaida (aus welcher Stadt Petrus/Andreas/und Philippus/die Jünger Christi bürtig waren Joh. I. 44.45.) Vnd sie brachten zu ihm einen Blinden/ und baten ihn/ daß er ihn anrühret. (und dadurch wider sehend machte.)

v. 23. Vnd er nam den Blinden bey der Hand/ und führet ihn hinaus vor den Flecken/ und spützet in seine Augen/und leget seine Hand auf ihn/ und fraget ihn/ob er etwas sehe?

v. 24. Vnd er sahe auf/und sprach: Ich sehe Menschen gehen/ als sehe ich Bäume [* Er siehet noch dunckel/ wie man von ferne Menschen für Bäume oder Stämme ansiehet. Also ist auch unser Anfang Christum zu erkennen schwach/ wird aber immer stärcker und gewisser *]

v. 25. Darnach leget er abermal die Hände auf seine Augen/ und hieß ihn abermal sehen [* das ist/ Er sprach: Wie sihestu nun *] und er ward wider zu recht bracht/ daß er alles scharff (in die ferne und doch eigentlich) sehen konte (wiewol der HErr im Augenblick/ das Gesicht völlig schencken können/ wie ers andern gethan hat/ so hat er doch hier seine Cur mählich fortgesetzet/ daß desto mehr seine Krafft erkennet/ je länger dieselbe an ihm gewürcket/ und daß unsere geistliche Erleuchtung abgebildet würde/ wie sie von Tag zu Tag zuneme 2. Cor. III. 18. c. IV. 16.)

v. 26. Vnd er schicket ihn heim/ und sprach: Gehe nicht hinein in den Flecken/ sage es auch niemand drinnen. (Vergl. Matth. IIX. 45.)

Der Dritte Theil.

Unterricht von Christi Person/ Leiden/und Bekäntnis.

v. 27. Vnd JEsus gieng aus und seine Jünger/ in die Märckte der Stadt Cæsareæ Philippi. Und auff dem Wege fragte er seine Jünger (sie desto besser zu unterweisen) und sprach zu ihnen: Wer sagen die Leute/ daß ich sey?

v. 28. Sie antworteten: Sie sagen/ du seyst Johannes der Täuffer/ etliche sagen/ du seyst Elias/ etliche du seyst der Propheten einer.

S v. 29

60

61 Vol. 3/V, col. 365–66. Mark 10:29–30. The missing words from the Biblical text of verse 29, as well as the following verse is full, are supplied in the opposite margin, so that it reads thus:

> . . . *Brüder und Schwester oder* Vatter und *Mutter oder* Weib *and Kinder and Aecker* um meinet Willen, und um des Evangelii Willen. V.30. Der nicht hundertfältig empfahe, itzt in dieser Zeit, Häuser u. Brüder, u. Schwestern u. Mütter u. Kinder, u. Äcker *mit Verfolgung* . . .

Here is an indication of Bach's concern for the integrity of the Biblical text. The error is an example of haplography, that is, the typesetter's eye went back to the second *Aecker* instead of the first and therefore omitted all the intervening words. Thus Bach fills in what is missing. Significantly, verse 30 speaks about the spiritual recompense the believer can expect in return for enduring difficulties and persecution for the sake of Christ and the Gospel. In all his disputes Bach could feel somewhat persecuted, and there may well be here an indication of the solace he found in the Word of Scripture that pointed him to Christ and the importance of the Gospel. See also no. 57.

61

61a

62 Vol. 3/V, col. 419–20. On Luke 1:45 (wrongly printed as v. 44). In Luther's commentary on the verse, the word *Jerusalem* is underlined and *Hebron* added to the margin. The quotation from Luther is taken from the *Hausspostille* of 1544. Bach had two separate editions of this collection of sermons on the church year, one in folio and the other quarto (Leaver C, nos. 7 and 28). The quotation is taken from the third part of the *Hausspostille,* the first sermon for the Feast of the Visitation:

62

> *It is right that Mary is honored not only for having general faith, which all Christians share and are blessed, that they have believed and found the grace of God through the fruit of the Virgin's womb, from which fullness we have all received grace upon grace (John 1:16), but also for special faith. For she has a special promise, which only applies to her, that she should give birth to Christ, the Son of God. Such promise she believes and does not allow herself to deviate from it, even if she does not understand it or know where it will lead. In this faith she makes a journey and goes to the mountains to her friend Elizabeth. As soon as she has heard from the angel that she would conceive in her womb and give birth to a Son, who will be great and will be known as the Son of the Highest (Luke 1:31–32), and that Elizabeth had also conceived a son in her old age, she makes this journey and goes straight to Elizabeth, without yielding or wavering, but is strong in faith, not in unbelief doubting the word of the angel, but is steady and strong in faith and knows above all that what God has promised through the angel will be fulfilled. Thus it is no joke but clearly in earnest that she believes that she is the mother of God and that Elizabeth has also conceived. Perhaps she does not go alone but Joseph goes with her, for it is further than the distance between Nazareth and Jerusalem, nevertheless, she will not be prevented from making the long*

> *and hard journey. Thus she acts by faith. We should follow this example, even if we do not have a similar special promise, as is Mary's, and cannot do what she does, we nevertheless have the general promise, which is both physical and spiritual. We should grasp the same Word and not doubt, but firmly believe that what God has said, that He will also do. For these two must be kept together, Word and faith. Faith cannot be without the Word, and, conversely, where the Word is there must also be faith.*

It is not exactly clear why Bach should substitute *Hebron* for *Jerusalem,* but this is another indication that he had a concern for Biblical topography (see no. 10). Bach composed at least two cantatas for the Feast of the Visitation, BWV 1 and *Siehe, eine Jungfrau ist schwanger* (see W. Neumann, *Sämtliche von Johann Sebastian Bach vertonte Texte* [Leipzig, 1974], pp. 159, 427). The verse provides the immediate Biblical context for Mary's Magnificat, which begins at the following verse (v. 46) and therefore has reference not only to Bach's large setting of the *Magnificat* (BWV 243), the cantata *Meine Seele erhebt den Herrn* (see Neumann, pp. 162, 435–36), but also to his approach to providing music for the service of Vespers, which included the singing of the canticle (see *Agenda, Das ist, Kirchen-Ordnung, Wie sich die Pfarrherren und Seelsorger in ihren Aemtern und Diensten verhalten Sollen. Für die Diener der Kirchen In Hertzog Heinrich zu Sachsen V. G. H. Fürstenthum gestellet Jetzo auffs neue aus Chur-Fürst Augusti Kirchen-Ordnung gebessert* . . . [Leipzig, 1712], p. 77).

63 Vol. 3/V, cols. 945–46, 947–48, 949–50. On John 19:30, 32, 34. There are two occurrences of underlining in these significant quotations from Luther. The quotations are taken from the Reformer's series of sermons on the chapter during 1528–29. On verse 30 Luther comments (the passage underlined is given in Roman type):

945 **Das Neunzehende Capitel.** 946

" einem ieden Narren eine neue Uberschrifft
" machen/wie der Titel einmal geschrieben ist/
" so sol er bleiben. Also muß des HERRN
" Titel auf dem Creutze gantz bleiben/nicht aus
" Pilati Vorsichtigkeit / sondern aus Gottes
" Schickung. Darumb/daß dieser Titel Christo
" allein gebühret. Hierauf folget/wie Christus
gebeten hat / für die / die ihn gecreutziget/ Luc. XXIII. 34.)

v. 23. Die Kriegs-Knechte aber / da sie JEsum gecreutziget hatten/ nahmen sie seine Kleider/ und machten vier Theil / einem jeglichen Krigs-Knechte ein Theil/ dazu auch den Rock. Der Rock aber war ungenehet / von oben an gewircket durch und durch.

v. 24. Da sprachen sie unter einander: Lasset uns den nicht zu theilen/ sondern darumb losen / wes er seyn sol. Auf daß erfüllet würde die Schrifft / die da saget: Sie haben meine Kleider unter sich getheilet / und haben über meinen Rock das Los geworffen. Solches thäten die Kriegs-Knechte. (S. Ps. XXII. 19. Matth. XXVII. 35. Marc. XV. 24. Luc. XXIII. 34. darauf folget des HErrn Verspottung und Lästerung/ Matth. XXVII. 39. folg. Marc. XV. 29. folg. Luc. XXIII. 35. folg. des einen Schechers am Creutze Bekehrung/ Luc. XXIII. 40. folg. Hr. Luth. T. IV. A. p. 687. Da machet S. Johannes einen sehr fleißigen Text von des HErrn Christi Rock und Kleidern / und saget / daß die Kriegs-Knechte / so Christum creutzigten/ seine Kleider zutrennet / und unter sich getheilet haben / seinen Rock aber haben sie unzutrennet gelassen / und darumb gespielet. Solche Historien wirfft der Evangelist hie mit ein/ vor des HERRN Abscheid / so es doch scheinet/ daß es nach des HErrn Christi Abscheid geschehen sey. Ohn zweiffel thut er solches umb der geistlichen Deutung willen/ wie er denn auch die Schrifft einführet/ und spricht/ daß die Schrifft dadurch erfüllet sey / die da saget: Sie haben meine Kleider unter sich getheilet etc. Psal. 22. Doch vergisset er auch nicht der Historien/ wie er diese Geschicht beschleusset / und spricht / solches thäten die Kriegs-Knechte / als solt er sagen/ es waren rechte verwegene Gesellen/ die solchen Durst und Muthwillen an dem unschuldigen Mann übeten. Wir wollen die gantze Deutung ietzt lassen anstehen / und bey der Historien bleiben. Nach der Historien zu reden/ ist durch dis Fürnehmen der Kriegs-Knechte angezeiget/ wie sicher / beständig und fest/ die Leute fahren/ welche Christum creutzigen/ diese Kriegs-Knechte fahren also mit des HErrn Kleidern/ als wäre er ein Schalck und Mörder.)

v. 25. Es stund aber bey dem Creutze JEsu seine Mutter / und seiner Mutter Schwester / Maria Cleophas Weib/ und Maria Magdalena.

v. 26. Da nun JEsus seine Mutter sahe/ und den Jünger dabey stehen/ den er lieb hatte/ spricht er zu seiner Mutter: Weib / siehe / das ist dein Sohn.

v. 27. Darnach spricht er zu dem Jünger: Sihe/ das ist deine Mutter. Und von Stund an nahm sie der Jünger zu sich. (Herr Luth. l. c. Der liebe HERR Christus wil die Welt gantz und gar gesegnen/ und bloß von ihr scheiden. Er hat nichts mehr auf Erden/ weder Geld noch Gut / weder Rock noch Kleider / sondern henget am Creutze bloß / hat nicht/ da er sein Haupt hinlege / hat auch nicht eines Fusses breit von der Erden / darauf er stürbe/ er liegt nicht auf einem Bett/ sondern hänget frey in der Lufft / allein hat er noch seine Mutter / und seine lieben Jünger / da scheidet er nun gantz und gar von der Welt/ und gibt seine Mutter auch hinweg/ und seinen liebsten Jünger / der ihm auf der Brust lag im Abendmahl. Solches ist ein grosser Schmertz/ wenn einer also dahin scheidet/ und sich weder Mutter noch Jünger/ noch etwas anders mehr auf Erden annehmen wel. Der liebe HErr muß nichts guts von der Welt halten / daß er ihr so gar Valete gibt. Zur Mutter spricht er: Weib/ sihe/ das ist dein Son/ zum Jünger spricht er: Sihe/ das ist deine Mutter/ und von Stund an nahm sie der Jünger zu sich. Das ist so viel gesagt / der Jünger Johannes nahm die Mutter JEsu an/ als seine eigene Mutter / nahm sie in sein Hauß/ pfleget und wartet ihr/ versorget sie/ daß sie hatte / daß sie bleiben möchte / als eine verlassene Wittwe/ die nun auch ihres einigen Sons beraubet war.)

v. 28. Darnach (nach dem eine grosse Finsterniß entstanden war/ von sechs biß zu neunen/ Matth. XXVII. 45. Marc. XV. 33. Luc. XXIII. 44. 45.) **als JEsus wuste/ daß schon alles vollbracht war/ dz die schrifft erfüllet würde/ spricht er: Mich dürstet.**

v. 29. Da stund ein Gefässe voll Essigs. Sie aber fülleten einen Schwam mit Essig/ und legten ihn umb einen Isopen/ und hielten es ihm dar zum Munde.

v. 30. Da nun JEsus den Essig genommen hatte/ sprach er: Es ist vollbracht. Und (nach dem er seinen letzten Seuffzer verrichtet hatte/ Vater/ in deine Hände befehl ich dir meinen Geist) **neiget das Häupt / und verschied.** (Luc. XXIII. 46. Matth. XXVII. 50. Marc. XV. 37. Hr. Luth. Allhie ziehen die Evangelisten hoch an/ daß "
unser lieber HERR JEsus Christus am "
Creutz ist verspottet / verspeiet/ und geschmä- "
het

63

Here the evangelists make much of this, that our dear Lord Jesus Christ is mocked, spat at, and reviled on the cross, and they describe this as worse suffering than His physical torment. For they bring in all the abuse and shame, that people walked by, mocked Him, and shook their heads and said: "If You are the Son of God, come down from the cross." The high priests, scribes, and elders mocked Him and said: "He has helped others, Himself He cannot help." Also the murderers who were crucified with Him reviled Him. In His suffering our dear Lord Christ had to put up with the truth of the proverb: "He who is afflicted need not worry about ridicule." Everything that Christ says and does has to become the butt of slander. Even in His prayer, "My God, My God, why hast Thou forsaken Me?" He cannot escape derision and misinterpretation. Add to this derision also the fact that they give Him vinegar to drink when He suffers burning thirst, as Scripture prophesied long before. They had brought along a vessel full of vinegar especially for Him, so that He might drink of it. The other malefactors they have supplied with good wine to drink, but Christ they give vinegar to drink and even mock Him scornfully, saying: "Why, He is thirsty; therefore give Him something to drink!" The situation here is this: No one else on earth is so wicked as Christ; He has to be the worst. No one pays attention to a single malefactor any longer, but the eyes and poisoned arrows of all are directed at Christ. But by departing this life with these words, "It is finished," our Lord indicates that all of Scripture has been fulfilled, as if He meant to say: "The world and the devil have done to Me whatever they could, and I have endured all that was necessary for the redemption of mankind and all that is prophesied and proclaimed in the prophets." Therefore everything is fulfilled and finished. This is what we should note well, that Christ's suffering is the fulfillment of Scripture and the accomplishment of the redemption of the human race. *It is finished; God's Lamb has been slaughtered and offered for the world's sin. The real High Priest has completed His sacrifice. God's Son has given and sacrificed His body and life as the ransom for sin. Sin is cancelled, God's wrath assuaged, death conquered, the kingdom of heaven purchased, and heaven is unbarred. All is fulfilled and completed, and no one may dispute it, as if anything remained to be fulfilled and completed.*

947 Evangelium S. Johannis. 948

" het worden / und machen ein grösser Leiden " draus / denn aus seiner leiblichen Marter; " Denn sie ziehen herein / alle Lästerung und " Schmach / daß die / so fürüber gangen sind / " ihn gelästert haben / und ihre Köpffe ge- " schüttelt / und gesagt: Bist du Gottes Son / " so steig herab vom Creutze. Die Hohen- " Priester / Schrifftgelehrten und Eltesten / " haben ihn verspottet / und gesagt: Andern hat " er geholffen / und kan ihm selber nicht helffen. " Auch die Mörder / die mit ihm sind gecreutzi- " get worden / haben ihn geschmähet. Es ist " dem lieben HErrn Christo in seinem Leiden " gangen / wie das gemeine Sprüchwort lau- " tet: Wer den Schaden hat / darff für das " Gespötte nicht sorgen. Alles / was Christus " hat / redet und thut / muß her halten / auch " sein Gebet / da er ruffet: Eli / Eli / Lama Asa- " bathani / mein GOtt / mein GOtt / warumb " hastu mich verlassen? kan nicht bleiben un- " verhönet / und unverkehret. Zu solcher Ver- " spottung gehöret auch / daß sie ihm Eßig zu " trincken geben in seinem grossen Durst / wie " die Schrifft lang zuvor geweissaget hat. Sie " hatten ein Gefäß mit Eßig umb seinen wil- " len hinaus getragen / auf daß sie ihn draus " tränckten; Den andern Schechern haben sie " guten Wein zu trincken gegeben / Christum " aber tränckten sie mit Eßig / und spotten sein " dazu hönisch / ja es dürstet ihn / gebet ihm doch " zu trincken. Denn hie gehets also zu / daß " niemand auf Erden so böse ist / als Christus / " er muß der ärgeste seyn: Hie siehet man kei- " nen Schecher mehr / sondern aller Augen und " gifftige Pfeile gehen auf Christum. Daß " aber der HErr verscheidet mit dem Wort / " es ist vollbracht / damit deutet er / daß alle " Schrifft erfüllet sey / als wolt er sagen: " Welt / Teuffel / haben an mir gethan / so viel " sie vermocht haben / so hab ich auch gelitten / " so viel zur Erlösung der Menschen von- " nöthen / und in der Schrifft durch die Pro- " pheten geweissaget und verkündiget ist. Dar- " umb ist alles erfüllet und vollbracht Solches " sollen wir wol mercken / daß Christus Leiden " der Schrifft Erfüllung / und der Erlösung " des Menschlichen Geschlechts Vollbringung " ist. Es ist vollbracht / Gottes Lamm ist für " der Welt Sünde geschlachtet und ge- " opffert. Der rechte HohePriester hat sein " Opffer vollendet / Gottes Son hat sein Leib " und Leben zur Bezahlung für die Sünde / da- " hin gegeben und aufgeopffert / die Sünde ist " getilget / Gottes Zorn versühnet / der Tod " überwunden / das Himmelreich erworben / " und der Himmel aufgeschlossen. Es ist alles " erfüllet und vollendet / und darff niemand " disputiren / als sey noch etwas dahinden zu " erfüllen und zu vollbringen.)

Der Dritte Theil.

Wie den Schechern / nicht aber JEsu die Bein gebrochen / sondern die Seite eröffnet sey / daraus Blut und Wasser geflossen / und von seinem Begräbniß.

v. 31. Die Jüden aber / dieweil es der Rüsttag war / daß nicht die Leichnam am Creutze blieben / den Sabbath über / (denn desselbigen Sabbaths-Tag war groß /) baten sie Pilatum / daß ihre Gebeine gebrochen / und sie abgenommen würden.

v. 32. Da kamen die Kriegs-Knechte / und brachen dem ersten die Beine / und dem andern / der mit ihm gecreutziget war. (Auf Christi Tod folget des Vorhangs des Tempels Zerreissung / Matth. XXVII. 51. Marc. XV. 38. Luc. XXIII. 45. Ein Erdbeben. Matth. XXVII. 52. Eröffnung der Gräber / v. 52. und Ausgehung etlicher / die begraben waren / v. 53. Bekehrung des Hauptmanns unterm Creutz / v. 54. Marc. XV. 39. Luc. XXIII. 47. anderer / die an die Brust geschlagen / Luc. XXIII. 48. Die Weiber von ferne gestanden / Luc. XXIII. 49. Herr Luth. Bey den Jüden war die Weise und Gewonheit / ja nicht allein Gewonheit / " sondern auch Gottes Gebot / daß der gecreu- " zigten oder gehenckten todte Leichnam am " Creutze nicht hengen / noch unbegraben blie- " ben / biß zu Niedergang der Sonnen / auf daß " die Erde nicht verunreiniget noch verflucht " würde. Denn also stehet geschrieben im Ge- " setz Mosi / 5. Mos. am XXI. Wenn iemand eine " Sünde gethan hat / die des Todes würdig ist / " und wird also getödt / daß man ihn an ein Holtz " henget / so sol sein Leichnam nicht über Nacht " an dem Holtz bleiben / sondern solt ihn dessel- " bigen Tags begraben. Denn ein gehänckter " ist verflucht bey Gott / auf daß du dein Land " nicht verunreinigest / das dir der HERR dein " GOtt giebt zum Erbe. Uber das war auch " vonnöthen / daß die Leichnam der gecreutzig- " ten oder Gehänckten / vom Creutz abgenom- " men würden für dem hohen Sabbath / auf " daß sie nicht unbegraben blieben / denn der " Sabbath ubertraff alle andere Feste / weil er " in den Zehen Geboten geboten war / darumb " eileten die Jüden / daß sie die Leichnam von " Creutzen abnehmen möchten / ehe denn der " grosse hohe Sabbath anfieng / welcher dar- " umb

63a

That Luther's summary of the meaning of the words "Es ist vollbracht" (It is finished) should be underlined here is highly significant. Luther states that these key words mean that the suffering and death of Christ are the fulfillment of the promises and prophecies of Scripture, that is, the redemption of sinful humanity. They are therefore the climax of the passion narrative as well as being a theological statement of what has taken place. The work of redemption is complete in the Savior's sacrifice of Himself. This Bach clearly understood, for he gives particular emphasis to the words "Es ist vollbracht" in the *St. John Passion* (BWV 245).

A notable feature of the structure of many of Bach's choral works is his use of symmetrical patterns of parallel movements arranged around a fundamental center point. This is especially evident in the *St. John Passion* (see F. Smend, *Bach-Studien: Gesammelte Reden und Aufsätze,* ed. C. Wolf [Kassel, 1969], pp. 11–23; R. A. Leaver, *J. S. Bach as Preacher: His Passions and Music in Worship* [St. Louis, 1984], pp. 31–33). At the heart of the *St. John Passion* is the chiastic structure in part two that centers on the chorale at No. 22:

- 18b. Chorus: Nicht diesen, sondern Barrabam (John 18:40)
- 21b. Chorus: Sey gegrüsset, lieber Judenkönig (John 19:3)
  - 21d. Chorus: Kreuzige, kreuzige! (John 19:6)
    - 21f. Chorus: Wir haben ein Gesetz (John 19:7)
      - * 22. Chorale: Durch dein Gefängnis, Gottes Sohn
    - 23b. Chorus: Lässest du diesen los (John 19:12)
  - 23d. Chorus: Weg, weg mit dem, kreuzige ihn! (John 19:15a)
- 23f. Chorus: Wir haben keinen König denn den Kaiser (John 19:15c)
- 25b. Chorus: Schreibe nicht: der Juden König (John 19:21)

Das Neunzehende Capitel. 949 / 950

umb groß und herrlich war / weil er in das hoheOsterfest fiel. Deñ gleich wie bey uns der Oster-Sontag viel höher gehalten wird/deñ ein schlechter gemeiner Sontag / also war bey den Jüden der OsterSabbath viel höher gehalten / denn ein schlechter Sabbath / ob schon der Sabbath für sich selbst / nach laut des dritten Gebots/heilig und höher gehalten werden muste. Aus der Ursach eileten die Jüden/ und baten den Landpfleger Pilatum/ daß er den gecreutzigten die Beine brechen / und die Leichnam von Creutzen abnehmen liesse. Und da Pilatus Befehl thät / kommen die Kriegs-Knechte / und brechen den zweyen Schechern die Beine/auf daß sie desto ehe stürben. Solches ist eine harte Pein gewesen / denn rechne du selbst/es ist kein Kinderspiel gewesen / daß sie die angenagelten/ verbluteten/verschmachteten Leichnam/so zerrissen und zerknirschet haben. Man hat sie võ neuen gemartert uñ am Creutz gerädert. Solche Pein und Marter wird dem lincken Schecher sauer und schwer ankommen seyn/ daß ihm am Creutze auch seine Gebeine gebrochen werden und er also mit grossen Schmertzen zur Hölle hinunter fahren sol. Widerumb dem rechten und frommen Schecher wirds leicht ankommen seyn / ob schon die Schmertzen des Leibes groß gewesen sind. Denn weil Christus/dem er vertrauet / und den er angeruffen hat / nun schon verschieden war / wird er mit Freuden des Todes erwartet haben / und gesagt: Frisch dran / lieben Kriegs-Knechte / O schlag tod / schlag tod / daß ich bald zu meinem HErrn und König in sein Reich und Paradeiß komme.)

v. 33. Als sie aber zu JEsu kamen/ da sie sahen/ daß er schon gestorben war/ brachen sie ihm die Beine nicht/ v. 34. Sondern d' Kriegsknechte einer öffnet seine Seite mit einẽ Speer/ und alsbald gieng Blut uñ Wasser heraus.

(in ziemlicher Menge/also/ daß man beydes unterschiedlich sehen und erkennen konte. H. Luth. So werden nun den beyden Schechern die Beine gebrochen / und gerädert am Creutze: Aber JEsu / weil er schon verschieden ist / werden die Beine nicht gebrochen / auf daß / wie S. Johannes sagt / die Schrifft erfüllet würde/ die da spricht: Ihr solt ihm kein Bein zubrechen. Er hat sollen das rechte Osterlamm seyn / welches man gantz essen solte. Aber der Kriegs-Knechte einer öffnete seine Seite mit einem Sper / und alsbald gehet Blut und Wasser heraus. Diß ist abermal ein groß Wunderwerck / so bey des HERRN Leiden und Sterben geschichet / daß aus seiner Seiten / da sie geöffnet wird / am Creutze Blut fleust. Natürlich ists nicht / daß aus einem todten Leichnam Blut fliessen sol. Denn wenn der Leib todt ist / geliefert und stocket das Blut im Leibe. Weil nun der HERR verschieden/und sein Leib tod ist/solt auch nach Art und Natur des todten Leichnams / sein Blut umbs Hertz sich geliefert haben. Daß nun Blut heraus fleust/ist wider die Natur/ und ein Wunderwerck / auf daß aber solch Wunderwerck desto grösser sey / fleusset aus seinem Leibe nicht allein Blut/sondern Blut und Wasser zugleich. Solch groß Wunderwerck am Creutz geschehen/ mit dem verstorbenen Leichnam JESU/ hat der Evangelist Johannes für andern Evangelisten/ nicht ohn Ursach / noch umbsonst angezeiget. Denn damit hat er nicht allein des blossen Wunderwercks gedencken / welches am Creutze geschehen / sondern auch einen hohen trefflichen Trost uns anzeigen / und einbilden wollen. Was ist nun/dz aus des HErrn JEsu Seiten am Creutze zugleich Blut und Wasser fleusset? Antwort: Unser Erlösung ist in dem Wunderwerck verborgen / wie es S. Johannes selbst deutet und auslegt in seiner 1. Epistel am V. Cap. Drey sind / die da zeugen / der Geist / und das Wasser / und das Blut / und die drey sind beysammen. Aus denselben dreyen Stücken werden allhie zwey Stück angezeiget / und beschrieben / Wasser und Blut / und die zwey Stück sol man wol von einander scheiden / ob sie schon beysammen sind. Das Blut / so aus des HERRN JESU Seiten fleust ist der Schatz unser Erlösung / die Bezahlung und Gnugthuung für unsere Sünde. Denn durch sein unschuldig Leiden und Sterben/ und durch sein heiliges theures Blut / am Creutze vergossen / hat unser lieber HERR JESUS CHRISTUS bezahlet / alle unser Schuld/ ewigen Tod und Verdamniß/ darin wir unser Sünde halben stecken. Dasselb Blut Christi vertrit uns bey GOtt/ und ruffet für uns ohn unterlaß zu GOTT/ Gnade/ Gnade / Vergib / Vergib / Ablaß/ Ablaß/ Vater/ Vater/ und erwirbt uns Gottes Gnade/ Vergebung der Sünde/Gerechtigkeit und Seligkeit. So ruffet das Blut JEsu Christi unsers einigen Mitlers und Fürsprechers ohn Aufhören/und für und für/ also/daß Gott der Vater solches seines geliebten Sons Ruffen und Fürbitt für uns/ ansiehet/und uns armen elenden Sündern gnädig ist. Denn er kan an uns keine Sünde sehen / ob wir schon voller Sünde stecken/ja eitel Sünde sind / inwendig und auswendig/ an Leib und Seel / vom Schedel an biß auf die Versen/ sondern siehet allein das theuer köstliche Blut seines lieben Sons unsers HErrn JEsu Christi / damit wir besprengt sind. Denn dasselbe Blut ist der gülden

Uu Gna-

63b

This chiastic structure is not only visible but also audible in that the music of 21d is repeated at 23d, and 21f at 23b, with only changes in key and the rhythmical adjustment made necessary by the different text. At the center is the chorale, which is not only the centerpiece of the second half of the *St. John Passion* but also the heart and focus of the entire work:

Durch dein Gefängnis, Gottes Sohn,
Ist uns die Freiheit kommen,
Dein Kerker ist der Gnadenthron,
Die Freistatt aller Frommen;
Denn gingst du nicht die Knechtschaft ein,
Müsst unsre Knechtschaft ewig sein.

Through Thy captivity, Son of God,
Freedom to us has come,
Thy prison is the throne of grace,
The refuge for all the faithful,
For if Thou hadst not been enslaved,
Our slavery would last forever.

If this chorale lies at the heart of the *St. John Passion*, then its climax is to be found in the words from John 19:30: "Es ist vollbracht." Again Bach stresses their importance by placing them within a chiastic structure:

- 28. Chorale: Er nahm Alles wohl in Acht
  - 29. Recit: Und von Stund an nahm (John 19:27b–30a)
    - * 30. Aria: Es ist vollbracht! (cf. John 19:30a)
  - 31. Recit: Und neigte das Haupt (John 19:30b)
- 32. Chorale: Jesu, der du warest tot, with the Aria: Mein teurer Heiland.

The symmetrical structure is emphasized by the framing of the meditative aria in the middle of the recitatives of Biblical narrative by two stanzas (20 and 34) of Paul Stockmann's passiontide hymn "Jesu Leiden, Pein und Tod," with its associated melody *Jesu Kreuz, Leiden und Pein,* by Melchior Vulpius. The first (at no. 28) anticipates the impending death of the Savior, with some remarkably descriptive harmonies in the last two lines. The second (at no. 32) meditates on the continuing significance of the death of Christ for the believer. Intertwined with and between the lines of the chorale is the calm and confident bass aria, which takes comfort in the security of the finished work of Christ expressed in the words "Es ist vollbracht." At the center (at no. 30) is the devastatingly beautiful meditation on these three last words of the Savior. But the grief-laden atmosphere is broken in the middle of the aria by the sudden fanfare: "The hero of Judah triumphs with might and has finished the fight" (cf. BWV 43:6, 92:3, 184:3). It is an allusion to Rev. 5:5: "Then one of the elders said to me, 'Weep not; lo, the Lion of the tribe of Judah, the Root of David, has conquered.' " This is Bach's musical exposition of "Es ist vollbracht," which approximates closely Luther's verbal exposition found underlined here: *that Christ's suffering is the fulfillment of Scripture and the accomplishment of the redemption of the human race* (cf. also BWV 159:4). See also no. 23.

Although there is no underlining in the next quotation, verse 32, col. 948–49, since it related directly to Bach's *St. John Passion,* we give it in translation. The source is the same as the previous passage:

> *Among the Jews the manner and custom—but not only the custom but also God's command—was that the corpses of the crucified and hanged did not remain on the cross and were not left unburied after sundown, so that the earth might not be defiled or cursed. For Deut. 21*[:22] *records: "If a man has committed a crime punishable by death and he is put to death, and you hang him on a tree, his body shall not remain all night upon the tree, but you shall bury him the same day, for a hanged man is accursed by God; you shall not defile your land which the Lord your God gives you for an inheritance." But it was also necessary that the bodies of those who were crucified or hanged be removed from the cross before the high Sabbath, so that they might not remain unburied. For that Sabbath was greater than all other festivals because it was commanded in the Ten Commandments. Therefore the Jews hurried to remove the bodies from the crosses before the great high Sabbath began, which was great and high because it fell in the great Easter festival. For just as among us Easter Sunday is considered greater than an ordinary Sunday, so among the Jews the Easter Sabbath was considered greater than an ordinary Sabbath, even though the Sabbath already by itself had to be considered holy and greater on account of the Third commandment. For that reason the Jews were in a hurry to ask the governor, Pilate, to let the legs of those crucified be broken and their bodies removed from the cross. And as soon as Pilate gives the orders, the soldiers come and break the legs of the two malefactors, so that they might die the sooner. This was painful torment, for, figure it out for yourself, it was by no means child's play when people thus mangled and crushed bodies already pierced with nails and bloodied and faint. Thus they were tormented anew and tortured on the cross. This torment and torture, to have his legs broken on the cross, must*

have been bitter and hard for the malefactor on the left, for thus he had to go down to hell in great pain. On the other hand, the good and pious malefactor on the right must have borne it with ease, even though the pains of body were intense. For because Christ, whom he trusted and to whom he had prayed, had already died, he must have waited for death with joy, saying: "Go to it, you dear soldiers. Beat me to death, beat me to death, so that I may soon come to my Lord and King in His kingdom and paradise.

The quotation from Luther continues on verse 34, col. 949–50, and there is some underlining (given here in Roman type):

Thus the legs of the two malefactors are now crushed and mangled on the cross. But because Jesus has already died, His legs are not broken, so that, as St. John says [John 19:36]*: "That the Scripture might be fulfilled, 'Not a bone of Him shall be broken.' " He was to be the true Easter Lamb, which was to be eaten intact* [see Ex. 12:9]. "But one of the soldiers pierced His side with a spear, and at once there came out blood and water." This again is a great miracle wrought in the Lord's life and death, that blood should issue from His side when it was opened on the cross. It is not natural for blood to flow from a corpse. For when the body is dead, the blood congeals and ceases to circulate in the body. Because the Lord has now passed away and His body is dead, also His dead corpse's blood in the heart should according to the custom of nature have given up its flow. That blood does issue forth is against nature and a miracle, but that the miracle may be even greater, not only blood but blood and water issue forth at the same time. This great miracle in the dead body of Jesus on the cross the evangelist John has recorded in his gospel in contrast to the other evangelists, but not without reason or purpose. For in doing so, he not only wanted to call to mind the miracle that occurred on the cross, but he also wanted to show us and impress on us a great and choice source of comfort. But what does this signify, that at the same time blood and water issue from the side of the Lord Jesus on the cross? Answer: Our redemption is concealed in this miracle, as St. John himself interprets and explains it in his first epistle, chapter 5[:8]*: "There are three witnesses, the Spirit, the water, and the blood; and these three agree." Of those three items, two are here mentioned and described, water and blood, and these two we should clearly distinguish, even though they are together. The blood that issues from the side of the Lord Jesus is the treasure of our redemption, the payment and ransom for our sin. For by means of His innocent suffering and dying and His holy, precious blood our dear Lord Jesus Christ paid for all our guilt, our eternal death and damnation, in which we are caught on account of our sin. This same blood of Christ represents us before God and cries out to God without ceasing for us:* "Grace! Grace! Forgive! Forgive! Indulgence! Indulgence! Father! Father!" *and gains for us God's grace, forgiveness of sin, righteousness, and salvation. Thus the blood of Christ Jesus, our only Mediator and Advocate, cries out without ceasing, forever and forever, so that God the Father accepts this cry and supplication of His dear Son for us and is gracious to us poor, miserable sinners. For He can see no sin in us, although we are crammed full of sin, yes, are nothing but sin, inside and outside, in soul and body, from head to toe; but He sees only the dear, precious blood of His dear Son Jesus Christ with which we are sprinkled. For this same blood is the golden cloak of grace in which we are clad and with which we appear before God, so that*

He cannot and will not look at us except as if we were His beloved Son Himself, full of righteousness, holiness, and innocence. On the other hand, the innocent blood of Christ possesses such virtue and power that it absolves, frees, washes, and cleanses us from all sin and iniquity, so that whoever is sprinkled with this blood and clad in it may confidently and joyfully appear before God, pray to Him, and confidently and without doubt hope that he will be heard, as St. Paul says, Eph. 3[:12]*: "In* [Christ] *we have boldness and confidence of access through our faith in Him." Indeed, such a person may not only appear before God, pray to Him, and expect to receive all good things from Him, but he may even boast that he is a son of God, whom all enemies and adversaries, indeed, any creature, cannot harm, and to whom all things must be subject, Rom. 8*[:39]*. But the evangelist adds that from the wounded side of Christ water issued forth together with the blood. This item we should also mark well. For even though the precious blood of Christ is our redemption, payment, and satisfaction before God and we are through its merit and intercession righteous and God's acceptable children, yet we are not perfectly and completely clean so far as our sinful nature is concerned. For the sin that lurks in our flesh and blood is astir without ceasing, and the filth of the old Adam wells up, defiles and pollutes us daily, and tempts us to evil desires, so that we daily sin, fall, stumble, and fail. This now calls for the water that flows forth from the wound of Christ in order that we may daily be cleansed from the remaining sins and the daily transgressions and failures. This water is Holy Baptism, the Sacrament and Holy Supper of our Lord Jesus Christ, and the precious Word of God which we preach and hear. This washes and cleanses us of the sins that daily stir in us and cause us to fall. Therefore we should attend to this blessed Word and the holy sacraments with all diligence and keep them in constant use, resist the sin within us, seek absolution, often receive the Sacrament of the body and blood of Christ, and constantly cleanse, wash, and furbish ourselves. Whenever I am assailed by weakness of faith, I am to say to myself: "Very well, I still feel much sin, weakness, and frailty within me, but I am baptized and I will take refuge in the dear Word, hear preaching, receive absolution, and partake of the Holy Sacrament; I will comfort and restore myself and cleanse and free myself of my weakness. When anger, impatience, worries about daily bread, and other sins assail me, I will do the same." In this way, by means of Baptism, absolution, the Sacrament, and the Word, I am to wash and cleanse myself daily of the sin that still always clings to me, so that I may resist these sings. This is therefore a constant washing and cleansing of the blessed water in us by which we bridle our evil lusts and desires, so that they do not lead us captive and do not gain control over our spirit; for without these, sin would be too strong for us, would overpower us and make us prisoners, and we would have to be submerged and lost in it. But here our dear Lord Jesus Christ has poured forth from his wound that efficacious water, our dear Baptism, that blessed Washing, and the Holy Sacrament of His body and blood, that medicine and a balm for our souls, and holy absolution and acquittal from sin, and the dear Word, so that we may thereby recover from every kind of temptation and may gain strength against sin. Therefore we should glory in the dear Word and the holy sacraments and stoutly insist on them against the devil and our own flesh and blood and say: "Though you, devil, be ever so angry and wicked, and* *you, flesh, be ever so mischievous and sinful and will not leave me alone, I am still baptized and have the Word of God. If you can badly defile and pollute me, I can bathe again and wash and cleanse myself." And such faith God recognizes in us, receives and keeps us in His grace for the sake of this faith. And though we be sinful and unclean and fall daily, nevertheless, God sees none of these sins but looks only at the blood of Jesus Christ, His Son, emblazoned on our foreheads and at Holy Baptism, in which we have put on Christ. This is the purity and holiness of Christians that depends on faith in Jesus Christ and on the satisfaction wrought by His holy, blessed blood and on the cleansing brought about through Baptism, through the Word, and through the Holy Sacrament. He who knows and understands this can withstand temptations and sins and in real faith stand firm and say: "I am a Christian, sprinkled with the blood of Christ and washed clean of sin and baptized in His name for salvation and eternal life."*

Objective and subjective realities meet in the cross of Christ. On the one hand there is the objective reality of the death of Christ, and on the other, the subjective reality of faith by which the believer makes the sacrifice of the cross his own. In the cross there is the objective demonstration of the grace of God, which needs to be received subjectively and experienced in the life of the individual Christian. So Luther's theme here is that although the death of Christ was once-and-for-all, its significance needs to be applied daily in Christian faith and life. At the heart of the message is the grace of God, which gives to the believer the assurance of forgiveness of sin. It is significant, indeed, that it is these words emphasizing the grace of God in the shed blood of the Savior that are underlined here.

There is also a connection with Bach's *St. John Passion* here, in that there are two places where the death of Jesus is especially applied to the individual and framed by the same two chorales:

- 14. Chorale: Petrus, der nicht denkt zurück
  - SERMON
- 15. Chorale: Christus, der uns selig macht

- 32. Chorale (with Aria): Jesu, der du warest tot
  - 33. Recit: Und siehe da, der Vorhang im Tempel (Matt. 27:51–52)
    - 34. Arioso: Mein Herz, in dem die ganze Welt
    - 35. Aria: Zerfliesse, meine Herz
  - 36. Recit: Die Juden aber John 19:31–37)
- 37. Chorale: O hilf, Christe, Gottes Sohn

Part one ends with the chorale "Petrus, der nicht denkt zurück," that is, stanza 10 of the hymn "Jesu Leiden, Pein und Tod," set to the melody *Jesu Kreuz, Leiden und Pein,* and part two begins with the first stanza of the hymn "Christus, der uns selig macht." In between came the Good Friday Vespers sermon, which, according to Leipzig custom, was on Isaiah 53 and Psalm 22 in alternate years (see *Leipziger Kirchen-Staat* [Leipzig, 1710], p. 25), the classic Old Testament passages that prefigure the crucifixion. The function of the sermon was to apply and relate to the hearers the meaning of the death of Christ in their own lives (see Leaver, *Bach as Preacher,* passim). Thus in Bach's setting of the *St. John Passion* the sermon was framed by these two chorales. Toward the end of the work the same two chorales recur with the same melodies but with different stanzas of the texts. Nos. 32 and 37 are respectively the final stanzas of the hymns, "Jesu Leiden, Pein und Tod," and "Christus, der uns selig macht" (see above on verse 32, where the chorale at no. 32 is shown at the end of the previous chiastic structure). These two stanzas frame the Biblical narrative and the arioso and aria, which apply the death of Christ to the life of the believer—exactly what Luther has done in the comment given here on this verse.

Luther particularly stresses the life of worship, expressed in Baptism, the Lord's Supper, hearing the preaching of the Word, etc., as the means whereby the grace of God is encountered by the individual. For the whole of his life Bach was involved in the worship of the Lutheran Church. Even when he was employed at the Calvinist court of Anhalt-Köthen, he and his family worshiped at the Lutheran Agnuskirche. All his children were baptized soon after their birth, and Bach was a regular visitor to the Lord's Table (see A. Oepke, "Johann Sebastian Bach als Abendmahlsgast," *Musik und Kirche* 24 [1954]: 202–08; G. Stiller, *Johann Sebastian Bach and Liturgical Life in Leipzig* [St. Louis, 1984], pp. 202–05; *BD* 2:19, 71, 124, etc.).

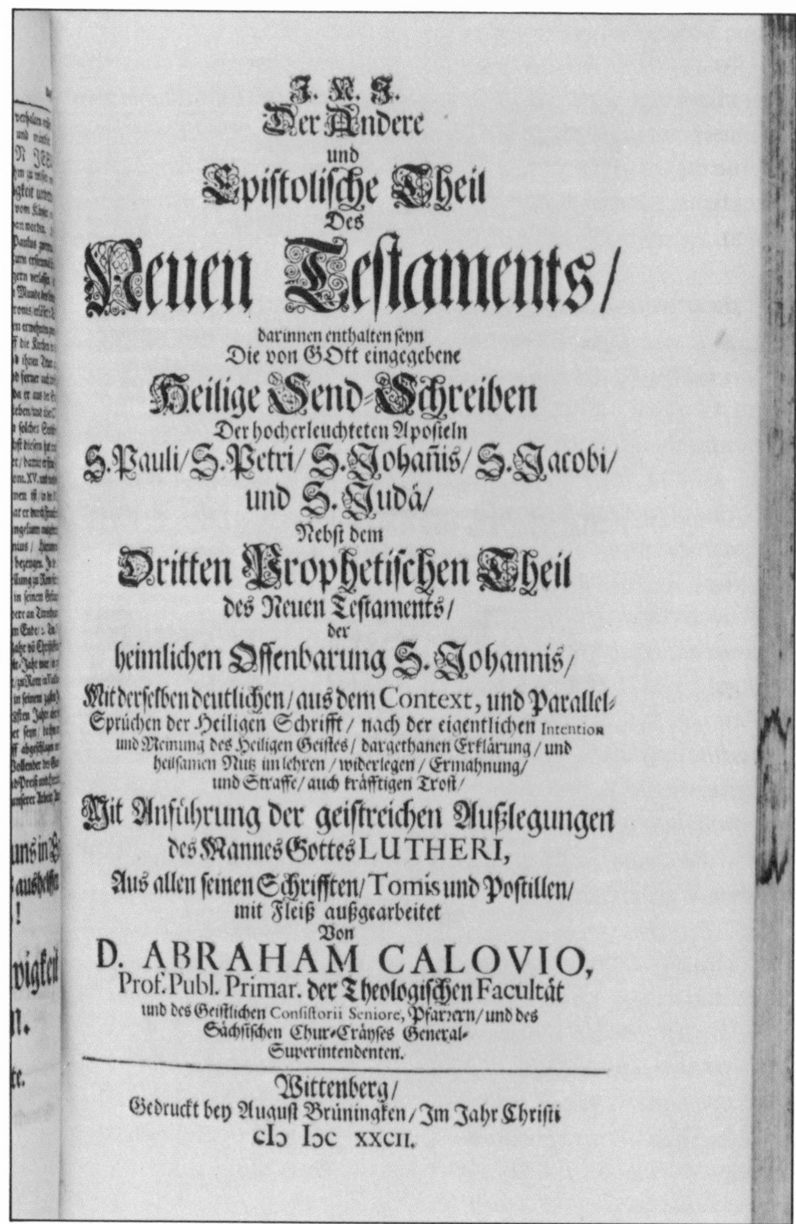
J. N. J.
Der Andere
und
Epistolische Theil
Des
Neuen Testaments/
darinnen enthalten seyn
Die von GOtt eingegebene
Heilige Send-Schreiben
Der hocherleuchteten Aposteln
S. Pauli/ S. Petri/ S. Johañis/ S. Jacobi/
und S. Judä/
Nebst dem
Dritten Prophetischen Theil
des Neuen Testaments/
der
heimlichen Offenbarung S. Johannis/
Mit derselben deutlichen/ aus dem Context, und Parallel-
Sprüchen der Heiligen Schrifft/ nach der eigentlichen Intention
und Meinung des Heiligen Geistes/ dargethanen Erklärung/ und
heilsamen Nutz im lehren/ widerlegen/ Ermahnung/
und Straffe/ auch kräfftigen Trost/
Mit Anführung der geistreichen Außlegungen
des Mannes Gottes LUTHERI,
Aus allen seinen Schrifften/ Tomis und Postillen/
mit Fleiß außgearbeitet
Von
D. ABRAHAM CALOVIO,
Prof. Publ. Primar. der Theologischen Facultät
und des Geistlichen Consistorii Seniore, Pfarrern/ und des
Sächsischen Chur-Crayses General-
Superintendenten.
Wittenberg/
Gedruckt bey August Brüningken/ Im Jahr Christi
cIↄ Iↄc xxcii.

64

64 The title page of the final part of the commentary, that is, Vol. 3/VI:

> *J.N.J. The second epistle part of the New Testament, in which are contained the holy epistles of the highly enlightened apostles St. Paul, St. Peter, St. John, St. James, and St. Jude, plus the third, prophetic part of the New Testament, the mystic Revelation of St. John, with the clear interpretation of these, presented according to the context and parallel passages of Holy Scripture, following the real intention and meaning of the Holy Spirit, for wholesome application in teaching, refutation, exhortation, denunciation* [cf. 2 Tim. 3:16], *and also rich consolation, together with quotation of the inspiring interpretations of that man of God, Luther, from all his writings, volumes, and postils, diligently developed by Dr. Abraham Calov, public professor, chairman of the theological faculty, senior pastor of the church consistory, general superintendent of Electoral Saxony. Wittenberg, printed by August Brüningken, in the year of Christ 1682.*

As with the other title pages, it states that the commentary has been taken essentially from the writings of Martin Luther.

65 Vol. 3/VI, col. 19–20. On Romans 1:17. Various underlinings and marks of emphasis are added to Calov's comment on the verse (the underlining here is given in Roman type):

> *In short: namely, the* principal cause of God's salvation *in* word and power is the Gospel, *which is the* means of salvation. *But the* meritorius cause *is* Christ *and the* means from our side is faith, *by which the revealed righteousness of Christ is received, but it is by faith alone: thus the* sinner *who* believes in Christ *is made righteous. The* form *is the* righteousness of Christ, *which becomes our own by faith. The* final cause *is life and eternal salvation.*

65

This is a statement of the principal causes of the justification of the sinner before God that one finds in classic Lutheran theology. For example, in Hutter's *Compendium*, which was the basic theological textbook from which Bach was taught at school (see W. Junghans, "Johann Sebastian Bach als Schüler der Partikularschule zu St. Michaelis in Lüneburg, oder Lüneburg eine Pflegstätte kirchlicher Musik," *Programm des Johanneums zu Lüneburg. Ostern 1870* [Lüneburg, 1870], p. 41), under the *locus* "De iustificatione" (XII. 4), there is the following statement:

> *There are three causes of our justification: (1) the grace of God; (2) the merit of Christ; (3) faith, by which these gifts of God promised in the Gospel are received* (L. Hutter, *Compendium locorum theologicorum* [Wittenberg, 1610]; ed. W. Trillhaas [Berlin, 1961], p. 52).

This in turn is based on a statement in the Formula of Concord (SD iii 25):

> *The only essential and necessary elements of justification are the grace of God, the merit of Christ, and faith which accepts these in the promise of the Gospel, whereby the righteousness of Christ is reckoned to us and by which we obtain the forgiveness of sins, reconciliation with God, adoption, and the inheritance of eternal*

life (The Book of Concord: The Confessions of the Evangelical Lutheran Church, trans. and ed. T. G. Tappert, et al [Philadelphia, 1959], p. 543).

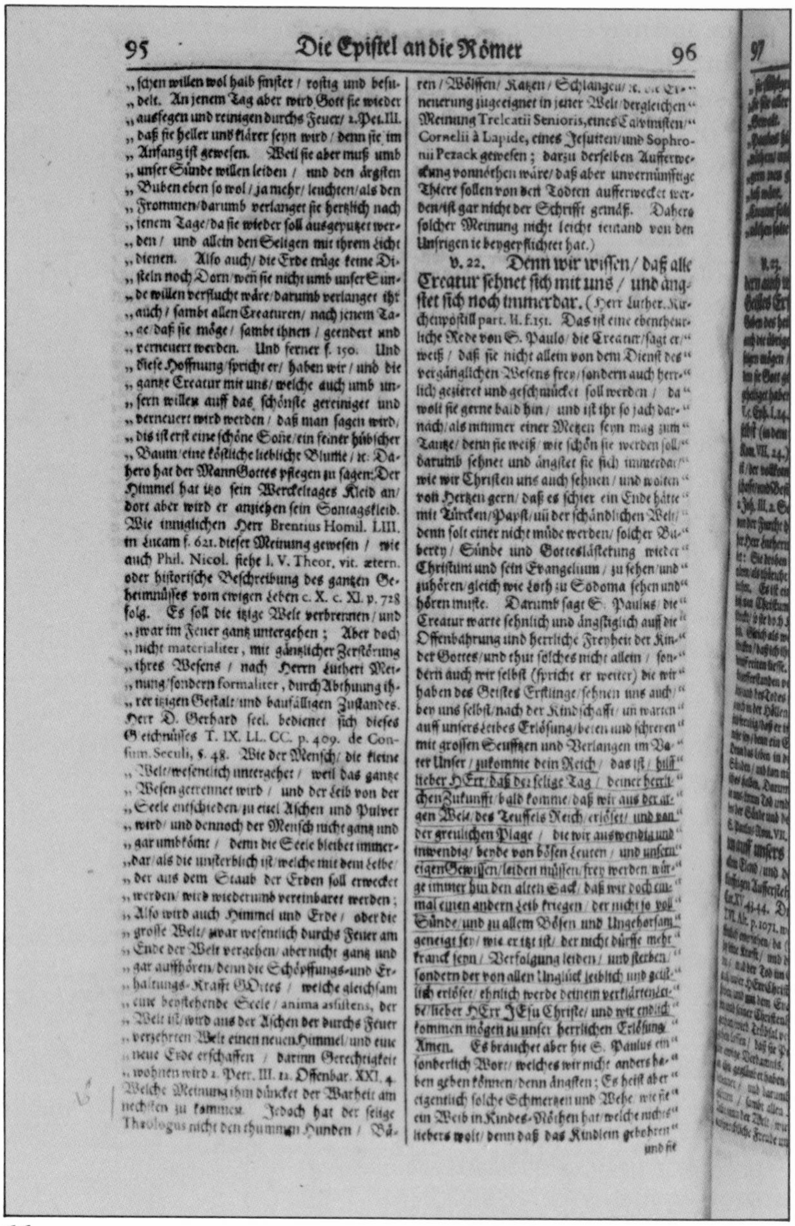
95 Die Epistel an die Römer 96

schen willen wol halb finster / rostig und besudelt. An jenem Tag aber wird Gott sie wieder aussegen und reinigen durchs Feuer/ 2. Pet. III. daß sie heller und klärer seyn wird / denn sie im Anfang ist gewesen. Weil sie aber muß umb unser Sünde willen leiden / und den ärgsten Buben eben so wol / ja mehr/ leuchten/ als den Frommen/ darumb verlanget sie hertzlich nach jenem Tage/ da sie wieder soll ausgeputzet werden / und allein den Seligen mit ihrem Licht dienen. Also auch/ die Erde trüge keine Disteln noch Dorn/ wen sie nicht umb unser Sünde willen verflucht wäre/ darumb verlanget ihr auch / sambt allen Creaturen/ nach jenem Tage/ daß sie möge / sambt ihnen / geendert und verneuert werden. Und ferner f. 150. Und diese Hoffnung/ spricht er/ haben wir / und die gantze Creatur mit uns/ welche auch umb unsern willen auff das schönste gereiniget und verneuert wird werden / daß man sagen wird/ dis ist erst eine schöne Soñe/ ein feiner hübscher Baum/ eine köstliche liebliche Blume / rc. Dahero hat der Mann Gottes pflegen zu sagen: Der Himmel hat itzo sein Werckeltages Kleid an/ dort aber wird er anziehen sein Sontagskleid. Wie inniglichen Herr Brentius Homil. LIII. in Lucam f. 621. dieser Meinung gewesen / wie auch Phil. Nicol. siehe l. V. Theor. vit. ætern. oder historische Beschreibung des gantzen Geheimnüsses vom ewigen Leben c. X. c. XI. p. 728 folg. Es soll die itzige Welt verbrennen / und zwar im Feuer gantz untergehen ; Aber doch nicht materialiter, mit gäntzlicher Zerstörung ihres Wesens / nach Herrn Lutheri Meinung/ sondern formaliter, durch Abthuung ihrer itzigen Gestalt/ und baufälligen Zustandes. Herr D. Gerhard seel. bedienet sich dieses Gleichnüsses T. IX. LL. CC. p. 409. de Consum. Seculi, §. 48. Wie der Mensch/ die kleine Welt/ wesentlich untergehet / weil das gantze Wesen getrennet wird / und der Leib von der Seele entschieden/ zu eitel Aschen und Pulver wird/ und dennoch der Mensch nicht gantz und gar umbkömt / denn die Seele bleibet immerdar/ als die unsterblich ist/ welche mit dem Leibe/ der aus dem Staub der Erden soll erwecket werden/ wird wiederumb vereinbaret werden ; Also wird auch Himmel und Erde / oder die grosse Welt/ zwar wesentlich durchs Feuer am Ende der Welt vergehen/ aber nicht gantz und gar auffhören/ denn die Schöpffungs- und Erhaltungs-Krafft GOttes / welche gleichsam eine beystehende Seele / anima assistens, der Welt ist/ wird aus der Aschen der durchs Feuer verzehrten Welt einen neuen Himmel/ und eine neue Erde erschaffen / darinn Gerechtigkeit wohnen wird 2. Petr. III. 13. Offenbar. XXI. 4. Welche Meinung ihm düncket der Warheit am nechsten zu kommen. Jedoch hat der selige Theologus nicht den stummen Hunden / Bä-

ren / Wölffen/ Katzen / Schlangen/ rc. die Erneuerung zugeeignet in jener Welt/ dergleichen Meinung Trelcatii Senioris, eines Calvinisten/ Cornelii à Lapide, eines Jesuiten/ und Sophronii Pezack gewesen ; darzu derselben Aufferweckung vonnöthen wäre/ daß aber unvernünfftige Thiere sollen von den Todten aufferwecket werden/ ist gar nicht der Schrifft gemäß. Dahero solcher Meinung nicht leicht iemand von den Unsrigen ie beygepflichtet hat.)

v. 22. **Denn wir wissen/ daß alle Creatur sehnet sich mit uns / und ängstet sich noch immerdar.** (Herr Luther. Kirchenpostill part. II. f. 151. Das ist eine ebentheurliche Rede von S. Paulo/ die Creatur/ sagt er/ weiß / daß sie nicht allein von dem Dienst des vergänglichen Wesens frey/ sondern auch herrlich gezieret und geschmücket soll werden / da wolt sie gerne bald hin / und ist ihr so jach darnach/ als immer einer Metzen seyn mag zum Tantze/ denn sie weiß/ wie schön sie werden soll/ darumb sehnet und ängstet sie sich immerdar/ wie wir Christen uns auch sehnen / und wolten von Hertzen gern/ daß es schier ein Ende hätte mit Türcken/ Papst/ uñ der schändlichen Welt/ denn solt einer nicht müde werden/ solcher Buberey / Sünde und Gotteslästerung wieder Christum und sein Evangelium / zu sehen/ und zuhören/ gleich wie Loth zu Sodoma sehen und hören muste. Darumb sagt S. Paulus/ die Creatur warte sehnlich und ängstiglich auff die Offenbahrung und herrliche Freyheit der Kinder Gottes/ und thut solches nicht allein / sondern auch wir selbst (spricht er weiter) die wir haben des Geistes Erstlinge/ sehnen uns auch/ bey uns selbst/ nach der Kindschafft/ un warten auff unsers Leibes Erlösung/ beten und schreyen mit grossen Seufftzen und Verlangen im Vater Unser / zukomme dein Reich / das ist / hilff lieber HErr/ daß der selige Tag / deiner herrlichen Zukunfft/ bald komme/ daß wir aus der argen Welt/ des Teuffels Reich/ erlöset/ und von der greulichen Plage / die wir auswendig und inwendig/ beyde von bösen Leuten / und unsern eigen Gewissen/ leiden müssen/ frey werden. wir ge immer hin den alten Sack/ daß wir doch einmal einen andern Leib kriegen / der nicht so voll Sünde/ und zu allem Bösen und Ungehorsam geneigt sey/ wie er itzt ist/ der nicht dürffe mehr kranck seyn / Verfolgung leiden / und sterben/ sondern der von allen Unglück leiblich und geistlich erlöset/ ehnlich werde deinem verklärten Leibe/ lieber HErr JEsu Christe/ und wir endlich kommen mögen zu unser herrlichen Erlösung Amen. Es brauchet aber hie S. Paulus ein sonderlich Wort/ welches wir nicht anders haben geben können/ denn ängsten ; Es heist aber eigentlich solche Schmertzen und Wehe/ wie sie ein Weib in Kindes-Nöthen hat/ welche nichts liebers wolt/ denn daß das Kindlein gebohren

und sie

66

66 Vol. 3/VI, col. 95–96. On Romans 8:21–22. The "NB" alongside the comment on verse 21 in col. 95 is in a hand other than Bach's. However, the ink used for the underlining in col. 96 appears to have slightly more density and therefore may have been done by another hand at another time, perhaps Bach's, but there must be some element of doubt. The quotation from Luther's *Kirchenpostille* is taken from his second sermon on the Epistle for the Fourth Sunday After Trinity (the passage underlined is given here in Roman type):

Paul uses forcible language here. Creation is aware, he says, not only of its future deliverance from the bondage of corruption, but its future grandeur. It hopes for the speedy coming of its glory, and waits with the eagerness of a maiden for the dance. Seeing the splendor reserved for itself, it groans and travails unceasingly. Similarly, we Christians groan and intensely desire to have done at once with the Turks, the Pope, and the tyrannical world. Who would not weary of witnessing the present knavery, ungodliness and blasphemy against Christ and His Gospel, even as Lot wearied of the ungodliness he beheld in Sodom? Thus Paul says that creation groaneth and travaileth while waiting for the revelation and the glorious liberty of the children of God. "And not only so," he adds, "but ourselves also, who have the first fruits of the Spirit, even we ourselves groan within ourselves, waiting for our adoption, to wit, the redemption of our body." We pray, we cry with great longing, in the Lord's Prayer, "Thy kingdom come," *that is:* Help, dear Lord, and speed the blessed day of Thy second advent, that we may be delivered from the wicked world, the devil's kingdom, and may be released from the awful distress we suffer—inwardly from our own consciences and outwardly from the wicked. Afflict to the limit these old bodies of ours so long as we may obtain others not sinful, as these, not given to iniquity and disobedience; bodies that can never know illness, persecution or death; bodies delivered from all physical and spiritual distress and made like unto Thine own glorified body, dear Lord Jesus Christ. Thus may we finally realize our glorious redemption, Amen. *Paul uses a peculiar word here in the text, which we cannot render by any other in our language than "travail." It carries the idea of pains and pangs such as a woman knows in childbirth. The mother's ardent desire is to be delivered. She longs for it with an intensity that all the wealth, honor, pleasure and power of the world could not awaken. This is precisely the meaning of the word Paul applies to creation. He declares it to be in travail, suffering pain and anguish in the extremity of its desire for release. But who can discern the anguish of creation? etc. (SML* 8:116–17)

This longing for the Lord's return and for full redemption after death is a frequent theme in Bach's choral works (for example, see nos. 45, 46, 51, 52, 67, and P. F. Foelber, *Bach's Treatment of the Subject of Death in His Choral Music* [Washington, 1961]). This longing is sometimes explained as a personal and morbid preoccupation with death. In reality it is but part of a long tradition of devotional eschatology that is characteristic of both Luther and later Lutheranism.

This section of Romans 8, though not this actual verse, was set by Bach in his motet *Der Geist hilft unser Schwachheit auf* (BWV 226).

67 Vol. 3/VI, col. 281–82, 283–84. On 1 Corinthians 10:12. There are marks of emphasis and underlining in these two quotations from Luther, taken from his sermon on the Epistle for the Ninth Sunday After Trinity in the *Kirchenpostille*, and the *Fourteen Consolations* (the passage highlighted by marks of emphasis is given within the signs < >, and the words underlined are given in Roman type):

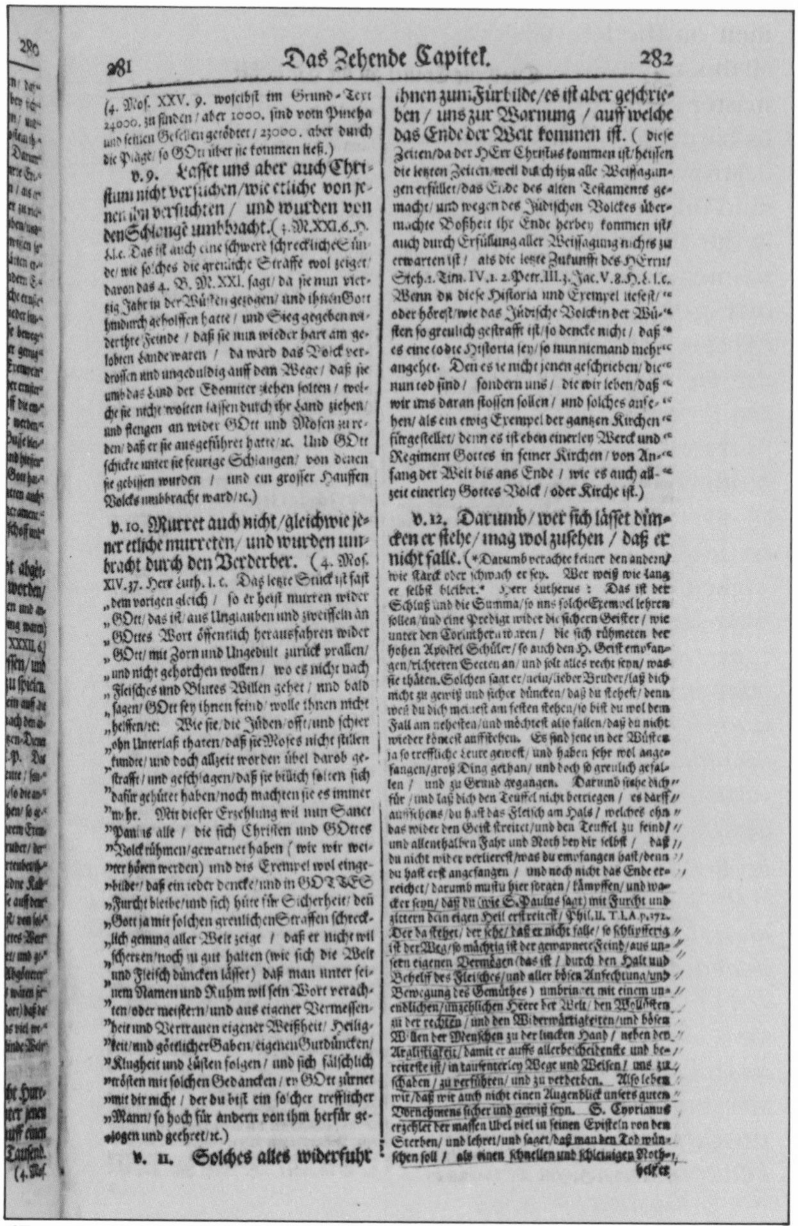
281 Das Zehende Capitel. 282

v. 9. Lasset uns aber auch Christum nicht versuchen / wie etliche von jenen ihn versuchten / und wurden von den Schlangē umbbracht.

v. 10. Murret auch nicht / gleichwie jener etliche murreten / und wurden umbracht durch den Verderber.

v. 11. Solches alles widerfuhr ihnen zum Fürbilde / es ist aber geschrieben / uns zur Warnung / auff welche das Ende der Welt kommen ist.

v. 12. Darumb / wer sich lässet düncken er stehe / mag wol zusehen / daß er nicht falle.

67

Here is summed up the teaching of the above examples. The sermon is directed against the self-confident. Some there were among the Christian Corinthians who boasted they were disciples of the great apostles, and who had even received the Holy Spirit, but who stirred up sects and desired to be commended in all their acts. To these Paul would say: "No, dear brother, be not too secure, not too sure where you stand. When you think you stand most firmly you are perhaps nearest to falling, and you may fall too far to rise again. They of the wilderness were worthy people and began well, doing great deeds, yet they fell deplorably and were destroyed. <Therefore, be cautious and suffer not the devil to deceive you. You will need to be vigilant, for you are in the flesh, which always strives against the spirit; and you have the devil for an enemy, and dangers and difficulties beset you on all sides. Be careful lest you lose what you have received. You have only made a beginning; the end has yet to be attained." So we must be wary and steadfast, that we may, as Paul has it, work out our own salvation with fear and trembling, *Phil. 2*[:12]. (*SML* 8:195). "Let him who stands take heed that he does not fall." The path is so very slippery and the foe is so very powerful, armed as he is with our own strength (that is, the aid given by our own flesh and all our evil desires), attended by the countless armies of the world, its pleasures and lusts on the right hand, its hardships and the evil intentions of

men on the left. Besides all this, this foe is himself a master in the art of doing us harm, of reducing and destroying us in a thousand different ways. Such is our life that not for a moment are we safe in our good intentions. *Cyprian, who in his treatise* De mortalitate *mentions many of these matters, teaches that* death is to be wished for as a> quick means of escape from these evils, wicked things, vexations, and encumbrances. ***And it is true that wherever there have been high-minded men who gave deep thought to these infinite perils of hell, we see that in contempt of life and death (that is, of all the evils mentioned before), they <desired to die and be delivered both from the evil of the sins into which they are now held . . . and from the evil of the sins into which they are still able to fall.>*** (LW 42:129–30)

On the question of falling away from the faith, see also nos. 33 and 69; on longing for death, see nos. 45, 46, 51, 52, 66.

283 Die Erste Epistel an die Corinther 284

Der Ander Theil.

Wie und warumb der Götzendienst zu fliehen / sonderlich wegen Niessung des Leibes und Blutes Christi.

67a

68 Vol. 3/VI, col. 767–68, 769–70. On Colossians 3:16. There is no marginal comment, underlining, or marking here, but it is the key passage in the New Testament that deals with the function of singing in worship, which is given here with Luther's commentary. In the subject index at the end of Vol. 3/VI, this is the only reference under the heading "Lieder." The quotation from Luther is taken from his Kirchen postille sermon on the Epistle for the Fifth Sunday After Epiphany:

> v. 16. Let the word of Christ dwell in you richly, teach and admonish one another in all wisdom, and sing psalms and hymns and spiritual songs *(1 Cor. 14:26; Eph. 5:19. Herr Luther: "This verse appropriately follows the injunction to be thankful. Paul would say: Be careful to honor teachers and preachers, begin grateful that they handle the Word and may richly impart it to you. I do not imagine Paul refers to the giving of the Word from heaven, for it is not within man's power to so give it; God alone can commit it to us. So He has done and continues to do. On every occasion when He permits the Gospel to be preached, He showers the message upon us abundantly, withholding no essential knowledge. But after it is given, we ought to be thankful and to faithfully read and hear it, sing and speak it, and meditate upon it day and night. And it should be our part to secure teachers enough to minister it to us liberally and continuously. This is what is meant by letting the Word of God dwell among us richly. . . . As I see it, the apostle's distinction of the three words—psalms, hymns, and spiritual songs—is this: 'psalms' properly indicates those productions of David and others constituting the psalter* [see notes on no. 44]; *'hymns' refers to the songs of the prophets occasionally mentioned in the Scriptures—songs of Moses* [see no. 18], *Deborah, Solomon, Isaiah, Daniel, Habakkuk, with the Magnificat, Benedictus, and the like, called* Canticles; *'spiritual songs'*

68

are those not written in the Scriptures but of daily origin with men. Paul calls these latter 'spiritual' to a greater degree than psalms and hymns, though he recognizes those as themselves spiritual. He forbids worldly, sensual, and unbecoming songs, desiring us to sing of spiritual things. It is then that our songs are calculated to benefit and instruct, as he says. But what is the significance of Paul's phrase 'with grace'? I offer the explanation that he refers to the grace of God and means that the singing of spiritual songs is to be voluntary, uncompelled, spontaneous, rendered with cheerfulness and prompted by love; not extorted by authority and law, as is the singing in our churches today. No one sings, preaches or prays from a recognition of mercy and grace received. The motive is hope for gain, or a fear of punishment, injury and shame; or again, the holiest individuals bind themselves to obedience, or are driven to it, for the sake of winning heaven, and not at all to further the knowledge of the Word of God—the understanding of it richly and in all wisdom, as Paul desires it to be understood. I imagine Paul has in mind the grace or graciousness of songs when he says in Eph. 4[:29]*: 'Let no evil talk come out of your mouths, but only*

768 | 769 Das Dritte Capitel. 770

68a

such as is good for edifying, as fits the occasion, that it may impart grace to those who hear.' Likewise should songs be calculated to bring grace and favor to them who hear. Foul, unchaste and superfluous words have no place therein, nor have any inappropriate elements, elements void of significance and without virtue and life. Hymns are to be rich in meaning, to be pleasing and sweet, and thus productive of enjoyment for all hearers. The singing of such songs is very properly called in Hebrew singing 'with grace,' as Paul has it. Of this character are the psalms and hymns of the Scriptures; they are good thoughts presented in pleasing words. Some songs, though expressed in charming words, are worldly and carnal; while others presenting good thoughts are at the same time expressed in words inappropriate, unattractive, and devoid of grace.") and spiritual songs [*with grace*] in your hearts to God. *(Herr Luther: "St. Paul does not mean that the mouth should be silent, but that the words of the mouth proceed from the heart sincerely and fervently; not hypocritically, as Isaiah 29*[:13] *says: 'This people draw near with their mouth and honor Me with their lips, while their hearts are far from Me.' So St. Paul would have the Word of God dwell among Christians generally, and richly be spoken, sung, and meditated upon everywhere; and that understandingly and productive of spiritual fruit, the Word being universally prized. He would that men thus sing unto the Lord heartfelt praise and thanks. He says let the Word 'dwell' among you. Not merely lodge as a guest for a night or two, but abide with you forever. He is constantly apprehensive of human doctrines.")* (Based on *SML* 7:87–91)

Note the emphasis on the role of music in the proclamataion of the Word, that music is identified with the Gospel rather than the Law, and that music making among people of God is a sharing in the spiritual benefits of God's grace. See nos. 26, 41, 42, 44, 54.

69 Vol. 3/VI, col. 815–16, 817–18. On 2 Thessalonians 2:3. There is no marking, underlining, or marginalia here, but it is an important passage with regard to Bach, since 2 Thess. 2:3–8 was the Epistle appointed for the Reformation Festival, which was celebrated each year on 31 October (cf. nos. 56, 74). In his comment on verse 3 Calov picks up the statement concerning apostasy and in col. 817 draws attention to the book by Nicolas Hun-n[ius]: *Apostasia Romanae Ecclesiae, ab Antiqua, Apostolica, vereque Christiana puritate salutaris doctrinae, fidei, cultus & Religionis,* which was written in 1632 while the author was superintendent minister in Lübeck. The volume was later translated into German and issued as *Apostasia Ecclesiae Romanae, Oder Abfall Der Römischen Kirchen von Der alten Apostolischen, und wahrhafften Christlichen Reinigkeit der heilsamen Glaubens-Lehre, Gottesdienst und Religion* (various editions published in Lübek, 1655, 1664, 1676, 1677, 1708). Bach owned a copy of one of these German editions (see Leaver C, no. 49; C. Trautmann, "Ansätze zu ideell-idiologischen Problemen um Johann Sebastian Bach," *Kerygma und Melos: Christhard Mahrenholz 70. Jahre,* ed. W. Blankenburg, et al [Kassel, 1970], p. 241). See further on no. 74.

69

Der Andere Theil.
Vom Anti-Christ/ und dessen Offenbarung/ Zerstörung und lügenhafften Wundern.
v. 3. Lasset euch niemand verführen in keinerley Weise. Denn er kömt nicht/ es sey denn/ daß zuvor der Abfall (das ist/ ein greulicher Abfall von der Evangelischen

69a

817 Das Ander Capitel. 818

69b

817 Das Ander

schen Lehre Christi/ nicht etwa von einem Punct/
sondern fast von allen Artickeln des Glaubens/
vergl. 1. Tim. IV. 1. 1. Joh. II. 18. Offenb. XIII. 15.
Hieher gehöret sel. Hn. D. Nicol. Hunnii Apostasia Rom. Eccles. ab antiqvâ Apostolicâ puritate, Et probatio, qvod Eccles. Roman. non sit
Christiana.) komme/ und offenbaret werde der Mensch der Sünden/ (der unzeh-
lich viel Sünden verursachet. H. Lutherus han-

69c

70 Vol. 3/VI, col. 837–38. On 2 Thessalonians 3:12. There are marks of emphasis and underlining in the quotation from Luther, taken from his *Commentary on the Psalms of Degrees* (on Psalm 127:2):

> *You should go no further than the outward man, that is, the heart and mind should not be bound thereby. For care should extend and grieve no further than the outward man, that is, the outward man is not idle or indolent, but is rather diligent and set in his calling with labors, studies, writings, cares, as an instrument. Thus must the hands work, but along with and under this labor the heart should sigh and cry to God the Lord for aid and blessing, so that, while the outward man is employed in his labor, the heart, at the same time and instead of cares, lifts its prayer to God and says thus:* Lord, I accept my calling and do what You have commanded, and will in all my work surely do what You will have done; only help me to govern my home, help me to regulate my affairs, etc.

This is the second prayer to have been underlined in this way (see no. 66). The understanding that while a man works at his profession and calling he should also pray links with Bach's custom of writing "J. J." (*Jesu Juva*—Jesus help me) at the head of his full scores (see the note on no. 1).

70

71 Vol. 3/VI, col. 1037–38, 1039–40. On 1 Peter 5:6–7. Marks of emphasis and numerous underlinings have been added to these extended quotations from Luther's sermon on the Epistle for the Third Sunday After Trinity from the *Kirchenpostille* (passages marked for emphasis are enclosed by the signs < >, and the words underlined are given in Roman type); first, on verse 6:

71

This is the last part and conclusion of the epistle of St. Peter. It is an exhortation to good works, such as a Christian, or believer, should practice. It is evident that the doctrine of the Gospel is not such as is charged by some, forbidding good works, or not earnestly commanding or urging them. Most diligently and repeatedly it urges the doctrine of works—such works as are, indeed, good works. There are in this epistle four natural heads which furnish us four good sermons. The first is of humility. The apostle has, in the verses immediately preceding our text, exhorted the elders, that is, pastors and preachers, to be in their lives "ensamples to the flock," not "lording it over the charge allotted" to them, *but using their office for the service of others. And here in our text he exhorts the others, especially the young, to "be subject unto the elder." And, in general, he admonishes all to "gird" themselves* "with humility, *to serve one another." So Paul likewise admonishes that we should honor one another. Humility is* the noblest and sweetest virtue love *brings forth, and it is* the most essential to peace and discipline. *But especially does it become and* adorn the young, *making them pleasing and precious* to God and men, bringing forth an abundance of good fruits. *If mankind could be led so to believe this that the virtue of humility would be generally practiced, it would be well everywhere. This would* be a beautiful world, *filled with discipline and good works.* I would much prefer to see a city in which the young are reared in this virtue than a hundred monasteries of barefooted and Carthusian friars, though they lived ever so strictly. *Alas! the greatest and most <frequent complaint heard anywhere is concerning the disobedience, wantonness and pride of the younger generation found in all ranks.> Therefore it is necessary to use all diligence that this exhortation be instilled into the hearts of the young and urged upon them, in the hope that it may benefit them. First of all St. Peter presents the divine command. We are not left* to our own good pleasure *in the matter—to show humility or not, as we please. God earnestly asks it of us, and asks that we do it lovingly and willingly. Otherwise his anger will be poured out upon us and we will have <no happiness nor favor, not even among men.>* For everyone is a foe to pride and arrogance. These offenses are condemned by the whole world, even by strangers whom they do not concern. *<One may be guilty of pride and not see his own shame, yet he cannot suffer it in another; he will hate and condemn that one. This vice hurts* no one save himself. *He makes himself hateful and contemptible before God and men. Everyone calls him a great, proud bag of filth and cries*

1039 Die Erste Epistel S. Petri. 1040

71a

shame upon him. God metes out judgment and scorn to him, witnessing that he will not let this vice go unpunished, but will put the offender to shame. As St. Peter here says: "God resisteth the proud."> . . . *St. Peter uses for his purpose a peculiar term when he says,* "Gird yourselves with humility." *"Gird" has the meaning of being bound or joined together most firmly; or, as a garment, most carefully woven through and through so that it cannot tear. He illustrates by this term how Christians, with all diligence, should strive after the virtue, and manifest and practice it among themselves, as if upon them as a band it* *was a special obligation. Thus, he says, must you be entwined together and bound to each other, and your hands clasped together. So must you be joined by humility, which cannot be dissolved, dismembered, or torn, <even though occasion be given one, here and there, incited by the devil, or the evil word of someone else, to fly into a passion, and grow defiant and boastful, as if to say: Must I suffer such things at the hands of this man? But rather say to yourselves: We are Christians, and must bear with each other and yield, in many things; for we are all one body, and we are placed together here on earth for the sole reason that we may, through love, serve on another.> And each should recognize his own* weakness. He should remember that God has given others also something and can give them yet more, and that therefore he should gladly serve and yield to others, remembering that he needs their help. *<Each one is created for the sake of others, and we are all to serve one another. God gives the same grace and salvation to all, so that none may exalt himself above his neighbor; or, if he lift himself up, that he lose the grace conferred and fall into deeper condemnation.> Therefore we must* hold fast to this humility, *so that the unity may not be destroyed. For the devil seeks to destroy this also, and uses every possible means to lead people to despise each other and to be proud and insolent in their treatment of each other. And these are things to which flesh and blood, even without special incitement, are inclined. . . . <For, if thou beginnest something in thine own power, and wisdom, and haughtiness, think not he will grant thee success and blessing to carry out thy purpose.> On the other hand, if thou humblest thyself, and beginnest aught in accordance with His will, in the fear of God and trusting in His grace, there is given thee the promise, "He giveth grace to the humble." So, then, thou shalt not only have favor with men, but success shall crown thy efforts. Thou shalt prove a useful man, both to God and to the world, and shalt complete and maintain thy work despite the resistance of the devil. For where God's grace is, there his blessing and protection must follow, and his servant cannot be overthrown or defeated. Though he be oppressed for a time, he shall finally come forth again and be exalted. So St. Peter concludes by saying: "Humble yourselves, therefore, under the mighty hand of God, that He may exalt you in due time." St. Peter shows in these words what true humility is and whence it comes. The heart, through knowledge of its sin, becomes terrified in the presence of God's anger and anxiously seeks grace. Thus humility is born, not merely external and before men, but of the heart and of God, from fear of God and knowledge of one's own unworthiness and weakness. He who fears God and "trembles at His Word" (as Is. 66[:5] says), will surely defy or hector or boast against nobody.* Yea, he will even manifest a gentle spirit toward his enemies. Therefore, he finds favor both with God and men. *The cause of this, St. Peter says, shall be "the mighty hand of God." . . . But again, let the proud fear, even though He permit them to go unpunished and to continue in their boastful course for a time. He watches their lives, and, when the proper time comes,* He will descend all too heavily upon them, *so that they cannot bear it. <He has already stretched forth His mighty hand, both to cast down the godless and to exalt the humble.>* (Based on *SML* 8:57–59, 62–63, 66–68)

Note the reference to words from the Magnificat at the very end of the quotation (see no. 62). The commentary on the following verse (verse 7) continues from where the previous quotation given above left off:

> *What will become of him who lives a God-fearing and humble life, suffering the insolence, pride and wantonness of the world? Or, where will he find protection and defense, to abide in his godly ways? We see daily how the pious are harassed and persecuted, and are trod on by the world. The apostle says: "Ye Christians must endure temptation and adversity, want and need, both physical and spiritual, in the world, and your heart is oppressed with anxieties and cares, and ye think within yourselves: O, what will become of me? How shall I be supported? What if I should die?" (For the world only concerns itself about how it may be enriched and filled, anxious, unbelieving consciences would, through themselves and their own good works, seek to have a gracious God and to die in peace.) "In view of all this," he says, "only hearken, I will counsel and instruct you aright as to what disposition you should make of your troubles." There is a brief passage in the 55th Psalm* [verse 22], *which reads: "Cast thy burden upon the Lord, and He will sustain thee: He will never suffer the righteous to be moved." Follow this advice. Let not your burden rest upon yourselves; for you cannot bear it, and must finally perish beneath its weight. But, confident and full of joy, cast it from you and throw it on God, and say: Heavenly Father, Thou art my Lord and God, who didst create me when I was nothing; moreover hast redeemed me through Thy Son. Now, Thou hast committed to me and* laid upon me, this office or work, and things do not go as well as I would like. There is so much to oppress and worry, that I can find neither counsel nor help. Therefore I commend everything to Thee. Do Thou supply counsel and help, and be Thou, Thyself, everything in these things. (*SML* 8:68–69)

The underlinings and markings of these passages are most significant. They are similar to those of no. 57. There the question was one of being angry if the integrity of one's office or profession demand it, but such anger should nevertheless, be tempered by a forgiving attitude; here it is the question of humility and the danger of "flying into a passion" in an attitude of belligerent defiance. This was always a problem for Bach, who felt he had to suffer persecutions and misunderstandings on many counts (see note on no. 57). Therefore, if these are his markings, it suggests that he was aware of his own "weakness," a word specifically underlined in the quotation on verse 6 above. It also suggests that he sought to deal with the problem in a prayerful way; the underlining in the quotation on verse 7 emphasizes the words of yet another prayer (see also nos. 66, 70).

72 Vol. 3/VI, col. 1297–98. On James 3:2. Marks of emphasis and underlinings have been added to two quotations from Luther (the passage with marks of emphasis is enclosed by the signs < >, and the words underlined are given in Roman type):

> So, even if pious men should err a little in such confused cases, God will be satisfied with their error, because their intentions are sincere and true, and they are not seeking advantage for themselves or knowingly speaking against the established laws, and He will bury it all in the Lord's Prayer when we say: "Forgive us our trespasses." <*In the same way every government must often make mistakes and cannot help it, but nonetheless does not give up its office or despair of it on that account. This life is too sinful and too blind! Even though we do our best, we make mistakes in many things which we must commend to God and say with King David in Psalm 19*[:12]: *"Who can discern his errors? Cleanse Thou me from hidden faults," etc., and James 3*[:2]: *"For we all make many mistakes," etc., so that God may find an opportunity to forgive our errors and sins and to show us His mercy.*> ("On Marriage Matters," *LW* 46:288). *For the Supper need not be denied to those who sometimes fall and rise again, but grieve over their lapse. Indeed, we must realize that it was instituted just for such people so that they may be refreshed and strengthened. "For in many things we offend all" James 3*[:2]. *And* we "bear one another's burdens," [Gal. 6:2], since we are burdening one another. ("An Order of Mass and Communion" [*Formula Missae*], *LW* 53:33).

72

As with many of the other instances of underlining, the subject matter so marked out here deals with the meaning and application of the Gospel in forgiveness and grace (see especially no. 66, where the passage underlined has a similar reference to the Lord's Prayer).

73 Vol. 3/VI, col. 1419–20. On Revelation 12:14. *Prag* has been corrected to *Augsburg* in Calov's commentary on the verse. The reference is to the religious peace of Augsburg 1555, according to which Lutherans were granted the legal right to practice their faith in Germany alongside Roman Catholics.

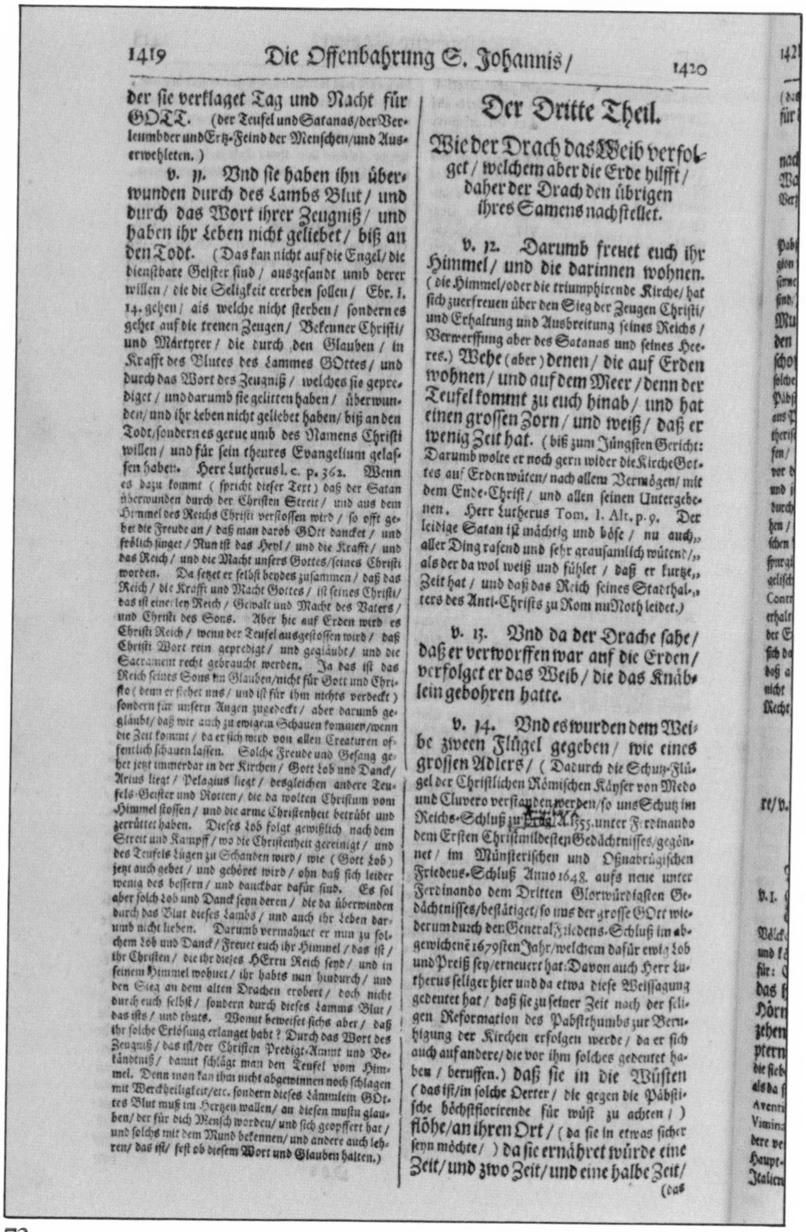

1419 Die Offenbahrung S. Johannis/ 1420

der sie verklaget Tag und Nacht für GOTT. (der Teufel und Satanas/der Verleumbder und Ertz-Feind der Menschen/und Auserwehleten.)

v. 11. Und sie haben ihn überwunden durch des Lambs Blut/ und durch das Wort ihrer Zeugniß/ und haben ihr Leben nicht geliebet/ biß an den Todt. (Das kan nicht auf die Engel/ die dienstbare Geister sind/ ausgesandt umb derer willen/ die die Seligkeit ererben sollen/ Ebr. 1. 14. gehen/ als welche nicht sterben/ sondern es gehet auf die treuen Zeugen/ Bekenner Christi/ und Märtyrer/ die durch den Glauben/ in Krafft des Blutes des Lammes GOttes/ und durch das Wort des Zeugniß/ welches sie geprediget/ und darumb sie gelitten haben/ überwunden/ und ihr Leben nicht geliebet haben/ biß an den Todt/ sondern es gerne umb des Namens Christi willen/ und für sein theures Evangelium gelassen haben. Herr Lutherus l. c. p. 362. Wenn es dazu kommt (spricht dieser Text) daß der Satan überwunden durch der Christen Streit/ und aus dem Himmel des Reichs Christi verstossen wird/ so offt gehet die Freude an/ daß man darob GOtt dancket/ und frölich singet/ Nun ist das Heyl/ und die Krafft/ und das Reich/ und die Macht unsers Gottes/ seines Christi worden. Da setzet er selbst beydes zusammen/ daß das Reich/ die Krafft und Macht Gottes/ ist seines Christi/ das ist einerley Reich/ Gewalt und Macht des Vaters/ und Christi des Sons. Aber hie auf Erden wird es Christi Reich/ wenn der Teufel ausgestossen wird/ daß Christi Wort rein geprediget/ und gegläubt/ und die Sacrament recht gebraucht werden. Ja das ist das Reich seines Sons im Glauben/ nicht für Gott und Christo (denn er siehet uns/ und ist für ihm nichts verdeckt) sondern für unsern Augen zugedeckt/ aber darumb gegläubt/ daß wir auch zu ewigem Schauen kommen/ wenn die Zeit kommt/ da er sich wird von allen Creaturen offentlich schauen lassen. Solche Freude und Gesang gehet jetzt immerdar in der Kirchen/ Gott Lob und Danck/ Arius liegt/ Pelagius liegt/ desgleichen andere Teufels-Geister und Rotten/ die da wolten Christum vom Himmel stossen/ und die arme Christenheit betrübt und zerrüttet haben. Dieses Lob folgt gewißlich nach dem Streit und Kampff/ wo die Christenheit gereinigt/ und des Teufels Lügen zu Schanden wird/ wie (Gott Lob) jetzt auch gehet/ und gehöret wird/ ohn daß sich leider wenig des bessern/ und danckbar dafür sind. Es sol aber solch Lob und Danck seyn deren/ die da überwinden durch das Blut dieses Lambs/ und auch ihr Leben darumb nicht lieben. Darumb vermahnet er nun zu solchem Lob und Danck/ Freuet euch ihr Himmel/ das ist/ ihr Christen/ die ihr dieses HErrn Reich seyd/ und in seinem Himmel wohnet/ ihr habts nun hindurch/ und den Sieg an dem alten Drachen erobert/ doch nicht durch euch selbst/ sondern durch dieses Lamms Blut/ das ists/ und thuts. Womit beweiset sichs aber/ daß ihr solche Erlösung erlanget habt? Durch das Wort des Zeugniß/ das ist/ der Christen Predigt-Ammt und Bekändtniß/ damit schlägt man den Teufel vom Himmel. Denn man kan ihm nicht abgewinnen noch schlagen mit Werckheiligkeit/etc. sondern dieses Lämmlein GOttes Blut muß im Hertzen wallen/ an diesen mustu glauben/ der für dich Mensch worden/ und sich geopffert hat/ und solchs mit dem Mund bekennen/ und andere auch lehren/ das ist/ fest ob diesem Wort und Glauben halten.)

Der Dritte Theil.

Wie der Drach das Weib verfolget/ welchem aber die Erde hilfft/ daher der Drach den übrigen ihres Samens nachstellet.

v. 12. Darumb freuet euch ihr Himmel/ und die darinnen wohnen. (die Himmel/ oder die triumphirende Kirche/ hat sich zu erfreuen über den Sieg der Zeugen Christi/ und Erhaltung und Ausbreitung seines Reichs/ Verwerffung aber des Satanas und seines Heeres.) Wehe (aber) denen/ die auf Erden wohnen/ und auf dem Meer/ denn der Teufel kommt zu euch hinab/ und hat einen grossen Zorn/ und weiß/ daß er wenig Zeit hat. (biß zum Jüngsten Gericht: Darumb wolte er noch gern wider die Kirche Gottes auf Erden wüten/ nach allem Vermögen/ mit dem Ende-Christ/ und allen seinen Untergebenen. Herr Lutherus Tom. 1. Alt. p. 9. Der leidige Satan ist mächtig und böse/ nu auch „aller Ding rasend und sehr grausamlich wütend/ „als der da wol weiß und fühlet/ daß er kurtze „Zeit hat/ und daß das Reich seines Stadthal-„ters des Anti-Christs zu Rom nu Noth leidet.)

v. 13. Und da der Drache sahe/ daß er verworffen war auf die Erden/ verfolget er das Weib/ die das Knäblein gebohren hatte.

v. 14. Und es wurden dem Weibe zween Flügel gegeben/ wie eines grossen Adlers/ (Dadurch die Schutz-Flügel der Christlichen Römischen Käyser von Medo und Cluvero verstanden werden/ so uns Schutz im Reichs-Schluß zu Prag A. 1555. unter Ferdinando dem Ersten Christmildesten Gedächtnisses/ gegönnet/ im Münsterischen und Oßnabrügischen Friedens-Schluß Anno 1648. aufs neue unter Ferdinando dem Dritten Glorwürdigsten Gedächtnisses/ bestätiget/ so uns der grosse GOtt wiederum durch den General-Friedens-Schluß im abgewichenē 1679sten Jahr/ welchem dafür ewig Lob und Preiß sey/ erneuert hat: Davon auch Herr Lutherus seliger hier und da etwa diese Weissagung gedeutet hat/ daß sie zu seiner Zeit nach der seligen Reformation des Pabstthumbs zur Beruhigung der Kirchen erfolgen werde/ da er sich auch auf andere/ die vor ihm solches gedeutet haben/ beruffen.) daß sie in die Wüsten (das ist/ in solche Oerter/ die gegen die Päbstische höchstflorirende für wüst zu achten/) flöhe/ an ihren Ort/ (da sie in etwas sicher seyn möchte/) da sie ernähret würde eine Zeit/ und zwo Zeit/ und eine halbe Zeit/ (das

73

74 Vol. 3/VI, col. 1431–32, 1433–34, 1435–36. On Revelation 14:6–8. There is neither marking, underlining, nor marginalia here, but it is an important passage with regard to Bach, since Revelation 14:6–8 was the Gospel appointed for the Reformation Festival, which was celebrated each year on 31 October (cf. nos. 56, 69). This passage was chosen for this purpose because at Luther's funeral his colleague Johann Bugenhagen, in a notable sermon, identified Luther as the "other angel with an eternal Gospel to proclaim," which is the subject of verse 6. As part of his commentary on the verse Calov quotes Luther's statement in which he accepts his prophetic role:

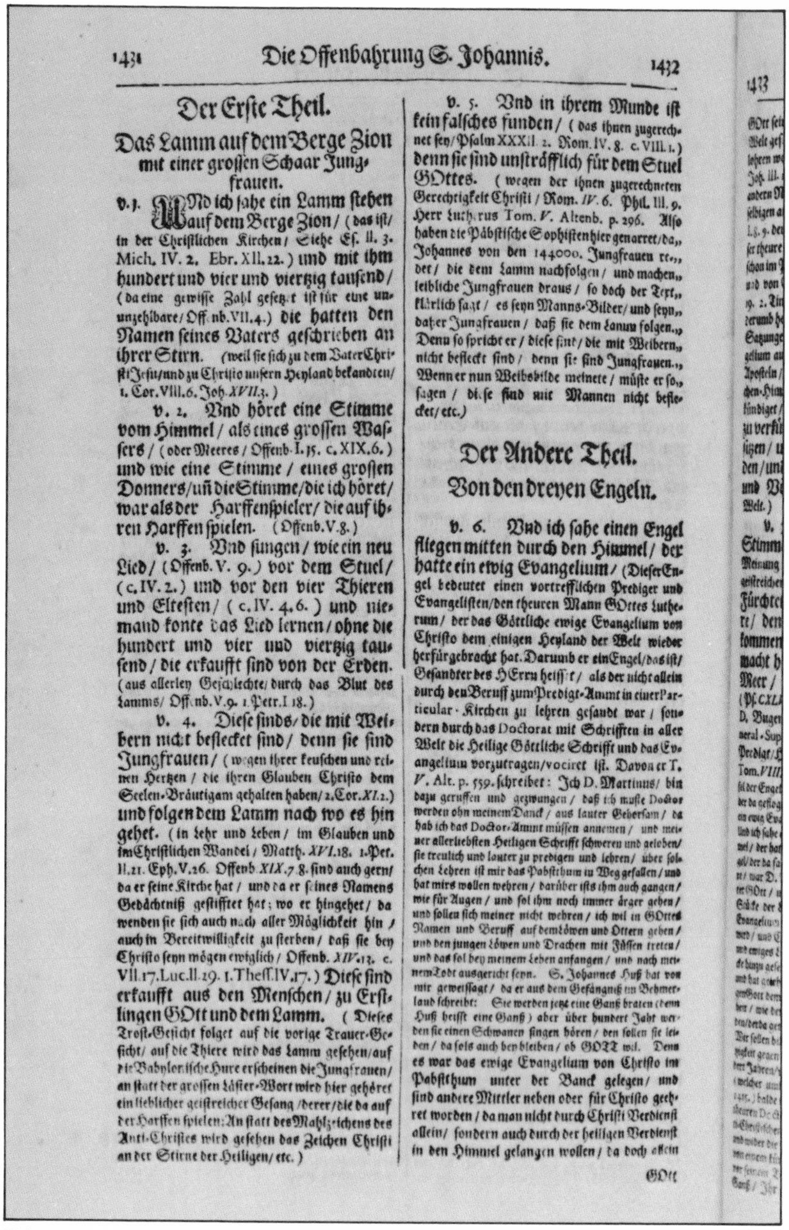

> *I, Dr. Martinus, have been called to this work and was compelled to become a doctor, without any initiative of my own, but out of pure obedience. Then I had to accept the office of doctor and swear a vow to my most beloved Holy Scriptures that I would preach and teach them faithfully and purely. While engaged in this kind of teaching, the papacy crossed my path and wanted to hinder me in it. How it has fared is obvious to all, and it will fare still worse. It shall not hinder me. In God's name and call I shall walk on the lion and the adder, and tread on the young lion and dragon with my feet* [cf. Psalm 91:13]. *And this which has been begun during my lifetime will be completed after my death. St. John Huss prophesied of me when he wrote from his prison in Bohemia, "They will roast a goose now (for 'Huss' means 'a goose'), but after a hundred years they will hear a swan sing, and him they will endure." And that is the way it will be, if God wills.* (*LW* 34:103–04)

74

On verse 7, at the head of a number of quotations from various sources, Calov quotes from Bugenhagen's funeral sermon for Luther:

> *He* [Luther] *was without doubt the angel of Rev. 14 that flew in the midst of heaven with an eternal Gospel, etc. As the text says: "Then I saw another angel flying in mid-*

heaven, with an eternal Gospel," etc. This angel says: "Fear God and give Him glory." These are the two main points of Dr. Martin Luther's teaching, the Law and the Gospel, through which the whole of Scripture is opened and Christ is known, our righteousness and eternal life. These two things he has clearly established (now that the time of his judgment is come) and has taught about real prayer and calling on God the heavenly Father in spirit and in truth. As the angel of Rev. 14 also says: "Worship Him who made heaven and earth," etc. Therefore, we should rightly recognize God's goodness and mercy towards us, that a hundred years after the death of St. John Huss (who died for the truth in the year 1415), He, by His Spirit, raised up this beloved Doctor Martin Luther against the teaching of Anti-Christ, the wretched and satanic papacy, and the devil's doctrine. This John Huss prophesied when he spoke, before his death, of a coming "swan." "Huss" in Bohemian means "goose." "So," says John Huss, "they may roast a goose now, but God will raise up a swan they will neither burn nor roast." And against their many cries, that he cannot know the answers of the future, he said: "After a hundred years I will answer you." This he has sincerely done through our dear father, Dr. Luther, in the year following a hundred years.

1433 **Das Vierzehende Capitel.** 1434

GOtt seinen eingebohrnen Son zum Heyland der Welt gesand / daß/die an ihn gläuben/ nicht verlohren werden / sondern das ewige Leben haben/ Joh. III. 16. 1. Joh. IV. 14. 16. und in keinem andern Namen sonst Heyl ist / Gesch. *IV.* 12. demselbigen auch der Fluch angekündiget wird, Gal. I. 8. 9. der ein ander Evangelium prediget. Dieser theure Lehrer hat das ewige Evangelium / das schon im Paradieß verkündiget war / 1. Mos. *III.* 15. und von Ewigkeit bestimmet gewesen / 1. Petr. I. 19. 2. Tim. I. 9. nach seiner Verdunckelung wiederumb herfür gebracht / er hat nicht Menschen-Satzungen geprediget / sondern das reine Evangelium aus den Schrifften der Propheten und Aposteln / und ist damit mitten durch den Kirchen-Himmel geflogen / und allenthalben es verkündiget / wie hier solches angedeutet worden /) **zu verkündigen denen / die auf Erden sitzen / und wohnen / und allen Heyden / und Geschlechten / und Sprachen / und Völckern /** (hin und wieder in aller Welt.)

v. 7. **Und sprach mit grosser Stimme:** (die jederman hören / und derer Meinung in allen Theilen der Welt aus seinen geistreichen Schrifften vernemen kunte /) **Fürchtet GOtt / und gebet ihm die Ehre / denn die Zeit seines Gerichts ist kommen / und betet an den / der gemacht hat Himmel und Erden / und Meer / und die Wasser-Brunnen.** (Ps. *CXLVI.* 6. Gesch. *XIV.* 7. Das erkläret Herr D. Bugenhagius der Eltere sel. vormals General-Superintendens allhier / in seiner Leicht-Predigt / Herrn D. Luthero sel. allhier gehalten / Tom. *VIII.* Altenb. p. 864. Er war ohne Zweifel der Engel / davon in der Offenb. XIV. Cap. stehet / der da geflogen hat mitten durch den Himmel / und hatte ein ewig Evangelium / etc. Wie denn der Text saget: Und ich sahe einen Engel fliegen mitten durch den Himmel / der hatte ein ewig Evangelium / etc. Dieser Engel / der da saget / fürchtet Gott / und gebet ihm die Ehre / war D. Martinus Luther: Und das hie stehet / fürchtet GOtt / und gebet ihm die Ehre / das sind die zwey Stücke der Lehre D. Martini Luthers / das Gesetz und Evangelium / durch welche die gantze Schrifft geöffnet wird / und Christus erkandt wird / unser Gerechtigkeit und ewiges Leben / zu welchen zweyen er auch diß Stücke hinzu gesetzt hat (die Zeit seines Gerichts ist kommen) und hat gelehret vom rechten Gebet und Anruffung gegen Gott dem Himmlischen Vater im Geist und der Warheit / wie der Engel Offenb. *XIV.* auch saget: Betet an / den / der da gemacht hat Himmel und Erden / etc. Item: Wir sollen billig erkennen Gottes Güte und Barmhertzigkeit gegen uns / und Gott dancken / daß er nach hundert Jahren / von dem Tode des heiligen Johannes Huß / (welcher umb der Warheit willen getödtet ist / Anno 1415.) balde uns erwecket hat durch seinen Geist diesen theuren Doctorem Martinum Lutherum, wider die Anti-Christischen Lehre / des leidigen Satanischen Pabsts / und wider die Teufels-Lehren / wie denn Johannes Huß von einem künfftigen Schwane selbst geprophezeyet hat vor seinem Tode: Denn Huß heist auf Böhmisch eine Ganß / Ihr bratet / (saget Johann Huß) jetzt eine Ganß / Gott wird aber einen Schwan erwecken / den werdet ihr nicht brennen noch braten. Und da sie wider ihn viel schryen / daß er ihnen nicht könte antworten / sol er gesagt haben: Nach hundert Jahren wil ich euch antworten / das hat er redlich gethan durch unsern lieben Vater D. Lutherum / und eben angefangen im folgenden Jahr nach hundert Jahren. Und diß ist nicht hie allein geschehen / sondern unter allen Völckern und Sprachen. Bellarminus traun der vortreffliche Cardinal betauret selbst / daß Lutherus mit seiner Lehr so geschwind in alle Länder durchgebrochen / und nicht vergnüget mit dem Abend und Nordischen Reichen / auch in den Morgen und Mittags-Ländern / zu den Griechen / in Indien / in die neue Welt selbst durchgedrungen / daß sie bald Deutschland eingenommen / darauf plötzlich gegen Mitternacht und Orient sich gewendet / Dännemarck / Norwegen / Schweden / Gothen / Ungern eingenommen / so wol in den Occident, und gegen Mittag in gleicher Eil geflogen / und Franckreich / Engeland / Schottland / die gewaltig blühende Reiche / in kurtzer Zeit gewonnen / auch durch die Alpen in Welschland eingebrochen / so wol bey den Flüssen einen sichern Sitz erhalten habe / Orat. ad T. IV. Oper. und præf. Tom. I. Controv. Wie sie auch in Spanien durchgedrungen / berichtet der sel. Herr Phil. Nicolai, de Regn. Christ. c. 1. Und der vorneme Frantzösische Historicus, Jac. August. Thuan. L. XXIII. Wie freudig aber dieser Engel das Evangelium bekandt / ist aus Tom. V. Jenens. German. in der Glosse auf das vermeinte Käyserliche Edict p. 298. zu sehen: Weil ich sehe / daß diesen Haupt-Artickel der Teufel immer muß lästern / durch seine Säu-Lehrer / und nicht ruhen und aufhören kan / so sage ich D. Martin Luther / unsers HErrn JEsu Christi unwürdiger Evangelist / daß diesen Artickel (der Glaub allein ohn alle Werck macht gerecht für Gott /) sol lassen stehen und bleiben / der Röm. Käyser / der Türckische Käyser / der Tartarische Käyser / der Persen Käyser / der Pabst / alle Cardinäl / Bischöffe / Pfaffen / Mönche / Nonnen / Könige / Fürsten / Herren / alle Welt sammt allen Teufeln / und sollen das Höllische Feuer dazu haben auf ihren Kopff / und keinen Danck dazu. Das sey mein D. Luthers Einsprechung vom Heiligen Geist / und das rechte H. Evangelium. Denn da stehet der Artickel / den die Kinder beten / Ich gläube an JEsum Christum / gecreutziget / gestorben / etc. Es ist ja niemand für unser Sünde gestorben / denn allein JEsus Christus GOttes Son / Allein JEsus GOttes Son / noch einmal / sage ich / Allein JEsus Gottes Son hat uns von Sünden erlöset / das ist gewißlich war / und die gantze Schrifft / und solten alle Teufel und Welt sich zureissen und bersten / so ists ja war. Ist ers aber allein / der Sünde weg nimmt / so können wirs mit unsern Wercken nicht seyn / so ists ja unmüglich / daß ich solchen einigen und allein Erlöser von Sünden / JEsum anders denn mit dem Glauben fassen und erlangen müge. Mit Wercken ist und bleibet er unergriffen. Weil aber allein der Glaube / für und ehe die Werck folgen / solchen Erlöser ergreiffet / so muß es war seyn / daß allein der Glaube für und ohn Werck solche Erlösunge fasse / welches nichts anders seyn kan / denn gerecht werden. Denn von Sünden erlöset / oder Sünde vergeben haben / muß nicht anders seyn / denn gerecht seyn oder werden etc. Aber nach solchen Glauben oder empfangener Erlösung / oder Sünden Vergebung / oder Gerechtigkeit / folgen alsdenn gute Wercke / als solches Glaubens-Früchte. Das ist unsere Lehre / und also lehret

74a

On verse 8, which states that "Babylon is fallen," Calov, following Luther (N.B. Luther's treatise of 1520, "The Babylonian Captivity of the Church" [*LW* 36:11–126]), identifies Babylon as the Roman Church. In doing so, he refers to two classic statements against the doctrines and practices of the Church of Rome, and copies of both were in Bach's own personal library. The first is *Examen Concilii Tridentini* by Martin Chemnitz (Leaver C, no. 5). It is a massive and detailed refutation, point by point, of the decrees of the Council of Trent. It was and remains the fundamental statement of Lutheran theology set against the doctrines of the

Church of Rome. See also Calov's comments on this important work given in Appendix 1, p. 179. The other book Calov has referred to before: N. Hunnius's *Abfall der Römischen Kirchen* (see no. 69). That Bach should own both books referred to here by Calov indicates how seriously he took the Lutheran Reformation and provides the background for our understanding of the cantatas he composed for the annual Reformation Festival (BWV 79, 80, 76 [second part], and possibly 129), for the bicentenary of the Augsburg Confession in 1730 (BWV 190a, 120b, Anh. 4), and those cantatas that were performed when the Reformation Festival fell on a Sunday (for example, BWV 5, 49, 163).

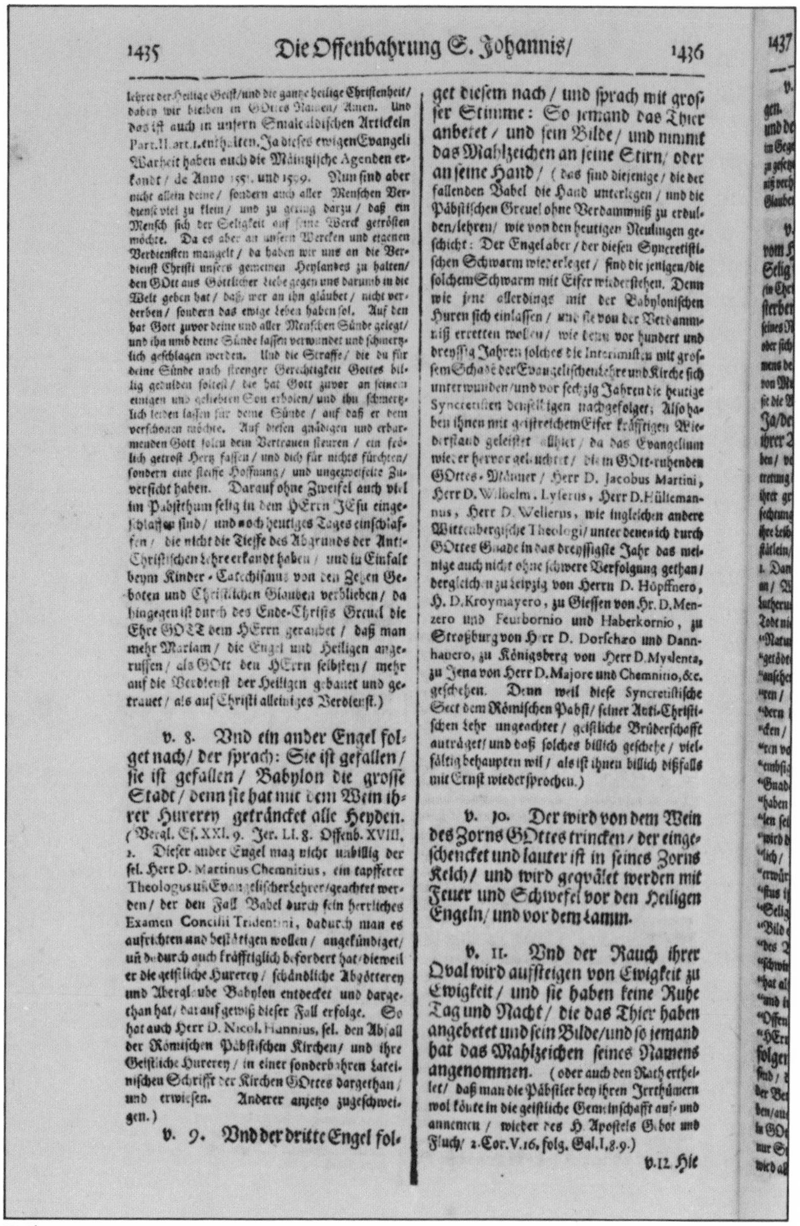

1435 Die Offenbahrung S. Johannis/ 1436

lehret der Heilige Geist/und die gantze heilige Christenheit/ dabey wir bleiben in GOttes Namen/ Amen. Und das ist auch in unsern Smalcaldischen Artickeln Part.II.art.1.enthalten. Ja dieses ewigen Evangeli Warheit haben auch die Mäintzische Agenden erkandt/ de Anno 1551. und 1599. Nun sind aber nicht allein deine/ sondern auch aller Menschen Verdienst viel zu klein/ und zu gering darzu/ daß ein Mensch sich der Seligkeit auf seine Werck getrösten möchte. Da es aber an unsern Wercken und eigenen Verdiensten mangelt/ da haben wir uns an die Verdienst Christi unsers gemeinen Heylandes zu halten/ den GOtt aus Göttlicher Liebe gegen uns darumb in die Welt geben hat/ daß wer an ihn gläubet/ nicht verderben/ sondern das ewige Leben haben sol. Auf den hat Gott zuvor deine und aller Menschen Sünde gelegt/ und ihn umb deine Sünde lassen verwundet und schmertzlich geschlagen werden. Und die Straffe/ die du für deine Sünde nach strenger Gerechtigkeit Gottes billig gedulden soltest/ die hat Gott zuvor an seinem einigen und geliebten Son erholen/ und ihn schmertzlich leiden lassen für deine Sünde/ auf daß er dein verschonen möchte. Auf diesen gnädigen und erbarmenden Gott solt du dein Vertrauen steuren/ ein frölich getrost Hertz fassen/ und dich für nichts fürchten/ sondern eine steiffe Hoffnung/ und ungezweifelte Zuversicht haben. Darauf ohne Zweifel auch viel im Pabstthum selig in dem HErrn JEsu eingeschlaffen sind/ und noch heutiges Tages einschlaffen/ die nicht die Tieffe des Abgrunds der Anti-Christischen Lehre erkandt haben/ und in Einfalt beym Kinder-Catechismus von den Zehen Geboten und Christlichen Glauben verblieben/ da hingegen ist durch des Ende-Christs Greuel die Ehre GOTT dem HErrn geraubet/ daß man mehr Mariam/ die Engel und Heiligen angeruffen/ als GOtt den HErrn selbsten/ mehr auf die Verdienst der Heiligen gebauet und getrauet/ als auf Christi alleiniges Verdienst.)

v. 8. **Und ein ander Engel folget nach/ der sprach: Sie ist gefallen/ sie ist gefallen/ Babylon die grosse Stadt/ denn sie hat mit dem Wein ihrer Hurerey geträncket alle Heyden.** (Vergl. Es. XXI. 9. Jer. LI. 8. Offenb. XVIII. 2. Dieser ander Engel mag nicht unbillig der sel. Herr D. Martinus Chemnitius, ein tapfferer Theologus und Evangelischer Lehrer/ geachtet werden/ der den Fall Babel durch sein herrliches Examen Concilii Tridentini, dadurch man es aufrichten und bestätigen wollen/ angekündiget/ und dadurch auch kräfftiglich befordert hat/ dieweil er die geistliche Hurerey/ schändliche Abgötterey und Aberglaube Babylon entdecket und dargethan hat/ darauf gewiß dieser Fall erfolge. So hat auch Herr D. Nicol. Hunnius, sel. den Abfall der Römischen Päbstischen Kirchen/ und ihre Geistliche Hurerey/ in einer sonderbahren Lateinischen Schrifft der Kirchen GOttes dargethan/ und erwiesen. Anderer anjetzo zugeschweigen.)

v. 9. **Und der dritte Engel folget diesem nach/ und sprach mit grosser Stimme: So jemand das Thier anbetet/ und sein Bilde/ und nimmt das Mahlzeichen an seine Stirn/ oder an seine Hand/** (das sind diejenige/ die der fallenden Babel die Hand unterlegen/ und die Päbstischen Greuel ohne Verdammniß zu erdulden/lehren/ wie von den heutigen Neulingen geschicht: Der Engel aber/ der diesen Syncretistischen Schwarm wiederleget/ sind die jenigen/die solchem Schwarm mit Eifer wiederstehen. Denn wie jene allerdings mit der Babylonischen Huren sich einlassen/ und sie von der Verdammniß erretten wollen/ wie denn vor hundert und dreyssig Jahren solches die Interimisten mit grossem Schade der Evangelischen Lehre und Kirche sich unterwunden/ und vor sechzig Jahren die heutige Syncretisten denselbigen nachgefolget; Also haben ihnen mit geistreichem Eifer kräfftigen Wiederstand geleistet allhier/ da das Evangelium wieder hervor geleuchtet/ die in GOtt-ruhenden GOttes-Männer/ Herr D. Jacobus Martini, Herr D. Wilhelm. Lyserus, Herr D. Hülsemannus, Herr D. Wellerus, wie ingleichen andere Wittenbergische Theologi/ unter denen ich durch GOttes Gnade in das dreyssigste Jahr das meinige auch nicht ohne schwere Verfolgung gethan/ dergleichen zu Leipzig von Herrn D. Höpffnero, H. D. Kroymayero, zu Giessen von Hr. D. Menzero und Feurbornio und Haberkornio, zu Straßburg von Herr D. Dorschæo und Dannhauero, zu Königsberg von Herr D. Myslenta, zu Jena von Herr D. Majore und Chemnitio, &c. geschehen. Denn weil diese Syncretistische Sect dem Römischen Pabst/ seiner Anti-Christischen Lehr ungeachtet/ geistliche Brüderschafft anträget/ und daß solches billich geschehe/ vielfältig behaupten wil/ als ist ihnen billich dißfalls mit Ernst wiedersprochen.)

v. 10. **Der wird von dem Wein des Zorns GOttes trincken/ der eingeschencket und lauter ist in seines Zorns Kelch/ und wird gequälet werden mit Feuer und Schwefel vor den Heiligen Engeln/ und vor dem Lamm.**

v. 11. **Und der Rauch ihrer Qual wird auffsteigen von Ewigkeit zu Ewigkeit/ und sie haben keine Ruhe Tag und Nacht/ die das Thier haben angebetet und sein Bilde/ und so jemand hat das Mahlzeichen seines Namens angenommen.** (oder auch den Rath ertheilet/ daß man die Päbstler bey ihren Irrthümern wol könte in die geistliche Gemeinschafft auf- und annemen/ wieder des H. Apostels Gebot und Fluch/ 2. Cor. V. 16. folg. Gal. I. 8. 9.)

v. 12. Hie

74b

75 Vol. 3/VI, col. 1501–02. The final page of the comentary. Calov's final words are:

With this wish [Rev. 22:21: "The grace of the Lord Jesus be with all the saints. Amen."] *St. John brings to an end this Secrets-Book, and with it I close, in the name of Jesus, not only the exposition of this book but also of the whole Holy Scripture. For this I praise the name of the Tri-Une God, for granting grace and strength of body and soul and spirit, with the four beasts of Rev. 4:8–9:*

"Holy,
Holy,
Holy,
is the Lord God Almighty, who was, and is, and is to come!" They give praise and glory and thanksgiving to Him who sits on the throne, who lives from eternity to eternity.
Amen, Amen!
The end of the Revelation of St. John, and the whole of the New Testament.

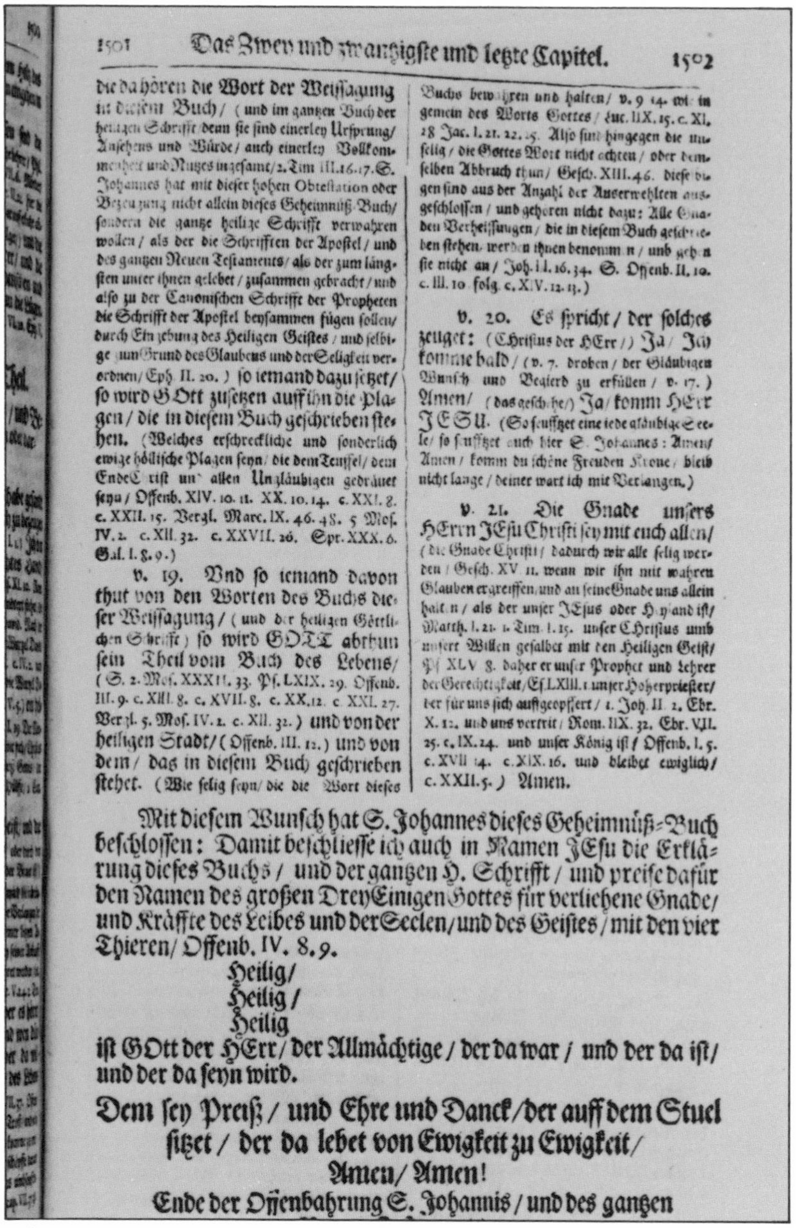
1501 Das Zwey und zwantzigste und letzte Capitel. 1502

die da hören die Wort der Weissagung in diesem Buch / (und im gantzen Buch der heiligen Schrifft / denn sie sind einerley Ursprung / Ansehens und Würde / auch einerley Vollkommenheit und Nutzes insgesamt / 2. Tim III. 16. 17. S. Johannes hat mit dieser hohen Obtestation oder Bezeugung nicht allein dieses Geheimnüß-Buch / sondern die gantze heilige Schrifft verwahren wollen / als der die Schrifften der Apostel / und des gantzen Neuen Testaments / als der zum längsten unter ihnen gelebet / zusammen gebracht / und also zu der Canonischen Schrifft der Propheten die Schrifft der Apostel beysammen fügen sollen / durch Eingebung des Heiligen Geistes / und selbige zum Grund des Glaubens und der Seligkeit verordnen / Eph. II. 20.) so iemand dazu setzet / so wird GOtt zusetzen auff ihn die Plagen / die in diesem Buch geschrieben stehen. (Welches erschreckliche und sonderlich ewige höllische Plagen seyn / die dem Teuffel / dem EndeChrist und allen Ungläubigen gedräuet seyn / Offenb. XIV. 10. 11. XX. 10. 14. c. XXI. 8. c. XXII. 15. Vergl. Marc. IX. 46. 48. 5 Mos. IV. 2. c. XII. 32. c. XXVII. 26. Spr. XXX. 6. Gal. I. 8. 9.)

v. 19. Und so iemand davon thut von den Worten des Buchs dieser Weissagung / (und der heiligen Göttlichen Schrifft) so wird GOTT abthun sein Theil vom Buch des Lebens / (S. 2. Mos. XXXII. 33. Ps. LXIX. 29. Offenb. III. 9. c. XIII. 8. c. XVII. 8. c. XX. 12. c. XXI. 27. Vergl. 5. Mos. IV. 2. c. XII. 32.) und von der heiligen Stadt / (Offenb. III. 12.) und von dem / das in diesem Buch geschrieben stehet. (Wie selig seyn / die die Wort dieses Buchs bewahren und halten / v. 9. 14. wie in gemein des Worts Gottes / Luc. IIX. 15. c. XI. 28 Jac. I. 21. 22. 25. Also sind hingegen die unselig / die Gottes Wort nicht achten / oder demselben Abbruch thun / Gesch. XIII. 46. dieselbigen sind aus der Anzahl der Auserwehlten ausgeschlossen / und gehören nicht dazu: Alle Gnaden Verheissungen / die in diesem Buch geschrieben stehen / werden ihnen benommen / und gehen sie nicht an / Joh. III. 16. 34. S. Offenb. II. 10. c. III. 10 folg. c. XIV. 12. 13.)

v. 20. Es spricht / der solches zeuget: (Christus der HErr /) Ja / Ich komme bald / (v. 7. droben / der Gläubigen Wunsch und Begierd zu erfüllen / v. 17.) Amen / (das geschehe /) Ja / komm HErr JESU. (So seufftzet eine iede gläubige Seele / so seufftzet auch hier S. Johannes: Amen / Amen / komm du schöne Freuden Krone / bleib nicht lange / deiner wart ich mit Verlangen.)

v. 21. Die Gnade unsers HErrn JEsu Christi sey mit euch allen / (die Gnade Christi / dadurch wir alle selig werden / Gesch. XV. 11. wenn wir ihn mit wahren Glauben ergreiffen / und an seine Gnade uns allein halten / als der unser JEsus oder Heyland ist / Matth. I. 21. 1. Tim. I. 15. unser Christus umb unsert Willen gesalbet mit den Heiligen Geist / Ps. XLV. 8. daher er unser Prophet und Lehrer der Gerechtigkeit / Es. LXIII. 1. unser Hoherpriester / der für uns sich auffgeopffert / 1. Joh. II. 2. Ebr. X. 12. und uns vertrit / Röm. IIX. 32. Ebr. VII. 25. c. IX. 24. und unser König ist / Offenb. I. 5. c. XVII. 14. c. XIX. 16. und bleibet ewiglich / c. XXII. 5.) Amen.

Mit diesem Wunsch hat S. Johannes dieses Geheimnüß-Buch beschlossen: Damit beschliesse ich auch in Namen JEsu die Erklärung dieses Buchs / und der gantzen H. Schrifft / und preise dafür den Namen des großen DreyEinigen Gottes für verliehene Gnade / und Kräffte des Leibes und der Seelen / und des Geistes / mit den vier Thieren / Offenb. IV. 8. 9.

Heilig /
Heilig /
Heilig
ist GOtt der HErr / der Allmächtige / der da war / und der da ist / und der da seyn wird.

Dem sey Preiß / und Ehre und Danck / der auff dem Stuel sitzet / der da lebet von Ewigkeit zu Ewigkeit /
Amen / Amen!
Ende der Offenbahrung S. Johannis / und des gantzen

75

76 Vol. 3/VI, Sig. Nnnjv verso. The beginning of the subject index that follows the Scripture index. Note that it is clearly stated that the commentary is first by Luther and second, and by implication only when nothing by Luther on the subject could be found, by Calov. See also nos. 33, 54, and nos. 1, 2, 3, 43, 47, 53, 55, 64.

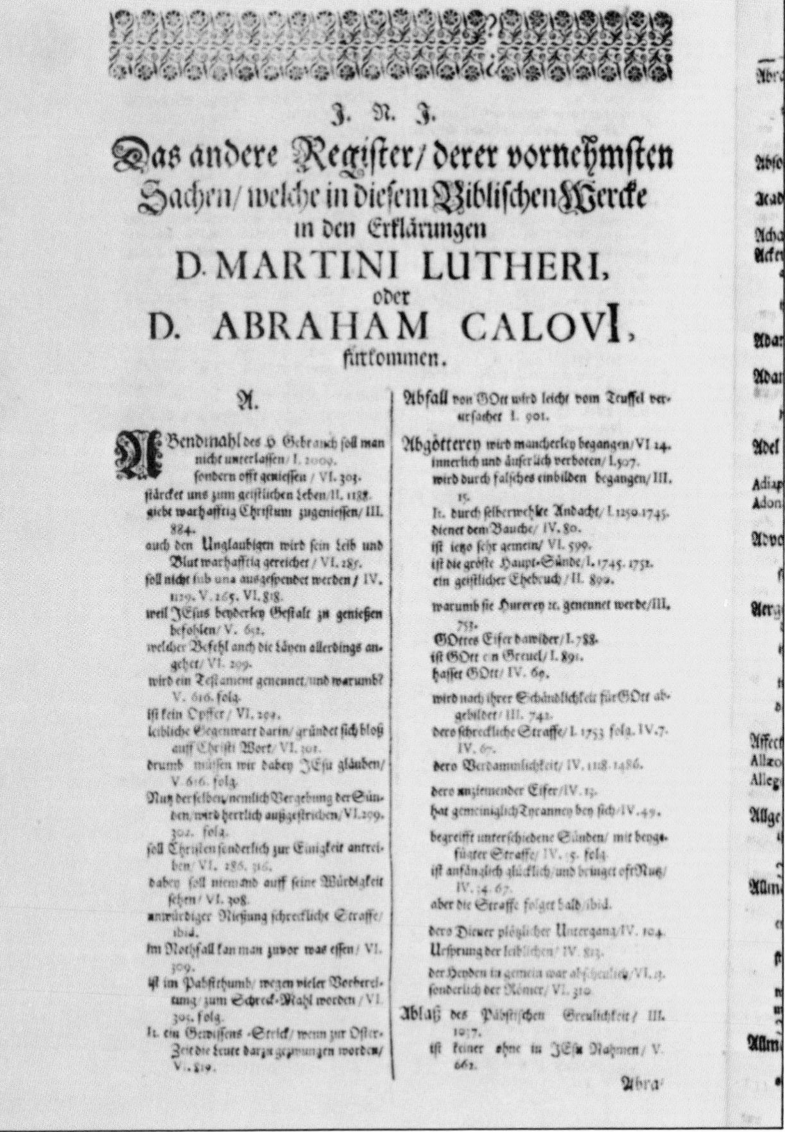

J. N. J.

Das andere Register/ derer vornehmsten Sachen/ welche in diesem Biblischen Wercke in den Erklärungen

D. MARTINI LUTHERI,

oder

D. ABRAHAM CALOVI,

fürkommen.

A.

Abendmahl des h. Gebrauch soll man nicht unterlassen/ I. 2009.
sondern offt geniessen / VI. 303.
stärcket uns zum geistlichen Leben/ II. 1188.
giebt warhafftig Christum zugeniessen/ III. 884.
auch den Unglaubigen wird sein Leib und Blut warhafftig gereichet / VI. 285.
soll nicht sub una ausgespendet werden / IV. 1129. V. 165. VI. 818.
weil JEsus beyderley Gestalt zu geniessen befohlen/ V. 652.
welcher Befehl auch die Läyen allerdings angehet/ VI. 209.
wird ein Testament genennet/ und warumb? V. 616. folg.
ist kein Opffer / VI. 294.
leibliche Gegenwart darin/ gründet sich bloß auff Christi Wort/ VI. 301.
drumb müssen wir dabey JEsu gläuben/ V. 616. folg.
Nutz derselben/ nemlich Vergebung der Sünden/ wird herrlich außgestrichen/ VI. 299. 302. folg.
soll Christen sonderlich zur Einigkeit antreiben/ VI. 286. 316.
dabey soll niemand auff seine Würdigkeit sehen / VI. 308.
unwürdiger Niessung schreckliche Straffe/ ibid.
im Nothfall kan man zuvor was essen/ VI. 309.
ist im Pabstthumb/ wegen vieler Vorbereitung/ zum Schreck-Mahl worden / VI. 305. folg.
It. ein Gewissens-Strick/ wenn zur Oster-Zeit die Leute darzu gezwungen worden/ V. 819.

Abfall von GOtt wird leicht vom Teuffel verursachet I. 901.

Abgötterey wird mancherley begangen/ VI. 14.
innerlich und äuserlich verboten/ I. 507.
wird durch falsches einbilden begangen/ III. 15.
It. durch selbererwehlte Andacht/ I. 1250. 1745.
dienet dem Bauche/ IV. 80.
ist ietzo sehr gemein/ VI. 599.
ist die gröste Haupt-Sünde/ I. 1745. 1752.
ein geistlicher Ehebruch / II. 892.
warumb sie Hurerey &c. genennet werde/ III. 753.
GOttes Eifer dawider/ I. 788.
ist GOtt ein Greuel/ I. 891.
hasset GOtt/ IV. 69.
wird nach ihrer Schändlichkeit für GOtt abgebildet/ III. 742.
dero schreckliche Straffe/ I. 1753 folg. IV. 7. IV. 67.
dero Verdammlichkeit/ IV. 118. 1486.
dero unziemender Eifer/ IV. 13.
hat gemeiniglich Tyranney bey sich/ IV. 49.
begreifft unterschiedene Sünden/ mit beygefügter Straffe/ IV. 15. folg.
ist anfänglich glücklich/ und bringet offt Nutz/ IV. 14. 67.
aber die Straffe folget bald/ ibid.
dero Diener plötzlicher Untergang/ IV. 104.
Ursprung der leiblichen/ IV. 813.
der Heyden in gemein war abscheulich/ VI. 13.
sonderlich der Römer/ VI. 310.

Ablaß des Päbstischen Greulichkeit / III. 1057.
ist keiner ohne in JEsu Nahmen/ V. 662.

Abra-

76

77 Vol. 3/VI, Sig. Ddddij recto. The first page of Errata, of which Bach has underlined parts in red ink, presumably as he checked these errors in the early columns of Vol. 1/I. In particular, he has underlined the omission from the quotation of Luther on col. 33, which he also entered into the margin at that place (see no. 5). Since both are in red ink, the markings here and there were probably made at the same time. See further the Introduction, p. 33.

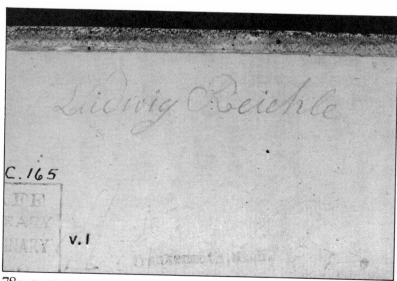

ENDE.

Druck=Fehler.

Was im Text versehen / kan alles aus einer Hauß=Bibel geändert werden. Auch kan ein jeder die unrechten oder versetzten Buchstaben selbst corrigiren. Hier werden nur die angemerckt / so den sensum corrumpiren möchten.

TOM. I.

PAg. 1. l. 6. à f. Ebal. p. 3. lin. antep. & ult. ließ: des Weibes schmertzliche Geburt/und des Mannes saurer Schweiß/ pag 5. l. 38. 1. Joh. I. 1. l. 46. Ebr. XI. 6. pag. 7. lin. 20. à f. v. feine l. feuchte lin. 18. à f. v. da l. war l. 17. à fin. l. umbringet war / und wo die Tieffe war / da ... p. 8. l. 42. Spr. IIX. 30. p. 9. l. 10. v. anführet l. anfähet l. 40. αἰῶνας. l 53. und 54. del. Mos. XX. 10. 11. p. 11. l. 22. ungeschmückt lin. 39. v. Tage l. läge pag. 14. lin. 32. v. Spanne l. Spange pag. 15. l. 4. à. f. v. und l. sind pag 19. l. 15. daran pag. 23. lin. 38. n. Adam adde: die Heva l. 59. in ihm pag. 24 lin. 20. n. gewest adde: noch davon gegangen ist / sondern ist alles am schönsten gewest. l. 39. n. abgelegt adde: und angethan das himmlische / hätte auch abgelegt pag. 25. lin. 1. n. den adde: Menschen in diesem p. 26. lin. 1. welcher lin. 23. n. bald adde er pag. 28. l. 9. als welches lin. 33. folg. ließ: dabey aber einen Versen=Stich leiden solte / v. 14. 15. von des Weibes Schmertzen in der Geburth / und des Mannes Schweiße in der Arbeit / sammt ihrer beyden Todt / v. 16-19. pag. 30. l. 30. durch die pag 32. l. 26. Rom. VII. 18. lin. 43. ließ: abgeschiedenes von der Natur / das von aussen hinzu kommt / und ohne Verletzung der Natur wider kan abgethan werden. pag. 35. l. 43. schau trüg. pag. 38. l. 17. n. Hoffnung adde: und also lebet und überwindet durch die Hoffnung l. 48. die ihnen pag. 39. lin. 12. zutreten werden pag. 42. lin. 26. n. durch den adde: Glauben an die Vergebung der Sünden / durch den l. 32. n. Farbe adde: seinem Weibe pag. 44. lin. 34. n. Angesicht adde: es sey ein Menschlich / oder ander Angesicht lin. 45. Matth. XXIIX. pag. 47. lin. ult. vom Himmel zeugete pag. 48. lin. 32. n. Cain adde: nicht lin. 44. n. eine adde: heuchlerische und pag. 49. lin. 42. sicher dahin pag. 53. lin. 20. n. jaal adde: das ist / hat angefangen / oder hats gewaget pag. 56. l. 41. vor Geburth l. Leben. pag. 60. lin. 3. à fin. v. auch l. durch pag. 61. lin. 5. v. gewisse l. gemeine pag. 67. lin. 31. 32. l. Nun ists noch Wunder / pag. 71. l. 21. v. Weg l. Wog. pag. 76. lin. ult. v. Sünde l. Sündfluth pag. 77. lin 4. à fin. v. Sündfluth l. Schöpffung p. 78. lin. 50. ließ: Wie der Weyarn die Küchlein / der Wolff die Schaffe frist pag. 84. l. 5. Babylonische Zerrüttung lin. 27. vor Abraham l. Thara lin. 31 vor Aufang l. Nachkommen lin. 45. welcher pag. 85. l. 6. Tuiscones pag. 87. lin: 42. Cæsarea pag 89. lin ... Zerstreuung der Völcker pag. 96. l. 4. 1. Mos. XIIX. 18. c. XXII. 18. pag. 102. lin. 15. à fin. n. hat adde darin er sich mit den seinen zur Ruhe setzen möchte pag. 113. lin. 19. verheisset ihr lin. 35. sonderliche lin. 39. n. gewiß ist / adde: zweiffelt er nun der Mutter halber / hat auch solches l. 40. del. hat pag. 136. lin. 5. à f. Bela pag. 137. v. Wiewol l. Dieweil lin. 43. n. Wetter adde durch der Engel Dienst sey erreget worden: Was aber gemeiniglich in einem Wetter und Ungestümigkeit pag. 138. lin. 33. ohne Verzug l. 44. l. und hat vielleicht pag. 139. l. 10. v. Zeugniß l. Zeichen lin. 24. 1. Mos. XXIIX. 22 p. 143. l. 38. und 39. del. sammt ihrer beyden Beschenckung pag. 144. lin. 15. n. Lande adde: sind gefunden worden / darumb wird er gedacht haben / wo in diesem gelobten Lande pag. 146. lin. 12. l. dir / sagt der König zu der Sarah / gebe ich auch nicht lin. 20. del. von pag. 157. lin. 6. v. der l. wie er lin. 35. v Und das / l. Unterdeß p. 158. l. 3.

Dddd ij Verzug

77

78 Various signatures and marks of ownership other than Bach's.

78a *Inside the front cover of Vol. 1/I: the signature of Ludwig [Michael] Reichle.*

78b *Flyleaf of Vol. 2/III: the inscription: "Halt im Gedächtnis Jesum Christ. Ludwig Reichle." This is a quotation from 2 Tim. 2:8, which is also the opening of BWV 67.*

78c *Flyleaf of Vol. 3/V: the signature of Ludwig Michael Reichle.*

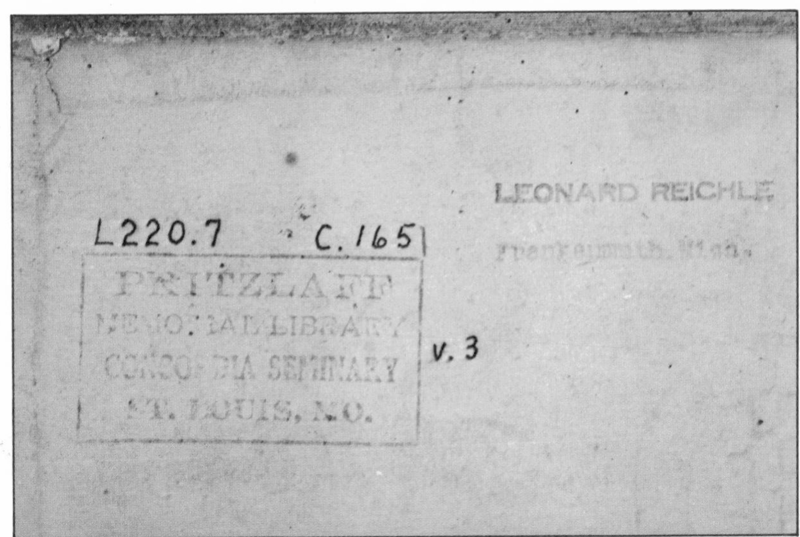

78d *Flyleaf of Vol. 3/V: the ownership stamp of Leonard Reichle.*

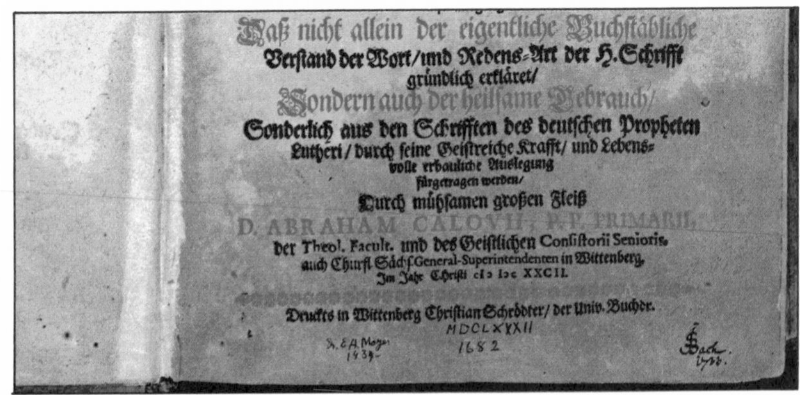

Waß nicht allein der eigentliche Buchstäbliche
Verstand der Wort/und Redens-Art der H. Schrifft
gründlich erkläret/
Sondern auch der heilsame Gebrauch/
Sonderlich aus den Schrifften des deutschen Propheten
Lutheri/durch seine Geistreiche Krafft/ und Lebens-
volle erbauliche Auslegung
fürgetragen werden/
Durch mühsamen großen Fleiß
D. ABRAHAM CALOVII, P.P. PRIMARII,
der Theol. Facult. und des Geistlichen Consistorii Senioris,
auch Churfl. Sächs. General-Superintendenten in Wittenberg,
Im Jahr Christi CIↃ IↃC XXCII.
Druckts in Wittenberg Christian Schrödter/ der Univ. Buchdr.
MDCLXXXII
1682

78e *Title page of Vol. 2/III: the signature "Dr. E. A. Mayer 1934."*

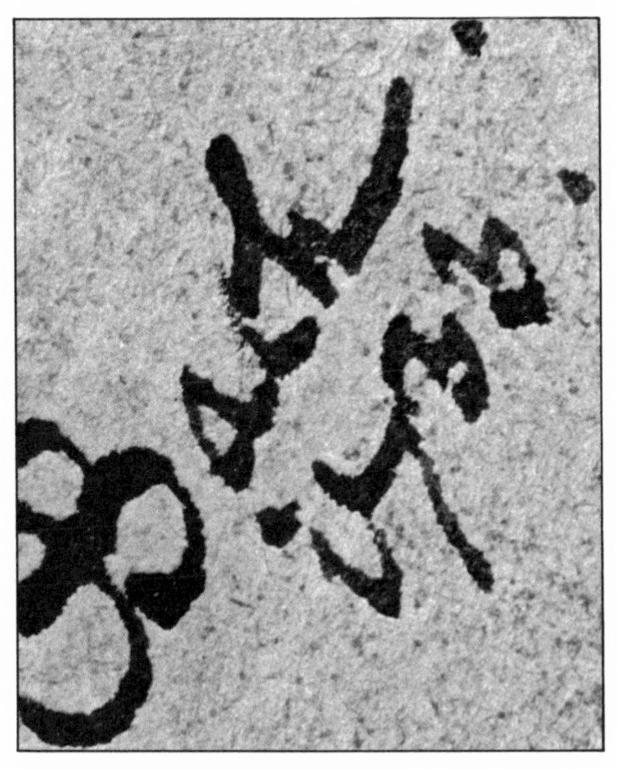

Appendix 1

[fol. † recto]

Illustrious and All-Powerful Elector [Johann Georg III of Saxony], Gracious Lord and Gracious and All-Powerful Electress [Anna Sophia], Gracious Lady

Since no greater treasure can be found on earth than the Word of God, through which we all have received the highest good, the soul's salvation and blessedness (2 Tim. 3:15; John 17:3; 1 Peter 1:9), and the precious and greatest promises are presented to us, namely that through the same we become partakers of the divine nature (2 Peter 1:4), the Word of God, Holy Scripture, is to be considered the pearl of great price for which we are to sell all that we have and buy it, [fol. † verso] according to the Lord's direction in Matthew 13:46. Oh, how "the man after God's own heart" [1 Sam. 13:14] rejoices over the Word of God! How he celebrates and exults in his excellent hymn of praise [Ps. 119], which through the inspiration of the Holy Spirit he has artistically organized according to the golden alphabet of its original language and where in all its 176 verses a beautiful laudation concerning the loftiness, dignity, and usefulness of Holy Scripture is introduced. "In the way of Thy testimonies I delight," he says in verse 14, "as much as in all riches." How diligently he expresses the desires in verse 5: "O that my ways may be steadfast in keeping Thy statutes!" And in verse 20: "My soul is consumed with longing for Thy ordinances at all times." In verse 24: "Thy testimonies are my delight, they are my counselors." Verse 36: "Incline my heart to Thy testimonies, and not to gain!" Verse 40: "Behold, I long for Thy precepts; in Thy righteousness give me life!" Verses 46–48, 54, 82: "I will also speak of Thy testimonies before kings, and shall not be put to shame; for I find my delight in Thy commandments, which I love. I revere Thy commandments, which I love, and I will meditate on Thy statutes . . . . Thy statutes have been my songs in the house of my pilgrimage . . . . My eyes fail with watching for Thy promise; I ask, 'When wilt Thou comfort me?' " Again in verses 98–103, 72, 144–45, 164, 167: "Thy commandment makes me wiser than my enemies, for it is ever with me. I have more understanding than all my teachers, for Thy testimonies are my meditation. I understand more than the aged, for I keep Thy precepts. I hold back my feet from every evil way, in order to keep Thy Word. I do not turn aside from Thy ordinances, for Thou hast taught me. How sweet are Thy words to my taste, sweeter than honey to my mouth! . . . The law of Thy mouth is better to me than thousands of gold and silver pieces . . . . Thy testimonies are righteous forever; give me understanding that I may live. With my whole heart I cry; answer me, O Lord! I will keep Thy statutes . . . . Seven times a day I praise Thee (that is, not twice or three times, but often) for Thy righteous ordinances . . . . My soul keeps Thy testimonies; I love them exceedingly." [fol. †2 recto] King David did indeed receive many splendid treasures from his enemies as well as from his friends and from those whom he placed under his dominion, such as the crown of the Ammonites, which was worth up to nine thousand ducats because of its gold, its precious stones, and its artistic workmanship, the crown David captured with the help of Joab (2 Sam. 12:30). But what was that to him compared with the Holy Scripture of God, the precious prize of the Word of God? He bears witness about this in Psalm 119:72, 127, 162: "The law of Thy mouth is better to me than thousands of gold and silver pieces . . . . Therefore I love Thy commandments above gold, above fine gold . . . . I rejoice at Thy word like one who finds great spoil." And in Psalm 19:9–10, he says: "The ordinances of the Lord are true and righteous altogether. More to be desired are they than gold, even much fine gold."

The Holy Spirit celebrates King Solomon's great understanding and wisdom and largeness of heart as having been "like the sand on the seashore." And He also testifies that his wisdom "surpassed the wisdom of all the people of the east, and all the wisdom of Egypt," indeed, that he was "wiser than all other men" (1 Kings 4:29–31). And because of his immeasurable riches he is praised because he "excelled all the kings of the earth" no less on account of his riches than on account of his wisdom (1 Kings 10:23), for all of the drinking vessels in his royal residence "of the House of the Forest of Lebanon were of pure gold; silver was not considered as anything in the days of Solomon" (1 Kings 10:21; 2 Chron. 9:20). For King Solomon "made silver as common in Jerusalem as stone" (1 Kings 10:27). And behold, this wisest of all kings considers all wisdom and all riches as nothing in comparison with Holy Scripture, when in Proverbs 3:13[–26] he can hardly find words enough to describe the dignity, the treasures, and the wonderful utility of Scripture in these words: "Happy is the man who finds wisdom, and the man who gets understanding, for the gain from it is better than gain from silver and its profit better than gold. She is more precious than jewels, and nothing you desire can compare with her. Long life is in her right hand; [fol. †2 verso] in her left hand are riches and honor. Her ways are ways of pleasantness, and all her paths are peace. She is a tree of life to those who lay hold of her; those who hold her fast are called happy . . . . My son, keep sound wisdom and discretion; let them not escape from your sight, and they will be life for your soul and adornment for your neck. Then you will walk on your way securely and your foot will not stumble. If you sit down, you will not be afraid; when you lie down, your sleep will be sweet. Do not be afraid of sudden panic, or of the ruin of the wicked, when it comes; for the Lord will be your confidence and will keep your foot from being caught." Therefore also Solomon splendidly celebrated the remembrance of his father on account of the latter's love of the Word of God. Would God that he had always followed it! In Proverbs 4:4[–10, 13, 18] he says: "He taught me, and said to me, 'Let your heart hold fast my words; keep my commandments, and live; do not forget, and do not turn away from the words of my mouth. Get wisdom, get insight. Do not forsake her, and she will keep you; love her, and she will guard you. The beginning of wisdom is this: Get wisdom, and whatever you get, get insight. Prize her highly, and she will exalt you; she will honor you if you embrace her. She will place on your head a fair garland; she will bestow on you a beautiful crown.' Hear, my son, and accept my words, that the years of your life may be many . . . . Keep hold of instruction, do not let go; guard her, for she is your life . . . . The path of the righteous is like the light of dawn, which shines brighter and brighter until full day."

The wise teacher of morals, Sirach, together with the Jewish church, praised the Book of the Covenant of God (the Old Testament), and the law that Moses bequeathed to the House of Jacob as its treasure, in the following words ([Ecclesiasticus] Chapter 24:37–38 [28–29]): "Just as the first man did not know her perfectly, the last one has not fathomed her; for her thought is more abundant than the sea, and her counsel deeper than the great abyss." [fol. †3 recto]

What shall we say about the esteemed Christian church and its distinguished teachers? The ancient church father Irenaeus writes in Book Five: "We must take refuge in the church and be nurtured in its bosom and be nourished with the divine Scriptures. For the Paradise of the churches is established in this world. Of all of the trees of Paradise, the Spirit of God says, you will eat, that is, of all the divine Scriptures you may partake." St. Jerome writes about this in his comment on Psalm 147: "The divine Word is extremely rich and contains all manner of spiritual delight. Whatever you desire and want to have you can find in the Word of God, as the Jews teach; for when they ate the manna, it brought them a great variety of flavors in their mouth, according to every man's wishes." St. Augustine says in his Second Letter to Volusius: "There is such a depth in the divine Scripture that I would daily desire to grow in it, even if I from the beginning of childhood through extreme old age wanted to study with the best leisure, greatest zeal, and better talents. Not as if one had to arrive at those things that are necessary for salvation with such great difficulty, but that when everybody has learned to understand faith from it, without which one cannot live a pious and righteous life, there are still so many things left over and surrounded by such a variety of the dark mystery among those who want to understand it! This has to do not only with the words in which these things are reported but also with the matters themselves which one should understand. In these things so lofty a wisdom lies hidden that even the most stouthearted, the most ingenious, and the most eager find that Holy Scripture somewhere bears witness that if a person wants to complete the job, he must first begin at the right place." Gregory the Great expresses this well and says much in few words in his Eighth Sermon on Ezekiel: "Holy Scripture shows its greatness as it builds morality. It shows its loftiness in its promise of merciful forgiveness. It shows its fierce form in the terror of its punishments. For it is sincere in its commandments, lofty in its promises, and fearful in its threats." The bishop of Constantinople, John, he of the "golden mouth" [Chrysostom], so named because of his "golden" oratorical ability, writes the following commentary on Matthew 24, as it would appear in German: "In Scripture an ignorant person finds what he should learn, a malicious person what he should fear, and an energetic person what he may expect as the reward of grace, a fainthearted person the foods that produce an average righteousness, which, though they will not make the soul stout, at least will not let the same die. But he who is of stout heart will find there the spiritual foods that will soon convert him to an angelic disposition. He who has been wounded by the evil foe will find there medicines and healing through repentance." In a separate sermon about Paradise he writes: "A field or a garden is indeed lovely, but much more lovely is the reading of Holy Scripture; for in the former flowers are found that wither in time, but in the latter there are passages that remain for an everlasting strength of life." In the same way Cyril in the Greek church of Alexandria taught about his matter; "As when farmers or gardeners in due time pick flowers of the loveliest fragrance and bring them, nicely arranged in little flower pots, to their lords, who receive them with amiable and thankful hearts, so we, too, who have assumed the teaching profession produce from divine Scripture as from a field not flowers that soon wither away and are only beautiful to behold, but flowers of the Word and of doctrine that encompass the unfading beauty of godliness through the Holy Spirit in Jesus Christ and with consummate loveliness and profusion present the fragrance of His mystery for a most pleasant aroma, as it is written, 'We are the aroma of Christ to God . . . from life to life'" [2 Cor. 2:15–16]. To which also Olympiodorus agrees, commenting on Ecclesiastes: "The divine Scripture is like a fruitful and fragrant field which, like Paradise, is planted with the best trees and bears a hidden treasure within it."

With these songs of praise of the old teachers of the church the sainted Herr Luther agrees beautifully as he writes in the German Altenburg edition, Vol. I, p. 92:

> *The holy Word of God has many names in Scripture because of its countless virtues and effects, for it is indeed all things and almighty. It is called a spiritual sword with which to battle against the devil and all spiritual enemies. It is called light, morning rain, evening rain, heavenly dew, gold, silver, medicine, raiment, jewelry,* [fol. †3 verso] *etc. It is in the same vein also called bread with which the soul is fed, strengthened, and made strong and stout. And we should not understand mere bread here; for in the same way as Scripture by means of physical bread expresses all manner of foods for the body and shows how precious they are, so it also by means of spiritual bread refers to all the foods of the soul, which are countless indeed. For there are various kinds of souls on earth, and each of them individually does not have one and the same need and skill, and yet the Word of God abundantly satisfies every one of them and its individual needs. For if the foods of all kings that ever lived and ever will live were heaped together, they could not in the least be compared with the most insignificant Word of God. That is why the Lord Christ in the Gospel calls it a royal banquet and in Isaiah a precious, choice, and splendid meal.*

But how we should read the divine Holy Scripture with understanding and profit has been demonstrated to us thoroughly by our beloved man of God, Luther, a man who from his own experience more than others learned these things. If we are once sure that the Word of God has been inspired by God for our salvation, he says, then we must esteem it precious, lofty, and valuable. About this he writes (Altenburg ed., V, 945):

> *That is the precious treasure that brings all salvation with it both in this life and the next, and does so in so rich a manner that whosoever has it is happy on account of it even in poverty and misery and would not give it up for all the world's goods but would prefer to be in death with it rather than live in revelry. But there are few who really have it. Therefore David has listed this blessing at the end, where a song would resound best of all. But who will adequately describe the greatness of this blessing? For who can completely detail all the virtue and power of the divine Word, when all Holy Scripture, sermons, and Christian books do nothing but praise the Word of God, as we ourselves also do daily with writing, reading, preaching, singing, writing poetry, and painting. For this blessing remains and also saves us when those other blessings vanish and when through death we leave them behind and part from them. But this blessing does not forsake us and does not part from us, but it breaks through death with us and draws us out of death and brings us to eternal life, where there will be no dying nor worry about death.*

We should also constantly remember and keep in view the well-known words of advice of Doctor Martin Luther in his preface to Master Johann Spangenber's Postil:

> *You must watch, study, give attention to reading. Indeed, you cannot overdo reading in Scripture, and what you do read you can never understand to excess, and what you*

understand well you can never teach to excess, and what you teach well you can never put into practice to excess. Believe the fellow who has tried it! It is the devil, the world, and our flesh that rage and storm against us.

If we want to grasp the proper meaning of the divine Word, we must read the same not only superficially but with the greatest diligence, as "the implanted Word, which is able to save your souls" (James 1:21), about which Luther, commenting on Psalm 117 (Altenburg ed., V, 252), says:

*This is what all the words of God demand, that we do not simply run over them and imagine that we have understood them perfectly in their very depth. That is the way the irresponsible, sated, tired spirits act when they have once heard a Word of God. Immediately it has to become old-fashioned, and people gape at something new as if they already knew everything they have ever heard. But this is a dangerous plague and a wicked secret trick of the devil, who by it has long made people secure, prying, and fit for every kind of error and sedition. This is actually the vice generally called sloth (*acedia*), being too lazy to attend worship. Against this Paul admonishes us in Romans 12:11 to be "aglow with the Spirit," and in Revelation 3:15*[–16] *we read: "Would that you were cold or hot! So, because you are lukewarm, and neither cold nor hot, I will spew you out of my mouth." It is true too that such half-hearted people are the most useless people on earth, and it would be better for them if they had no abilities at all, for they are obedient to no one, know everything better than the rest of the world, know how to evaluate all art and literature; in short, they* [fol. †4 recto] *cannot teach anyone anything worthwhile, and they also let no one else teach them anything. They have swallowed the whole schoolbag, which admits no teacher, and yet they haven't a single book in it that would permit them to teach others properly. Such hopelessly muddled people the devil now has in special supply among the sects, where there is not a single scribbler who, hearing a sermon or having been made able to read a German chapter, forthwith proclaims himself a doctor, crowns his ass, holds concourse with himself, and decides that he now knows everything better than all others who teach him. Master Know-It-All is their name, people who can bridle the steed at its tail. All this, I say, is due to the fact that people read or hear the Word of God so thoughtlessly instead of with fear, humility, and industry. This devil and temptation I have often felt in my own case, and even today I can hardly sufficiently guard and sign myself* [with the sign of the cross] *against it, as I freely admit for the sake of giving an example to whomever it may please, even though I am now already an old doctor and preacher and surely know, or should know, as much about Scripture as all of these know-it-alls know. Still I must become a child and every day early in the morning must recite aloud the Ten Commandments, the Creed, the Lord's Prayer, and all the favorite psalms and Scripture passages that I want to hear, yes, just as we teach and train our children now, even though beyond that I daily work in Scripture and carry on warfare against the devil. Nor may I say in my heart: The Lord's Prayer is old stuff, you know all about the Creed, etc., but I learn something from them every day and remain a student of the Catechism. I also feel that it is really true what Psalm 147*[:5] *says: "His understanding is beyond measure." And the man of wisdom says: "He who drinks of me will always be thirsty for me, etc." If this is my situation, how must it be for those secure, self-satisfied masters of conceit, who neither struggle nor act at all?*

Also, that man of God has prescribed the manner in which people should study theology from the Word of God by writing the following in his preface to the Wittenberg and Jena edition, Vol. I:

I want to show you a proper way to study theology, in which I have exercised myself. If you follow my direction, you will be learned enough so that, if need be, you yourself could produce books that would be just as good as those of the fathers and the councils, just as I (in God) have presumed and without arrogance and lies pride myself to say that I would not be far inferior to some of the fathers when it comes to writing books; but of course when it comes to life, I cannot compete with them. And if this method is the one the sainted King David teaches in Psalm 119 (and no doubt is adopted also by all the patriarchs and prophets), you will find three rules that are presented throughout the psalm. They are oratio, meditatio, tentatio *(prayer, meditation, temptation). In the first place, you should know that Holy Scripture is a book that makes the wisdom of all other books appear as foolishness because none of them teaches about eternal life, save this one. Therefore you must forthwith despair of your own intellect and understanding, for with these you will not attain to eternal life, but with such presumption you will only cast yourself and others with you down from heaven (as Lucifer did) into the abyss of hell. No, you must kneel down in your chamber and with true humility and seriousness pray to God that through His dear Son He would grant you His Holy Spirit, who may enlighten and lead you and give you understanding. As you see, David in the psalm referred to prays: "Teach me, Lord, instruct me, lead me, show me," and other words to the same effect, even though he knows the text of Moses and other books very well and has heard and read them daily. Still he wants the true Master of Scripture to be given in addition, so that he may be no means by his own intellect come to grief and become his own teacher, for that is how sectarian spirits are born, who imagine that Scripture is subject to them and may easily be understood by their intellect, as if it were Marcolvus or the Fable of Aesop, for which they need no Holy Spirit. In the second place, you are to meditate, that is, not only in your heart but also externally deal with and pass back and forth the oral sound and literal word in the book, reading it again and again, carefully noting it and pondering what the Holy Spirit means by it. And take care that you do not grow weary and think that reading it, hearing it, and saying it once or twice is enough and that you understand it all thoroughly, for that will never produce an extraordinary theologian but rather someone who is like untimely fruit that drops before it is half ripe. Therefore you see David in the psalm always stating that he wants to speak, evaluate, say, sing, hear, and read day and night, and yet always nothing but God's Word and commandments. For God does not want to give you His Spirit without the external Word. Be guided by that, for He did not prescribe it in vain that there should be external writing, preaching, reading, hearing, singing, saying, etc. In the third place, there is temptation. This is the touchstone, for this teaches you not only to know and to understand but also to experience how genuine, how truthful, how sweet, how lovely, how powerful, and how comforting the Word of God is, wisdom above all wisdom. Therefore you see how David in the psalm referred to complaints so often about all kinds of enemies, wicked princes or tyrants, false spirits and sects* [fol. †4 verso] *that he has to put up with and that therefore he meditates, that is, contemplates, God's Word in every way (as we have said), for as soon as God's Word comes alive in you, the devil will afflict you and make you a full-fledged doctor and teach you through his temptation to seek God's Word and love it. I myself (to mix mouse dirt among the pepper) am heavily indebted to my papistic friends that they through the devil's assaults so assail, corner, and frighten me that they have made a pretty good theologian out of me, which I would not have become otherwise. And what they on their part have won in dealing with me, those honors, that victory and triumph, I gladly let them have, for that is the way they wanted it. So there you have David's rule; if you now study to follow his example, you will also sing and exult with him in this psalm: "The law of Thy mouth is better to me than thousands of gold and silver pieces." Again: "Thy commandment makes me wiser than my enemies, for it is ever with me. I have more understanding than all my teachers; for Thy testimonies are my meditation. I understand more than the aged, for I keep Thy precepts, etc." You will find out how stale and rotten the books of the fathers will taste to you, and you will not only despise the books of the enemies but also in writing and teaching both of these will please you less and less. Once you have arrived at this point, you may confidently hope that you have begun to be a proper theologian who may teach not only the young, imperfect Christians but also the growing and the mature ones, for the church of Christ has all kinds of Christians in it, young, old, weak, sick, healthy, strong, bright, dull, simple, wise, etc.*

Therefore the dear man of God in his beautiful address "To the Councilmen in Germany That Children Are to Be Kept in School" (Jena ed., II, German) admonishes: "Besides, we should diligently teach languages, for although the dear apostles of the Lord Christ were splendid and outstanding people, nevertheless, before they began to preach publicly, God the Holy Spirit taught them languages, yes, brought these languages down from heaven," as Doctor Luther had a way of saying. In "Concerning Adoration of the Sacrament" (Vol. II, p. 220; VI, p. 231), to the Waldensians in Bohemia and Moravia, he writes near the end:

And if I should be able to accomplish it among you, I would ask that you cease to despise the languages so but, because you could well do it, let your preachers and gifted boys always be instructed well in Greek and Hebrew. I certainly know too that he who is to preach from Scripture and expound it and does not have the aid afforded by the Latin, Greek, and Hebrew languages but must do it solely on the basis of his mother tongue, will make many an egregious error, for I know how these languages help immeasurable to get at the pure understanding of divine Scripture. Augustine, too, felt this and expressed himself to the effect that there should be people in the church who know Greek and Hebrew, especially those who deal with the Word, for the Holy Spirit wrote the Old and the New Testament in these two languages.

Again (p. 474):

Now, to the extent that the Gospel is dear to us, so let us diligently promote the languages. For God did not for nothing let His Scripture be written in these two languages, the Old Testament in Hebrew and the New Testament in Greek. Those languages which God did not despise but chose above all others for His Word we should honor too above all others. For St. Paul proclaims it as a special honor and advantage of the Hebrew language that God's Word is given in it, when he says in Romans 3:1–2: "What advantage has the Jew? Or what is the value of circumcision? Much in every way. To begin with, the Jews were entrusted with the oracles of God." King David also proclaims that in Psalm 147:19[–20]*: "He declares His Word to Jacob, His statues and ordinances to Israel. He has not dealt thus with any other nation; they do not know His ordinances." And that is why the Hebrew language is called holy. St. Paul in Romans 1:2 speaks of "holy" Scripture no doubt because of the holy Word of God there expressed. Therefore we may also call the Greek language holy, I suppose, because it was chosen above others that the New Testament might be written in it. And from it as from a fountain* [the Gospel] *has, through translation, flowed on to other languages and has hallowed them too. Let this be said: We will probably not retain the Gospel* [fol. †† recto] *without the languages. The languages are the sheath in which the sword of the Spirit is kept. They are the chest in which we retain the jewel. They are the vessel in which we store this drink. They are the pantry in which this food is found. And as the Gospel itself testifies, they are the baskets in which we keep these loaves and fishes. But on the contrary*

(further, p. 476),

it was a foolish undertaking to presume to learn to know Scripture through the commentaries of the fathers, by reading many books and glosses. We should have addressed ourselves to the languages instead. For the dear fathers were without the languages and therefore they sometimes expended a lot of effort on a single verse by means of many words, and yet in the final analysis they did not reflect the meaning but guessed at half of it and missed half of it. And now you chase after the same with great pains, whereas you could meantime through the languages give better information to him whom you now follow. For like the sun against the shade, so is the language against the glosses of all the fathers. Since, then, it behooves Christians to exercise themselves in Scripture as their own book and it is a sin and a shame that we do not know our own book nor are acquainted with God's language and Word, it is an even greater sin and shame that we do not learn the languages.

The following important guidelines the sainted Herr Luther always had in mind in his spirited commentary on Holy Scripture, and I have purposely taken note of them in this German Biblical and Lutheran interpretation. (1) The text is carefully read through and scrutinized a number of times in the manner in which pits and strata in mines and quarries are examined with the greatest care. (2) Each word's basic meaning and sense, as well as that of each expression in its usual meaning and according to customary usage in Scripture, is noted, and both of these in the primary and original language, and from this point of view it is discussed. (3) The context has been considered carefully, and so have the intention, the argument, and the purpose of the Holy Spirit, so that this may by all means be maintained and we may not depart from it. (4) I have taken the parallel passages into account, those that elucidate not only the words but also the phrases and expressions, especially when the same argument and the same material is treated somewhere else in Scripture. (5) Also the customs of people and countries have to be considered. (6) Especially careful note is taken of the subject spoken on, so that when the literal sense is to be assumed to be about Christ and the Holy Spirit is actually speaking, the text may not be applied to David or other persons, or left is doubt as to whom it does apply. (7) We have to consider the places in the cities, villages, and regions, so that no mistakes might occur in the stories. (8) The same applies to persons and names, which are often given in [fol. †† verso] various ways. (9) Especially the analogy of faith has to be considered in keeping with the reminder of Paul in Romans 12:6, "If prophecy, in proportion to our faith." (10) For the prophecies of the Old Testament we have to keep in mind the fulfillment to be found in the New Testament, so that the harmony of Holy Scripture may everywhere be apparent. (11) Likewise the figures and types of the Old Testament cannot be neglected, so that the shadows of things to come and the types may be understood and explained by means of their opposites and antitypes. (12) No less, the other passages that are interpreted and explained in the New Testament have to be noted, so that we may not diverge from the Holy Spirit's own interpretation, for this is of course certain, that there is no better interpreter of Holy Scripture than the Holy Spirit Himself. The Holy Spirit Himself reminds us (2 Peter 1:20–21): "First of all you must understand this, that no prophecy of Scripture is a matter of one's own interpretation, because no prophecy ever came by the impulse of man, but men moved by the Holy Spirit spoke from God." (13) Therefore I was everywhere very careful that the single literal interpretation of Holy Scripture remain final and that nowhere a twofold interpretation, as, for instance, the literal sense and the mystical sense, that is, the spiritual understanding, be brought in, as some Bible interpreters now and then go in for, especially the Papists and in part also the Reformed, and this can occasionally be seen in the popular German and Latin "paraphrases." Just as there is only one form and substance for a thing, so there is also only one meaning of a word and a text, for the meaning is the form of the word. What would finally become of Holy Scripture if people wanted to receive and understand words and passages not in one meaning but in two? Would Scripture in this shape not become ambiguous and doubtful? And couldn't we in that case liken them, together with the Papists, to the oracle of Apollo at Delphi? For the papistic twofold sense actually originated with the Jews, was continued by Origen, and actually propagated by the Papists in the darkness of the kingdom of the Antichrist. [fol. †2 recto]

On this subject Herr Luther should really have been heard in our church, as he purposely has reminded us in his comment on Psalm 21 (Altenburg ed., II, p. 727):

The mystery of iniquity had begun to show itself and exert its influence already in the time of St. Paul, in this way, that the single interpretation of the simple Scripture was divided into many meanings, an evil we may presumably credit to Origen and later to his successor, Jerome, those two saintly and select men, it seems to me. For about at the same time the elect began to be misled into error, so that they pressed and forced the passage of St. Paul (2 Cor. 3:6), "The [letter] *kills, but the Spirit gives life," to a point where they interpreted the "letter" to be the meaning of the story and the "Spirit" to be the mystical interpretation. This was an altogether too unfortunate attempt at imitating St. Paul, who in Galatians 4 uses the mystical sense and meaning concerning Abraham and his two wives but does not call it either "letter" or "Spirit." In the same way Philo, too, writes, as Eusebius says in his history, that the Christians in Alexandria did such things. In this city there was a famous Christian school after the pattern of the one that was in Antioch in apostolic days. Origen no doubt followed this school, and when he added much of his own thought, he fell altogether too far, soaring so high as to have people teach that they should disregard the Scriptural sense and the letter and accept only the mystical sense and spirit. But the very Spirit of God withstood him there, for it was still very much alive in the congregation at that time, and it opposed him with power and condemned all his books there. To this development apostate Porphyry made a heavy and definite contribution, so that Christian art and teaching fell into ill repute and report. But when the apostolic fathers disappeared from the scene and the Christians in time became rather careless and no longer diligently searched Scripture, Scripture itself gradually began to be torn and corrupted in many ways. This went on until the great schools arose and the kingdom of the Antichrist was established through the hand and power of the Roman bishops, for now not the mystery of iniquity but iniquity itself was in operation, and the abomination now publicly stood in the holy place. Result: since Christ and faith had now been exterminated, the apostles of the pope first began with Thomas Aquinas and Nicholas de Lyra to promulgate throughout the world the fourfold sense of Scripture, that is, the literal, the moral, the spiritual, and the mystical, and thus the cloak of Christ was divided into four parts, so that each sense has its individual proponents, researchers, masters, and teachers, like brave mercenaries and bold perverters of Holy Scripture.*

And in volume VI of the last commentary on Galatians, page 799, Luther says:

The idle nonscholars and the inexperienced monks and sophists dreamed up a church triumphant, a ruling church, purporting that Scripture had a fourfold sense and interpretation: the first, which the letter posits, which they call the literal sense; the second, which they call tropological, in which Scripture is held up as an example to people to admonish them to follow it; the third, the allegorical, which is a mystical, hidden meaning; the fourth, the anagogical, in which the sense is applied to entirely heavenly objects and beyond this life. And according to this fourfold sense or meaning they have interpreted almost every word of Holy Scripture. Thus if we now want to deal with Jerusalem according to the first, the literal, sense, it is the physical city in Judea. According to the second sense, it tropologically means a clean conscience. According to the allegorical sense, it is supposed to mean the church that is on the field of battle here in the life on earth and must constantly be at war. According to the anagogical sense it means the heavenly fatherland, or the ruling church beyond this life in heaven. With these clumsy, preposterous, trumped-up, garrulous obscenities, through which they have torn Scripture into such a variety of sense and meaning, they have brought about the pitiful condition that a person could not teach and instruct consciences reliably and completely on any point at all.

And again (Altenburg ed., II, 728) Luther, commenting on Psalm 22, says:

Isn't it a godless thing to divide and tear

apart Holy Scripture in this manner, so that you credit the literal sense neither with faith nor morals nor hope but insist that the historical sense alone is of no value and that you ascribe faith, but not morals or hope, to the spiritual sense, and morals to the moral sense, and hope to the mystical sense? It's as if St. Paul did not speak differently to Timothy in 2 Timothy 3:16–17, where he says: "All Scripture is inspired by God and profitable for teaching, for reproof, for correction, and for training in righteousness, that the man of God may be complete, equipped [fol. ††2verso] *for every good work." Tell me, kind sir, what are they doing as they tear Scripture apart except to reveal that they know absolutely nothing about Scripture, neither concerning faith or hope or good morals? That is why they have not adduced and treated for the teaching of faith (as Hebrews 11 does) the history and the stories of the named patriarchs, Abraham, Isaac, and other sainted fathers of the entire people of Israel, but they have despised this as so much dead history, something that has indeed happened but now has no meaning for them. Instead, they have dreamed up and invented I know not what interpretations and senses of faith, morals, and hope. By means of this ungodly procedure they have taken away and torn up this garment for us, and they have dressed and clad us, instead of with the raiment of Christ, with the spider's web (Is. 59:6), that is, human rules and commandments that surpass all abominations, even the* Ethics *of Aristotle, the godless heathen. Thus we see that Scripture did remain in the papacy but that it was torn apart and by their fourfold division was changed and transformed into wicked, useless, fragmented, and uncertain bones of contention which serve neither the doctrine of faith nor that of hope nor that of morals any longer. Furthermore, finally such crudity and want of sense gained the upper hand and took over that they no longer understood even the words of the grammar. And whenever they found a figurative expression, they converted it into a spiritual sense so that a person did not know what they meant. And if the Spirit had not in advance announced and prophesied that this rending of Scripture would stand within the confines and the number of these four senses, surely they would have set up many varieties of meaning and used many varied figures of speech, that is, flowery ways of speaking and veiled words, since they did not have enough brains, wit, and understanding that they could have taken the spiritual, mystical, and moral sense for one and the same thing.*

And especially in the golden commentary on Genesis, in his last comment on chapter 15, verse 7 (Altenberg ed., IX, p. 385), Luther writes:

> *The Latin church has few people who have written about Moses. Lyra is the foremost one, and from him later others emerged, as for instance Hugo. Lyra in this text proposes a rule that he considers very important for the understanding of Scripture, namely that many passages in Scripture are to be understood in a twofold manner: first, according to the letter and as applying to earthly and physical things; second, applying to spiritual and eternal things. And he lists this text in this category. In the theological schools it is a well-known rule that Scripture is to be understood in a fourfold way: first, according to the historical or literal sense; second, in relation to the example and life of good morals; third, according to the heavenly meaning; fourth, according to the allegory, or mystical meaning. I am of course content to let everyone be right in his sense and understanding, but our energy is to be directed primarily to this, if we want to deal correctly with Scripture, that we have one simple, honest, and certain historical sense. For I consider it not only dangerous and useless for teaching to interpret Scripture in more than one sense and meaning, but it also diminishes and weakens the name and reputation of Scripture, which should forever and ever remain in one sure sense and meaning. Thus, even though I don't want to oppose Lyra's meaning in this case, I also do not want to follow him in expounding this text, as if it were a prophecy concerning the land of Canaan, but not primarily, for primarily this text speaks of a sure spiritual*

prophecy and of eternal life. Thus Lyra also says that this passage is Psalm 89:26–27, "He shall be My Son, and I will be His Father," is to be understood, up to a point, but not primarily, as applying to Solomon, David's son, but primarily it is to be understood as applying to Christ. With this explanation Lyra means to be of some help to people who study Scripture, so that they may be able to help themselves in the case of unclean passages. But I hold the contrary view and conclude that in the church it is not without danger and useless to follow this rule. For in Scripture we should everywhere see to it that we have one sure and simple meaning of the story, and he who alters this or departs from it should know that he has departed from Scripture and is following an uncertain and doubtful sense. Therefore, so far as this text is concerned, it is certain that Moses is at the same time speaking about spiritual possessions, but not, as Lyra thinks, with the same words but with different words, so that he speaks of spiritual possessions with one set of words but of physical possessions with another set of words. And this he also does above in chapter 12. There God speaks about the possession of the land of Canaan, but at the end He adds this little statement: "In you all the families of the earth shall be blessed," which is really and clearly a spiritual statement of a prophecy of Christ. And it would surely be a crude and harmful mistake if Lyra, following his canon, or rule, wanted to apply and draw these words to another meaning and make of the spiritual blessing, which it is here primarily, also a physical blessing up to a point. Therefore in this instance [Gen. 15:7] it is the primary, single, and peculiar sense of the passage that God is speaking of the physical [fol. ††3 recto] prophecy of the land of Canaan, and no twofold sense of the story or letter can be granted or admitted. But if someone here wanted to ruminate in the way of allegory and wanted to convert Ur of the Chaldees into hell, sin, and death and the land of Canaan into life eternal, he would, as no one could doubt, be following a strange sense, one in no way inherent in these words. Even though allegory is not completely unfit and inconvenient for teaching, yet this sense and interpretation is weak, and nothing can be accomplished by it, for if it were proper, one could think up many such interpretations in passages of Scripture, just as one can invent many shapes and forms and impress them on wax. But we should be concerned that we may have one sure and true sense of Scripture which can be no other than that of the letter and the story. Thus therefore Moses spoke earlier of the spiritual prophecy of the land of Canaan, and here there is no need for anyone to say that Ur means sin and the Promised Land means immortality; for this Moses said previously about Abraham, that his faith was reckoned to him as righteousness, that is, that through faith his sin was forgiven and eternal life was granted to him. Therefore also the letter, when handled properly, by itself bestows and proclaims that Abraham is an heir of righteousness, that is, that through faith his sin was forgiven and eternal life was granted to him. Therefore also the letter, when handled properly, by itself bestows and proclaims that Abraham is an heir of righteousness and eternal life through Christ, and because Abraham is not alone but has a promise of seed and progeny, and his seed and progeny is what is the result of the promise, that is, he who believes the promise, therefore Paul applies the prophecy of a physical blessing to the believers among the Gentiles, for because the entire transaction is dependent on the fact that Abraham believed God and that that was counted to him as righteousness, that through faith he is righteous and has become an heir of the eternal kingdom, from that Paul deduces this general understanding, and from it that everyone who believes the promise as Abraham did is an heir of the eternal kingdom and is righteous, whether he is of the physical or carnal seed of Abraham or not. And if Paul had not drawn this sense from the simple understanding of the letter, he would never have seen it. In the Epistle to the Galatians he tells us: Those who are of faith are blessed with believing Abraham; again, those who are of faith are Abraham's children; again, those who oper-

> *ate with the works of the Law are under wrath, etc. Where does Paul get this argument? Actually from this text, which all of us would have passed by as a useless and despised text. Therefore all of us primarily owe all honor to St. Paul as the greatest teacher and master of Holy Scripture, and we are obliged to follow him and are determined in no way to let the lying sophists lead us away from his teaching and understanding. This is what I wanted to say for the sake of the young people and those still inexperienced in Scripture. For when these come up against such statements and interpretations of the fathers and the teachers, they think they have found pearls, when actually they are not free from danger and tend to lead away from the right understanding of Scripture, that is, direct us away from the letter and the historical understanding, which alone we should retain, insist on, and consider our foundation.*

Therefore we must surely restrict ourselves to the single literal understanding of the Holy Spirit in all passages of Holy Scripture, so that God's Word and the sense of the Holy Spirit may not become uncertain. On this foundation everything may then be built and used as so much more certain and thorough. And that is why Holy Scripture has been given by God. (14) [Continuing the numeration which last appeared on p. 168 above.] We must use God's Word for wholesome teaching in the articles of faith, all of which must have a firm foundation in both the Old and the New Testament; for we are built on the foundation of the prophets and the apostles (Eph. 2:20; 2 Peter 3:2). And the wall of the heavenly Jerusalem has 12 foundations and in them the names of the 12 apostles of the Lamb (Rev. 21:14). (15) With Holy Scripture we are to refute all error and heresy with which unbelievers and irresponsible people throw Holy Scripture into confusion "to their own destruction" [fol. ††3 verso] (2 Peter 3:16). (16) We must use Holy Scripture for the improvement of the sinful life through godly renewal. (17) It should also be used for correction or for instruction in righteousness, which is in Christ Jesus. (18) Also for comfort in all affliction and temptation; "for whatever was written in former days was written for our instruction, that by steadfastness and by the encouragement of the Scriptures we might have hope" (Rom. 15:4).

(19) And because it appears as if Scripture here and there contradicts itself, therefore it is necessary that the passages that seem to be contrary to each other be compared in order that this foundation may everywhere remain immovable and nowhere in the divine Holy Scripture a falsification or error may be admitted, for "it is impossible that God should prove false" (Heb. 6:18), and "the ordinances of the Lord are true, and righteous altogether" (Ps. 19:9). (20) Therefore also we should in no Biblical history and also in none of the chronologies make room for faults and errors, as some do; in fact, not even doubt should be admitted. But the computations of time in Holy Scripture must be correct and honored, just as it is correct everywhere in truth. (21) Above all, we must observe the chief message of Holy Scripture, Christ Jesus, that we may keep Him in both the Old Testament and the New Testament and search out how in Him alone all believers of all time have sought and found true righteousness, life, happiness, and salvation. See Genesis 3:15; 4:1; 12:3; 18:18; 22:18; 26:4; 28:14; 49:10; Job 19:25; Isaiah 53:11; Habakkuk 2:4; Luke 24:26–27, 44f.; John 5:39; 20:31; Acts 10:43; 13:37–38; 15:11; Romans 1:16–17; 3:21–22; 10:4; 1 Corinthians 15:1–4; etc.

Holy Scripture must also be and remain as it is provided by the exalted divine Majesty, a real regal form and royal memorandum (Deut. 17:14ff.). Note how specifically the king and regent was ordered to take the Law, that is, the diving Holy Scripture, from the priests and Levites and write it in a book which should be in his possession and [fol. ††4 recto] in which he should read throughout his life. He should not, as the pope orders contrary to God's commandment, stand aloof from Holy Scripture, as if he as a layman were not, and only the clergy were, entitled to read Holy Scripture, but here (Deut. 17:19[–20]) God commanded Moses regarding the king of the people of God: "[The king] shall [with all diligence] read in it all the days of his life, that he may learn to fear the Lord his God, by keeping all the words of this Law and these statutes, and doing them; that his heart may not be lifted up above his brethren, and that he may not turn aside from the commandment, either to the right hand or to the left." And then this beautiful promise is added in verse 20: "So that he may continue long in his kingdom, he and his children, in Israel." This was carefully spelled out also for Joshua, the Israelite regent, by God, the All-Highest (Joshua 1:7–8): "Be strong and very courageous, being careful to do according to all the Law which Moses My servant commanded you; turn not from it to the right hand or to the left, that you may have good success wherever you go. This book of the Law shall not depart out of your mouth, but you shall meditate on it day and night, that you may be careful to do according to all that is written in it; for then you shall make your way prosperous, and then you shall have good success."

On this account it is indeed surprising and to be lamented that the Roman Antichrist dared to forbid even princes and lords to read in the Bible, while Cardinal Stanislaus Hosius (Vol. I, p. 664) unashamedly and insanely adds the reason "by express command of the Word of God." Similarly the *Censura Coloniensis* (p. 23) states: "That which is holy may not be given to dogs" [Matt. 7:6]. Herr Luther speaks very eloquently about this in his commentary on Deuteronomy (Altenburg ed., V. 1088):

> *About Solomon it is written that he had a wealth of gold and silver that his father had bequeathed to him and he himself had gathered such as no other king had; but herein lies the power of the commandment, as the text says, that his heart may not turn aside, that is, that he may not gather all this and make it a source of confidence, for the Lord desires that a king be God-fearing and that the people trust in God's Word alone. Therefore He takes all the things away on which people place their reliance. If they do not rely on them but use them in faith to God and have a sufficiency in His Word, they shall suffer no harm, as indeed the most pious, richest, and most powerful King David exults and says: "Not in my bow do I trust, nor can my sword save me"* [Ps. 44:6]; *and again: "With God we shall do valiantly; it is he* [fol. ††4 verso] *who will tread down our foes"* [Ps. 60:12]. *And again: "Who will bring me to the fortified city? . . . O grant us help against the foe, for vain is the help of man!"* [Ps. 60:9–11]. *And there are many other such passages. David does not deny that he has bows and sword and men, but he says he will not put his trust in them. That is why Moses commands that the king read this book Deuteronomy diligently, in order to learn to fear the Lord at all times. That is, he commends to him the Word of faith, which he abundantly presents in this book, as we have seen, so that the king's heart may not exalt itself above his fellows with superfluity of possessions and may not become presumptuous on account of his power or riches, but may fear the Lord, whose "delight is not in the strength of the horse, nor His pleasure in the legs of a man"* [Ps. 147:10], *and on the other hand, that he may not despair when his cause is lost and his enemies prevail, as he says here* [Deut. 17:20]: *He should not turn aside to the right or to the left but should honestly and firmly stride along between prosperity and adversity, between power and weakness, between honor and dishonor, and should faithfully and stoutly adhere to the Word of God alone.*

But the records amply show how dreadfully the divine Holy Scripture was despised, violated, and condemned. Thus Elias Hasenmüller, in his *Historia Jesuitica* (VI, 146) noted that a Jesuit priest by the name of Henricus, a governor and steward in Ingolstadt in 1584, publicly said to his students: "To be delighted to hear many sermons and to take much and frequent pleasure in reading Scripture, that is truly not a sign of a good Catholic, but rather of heretics, people who amuse themselves with such things, just as an ape does with a nut. A true Catholic does not take much delight in sermons, which easily rustle past him like a wind, nor in the reading of Scripture, for it is a dead letter that he does not understand. No, his real interest is in hearing many masses" [none of which he really hears distinctly] "and repeatedly going to confession. He who despises or neglects this sins more grievously than he who in his whole life has never heard a sermon or seen a Bible." On 3 August 1583 in Rome, Father Fabricius exploded publicly with: "The heretics always hold the Bible up to us, but we have the pope as our Bible. If we follow him, we cannot err or be deceived. Also, the pope can interpret his own opinion himself, but the Bible cannot interpret its opinion at all." Indeed, in Landsberg on 6 April 1583 the eminent Spanish Jesuit, Gregory of Valencia, in all seriousness said to someone: "If you want to be a respectable Catholic, you must be sure not [fol. ††† recto] to be a student of the Bible or to read the Bible." To say nothing of the fact that so many people were pitifully tortured, burned, and buried alive only because they possessed or read a Bible and were therefore declared heretics and condemned, and that their Bibles were burned together with them, as we see it given in the *Martyrologium,* translated from the French in Herborn in 1617 and elsewhere to be found too. Thus the electors and princes and also other estates of the Augsburg Confession in their magnificent exposition of 1564, setting forth the reasons why they could not attend the Council of Trent called by Pope Pius IV, stated the following complaint, among other things:

> *Thirty years ago students of Holy Scripture had permitted themselves to be heard publicly before trustworthy people to the effect that they had faithfully attended the lectures of the theologians and had put in their full time, but that in all truth they well remembered that throughout the time of their complete course, that is, in their five of six years in schools of the theologians, they had never heard either Jesus or Christ mentioned or referred to with even a few words, but that they had had so much to do the Master of Sentences, Scotus, Bonaventure, Alexander of Alexandria, Thomas Aquinas, and other similar scholastics that the writings of the holy evangelists and apostles were never mentioned and that they much less had been able to study them diligently.*

In the same vein Herr Luther, in the chapter on the Bible in his *Table Talk,* testifies regarding Dr. Andreas Carlstadt that he did not begin to read the Bible until eight years after he had earned his doctorate. And many graduates of the Sorbonne and many old Paris University doctors confessed, yes, swore by God on high, that they were more than 50 years old before they knew what the New Testament was, as Robert Estienne reports in 1532 in his preface to the *Censura* of the Parisian theologians. Erasmus tells the story about Jacobus Latomus that he mercilessly charged a poor young student to read all of Lombard, Alexander, Scotus, Thomas, Bonaventure, Armachanus, Alrisiodorus, Holcot, Bricot, Peter of Aliacum, Occam, Durandus, Haymo, Carrensis, Aegidius, Tartarerus, etc., and in the study of them become an old man [*fol. ††† verso*] before studying the Old and New Testament. And Alphonso de Castro confirms in *Adversus Haereticos* I. 4. that because of the Lutherans and other heretics people in the last 300 years have forsaken the twaddle of the scholastics and have turned to studies of Holy Scripture to improve themselves. Sixtinus Amama, in his *Creation de Barbarie* relates that a doctor of theology, asked about the Decalog, denied that he had such a book in his library. Gerhardus Listrius Rheutensis admits that he knows many doctors of theology who before their 50th year had not yet read all the epistles of the New Testament, as they themselves admitted. Petrus Rodolphus a Tossignano, a Franciscan, writes in the preliminaries of his *Diction. Concionat. Pauper,* Chapter 35, that there are many theologians who have hardly read through the whole Bible. Even Erasmus, whom Leo X called his dear son and whom Paul III wanted to make a cardinal, whom Cardinals Sandoletus and Bembus also regarded very highly, laments in his *Epistola apologetica ad Martinum Dorpium* that he knows people who spent 80 years in the caprices of the scholastics without ever reading through the context of the gospels, as they themselves confessed to him, and that there are many theologians who never read the New Testament from beginning to end. Jacob Reihingius, an eminent Jesuit, while still a Papist, wrote in his *Apologia pro laqueis contrit.,* of the year 1623, page 84, that he lived among Jesuits in Ingolstadt for 14 years but that not on a single day did he or any of his fellow students hear them expound Scripture. Angelus Politianus says that he read the Bible through once, but that he had never misapplied his time more miserably. Cardinal Petrus Bembus writes that he read the Bible once, and if he should read it once more, he would ruin his Latin altogether. Henricus Cornelius Agrippa laments in his *Praefatio de vanitate scientiae* that many people not only despise Holy Scripture as boorish and idiotic but also persecute it. The Jesuit Hoffaeus has said that it is not necessary to read the Bible, because among Catholics the canons of the church are to take the place of the Bible. The

Jesuit Pietro said that reading the Bible would make a Lutheran heretic before it would make [*fol. †††2recto*] a Roman Catholic. The bishop of Salzburg once came upon a New Testament at an inn and, opening it at random, happened upon Paul's statement in Romans 3:28, "For we hold that a man is justified by faith apart from works of Law." He became angry and said: "O Paul, have you become a Lutheran too?" and threw the book away. In the same way also Johann Manlius, *L. C.,* Chapter III, page 30, relates that he had heard a monk preach who expounded Aristotle's *Ethics* and had a large audience. A licentiate of theology remarked: "Even if we lost all the prophetic and apostolic books, we could still replace the teaching of the Gospel from the *Ethics* of Aristotle." A doctor in Stuttgart preached along similar lines. And Didacus Stella writes about Luke 11 (p. 70) that many doctors and preachers turn the sermons they preach to the people into fables, human rules, poetry, and philosophy. And also the eminent Jesuit Franciscus Ribera, in his introduction to the prophet Joel, p. 183, laments that [*preachers*] much prefer to fill the ears of the people with pleasantries than with Scripture. The outstanding Jesuit and Cardinal Bellarmine complains (*De gemitu columbae,* II, Chapter LII, p. 197) that the papistic bishops confess that they did not apply their diligence to Holy Scripture but to jurisprudence and that they did not concentrate on sermons but busied themselves with matters of law. Indeed, Hostiensis and Panormitanus have a hard time deciding whether canon law or theology is more useful for a bishop. And above Chapter I or *De affinitate et consanguinitate* they give this solution: "Where there are heretics, theology is more useful, but where not, canon law is more useful."

And that is obviously why we find such magnificent magisterial and canonical expositions of many beautiful passages of Holy Scripture among them! Thus, for example, David à Mauden explained Job 21:7, "Ask the beasts . . . the birds of the air," in this way, that the prelates and wise men of the church are meant in these words and that God would not let them fall into error and so harm the church. [fol. †††2 verso] Antonius, the archbishop of Florence, expounded the Davidic statement of Psalm 8:68– (Part III, Subject 22, Chapter 5, par. 1) in this manner: "Thou hast put all things under his feet," that is, under the pope's feet; "all sheep," that is, the Christians; "and oxen," that is, the Jews; "and also the beasts of the field," that is, the Gentiles; "the birds of the air," that is, those who transcend the broad current of error and vice as such who are to be registered as saints; "and the fish of the sea," that is, the souls of the deceased, who pass their time in the bitterness of the wild sea and are to be rescued from the waters of punishment in hell by means of indulgences. Antonius Puccius said at the Lateran Council that the prophecy of Psalm 72:11, "May all kings fall down before Him; all nations serve Him!" is fulfilled in Leo X. Franciscus Turrianus, in *Against Sadeeln,* p. 14, tries to prove from the prophecy in Isaiah 49:23 that the pope's feet are to be kissed. "With their faces to the ground they shall bow down to you, and lick the dust of your feet." To prove the same thing, Joseph Serranus, also without rhyme or reason, cites the following passages in his book *About the Adoration of the Roman Pontiff's Feet* (Chapter II and III): Is. 60:14; 61:6; 66:11; Matt. 3:11; 28:9; Luke 7:44–45; 24:52; John 17:22; Acts 10:25; 14:18; Rev. 21:7 and therefore expounds these passages in extraordinarily splendid and magisterial style. Bozius, *De signis ecclesiae* (Book XV, Chapter 6), applied the words of Christ in Matthew 10:30, "But even the hairs of your head are all numbered," to the relics of the saints. Bellarmine, in the preface to his book *About the Roman Pontificate,* applied the passage Isaiah 28:16, "Behold, I am laying in Zion for a foundation a stone, a tested stone, a precious cornerstone," to the pope in Rome. Panigorolla, in *Disceptatio II,* Part I, states that the visible church has a visible head, the vicar of Christ on earth, and that this is he of whom Paul speaks in Ephesians 4:5, "one Lord." Johannes Zacharias, an Erfurt Papist theologian, at the Council of Costnitz against John Hus quoted the passage Ezekiel 34:10, "Behold, I am against the shepherds," in support of the primacy of the pope and fraudulently added the words "and not my people," which are not found in the Hebrew or the Greek or the Latin text. What Christ says about Himself Matthew 28:18, "All authority in heaven and on earth has been given to Me," [fol. †††3 recto] is applied to the pope in *Ceremon.,* I, *tit.* 7. The words of Christ in John 12:32, "And I, when I am lifted up from the earth, will draw all men to Myself," Jacobus de Terano, the chamberlain of Urban VI, in his tract *De monarch.* explains as follows: "All empires and kingdoms of the world I will win back and take them away from the emperors and kings and other princes, and I will do it with my soldiers, the apostles, and make them subject to my vicar, the pope in Rome." What is prophesied about Christ in 2 Samuel 7:13, "I will establish the throne of his kingdom forever," Johannes de Turrecremata, in *Summa de potest. eccles.* (I, Chapter 90), explains this way: "I will see to it that the kingdom of the pope will remain forever." The statement of Christ in Luke 12:42 concerning "the faithful and wise steward" the same author, in Book II, Chapter 80, interprets as follows: "I will set the pope over the entire house of Christ, that is, over the entire church." Similarly, in Book II, Chapter 8, he also understands the text in Revelation 4:2, "lo, a throne stood in heaven," as applying to the apostolic chair, and "heaven" as applying to the church militant; and the words "with one seated on the throne" as meaning the pope in Rome; and the words (verse 4) "Round the throne were twenty-four thrones, and seated on the thrones were twenty-four elders" as applying to the cardinals. At the Council of Trent the words in John 3:19, "The light has come into the world, and men loved darkness rather than light," were interpreted by the bishop of Bitonto as speaking of the pope; and at the Lateran Council in Rome, Simon Benignius, the bishop of Mandrusia, addressed Pope Leo with the words of Revelation 5:5, "Lo, the Lion of the tribe of Judah, the Root of David," saying: "For you, most blessed Leo, we have waited as for the Savior." In his Book VII, Paulus Aemylius relates that Sicilian legates addressed the pope as follows and he raised no objection: "Holy Father, thou that takest away the sin of the world, have mercy on us, thou that takest away the sin of the world, grant us thy peace." From the statement of Christ in Luke 9:56, "The Son of Man came not to destroy men's lives but to save them," Hardingus in his writing against Ivellus wants to prove that the substance of the bread in Communion does not disappear and come to naught. The words of Isaiah 63:3, "I have trodden the winepress alone, [fol. †††3 verso] and from the peoples no one was with me," the 1493 *Mariale* of Strasbourg (Book I, Chapter 3) misapplies as follows: "Although Mary, the Mother of mercy, assisted the Father of mercy in the work of our salvation, it is true, O Lord, that no man was with You, but only a woman was with You, and she has experienced in her heart all the wounds that You suffered in Your body." Henno interprets the angel's greeting to Mary in this way: *Ave* [Hail], that is, *A ve,* or *sine vae,* "without woe," because through the mother of mercy we are freed from many a woe. He also applies the Word of God in Genesis 2:18, "It is not good enough for the human race to have only a single advocate or mediator, because it has so many dangerous things to bring before God. "I will make him a helper fit for him," that is, the holy Virgin. The learned Jesuit Cornelius à Lapide complains that several new preachers are introducing a new way of interpreting Scripture in order to entertain the people. Thus he says that, for example, he has found a sermon book to say that David had much woman trouble, because in Psalm 70:1 he prayed for his wife: "Be pleased, O God, to deliver me." In Latin this reads: *Deus in adiutorium meum intende,* that is, "O God, hasten to my wife, make her ready and willing," for in Genesis 2:18 the wife is called *adiutorium*: "I will make him a helper fit for him." The Jesuit says further: "I have actually heard another [preacher] say that Moses died *super os Domini,*" therefore "in a kiss of the Lord." A third preacher, preaching on the text Lamentations 1:15–16, "The Lord has trodden as in a winepress the virgin daughter of Judah. For these things I weep," interprets: "The Holy Virgin is conceived without original sin, therefore I, Jeremiah, must weep, for I, though I am more than other men, who are born in such sin, am still inferior to the Virgin Mary, for she was neither born nor conceived in original sin." And this new manner of interpreting and preaching they defend on the basis of Matthew 13:52, "Every scribe who has been trained for the kingdom of heaven is like [fol. †††4 recto] a householder who brings out of his treasure," they say, not only things old but also things new. But he who does not bring forth new things, but only old ones, is not "trained for the kingdom of heaven" and is not fit to be a teacher of the New Testament. And such new interpretations God reveals to those who dedicate their entire lives to contemplation and to meditation on Holy Scripture! Such a scholar, "trained for the kingdom of God," that "part-time student" must also have been who, in his ninth sermon, interprets the words of Psalm 74:13, "Thou didst break the heads of the dragons on the waters," to mean: The devils are driven out and dispersed by means of holy water. So also another fellow, as Polydorus Vergilius reports in *De invent.,* Book IV, Chapter 9, interpreted the words of Hannah in 1 Samuel 2:8, "The pillars of the earth are the Lord's" [*Domini sunt cardines terrae*] to refer to the cardinals. Malderus, page 237, deduces from the words of Exodus 19:13, to the effect that not even an animal should touch the mountain, that no prelate should be censured by anyone. *Barbatia Consil.,* I, 5, concludes from Psalm 8:6, "Thou has put all things under His feet," that the pope has all power. And from John 10:16, "there shall be one flock," the conclusion is: "Therefore the pope has power over believers and unbelievers." Antoninus, archbishop of Florence, in his *Summa historia,* Part III, Lit. 23, Chapter 1, interprets the words of Zechariah 11:7, about the two staves, as applying to the orders of monks, the Dominicans and the Franciscans. The one called "Grace" he interprets to be the Dominican order; the one called "Union" [Bands] he interprets to be the Franciscan order, because the wore rope sashes. Cardinal Hosius, in his *Petricovienl. Confess.,* Chapter 10, concludes from the words of Isaiah 40:12, "Who has . . . enclosed the dust of the earth in a [three-finger] measure?" that the sign of the cross should be made with three fingers. Who can report all such innovations and corruptions of Holy Scripture that are found in the papacy? Most of them are so foolish or also so impious that one must be horrified. Who does not know that the entire Book of Psalms has been interpreted to point to Mary and that everything that the Holy Spirit had included there about the Lord has been transferred to the holy Virgin and Mother of the Lord, and that the pope and the Roman Church take delight in this? Who is ignorant of the fact that all of the papacy is founded on a shameful perversion of the Word of Holy Scripture? Take [fol. †††4 verso] the Word of Christ in Matthew 16:18, where the Rock, Christ, or the confession to Christ is made out to be Peter, and where the keys of the kingdom of heaven are interpreted to be the full power of Peter alone in the church and the entire world, when in fact the Rock, on which the church of Christ is built, is to be understood as no one else but Christ, the Rock that followed the Israelites in the desert and gave them to drink (1 Cor. 10:4). He alone is "the foundation stone, a tried stone," "the headstone of the corner" that is well founded, that the Lord Himself has laid in His church as the cornerstone and has made the foundation of the church, of faith, and of the salvation of the believers (Is. 28:16; Ps. 118:22; Matt. 21:42; Acts 4:11; Rom. 9:33; 1 Peter 2:6). This is the way the Lord Christ, St. Peter himself, and St. Paul interpret this Rock, as all those who believe in Christ Jesus and through faith in Him as the only foundation are built up will not be ashamed but be saved and receive eternal salvation. Compare Rom. 9:33; 10:11; Joel 2:33; Rom. 10:13; John 3:16; Hab. 2:4; Rom. 1:16; Gal. 3:11; Heb. 10:38. Therefore not only the ancient teachers of the church as one man both in the Greek church, namely Basil the Great, Theodoret, Cyril of Alexandria, Epiphanius, Chrysostom, and Theophylact, and in the Latin church, namely Tertullian, Ambrose, Hilary, Jerome, Augustine, Anselm, but also the Roman bishops themselves, such as Felix III and IV, Gregory the Great, Leo II, Adrian I, and Innocent II, understand this Rock to refer to Christ and that the keys of heaven were entrusted and given not only to Peter but to all the apostles, as Matthew 18:18 and John 20:23 clearly show. Especially Pope Anacletus specifically decreed in papal law that although Peter was the first to receive the power to bind and to loose, the other apostles received the same privilege and power "in like partnership or communion with him" [*pari cum eo consortio*]. This state of affairs even the famous Cardinal Bellarmine himself acknowledges, quoting it with approval from Cyprian in *Jus canonicum,* causa 24, quaestio 1. (After the death of Clement, in the first vote of the second conclave, Bellarmine received even more votes to become pope than any other cardinal in March 1605. Also later, after the death of Leo XI, who ruled only 26 days and died 27 April 1605, Bellarmine received even more votes, so that the eminent Cardinal Baronius in the conclave shouted: "Let us make Bellarmine pope. [fol. †††† recto] He is an excellent man," as we can see in printed form in a tract called *The Cardinal's Hat,* or *Report about the Cardinals, Their Origin, Growth, Present Position, Office, Condition, Function, Ceremonies, and Customs, as Well as What Has taken Place in the Conclave, or Election Chamber, for 200 Years.*) Bellarmine, in *De Rom. Pont.,* Book I, Chapter X, in the paragraph beginning *Loquitur,* states that the highest apostolic power of the church was given not to Peter only, but also to the other apostles and that the apostolic power was the highest and topmost power. This he acknowledged again in Book IV of the same work, Chapter 23, the last paragraph. Indeed, in Book I, Chapter 11, he had to admit that all the apostles were pastors and bishops of the entire church. And this, too, is a crude papal perversion, that the words of the Lord in John 21:15, "Feed my lambs," have been applied only to Peter and therefore to the Roman pope's general episcopacy over all of Christendom, even though the eminent Cardinal Cusanus interprets these words as applying to the feeding done by the Word and by example, as indeed the words do mean. And so, too, the eminent Jesuit Cardinal Bellarmine, whom we have just mentioned, in his *De Rom. Pont* (Book IV, Chapter 23), places Peter on the same level with the other elders and apostles of his time because he calls himself only a fellow elder and admonishes the elders to feed the flock of Christ and to be "examples to the flock" [1 Peter 5:1–3]. Is it not a contemptible perversion about which even the eminent Jesuit Cornelius à Lapide, in his "Preface to the Twelve Minor Prophets," page 7, laments that the words of David in Psalm 35:2, "Rise for my help," have been misinterpreted to mean, "See to it that my wife is compliant and obedient to me," for a wife is a help, and David had reason to pray to God daily because of his trouble with his wife. Likewise he complains that another had tried to prove from the words of Lamentations 1:15–16, "The Lord has trodden as in a winepress the virgin daughter of Judah. For these things I weep," that the holy Virgin was conceived without sin and that Jeremiah wept because he was only born without sin, yet was conceived in sin. Is it not a shameful falsification of Holy Scripture that the Jesuit Antonius Sanctarellus omitted the tiny negative word in the words of Paul, 2 Corinthians 10:8, and quoted thus: "our authority, which the Lord gave . . . for destroying you," when to the contrary the text says, "*not* for destroying you"? Who can deny that it is nothing but shameful mockery [fol. †††† verso] of the holy and divine original text that Cardinal Francisco Jimenez de Cisneros arranged the Complutensian [Polyglot] Bible in such a way, as he himself states, that he placed the Latin translation between the Hebrew and Greek texts for this reason, that Jesus was crucified between two malefactors, as if the Hebrew text in comparison with the Latin translation were to be considered like a murderer and malefactor beside Christ and opposed to the Lord Christ! Again (is it not mockery of the holy text) that, in order to guarantee the pope's domination over all the monarchs of the world, even the Lord's Word, clearly forbidding all domination among His disciples and denying it to them, was overturned and falsified? For the words of Luke 22:26, "But not so with you" (*Vos autem non sic*) were turned into [a question] "But you shall not?" that is, "But are you not to have dominion?" To this question the Lord Christ is supposed to have answered, "Of course!" meaning that He does not forbid dominion to His disciples and apostles but rather recommends it to them here. A Cardinal Albanus, in the preface to a collection of his writings, and Franciscus Bursatus, in his *Deliberations* (124, note 74), prattle away, saying that the Donation of Constantine the Great was made to the Roman pope, as they concoct it, and that this was previously announced by the Holy Spirit in 1 Chronicles 29:10–12 in these words: "Blessed art Thou, O Lord, the God of Israel our father, forever and ever. Thine . . . is the greatness, and the power, and the glory, and the victory, and the majesty; for all that is in the heavens and in the earth is Thine; Thine is the kingdom, . . . and Thou art exalted as head above all. Both riches and honor come from Thee, and Thou rulest over all. In Thy hand are power and might; and in Thy hand it is to make great and to give strength to all." But how does this fit the papacy in Rome, which not the Lord our God but the abominable Satan, the lying spirit, made great and powerful? For what is here advanced about the Donation of Constantine the Great is a fat, crude, and barren lie, and that applies also to what is said about the papacy, which was established not by God but by the devil, as Herr Luther beautifully proved in the Altenburg edition, Vol. 8, p. 418. Likewise, as Boniface VIII, in Book VI, in the chapter beginning *Unam sanctam de maj. et obed.,* rambles along as he establishes this decretal, that the fact that "all human creatures are subject to the pope is of course necessarily to be believed on pain of the loss of salvation" is prophesied in Jeremiah 1:10 (but everyone who has not been robbed of his mental powers sees how absurd this is). Platina, in his *Lives,* writes about the pope that he according to his good pleasure gave away secular kingdoms [fol. ††††2 recto] and again took them back when he felt like it. This power of the Roman pope and the submission of all men to his jurisdiction the Papists have ventured to maintain contrary to all sense on the basis of St. Paul in Romans 13:1, among other passages: "Let every person be subject to the governing authorities." But in this passage he is rather ordered to be obedient to the government as a matter of conscience, for Salmeron, Pererius, and Tolerus of the cardinals admit that Augustine (Letter 54, To the Macedonians), Chrysostom, and almost all the ancient interpreters understood that this text refers only to secular government and that the text itself demands such an interpretation as of a government that "does not bear the sword in vain." And that is how also Peter Lombard and the sholastics almost unanimously interpret the text. Thomas Aquinas adds the reason that some people in the first Christian church advanced the theory that they were not subject to secular government because of the liberty they had acquired from Christ. And Salmeron notes that the seditious heretics called Gaulonites taught this when they denied that taxes and obedience were owed to the emperor. So also the eminent Cardinals Cajetan and Bellarmine themselves commented that Paul's discourse in general has to do with all government (*Tract. de offic. princip. Christ.*, p. 36; especially Dr. Joh. Gerhard, *Confessio Catholica*, Book III, L. II, Art. VI, Chap. V, pp. 156f., etc.

These shameful perversions God in heaven finally had to avenge as a force that directly wars against His Holy Scripture, the Word of divine truth, and against the honor of His holy name. Therefore the holy and righteous God no longer could look on but sent his "angel flying in midheaven, with an eternal Gospel to proclaim to those who dwell on earth, to every nation and tribe and tongue and people; and he said with a loud voice, 'Fear God and give Him glory, for the hour of His judgment has come; and worship Him who made heaven and earth, the sea and the fountains of water' " [Rev. 14:6–7]. For Him another angel and man of God soon followed the first angel and great teacher, Dr. Martin Luther, namely Dr. Martin Chemnitz, [fol. ††††2 verso] who spoke words or produced writings with which he translated into reality what the former writer had announced in mystic revelation, namely what through and after the proclamation of that man of God, Martin Luther, should follow. To this end no less the second Martin, Dr. Chemnitz, cooperated, especially by means of his *Examination of the Council of Trent*, which, even up to the present hour of the papacy, the cardinals, archbishops, prelates, or any orders of monks, indeed, the whole Jesuit sect, countless though they be, have not been able to refute. Therefore, what that first angel said (Rev. 14:8), "Fallen, fallen is Babylon the great, she who made all nations drink the wine of her impure passion," has taken place in deed and truth [cf. no. 74].

By the grace of God, amid devoted prayer to God, faithful and diligent work in the Lord, and busy study of the holy Word of God, I have with all my strength and ability noted above in this holy Lutheran Bible more than 20 guidelines that are always to be taken into consideration in the study of Holy Scripture, and I have to that end also directed this Biblical work and have for it looked up and arranged with special diligence whatever is helpful from all the works of that dear man of God, Luther. For this undertaking especially Your Electoral Grace's most precious father, of electoral grace, now asleep in God, has supported me and with eager Christian and electoral encouragement, as well as most gracious promises of a publisher and of an effective dissemination for the common good of the church of Christ has been of help to me. And Your Electoral Eminence, too, has honored me with special electoral favor, particularly at the humble presentation of my Latin work, *Biblia Illustrata*, and in the gracious recommendation of this German Lutheran Bible, Your Eminent Electoral Grace has been content to promote the same throughout your honorable and laudable land through your worthy privy councillors. [fol. ††††3 recto] To this end not only gracious official notices to the consistories and superintendents in the entire electoral land encourage purchase of this work have gone out, but also a very gracious subsidy has been given from the government treasury, about one heller, to the publisher of this work, to promote the printing of copies for the coming public diet, for which may God provide peace and healthful weather! For this I herewith express my most loyal and humble thanks. Since it is my duty to extol such great grace and strive to preserve it, it is my privilege humbly to dedicate Volume I of this Biblical work to Your Electoral Highness, and I most humbly pray Your Electoral Grace to take note of it and graciously promote it, so that this "labor in the Lord may not be in vain" but achieve the wholesome purpose desired for the honor of the great God in heaven and for the propagation of the salutary evangelical doctrine renewed by Dr. Luther for the spread of the kingdom of Christ Jesus and for the destruction of the kingdom of the eastern and western Antichrist and all perversions and heresies, so that in Your Electoral Grace's lands, indeed in the entire blessed Christendom, the only divine truth and the true meaning of Holy Scripture may by God's gracious bestowal be maintained and even to the end of the world may be successful and God and His Son, Christ Jesus, may alone be glorified. This is the daily sign in which I join King David in Psalm 115:1: "Not to us, O Lord, not to us, but to Thy name give glory, for the sake of thy steadfast love and thy faithfulness!"

Most Gracious and All-Powerful Elector and Lord, that most praiseworthy Israelite, King David, gathered together an enormous treasure for building the temple and sanctuary of the Lord, which he bequeathed to the heir of his throne, King Solomon, with these words: "With great pains I have provided for the house of the Lord an hundred thousand talents of gold, a million talents of silver, and bronze and iron beyond weighing" [1 Chron. 22:14]. Because the gold and silver alone, without the bronze and iron, [fol. ††††3 verso] amount to 33,000 tons, or 3,300 millions of gold, to which he added another "three thousand talents of gold, of the gold of Ophir, and seven thousand talents of refined silver" (1 Chron. 29:4), and thus he brought together 33,650 tons of gold. The sum of these figures seems incredible to some other interpreters of Scripture, and therefore they argue against it. For Capello it seems inhuman and much too large for the pictures of the temple. And for the eminent English scholars Brerewood and Brian it seems unreliable because it surpasses the treasure of all other monarchs by far. But it is still correct and taken from the Holy Spirit's infallible explanation (Ex. 38:24–25 and Ezekiel 45:12) as well as proved in other places. And he who considers what glorious potentates, people, kingdoms, and lands David conquered; what enemies he defeated to take over their goods; what booty he took from them, as, for example, from Hadadezer, son of Rehob and king of Zobah [2 Sam. 8:3–5; 10:15–18]; what countless tribute and gifts he received from those who came under his power, for instance, the princes of the Philistines, the king of the Moabites, the Children of Amalek, the Children of Ammon, and from all of Edom; what he received from those who sought his friendship, as, for instance, what Toi, king of Hamath, gave him (2 Sam. 8:9–10); to say nothing of the silver and gold possessions that King David now and then dedicated himself and the silver and gold possessions that King Toi, mentioned above, presented to him through his son Joram, as may be read in 2 Samuel 8:10—a person who considers all this will not doubt the sum that the Holy Spirit recorded so definitely. Neither will he who will consider how King David also vigorously worked with gold and silver and also, in addition to these ores, with bronze, iron, and hardwoods to make wooden vessels, with onyx, set rubies, and colorful gems, and every type of precious stone and marble for the house of God (2 Chron. 29:2). Also the worshipful princes of the kingdom of Israel were not lacking in their voluntary contributions to the treasury of the house of the Lord but "gave for the service of the house of God five thousand talents and ten thousand darics of gold" (which makes 900 tons of gold and 2,000 Reichsthaler), "ten thousand talents of silver" (these come out to 1,050 tons of gold) "eighteen thousand talents of bronze, and a hundred thousand talents of iron," also many and various precious stones, about which King David was [fol. ††††4 recto] very happy and praised God and glorified Him before the whole congregation (1 Chron. 29:7–17): "O Lord our God, all this abundance that we have provided for building Thee a house for Thy holy name comes from Thy hand and is all Thy own. I know, my God, that Thou triest the heart, and hast pleasure in uprightness; in the uprightness of my heart I have freely offered all these things, and now have I seen thy people, who are present here, offering freely and joyously to Thee" [on such weights and measures, cf. nos. 51 and 52].

This was a splendid contribution (as noted above) toward the sanctuary of the Lord, the likes of which one does not again see in Holy Scripture or in profane history. Not unjustly do the Rabbinical scholars call Holy Scripture the sanctuary of the Lord, to indicate the honor that is due the Holy Bible. And it certainly is the real sanctuary and the most precious treasure. Therefore generous minds are ready and willing to spend something for the Holy Bible and the proper interpretation of Holy Scripture. There can be no doubt that this German Bible, to a great extent Luther's own work, will be dear and valuable to them as the highest treasure of the world. Besides, it will not be necessary for them to contribute so large a treasure as King David got together, not even such as the princes of Israel dedicated to the Lord. This sanctuary, though it is the most precious of all, does not cost a single ton of gold, no, not even half a ton or even a tenth of a ton of gold, but only half a penny, half of the shock, as the contributions now run here. How could therefore your praiseworthy land avoid investing voluntarily and with all its heart in the incredible benefit brought by this incomparable treasure to the glory of God and for the salvation of his church? From it a rich heavenly blessing and many thousands of rewards of grace will certainly follow.

Concerning Your Electoral Grace, Most Gracious Elector and Lord, as also concerning Your Electoral Grace, Most Gracious Electress and Lady, I am [fol. ††††4 verso] fully assured that the Holy Bible is thought of as your greatest treasure and most valuable possession, as indeed Your Electoral Grace and Your Gracious Eminence have the reputation everywhere in the world that the Holy Bible is dearer to you than many thousand pieces of gold and silver, for it is your only treasure and eternal inheritance and your heart's delight.

May God fulfill all of the heartfelt well-wishes that are offered in these solemn times of expressions of allegiance, and may He grant what Your Electoral Excellency's heart desires here in time and there in eternity for the sake of our dear Savior, Christ Jesus, the only Man of Grace and the eternal High Priest. Amen.

Wittenberg, 9 September, in the year of Christ 1681 [cf. nos. 51 and 56], the day set for the elector's—may God grant many blessings—entry into the electoral residence in Dresden after the gracious liberation of the same from the "infection," against which may God hereafter for time unimaginable protect it.

To Your Electoral Gracious and
Royal Highness

Your most humble servant
and faithful intercessor before God

Abraham Calov, Dr.

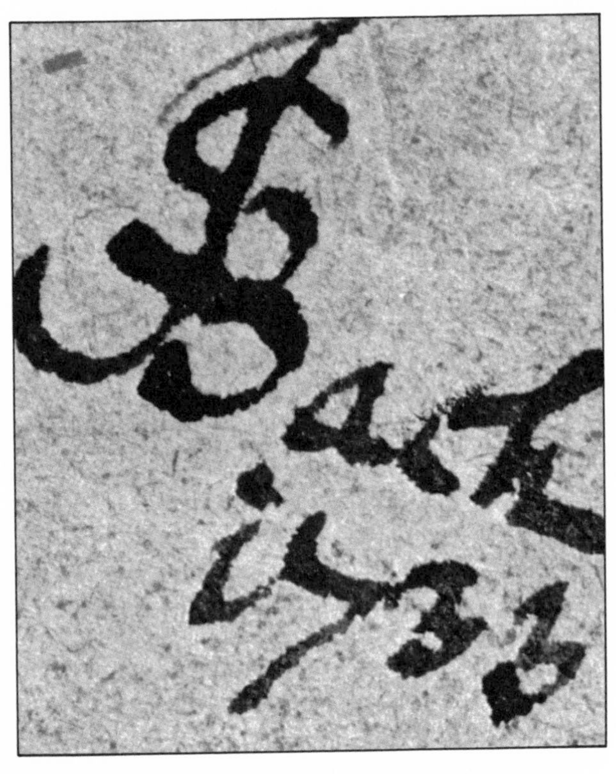

Appendix 2

[Vol. I/II, Col. 213–14]

J. N. J.
The Holy Book of Psalms

Preface to the Psalter of David

This holy book of David, king and prophet, properly confirms the divine saying of Isaiah 32:8: "He who is noble devises noble things," and this is inspired by the princely Spirit, for so David calls the Holy Spirit in Psalm 51:12, just as David testifies with fluent pen in 2 Samuel 23:2–3: "The Spirit of the Lord speaks by me, His word is upon my tongue. The God of Israel" (God the eternal Father) "has spoken to me" (what I have said through His Spirit, Acts 1:4; as it was inspired in me through His Spirit, 2 Tim. 3:16; 2 Peter 1:21; for "my tongue is like the pen of a ready scribe," Ps. 45:1), "the Rock of Israel has said to me" (in me and through me): "When one rules justly over men" (the Son of God, who "shall execute justice and righteousness in the land," Jer. 23:5; 33:15; whom David acknowledges as his Lord, Ps. 97:5, singing about Him in verse 2, "Righteousness and justice are the foundation of His throne," and in verse 6, "The heavens proclaim His righteousness; and all the peoples behold His glory"), "ruling in the fear of God" (as "the Spirit of the Lord shall rest upon Him, . . . the Spirit of knowledge and the fear of the Lord," Is. 11:1–3); and therefore David is praised by St. Paul for this, that he had the spirit of faith, 2 Corinthians 4:13, and his psalms the Lord Christ Himself, the great Prophet of the Lord and the self-sufficient eternal Wisdom, quoted, expounded, and, in addition to the books of Moses and the prophets, recommended to His disciples and apostles, the teachers of the whole world, as the only canonical Scripture of the Old Testament inspired by God, the rule of faith, and the life of the God of Israel (Luke 24:44–45; Gal. 6:16) and from them asserted the great article of faith regarding His divine nature and the exaltation to the right hand of God in His human nature (Luke 20:42) because David in the Book of Psalms (Ps. 110:1–2) bore witness to this and through the Holy Spirit said: "The Lord says to my lord: 'Sit at my right hand' " (Mark 12:36; Matt. 22:44). His Book of Psalms St. Peter introduced to the first disciples in public meeting from Psalm 69:25 and again from Psalm 109:8, according to Acts 1:20f.; and 2:25, 35, from Psalm 16:8f. and Psalm 110:2, quoted above. Also our heavenly Master, Rabbi, and Teacher, who came from God (John 3:2), repeatedly use this holy Book of Psalms as divine canonical Scripture to prove articles of faith, both in the days of His life in the flesh, as, for instance, Psalm 8:2 in Matthew 21:16; Psalm 23:1 in John 10:11; Psalm 41:9 in John 13:18; Psalm 35:19 in John 15:25; Psalm 82:6 in John 10:34; Psalm 109:8 in John 17:12; and Psalm 118:22 in Matthew 21:42 and Mark 15:34 and Luke 20:17; and on the cross Psalm 22:1 in Matthew 27:46 and Mark 15:34; Psalm 69:23 in John 19:29; Psalm 31:6 in Luke 23:46; and also after His [col. 215–16] exaltation (Rev. 2:27), whereupon, at the prompting of the Holy Spirit, the holy apostles and men of God likewise often introduce the holy Book of Psalms, both in their sermons and their writings, as the divine canonical Scripture and the unquestioned Word of God to prove their apostolic teaching. Thus St. Peter in Acts 2:25f. cites Ps. 16:8; in 1 Peter 2:25 and 5:4, Ps. 23:1; in 1 Peter 3:10, Ps. 34:13; in 1 Peter 2:7, Ps. 118:22; in 2 Peter 3:8, Ps. 90:4; in 1 Peter 2:23, Ps. 109:28; in 1 Peter 5:7, Ps. 55:24; in 2 Peter 1:19, Ps. 119:105. And St. John made use of this holy booklet no less, quoting from Ps. 22:19 in John 19:24; from Ps. 2:9 in Rev. 19:15. Also compare Ps. 32:1 and 1 John 1:9; Ps. 75:8 and Rev. 14:10 and 16:19; Ps. 78:24 and John 6:31. The other holy evangelists have likewise called the holy Book of Psalms to witness. St. Matthew 21:16 refers to Ps. 8:2; Matt. 27:39 to Ps. 22:7; Matt. 27:35 to Ps. 22:18. Also compare Matt. 13:35 with Ps. 78:4; Matt. 21:9 with Ps. 118:25–26; Matt. 27:34, 48 with Ps. 69:21; Matt. 27:43 with Ps. 22:8; Matt. 7:23 and 25:41 with Ps. 6:8. Likewise Mark 15:29 refers to Ps. 22:7; Mark 15:14 to Ps. 22:16. In the same way St. Luke 23:35 refers to Ps. 22:8; Luke 23:33 to Ps. 22:16; Luke 20:17 to Ps. 118:22. Also compare Luke 13:27 with Ps. 6:8; Luke 20:42 with Ps. 110:1. But more than others the highly inspired apostle Paul diligently made use of this beautiful Book of Psalms in his sermons and writings to certify his own apostolic and divine teaching, as may be seen by comparing Heb. 1:5 with Ps. 2:7; Eph. 4:26 with Ps. 4:4; Rom. 3:13 with Ps. 5:9; Heb. 2:6 with Ps. 8:4; 1 Cor. 15:27 with Ps. 8:6; Rom. 3:14 with Ps. 10:7; Rom. 3:10–12 with Ps. 14:1, 3 and Ps. 53:3; Acts 13:35 with Ps. 16:10; Heb. 2:13 with Ps. 18:3; Rom. 15:9 with Ps. 18:50; Ps. 19:5 with Rom. 10:18; Heb. 2:12 with Ps. 22:23; 1 Cor. 10:26, 28 with Ps. 24:1; Rom. 4:7 with Ps. 32:1; Heb. 11:13 with Ps. 39:12; Ps. 40:6 with Heb. 10:6; Rom. 8:36 with Ps. 44:22; Heb. 1:8 with Ps. 45:6; 1 Tim. 6:7 with Ps. 49:17; Acts 17:24 and 1 Cor. 10:26 with Ps. 50:12; Rom. 3:14 with Ps. 10:7; 1 Tim. 6:17 with Ps. 62:10; Rom. 2:6 and 1 Cor. 3:8 with Ps. 62:12; Eph. 4:8 with Ps. 68:18; Rom. 15:3 with Ps. 69:9; Rom. 11:7 with Ps. 69:23; Acts 14:16 with Ps. 81:12; Acts 13:22 with Ps. 89:20; 1 Cor. 3:20 with Ps. 94:11; Heb. 3:7 and 4:7 with Ps. 95:8; Heb. 1:6 with Ps. 97:7; Ps. 104:4 with Heb. 1:7; Heb. 1:10 with Ps. 102:25; Heb. 1:13 with Ps. 110:1 and 1 Cor. 15:25; Heb. 5:6 and 7:17 with Ps. 110:4; 2 Cor. 9:9 with Ps. 112:9; 2 Cor. 4:13 with Ps. 116:10; Rom. 15:2 with Ps. 127:1 [?]; Heb. 13:6 with Ps. 118:6; Rom. 3:13 with Ps. 140:3. From these comparisons we can see that St. Paul adduced and used the Psalms of David more than 50 times. All the disciples of the Lord kept the psalter in mind. Thus in Acts 4:25 they refer to Ps. 2:1, and those who received the Lord at His entrance into Jerusalem recalled Ps. 118:25–26, according to Matt. 21:9 and Mark 11:9. And St. Stephen in Acts 7:46 cites Ps. 132:5. Yes, even cursed Satan, in his temptation of the Lord (Matt. 4:6; Luke 4:10), quotes from Ps. 9:11. Accordingly, no other book of the Old Testament is so often cited in the New Testament as David's booklet of psalms and the inspiring prophet Isaiah.

Therefore there is no reason to doubt its divine authority, and no one has easily doubted it, except the godless Nicolaitans and the heretic Gnostics. And so, in the general church, this book was considered a glorious treasure, which the Hebrews, the Latins, and the Germans call a book of praise and thanksgiving. Also [col. 214—15, numeration error but continuous] in the Greek church it is called a book of hymns and songs of praise, because in it many inspiring and glorious psalms of praise and thanksgiving are to be found. Therefore the whole book is *called Psalterium, after the name of a musical instrument on which psalms, hymns, and songs of thanksgiving are accompanied* [underlined in red by Bach—see no. 44]. Many beautiful names have been given to it. Basil the Great called it a rich, common storehouse (*promptuarium*) of all good teaching, in which one can find what is useful to every man's salvation, where a treasury of perfect theologians and every good provision is concealed, where all the medicines to counteract the poison of the souls, to drive away evil spirits, and to maintain the protection of angels are given, all the means to usher in glorious days of celebration and joy, to present all kinds of spiritual sacrifices, *to voice all kinds of beautiful melodies and arrange angelic songs* [underlined by Bach]. Athanasius calls the psalter a short summary of the entire Holy Scripture. Augustine speaks of it as the protection of little boys, the pride of youth, the comfort of the aged, and an index and table of contents of the Old Testament. Herr Luther calls it an epitome and brief abstract of the whole Bible. Other pious theologians call it the scene of the works of God, a beautiful garden of roses, a lovely meadow full of beautiful flowers, a charming paradise in which not only fragrant flowers but also pleasing fruits are found, a vast sea in which costly pearls are present, but such as can be found only by those who endure the stormy winds of temptation; a heavenly school in which we address God the Lord; a clear mirror of divine grace, in which the most friendly countenance of the kindliest heavenly Father shines through; a spiritual anatomy of our soul that lays bare all its emotions and is the effective means of all the motions of the soul; a golden necklace and bracelet, made of the pure gold of doctrine, of the beautiful pearls of comfort, and of the precious gems of prayer and spiritual devotion. But our dear Herr Luther, as the most splendid German speaker and true Chrysostom, or "golden mouthed," has especially in his praise of the beautiful Book of Psalms produced his masterpiece in his preface, in which he primarily praises it:

> *Because no greater book of examples, or of stories of the saints on earth, has appeared or could appear. And if one should wish that from all the examples, legends, and stories the best would be read, collected, and published in the best way, it would have to be the present psalter. For here we find not only what one or two saints have done but what the very Head of all saints has done and what all saints still do: how they conduct themselves over against God, friends, and foes, how they act and behave in danger and tribulation. In addition, there is a variety of divine and salutary teachings and guidance in it. And the psalter ought to be near and dear alone for this reason, that it prophesies so clearly concerning the death and resurrection of Christ and describes His kingdom and the condition and character of all Christendom so well that one could well call it a miniature Bible in which everything that is contained in the whole Bible is expressed in the best and shortest way and is made and prepared to be a splendid enchiridion, or handbook. And so I think the Holy Spirit Himself wanted to take the trouble to put together a short Bible and pattern book of all of Christendom, or of all the saints, so that he who could not read the whole Bible would have almost the whole sum of it written in a small booklet. But beyond that it is the psalter's nobel virtue and characteristic that, whereas other books indeed rattle off much concerning the works of the saints but say little about their words, the psalter is exceptional and leaves such a pleasant and sweet taste when a person reads in it not only about the works of the saints but also about their words, how they spoke to God and prayed, and still speak and pray. The result is that the other legends and examples, compared with those of the psalter, have to appear to present completely vain and dumb saints but the psalter shows us real live saints, for it presents not only their*

works but also their heart and the basic treasure of their souls, so that we can see the foundation and source of their words and works, that is, their heart, what kind of thoughts they had, how their heart was disposed in every kind of experience, danger, and affliction. This the legends and examples that exalt only their works and miracles do not do and cannot do. For I cannot know where a person's heart stands even if I see or hear that he performs many wonderful works. But the psalter presents this information about the saints in the richest measure, so that we may be certain how their hearts stood and how they spoke to [col. 218–19, numeration error but continuous] *and God and to everyman. A human heart is like a ship on a wild sea, being assailed by the storm winds from the four corners of the earth: here fear and worry about an impending accident attacks; there the dread and sorrow of a present evil asserts itself; here hope and presumption waft in a promise of coming bliss; there the wind of security and happiness in present advantages shows itself. Such storm winds teach a person to speak seriously, to open one's heart, and to pour out the basic contents. For he who is in fear and affliction speaks altogether differently about mishaps than he does who soars along in joy; and he who floats along in joy speaks and sings altogether differently about joy than he who is stuck in fear. It's not from the heart, people say, when a sad person is to laugh or a happy person is to weep, that is, his heart's depth is not open to view, and it does not show itself. But what is most of the content of the psalter but such serious conversation during all such storm winds? Where do we find better words of joy than the psalms of praise or the psalms of thanksgiving furnish? That is where you look into the hearts of all saints as into beautiful and cheerful gardens, indeed, as into heaven, to see how charming and cheerful flowers of all kinds of beautiful thoughts toward God because of His kindness open up in them. On the other hand, where will you find more profound, more plaintive, more woeful words of sadness than the psalms of lamentation present? Again, here you look into the hearts of all believers as if into death, indeed, as if into hell. How dark and dismal it is here, full of every kind of sad look as the wrath of God! Furthermore, where the psalmists speak of fear and hope, they use such words as transcend any picture of fear and hope any painter could paint for you or any Cicero or orator could present. And as I said, the best thing is that they speak such words and expressions to God and with God. This brings a twofold earnestness and life into their words. For otherwise, when we speak to mere human beings in such situations, it's not really from the heart and it does not burn, live, and press so urgently.*

All of this we find in his beautiful preface to this golden book. It is well worth it that it be deeply impressed on our hearts so that we may always feel its flavor and strength. Accordingly, when a believing heart has tasted a proper flavor and a permeating strength, it will no doubt seem to be a lovely and salutary dew from heaven and a heart-reviving balm in all fear and impotence of his soul. Germane to this discussion also is Herr Luther's preface to the psalter of 1545, which may be found in part II of the sermons on the Psalms by Dr. Joachim Morlin, which was first prepared for the press in 1555 by Dr. Jerome Weller but is nowhere included in Luther's editions of the Psalms or in the volumes of his works:

It would only be fair that every Christian who wants to pray and exercise himself devotionally make the psalter his manual. And it would certainly also be good for every Christian to cultivate it again and again and to be so conversant with it that he would know it by heart, word for word, and always have it on his lips whenever he needs to talk about something or do something. In that case he would always choose or adduce a word from it as from a proverb, for it certainly is true that for everything a devout heart may wish to pray for it finds psalms and words so suitable and lovely that no human being, indeed not all human beings together, would be able to invent such a good mode, word, or devotion. Thus the psalter also teaches and comforts us in prayer, thus the Lord's Prayer leads to it, and the psalter leads to the Lord's Prayer, that one can be understood from the other beautifully and both harmonize charmingly. Therefore we should not only ban our former prayer books, which vainly made use of unchristian lies and abuses almost exclusively, even in the best prayers, where our Lord's suffering is brought in but not to engender faith but for a temporal use and application, but we should also see to it that none of the new prayers make their inroads again, for there is again a movement afoot according to which everybody, in keeping with his religiosity, wants to compose prayers paraphrasing the psalms and so see his own work praised and used in the church and among Christians, just as if the psalter and the Lord's Prayer were inferior and insignificant things. If these things are not understood and proper measures are not taken, both psalter and Lord's Prayer will fall into their former contempt. In part these people pray well, but the psalter and the Lord's Prayer should be better, indeed, the very best. He who learns to pray these aright prays much better than all others, especially since the psalter by the grace of God has been translated to German.

I have heard a story of a pious person to whom the Lord's Prayer had become so dear that she prayed the same with tears in her great devotion. In that case a bishop with the best of intentions wanted to improve her devotion and therefore took away the Lord's Prayer and gave her many good devotional prayers. But then she lost all devotion and had to get rid of all those devotional prayers and take up the Lord's Prayer again. I am of the opinion too that if anyone would earnestly make an effort with the psalter and the Lord's Prayer, he would soon send his devotional little prayers on vacation and say: "Alas, these don't have the juice, power, excitement, and fire that I find in the psalter. They leave me so cold and hard, etc." May our dear Lord, who has taught us to pray the psalter and the Lord's Prayer and has given them to us, [col. 220–21] *grant us His Spirit and grace that we may with enthusiasm and earnest faith pray diligently and without ceasing, for this is necessary, and He has commanded it and wants it done. To Him be praise, honor, and thanksgiving to eternity. Amen.*

So far as the classification of the holy psalter is concerned, the Syrian church and St. Athanasius divided the psalms into five categories. Some are didactic psalms, in which the entire theology about God the Holy Trinity, about Christ our Savior, and other articles of faith are given. Some are hortatory psalms, in which we are reminded of what we should do and what we should not do, to the glory of God and from the gratitude we owe, so that we may not fall away from His fatherly grace and forfeit our faith. Others are prophetic psalms, in which are found beautiful prophecies concerning the sending of the Son of God and the esteemed Holy Spirit, concerning the shape of the New Testament and the church of God. Some are prayer psalms, in which we have petitions in every kind of suffering and physical and spiritual need, especially painful and humble penitential psalms. And finally there are beautiful psalms of praise and thanksgiving, in which the purpose is to praise the name of God and to join the heavenly seraphim and the band of the elect, to line up and stand together in one chorus to praise and exalt the Holy Trinity. Of course, as Herr Luther has very well reminded us, in a single psalm there are occasionally found two, three, or all five items, or a single psalm may belong to all five classifications. Those, however, which are of one classification throughout are chiefly the prophetic psalms, of which there are no small number, such as Psalm 2, concerning the Passion and the general kingdom of Jesus; Psalm 8, concerning His humiliation and exaltation; Psalm 16, concerning His death and resurrection and His entry into eternal life; Psalm 18, concerning His reliance on God; Psalm 19, concerning the spread of His Word into all the world; Psalm 22, concerning his bitter suffering and crucifixion; Psalm 23, concerning His comforting office of Shepherd; Psalm 24, concerning this our King of glory; Psalm 31, concerning His death and His yielding up His soul; Psalm 35, concerning the undeserved enmity to Him; Psalm 40, concerning His salutary sacrifice for us; Psalm 41, showing how He was forsaken and troubled over it in the days of His flesh; Psalm 45, concerning the office, anointing, and preparation of Him who is our King, and in addition concerning His spiritual marriage with us and concerning the blessed distribution of His progeny; Psalm 46, concerning the preservation of His church, that "the city of God shall be made glad"; Psalm 47, concerning His victorius ascent to heaven; Psalm 48, concerning His resurrection and the outpouring of the gracious rain of the Holy Spirit after His glorious ascension into heaven; Psalm 69, concerning His fear of hell and the peculiar sensation of physical life; Psalm 72, concerning the spread of his kingdom and His seed; Psalm 89, concerning the majesty of the person and the office of Messiah; Psalm 93, concerning the extent of His kingdom; Psalm 95, how all the world is to hear His voice; Psalm 96, how all the world will sing to the honor of the Lord and rejoice over Him; Psalm 97, how He is to be exalted in all lands; Psalm 98, how His salvation is to be proclaimed everywhere and His righteousness is to be revealed before all peoples; Psalm 99, how righteousness will be loved in His kingdom; Psalm 100, how he makes us to be His people and "the sheep of His pasture"; Psalm 108, concerning the reestablishment of the kingdom of Messiah; Psalm 109, concerning the bitter suffering of Christ and the devilish wickedness of Judas, and concerning the condemnation of the latter; Psalm 110, [col. 222–23] concerning our Lord's sitting at the right hand of the Lord, His reign over his enemies, also concerning his peculiar priesthood after the manner of Melchizedek; Psalm 113, how the name of Christ is to be praised from the rising of the sun to the setting thereof; Psalm 117, concerning the call of the Gentiles; Psalm 118, concerning the victory of Christ and how the stone rejected by the godless people has become the head of the corner, on which account He will be received with joy by the believers at His entry for suffering.

The penitential psalms are quite well known: Psalms 6, 32, 38, 51, 102, 130, and 143. The psalms of thanksgiving, as also the didactic psalms, are found throughout the psalter, and they are those that were used particularly diligently by the Israelite kings. All psalms that have no title or list no name are ascribed to that king and prophet, David, and there are 51 of these, in addition to those that explicitly carry David's name in the superscription. Of the latter there are 72, and so those that are commonly ascribed to David number 123. According to their titles, the remaining 27 belong to the following: one, Psalm 90, to Moses; two, Psalms 72 and 127, to King Solomon; *twelve,* Psalms 50, 73, 74, 75, 76, 77, 78, 79, 80, 81, 82, 83, *to the prophet Asaph, King David's Capellmeister* [underlined in red by Bach—see no. 44]; one Psalm 89, to Ethan the Ezrahite; eleven, Psalms 43, 44, 45, 46, 47, 48, 49, 84, 85, 87, 88, to the sons of Korah. Several are ascribed to a certain Jeduthun, but we have no information about that, except that the title of Psalm 77 states: "A Psalm of Asaph for Jeduthun, to Be Performed," which seems to indicate that Asaph composed the psalm and appointed Jeduthun to perform the same. Similarly the title of Psalm 88 is to be interpreted to mean that the sons of Korah composed that psalm song and assigned it to Heman the Ezrahite for instruction and performance. For even though Heman and Jeduthun were prophets (1 Chron. 25:1), as *Heman* [underlined in red by Bach] is called a seer, that is, a prophet of the king "according to the promise of God to exalt Him" (1 Chron. 25:5; 2 Chron. 35:15), and *Jeduthun* [underlined in red by Bach] is called a seer of King Josiah, *yet they served in instrumental music making as they had been ordered by David for the work of their office to perform this "with lyres, with harps, and with cymbals"* [underlined in red by Bach] (1 Chron. 25:1, 6).

Otherwise the Book of Psalms of David—it is credited to him as the one who composed most of the psalms, namely 123, and 30 prophetic psalms and as the man raised up by "the anointed of the God of Jacob" (2 Sam. 23:1)—is divided into five parts by the Hebrews, as also the writings of Moses are and as there is among the Jews an appendix of five books to the books of Moses. This division is made because each part ends with an Amen. Part I contains the first 41 psalms and closes with Ps. 41:13: "Blessed be the Lord, the God of Israel, from everlasting to everlasting! Amen and Amen." Part II begins at Psalm 42, contains 31 psalms, and ends in Psalm 72:18, 19 with the hymn of praise: "Blessed be the Lord, the God of Israel, who alone does wondrous things. Blessed be His glorious name forever; may His glory fill the whole earth! Amen and Amen!" Part III begins with Psalm 73, contains only 17 psalms, and ends with Psalm 89:52: "Blessed be the Lord forever! Amen and Amen." Part IV begins with the psalm of Moses, Psalm 90, also contains 17 psalms, and ends with Psalm 106:48: "Blessed be the Lord, the God of Israel, from everlasting to everlasting! And let all the people say, 'Amen!' Praise the Lord!" Part V, the last part, begins at Psalm 107, [col. 224–25] contains 44 psalms, and Psalm 150, the last psalm, closes the whole psalter with these words of verse 6: "Let everything that breathes praise the Lord! Praise the Lord!" The content of each psalm Herr Luther has drawn up in the Altenburg edition of his works, vol. VI, pages 137ff.

Bibliography

Arnold, D. *Bach.* Oxford, 1984.

Axemacher, E. *"Aus Liebe will mein Heyland sterben." In Untersuchungen zum Wandel des Passionsverständnisses im frühen 18. Jahrhundert.* Beiträge zur theologischen Bachforschung 2. Stuttgart, 1984.

Besch, H. "Eine Auktionsquittung J.S. Bachs." In *Festschrift für Friedrich Smend zum 70. Geburtstag,* 74–79. Berlin, 1963.

———. *Johann Sebastian Bach: Frömmigkeit und Glaube.* Gütersloh, 1938.

Bibliotheca Mayeriana seu apparatus librarius Io. Frid. Mayeri. . . . Berlin, 1715.

Bitter, C. H. *Carl Philipp Emanuel und Wilhelm Friedemann Bach und deren Brüder.* Berlin, 1868.

———. *Johann Sebastian Bach.* 2 vols. Berlin, 1865. Abridged English version: *The Life of J. Sebastian Bach.* Trans. J. E. Kay-Shuttleworth. London, 1873.

Blankenburg, W. "Die Bachforschung seit etwa 1965, Teil III." *Acta Musicologica* 55 (1983) 1–58.

———. "In the Sign of Bach." *CTM* 21 (1950): 366–67.

———. "Theologische und geistgeschichtliche Probleme der Gegenwärtigen Bachforschung." *Theologische Literaturzeitung* 78 (1958): 391–410.

———. "Zwölf Jahre Bachforschung." *Acta Musicologica* 37 (1965): 95–158.

Blankenburg, W., and R. Steiger, eds., *Contate: Eine Handreichung für Pfarrer und Kirchenmusiker zum Schütz- und Bach-Gedenkjahr 1985.* Kassel, 1984.

Blume, F. "Outlines of a New Picture of Bach." *Music and Letters* 44 (1963): 214–27.

Buszin, W. E. "Lutheran Theology as Reflected in the Life and Works of J. S. Bach." *CTM* 21 (1950): 895–923.

Cox, H. H. "Bach's Bible." In *Bach in Bethlehem Today: A Conference Report,* ed. A. Mann, 31-35. Bethlehem, 1979.

Dadelsen, G. von. *Beiträge zur Chronologie der Werke Johann Sebastian Bachs.* Tübinger Bach-Studien 4/5. Trossingen, 1958.

Dürr, A. "New light on Bach." *The Musical Times* 107 (1966): 484–88.

———. *Zur Chronologie der Leipziger Vokalwerke J. S. Bachs.* 2d ed. Kassel, 1976.

Frick, M. "Three Volumes of Bach's Library Featured." *Quad* 10, no. 9 (16 Nov. 1961).

Foelber, P. F. *Bach's Treatment of the Subject of Death in His Choral Music.* Washington, 1961.

Freyse, C. "Fünfzig Jahre Bachhaus." *BJ.* 1957, 168–91.

Fuerbringer, L. E. *Eighty Eventful Years.* St. Louis, 1944.

———. *Persons and Events.* St. Louis, 1947.

———. "Das Schicksal eines Buches." *Der Lutheraner* 91 (5 March 1935): 76.

Geck, M. "Bachs Schriftverständnis." *Musik und Kirche* 40 (1970): 9–17.

Gerstenberg, W. *Composers' Autographs.* 2 vols. 2d ed. London, 1968.

Godman, S. "Bachs Bibliothek: Die noch vorhandenen Handexemplare." *Musica* 10 (1956): 756–61.

———. "Bach's Copies of Ammerbach's 'Orgel oder Instrument Tabulatur.' " *Music and Letters* 38 (1957): 21–27.

Gorali, M., B. Hirschowitz, and T. Turel. *The Old Testament in the Works of Johann Sebastian Bach.* Haifa, 1979.

Hammer, E. W. "Index, 1286 Pages: The Altenburg Luther." *The Lutheran Quarterly* 1 (1949): 213–24.

Herz, G. *Bach Sources in America.* Kassel and New York, 1984.

———. "J. S. Bach 1733: A 'New' Bach Signature." In *Studies in Renaissance and Baroque Music in Honor of Arthur Mendel,* ed. R. L. Marshall, 254–63. Kassel, 1974.

———. "Towards a New Image of Bach." *BACH* 1, no. 4 (Oct. 1970): 9–27.

Hoch, F. G. "Lost Volume of Bach Found in Thumb Home." *Detroit News* (2 Nov. 1935).

Leaver, R. A. "Bach's Understanding and Use of the Epistles and Gospels of the Church Year." *BACH* 5, no. 4 (Oct. 1975): 4–13.

———. "The Calov Bible from Bach's Library." *BACH* 7, no. 4 (Oct. 1976): 16–22.

———. *J. S. Bach as Preacher: His Passions and Music in Worship.* St. Louis, 1984.

———. "Leipzig's Rejection of J. S. Bach." *BACH* 3, no. 3 (July 1972): 27–39; ibid., no. 4 (Oct. 1972): 3–7.

———. "Number Associations in the Structure of Bach's *Credo* BWV 232." *BACH* 7, no. 3 (July 1976): 17–24.
See also entries in list of Abbreviations.

Leipziger Kirchen-Staat. Leipzig, 1710.

Leube, H. *Kalvinismus und Luthertum im Zeitalter der Orthodoxie.* Leipzig, 1928.

Marshall, R. L. *The Compositional Process of J. S. Bach: A Study of the Autograph Scores of the Vocal Works.* 2 vols. Princeton, 1972.

Miller, L. D. "J. S. Bach's Bible." *The Hymn* 25 (1974): 14ff.

Minear, P. S. "J. S. Bach and J. A. Ernesti: A Case Study in Exegetical and Theological Conflict." In *Our Common History as Christians: Essays in Honor of Albert C. Outler,* ed. J. Descher, L. T. Howe, and K. Penzel, 131–55. New York, 1975.

Neumann, W. *Sämtliche von Johann Sebastian Bach vertonte Texte.* Leipzig, 1974.

Oepke, A. "Johann Sebastian Bach als Abendmahlsgast." *Musik und Kirche* 24 (1954): 202–08.

Petzoldt, M., ed. *Bach als Ausleger der Bibel: Theologische und musikwissenschaftliche Studien zum Werk Johann Sebastian Bachs.* Berlin, 1985.

Pipping, H. *Sacer decadum septenarius Memorian Theologicorum nostra aetate clarissimorum renovatam exhibens.* Leipzig, 1705.

Preus, R. D. *The Theology of Post-Reformation Lutheranism.* Vol. 1. St. Louis, 1970.

Preuss, H. *Bachs Bibliothek.* Sonderdruck aus der Zahn-Festgabe. Leipzig, 1928.

———. *Johann Sebastian Bach der Lutheraner.* Erlangen, [1935].

Sauer, P. *The Life Work of Joahnn Sebastian Bach. Lecture delivered under the auspices of the Lyceum Committee of Concordia Seminary, St. Louis, Mo., November 23, 1928.* St. Louis, 1929.

Scheide, W. H. *Johann Sebastian Bach as a Biblical Interpreter.* Princeton, 1952.

Schulze, H.-J. "Marginalien zu einigen Bach-Dokumenten." *BJ.* 1961, 79–99.

Siegele, U. "Bachs Stellung in der Leipzig Kulturpolitik seiner Zeit." *BJ.* 1983, 7-50.

Siegmund-Schulze, W. *Johann Sebastian Bach.* Leipzig, 1976.

Sietz, R. "Die Orgelkompositionen des Schülerkreise um Johann Sebastian Bach." *BJ.* 1935, 33–96.

Smend, F. *Bach-Studien: Gesammelte Reden und Aufsätze.* Ed. C. Wolff. Kassel, 1969.

Spitta, P. *Johann Sebastian Bach.* 2 vols. Leipzig, 1873–80. English edition: *Johann Sebastian Bach: His Work and Influence on the Music of Germany, 1685–1750.* Trans. C. Bell and J. A. Fuller-Maitland. 3 vols. London, 1883–85.

Stevenson, R. M. "Bach's Quarrel with the Rector of the St. Thomas School." In *Patterns of Protestant Church Music,* 66–77. Durham, N.C., 1953.

Stiller, G. *Johann Sebastian Bach and Liturgical Life in Leipzig.* Trans. H. J. A. Bouman, D. F. Poellot, and H. S. Oswald, ed. R. A. Leaver. St. Louis, 1984.

Trautmann, C. "Ansätze zu ideell-ideologischen Problemen um Johann Sebastian Bach." In *Kerygma und Melos: Christhard Mahrenholz 70. Jahre,* ed. W. Blankenburg, et al, 237–45. Kassel, 1970.

———. "Bach's Bible." *American Choral Review* 14, no. 4 (Oct. 1972): 3–11.

———. *Ex libris Bachianis: Eine Kantate Johann Sebastian Bachs in Spiegel seiner Bibliothek.* Zurich, 1969.

See also entries in list of Abbreviations.

Vidal, P. *Bach les Psaumes, Passions, Images, et Structures dans l'Oeuvre d'Orgue.* Fontenay-sous-Bois, 1977.

Werthemann, H. *Die Bedeutung der alttestamentlichen Historien in Johann Sebastian Bachs Kantaten.* Tübingen, 1959.

Whitaker, W. G. *The Cantatas of Johann Sebastian Bach Sacred and Secular.* 2 vols. London, 1959.

Wilhelmi, T. "Bachs Bibliothek: Eine Weiterführung der Arbeit von Hans Preuss." *BJ.* 1979, 107–29.

Zehnder, H. F. *"Teach My People the Truth!" The Story of Frankenmuth, Michigan.* Frankenmuth, 1970.